Symbol and Idea in Henry Adams

Symbol and Idea in Henry Adams

BY

MELVIN LYON

UNIVERSITY OF NEBRASKA PRESS · LINCOLN

Publishers on the Plains

Manufactured in the United States of America

FOR
ROSEMARY
and our Children:
Cathy, David, Tommy,
and Susan

CONTENTS

Author's Note ix

Introduction 1

   I. The American Democratic Hero 13

   II. The Failure of Democracy as Ultimate Authority 25

   III. The Acceptance of Nature as Ultimate Authority 37

   IV. America Discovers Its National Identity 58

   V. Pessimistic Naturalism and the Childhood of Man 78

   VI. Pessimistic Naturalism and "The Fall" of Man 113

   VII. The Ultimate Symbols: I 140

   VIII. The Ultimate Symbols: II 191

   IX. The Pattern of Ideas 225

Appendix I. The Unity of the Dynamic Theory of History 231

Appendix II. "Feeling" and "Reason" after *Chartres* 241

Critical Notes 247

List of Works Cited 309

Acknowledgments 317

Index 319

AUTHOR'S NOTE

Two kinds of notes are used herein: footnotes and critical notes. The critical notes at the end of the text explore in more detail particular points in the text within the context of the relevant criticism and scholarship. Footnotes refer the reader to the appropriate critical note.

Symbol and Idea in Henry Adams

INTRODUCTION

The sensibility expressed in the writings of Henry Adams has eight or nine primary aspects: intellectualism; moralism; didacticism; a concern with contemporary and future relevance, and especially with relevance for the individual in relationship to society; historicism; scientism; and two elements—imagination and intuition (or feeling or instinct)—which are best discussed together and for that purpose may be called, collectively, subjectivism.[1] Of these the most basic aspect is intellectualism: throughout his work Adams' sensibility operates ultimately in terms of concepts. He changes his mind about how the most adequate concepts are derived from reality; he even loses most of his faith in the ability of concepts to affect and express reality; yet he is never satisfied with facts or intuitions (or images or feelings) until they are translated into abstract terms. The particular abstractions he is concerned with are largely determined by his insistence that ideas be relevant to the good life in his own time and the future, and his persistent attempt to persuade other men to achieve that life. Hence, he tends to embody his ideas in some more or less specific program for improving society. The lifelong focus of this tendency is national politics, although in later years its primary focus becomes university education.

Intellectualism, moralism, didacticism, and a concern for contemporary relevance function most independently of the other aspects of Adams' sensibility in his early essays. The subjects of these essays are contemporary rather than historical, but here, as always in his work, when the subject is not specifically historical it is at least set in a historical context. The importance of the past for Adams lies in its relevance to the present and future, for these, he believes, can be understood and directed—insofar as they can be directed—only by viewing them in relationship to the past. The past has such value because, in his view, the validity and value of ideas can be tested only by experience. History as the totality of past human experience, is the repository of such tests and thus a means of gaining perspective upon the present. Throughout his career Adams also tries to improve the ability of history, as an *account* of human experience,

[1] See critical note 1.

I

to demonstrate the relative value and validity of ideas by making it more scientific. At first, he emphasizes the rigorous use of the scientific method both in research and in presenting its results; later, he tries to develop laws of history analogous to those of natural science and based upon them. In these efforts he acts essentially not as a scientist but as a historian trying to adapt to his discipline the methods of reaching truth accepted as most valid by his age. This historicism reaches its most autonomous expression in *The Life of Albert Gallatin* and especially *The History of the United States During the Administrations of Thomas Jefferson and James Madison.*

Subjectivism becomes a primary aspect of Adams' sensibility later than the other seven aspects, although, like them, it is present in his work from the beginning.[2] The a priori moralism of his early essays[3] anticipates the importance of intuition (or instinct) as a means of knowing in his later work. Even more clearly related to the later work is Adams' recognition in these rationalistic essays that man has an affective and imaginative as well as rational side to his nature and that the most effective writing appeals to the whole man by making use of images as well as abstractions and by appealing to feeling as well as reason. Hence imagination and feeling as important aspects of expression appear in such early essays as "The New York Gold Conspiracy" and, in the middle period, in *The History*, whose greatness is due in part to its being a literary as well as a scientific work. Subjectivism is most autonomous in Adams' work in the novels, written as relief from the writing of *The History*. In *Democracy* the larger role of subjectivism appears in the greater importance of symbols in the work and in the appearance of a character who attaches as much importance to feeling as to thinking and makes her ultimate decisions on the basis of intuited moral principles. Yet subjectivism still remains largely under the control of intellectualism and didactic moralism, and a historical context is used to give greater veracity and conviction to the contemporary testing of ideas. In *Esther* there is a character who acts even more in terms of feeling than her counterpart in *Democracy*. Otherwise, the aspects of sensibility which appear

---

[2] I received a copy of Vern Wagner's *The Suspension of Henry Adams* (Detroit: Wayne State University Press, 1969) as the present work was going to press and hence have not been able to use his book. However, had I been able to, I would have added "humor" to my list of the primary aspects of Adams' sensibility.

[3] See George Hochfield's Introduction to Henry Adams, *The Great Secession Winter of 1860–61 and Other Essays*, ed. and with an introduction by George Hochfield, A Perpetua Book (New York: A. S. Barnes and Co., Inc., 1963), pp. xiii–xv; and Charles Andrew Vandersee, "The Political Attitudes of Henry Adams" (Ph.D. dissertation, UCLA, 1964), pp. 12, 88–89. Examples in Adams' texts are in *Great Secession Winter*, pp. 110, 258.

have much the same relationship as in the earlier novel—until the last one-fourth of the work, where intuition and imagination become freer from intellectualism than anywhere else in Adams' work. The character who relies on feeling gains ideas intuitively from a natural object functioning as a symbol whose meaning is never fully intellectualized. Here in a far more profound way than in the earlier works subjectivism becomes an aspect of perception as well as expression. This basic change continues in *Mont-Saint-Michel and Chartres* and *The Education of Henry Adams*, where subjectivism, though less free than in the novels, is more complex, more pervasive, and more important than in any of Adams' works except the last part of *Esther*. Now Adams himself has come to let intuition or feeling rather than reason lead him to subjects for contemplation. As always, contemplation leads to conceptualization, but now the participation of subjectivism in perception produces a balance between intellectualism and subjectivism—or a fusion of the two—in works which are the expression of a sensibility not on a holiday but functioning in its totality. Of all Adams' works, *The Education* most fully fuses the eight or nine principal aspects of his sensibility and thus represents its fullest fruition.

The essays on the theory of history return to the emphasis on intellectualism and didacticism of the early essays, and to the immediate emphasis in them and the novels on contemporary relevance. But historicism and scientism are strengthened and moralism weakened. There is another, even more basic difference: the essays present a conceptualized version of what was initially and remains essentially an intuitive and imaginative rather than rational response to reality.

Though all of the aspects of Adams' sensibility are involved in the present study, it is primarily concerned with the ideas which result from his intellectualism, with his symbolism—one aspect of his imagination —and especially with the relationship between his ideas and symbols. Most of his ideas are related to the most pervasive theme in his work— the problems of distinguishing in human experience between illusion and reality and of ascertaining the value of each for human life. He examines these problems in a context of human experience, more especially in a historical context (though this is sometimes in the background rather than the immediate foreground), where he finds certain versions of recurrent human ideas and attitudes brought to the test of different sets of circumstances and thus proved false or true, valuable or not. Up to 1892 American history is the context in which Adams tests the validity and the value of democracy as an ideal and a form of government. The specific questions this test involves are whether men are naturally good; to what extent their wills are free; whether men and their wills, or circumstances, are more important in bringing about historical change; and to what extent the aims of American democracy have been in harmony with historical circumstances in the eighteenth and nineteenth centuries. After 1892 world history becomes the context in which Adams is testing what he believes is the innate human belief in unity. He is concerned again with the extent to which man's will is free and efficacious, but now he also asks whether man can know absolute truth, to what extent man's belief in unity and desire for it are in harmony with reality, and whether religion or science approaches closer to truth.

In all of the major works in which these tests and their results appear (except *The Life of Albert Gallatin*), symbolism is a pervasive and often major literary technique. Following the usage of René Wellek and Austin Warren, I use "symbolism" in a broad sense to mean not only symbols but metaphors, similes, and significant images when they are used frequently or importantly in a single work or body of work.[4] Easily adaptable to this broad sense of the term and admirably suited to Adams' usage is M. H. Abrams' definition of a literary symbol: "a word or phrase signifying an object [a thing, a person, an event, or a place] which itself has significance; that is, the object referred to has a range of meaning beyond itself."[5] (Because I am principally concerned in this study with meanings rather than words, I use the term "symbol" to refer primarily to the object or event signified by the word rather than the word itself.) The special value of this definition for Adams' work is that it does not specify what the significance of a symbolic object must be, and, especially, that it does not limit significance to the multiplicity and ambiguity of reference which characterize Romantic and post-Romantic symbols. Although the importance Adams comes to ascribe in his later life to feeling and intuition is largely responsible for the great increase in the pervasiveness and importance of symbolism in *Chartres* and *The Education*, even in them the symbols are less Romantic than rationalistic. Their meanings may be multiple but, as in all of Adams' work, these meanings are specific rather than ambiguous. They are also concepts—or can be expressed in conceptual terms appearing in the text—and often are explicitly stated by the narrator.

Three examples will clarify Adams' usage. The flag is an important symbol in *The History*. "Flag" is a word referring to an object which is a sign and a symbol—and a symbolic gesture—in the world which Adams is recording and interpreting. But the same object also has a related literary meaning in the book: the tendency of any country—though

---

[4] René Wellek and Austin Warren, *Theory of Literature*, A Harvest Book (New York: Harcourt, Brace, and Co., 1956), p. 178.

[5] M. H. Abrams, *A Glossary of Literary Terms* (New York: Holt, Rinehart and Winston, Inc., 1963), p. 95.

particularly the United States—toward unity and political centralization, toward an effective national sovereignty. On a higher level of abstraction, the flag seems to represent unity in general. Adams' use of the symbol to mean a unifying tendency is specific and explicit; his use of it to mean unity is also specific though only implied. A different and better known symbol is the Virgin in *Chartres* and *The Education*. In the medieval world, she was considered not a symbol but a fact. In Adams' work, she is a symbol for the sexual force of woman and its expression in the emotion of love. As such, she is also explicitly a symbol for unity in the form human beings find most desirable when their sense of unity is strongest and their desire for it most intense. In this case, even more clearly than in that of the flag, the symbolic object is significant on two levels of abstraction, but in this case the significance on both levels is specific and explicit. In *The Education*, the death of Adams' sister is also a symbol in two worlds, the world of Adams' life and that of the book—though in this case (as the event is presented in the book) there is not the disparity between the meaning of the symbol in the two worlds that there is in the case of the flag and the Virgin. Adams intermixes description of the event with a full statement of its significance for him. It is his first full realization that reality is chaos. As such, it is also the climactic example of the experience which he repeatedly undergoes throughout *The Education* and eventually decides is the essential process in man's relationship with reality: the disintegration of human unity into nature's chaos. This event both epitomizes and symbolizes the multiple variety of such experiences in the book. Moreover, since the Henry Adams who is the subject of *The Education* is also Everyman and his story is that of mankind, the death of this particular woman becomes a universal symbol for all men's relationship with nature.

The emphasis upon ideas in these symbols is characteristic of Adams' use of symbolism. It is most strongly stated by him in a letter he wrote in 1912: "Symbolism is a wide field. It is, in fact, the whole field of art. No artist ever thought of anything else until the Dutchmen came down to portraits and landscapes in their own Dutch spirit. You have a sort of a symbolic monument in every picture that the Italians ever painted, and every statue the Greeks ever sculped. Every coin was a symbol, and every line meant an idea." [6] Here Adams suggests a conception of both symbolism and art. Most works of art are symbolic embodiments of an idea or a number of ideas. The primary pleasure art gives lies not in the aesthetic

[6] HA to Florence Keep, March 15, 1912, in Henry Adams, *Henry Adams and His Friends: A Collection of His Unpublished Letters*, comp. with a biographical introduction by Harold Dean Cater (Boston: Houghton Mifflin Co., 1947), p. 732; hereafter cited as Cater.

contemplation of its form but in intellectual penetration through the work considered as a symbol to its animating concept. This statement reiterates Adams' lifelong insistence upon formulating all of his experience in conceptual terms. It also suggests a distinction drawn by Henry Nash Smith between two ways of using symbols. Discussing the historian Frederick Jackson Turner's use of metaphors, Smith says that ordinarily Turner used them "to illustrate and vivify his logical propositions rather than as a structural principle or a means of cognition: that is, he used them rhetorically not poetically." [7] Adams' 1912 letter suggests that most works of art are basically rhetorical symbols, that form is subordinate to content (the two being considered separable), and that content is ultimately an idea or a set of ideas. In this view symbolism is essentially a matter of expression rather than conception and hence compatible with art controlled by ideas and a didactic intention.

This notion of symbolism appears in an extreme form in a letter Adams wrote when *The Education* was first published, in which he says that everything in that work is sugar-coating except for the story of education which it contains. Here Adams is not only asserting the primacy of ideas; he is also derogating the value even of rhetorical symbolism. This view is rare in his work except in connection with his dynamic theory of history in its abstract form (and especially with "The Rule of Phase Applied to History" and "A Letter to American Teachers of History"). Indeed, in another letter about *The Education* he contradicts himself by saying that the book was written purely as a literary experiment for the sake of educating himself "in the possibilities of literary form." [8]

The wholly rhetorical view of symbolism also has some relevance to Adams' use of image, metaphor, simile, and symbol in the essays which preceded *The Life of Albert Gallatin*. In these essays, idea and image are easily separable and the image is used primarily in a rhetorical way to vivify or illustrate the idea. Yet even here Adams is frequently also interested in the power of the figure to add to the reader's total grasp of the idea by suggesting its emotional correlate. In his first post-college essay, for example, "The Great Secession Winter of 1860–61," he says of the Virginia election of 1860 that "the country began to wake from its despair. Slowly the great ship seemed to right itself, broken and water-logged it is true, but not wrecked." [9] Here the second metaphor functions primarily

---

[7] Henry Nash Smith, *Virgin Land: The American West as Symbol and Myth* (Cambridge, Mass.: Harvard University Press, 1950), p. 253.

[8] HA to Whitelaw Reid, Sept. 9, 1908. Cf., HA to John Franklin Jameson, Mar. 20, 1909. HA to Edith Morton Eustis, Feb. 28, 1908 [?], in Cater, p. 622, pp. 649–650, 614–615.

[9] Henry Adams, "The Great Secession Winter of 1860–61," in *Proceedings*, Massachusetts Historical Society, XLIII (1909–1910), 680 [reprinted in *Great Secession Winter*, pp. 3–31].

as a rhetorical heightening of the idea suggested by the first metaphor. Yet it also functions, to some extent, poetically, as a mode of cognition, in the sense that it involves the reader in the emotional aspect of the total fact. Fifteen years later, in "The New York Gold Conspiracy," Adams moves farther in the direction of a poetic use of figures when he makes the climax of his characterization of Jay Gould a comparison of Gould with a spider. This comparison is more central to the essay in which it appears than the ship metaphor was, because Gould is the principal person in "The Gold Conspiracy" whereas the Virginia election was only a small part of the earlier essay. (In *John Randolph* [10] Adams' characterization of Randolph as a Virginian Don Quixote is a more complex and comprehensive—though less autonomous—figure, which operates in a similar way.) The spider analogy, unlike the ship figure, also suggests much that is not explicitly stated. It is a more subtle and complex figure, less tied to any particular passage in the essay in which it appears, and hence able to function more autonomously. As a result, it comes closer to having equal importance with the ideas and facts in the essay than the ship does.

In *The History* the symbols have no obvious structural importance. All but one appear briefly for the first and last time in the last chapter of the nine-volume work, where individually they are summary representations of various important aspects of American life. In this role their meanings are specific and explicit, their function, rhetorical. The other symbol does not appear in the last chapter and its significance is never made explicit, but its individual function is also rhetorical. Yet when all four symbols are considered together, they also seem to function, below the level of statement, both structurally and as a means of cognition. Thus considered they break into two pairs, each presenting the two aspects of *The History*'s principal theme: the tendency for power in America to become at once democratic and centralized. From this perspective, the symbols are the final expression of the work's cumulative meaning, and their implicit relationship to one another is an expression of its overall thematic structure. The minor role that symbols play in the body of the work is due to Adams' avowed purpose of arriving inductively at historical truth by stating facts in their chronological sequence. Yet when he ends the work with a series of questions rather than answers, he does so not because his method had failed to yield conclusions but because he has decided not to state them. [11]

[10] I have chosen not to explicate *John Randolph* (1882) in the present text because it seems to me its basic symbolism has already been treated in Henry Rule, "Henry Adams' Attack on Two Heroes of the Old South," in *American Quarterly*, XIV (Summer, 1962, Part I), 180–183.

[11] HA to Brooks Adams, June 5, 1895, in Henry Adams, *Letters of Henry Adams (1892–1918)*, ed. Worthington Chauncey Ford (Boston: Houghton Mifflin Co., 1938), p. 70; hereafter cited as Ford (1892–1918).

This fact explains in part why the symbols are never brought together. It also suggests the way in which they operate, nonetheless, as a means of cognition: they suggest meanings which Adams was aware of but wished to hide or at least to leave implicit.

The symbols in the novels have a more poetic function than do the earlier symbols. As in all of Adams' work, however, they are tightly controlled—with one possible exception—by a body of clearly defined concepts explicitly stated in the work. In *Esther* three of the four major structural divisions determined primarily by the action also involve in a crucial way the three major symbols of the work. One symbol in each novel also functions as a means of cognition for the chief character in the novel. In both cases, most of what the protagonist learns is stated or suggested earlier in the book. In *Esther*, however, the main character's discovery of her own idea of reality through personal confrontation with a symbol adds a great deal both to what she and the reader know of her. Also in this novel, for the first time in Adams' work (and the last, with the possible exception of *The Education*), the conceptual basis for a symbol is not made clear in the book. Of all Adams' major symbols, Niagara Falls, Esther's symbol for reality, has the most ambiguity and multiplicity of reference. Yet it too is set in a rational context which at least points toward an explication of its meaning in abstract terms.

Chartres and *The Education* are the culmination of Adams' use of symbolism. In them the symbolism is more pervasive, more complex, more important, and more poetic than in any other of his works. In them, too, the symbols are valued more equally with their conceptual meanings than in Adams' other works (with the exception of the falls in *Esther*). In part, this is the climax of Adams' steady movement away from a purely rational sense of reality to an increasing belief that irrational elements are essential to any adequate version of such a sense. Following Henri Bergson, Adams comes to believe that intuition and imagination rather than reason should guide the sensibility to objects for contemplation. Thus, as in Esther's experience with the falls, imagination is not only a matter of expression but basic to perception as well. This change of belief means that symbolism becomes more integral to Adams' expression than it has been before, that it has a more poetic and less simply a rhetorical function. Yet, though reason is now viewed as subsequent rather than precedent in the functioning of sensibility, it is no less active. Adams continues to extract a clearly formulated abstraction from every imaginative perception and to make an abstraction the basis of every element of imaginative expression. The primary changes from the early work are an increase in the number of symbols used, their fuller development, and something closer to equality of importance between symbol and idea than has previously existed. Such a balance is most continuously achieved in *Mont-Saint-Michel and Chartres*. There the pervasive conceptual significance of the great number and complexity of symbols is made clear and definite (though not always obvious) throughout. *The Education* is more complex. As a whole it is controlled more fully and explicitly by the theory of history which is its basis and that of *Chartres* (at least in part) than the earlier book. Indeed, from one perspective, *The Education* is a demonstration of how the total experience of Henry Adams finds viable rational formulation in the theory, concluding in the penultimate two chapters with the theory in abstract form. Yet if *The Education* is more abstract than *Chartres* in its external form, it is less abstract in its individual parts. Its persons, events, and objects are almost all symbolic,[12] but they operate more independently of their conceptual significance than the symbols in *Chartres*. In part this is because the autobiographical nature of *The Education* limits the extent to which its material can be organized in a rationally coherent way. Close reading seems to demonstrate that such coherence does exist, despite a more pervasive use of paradox and an even greater complexity than appear in *Chartres*, but the immediate effect of the greater subtlety and decreased explicitness of rational coherence is to minimize its impact and give to the tangle of facts, allusions, ironies, and figures of which the work often seems to consist the most *symboliste* quality that appears in Adams' work.

There are other passages, however—and these the finest in the book—in which Adams achieves an intermingling of image and idea which represents his highest achievement as an artist. The best of these passages is his description of his sister's death. In it the facts of the event and Adams' interpretation of its significance are each presented in some detail. Yet while fact and interpretation to some extent exist separately, ultimately each moves—under the impetus of an intensity of emotion which renders facts luminous with significance and generates images from ideas —toward a moment of vision in which Adams' final view of reality and man's fate receives the most vivid and complete embodiment in his work.

Of these three aspects of Adams' use of symbolism in *The Education*, the abstract, the *symboliste*, and the balance and fusion of idea and image, the abstract is the most important for his later work. As described in *The*

[12] A brilliant discussion of Adams' use of symbolism in *Chartres* and *The Education*, contrasting its use in the two works and comparing and contrasting Adams' usage with that of medieval allegorists and mystics, modern symbolists and stream-of-consciousness writers, appears in John Brunner, "Henry Adams: His Decline and Fall" (Ph.D. dissertation, UCLA, 1956), pp. 195, 366–371, 384–386, 395–400. A brief account of the use of symbolism in *The Education* appears in Gene H. Koretz, "Augustine's *Confessions* and *The Education of Henry Adams*," in *Comparative Literature*, XII (Summer, 1960), 200–202.

Education, his theory of history is a rationalization of what is basically an act of will and imagination. Yet the works he chooses to write after *The Education* (*The Life of George Cabot Lodge* was written as a favor to Lodge's family) are restatements of the theory severed from the autobiographical context in which it first appears and thus even more abstract than the statement in *The Education*. Near the end of *The Education*, Adams writes that "images are not arguments, rarely even lead to proof, but the mind craves them, and, of late more than ever, the keenest experimenters find twenty images better than one, especially if contradictory; since the human mind has already learned to deal in contradictions."[13] The purpose of such images is to make difficult abstractions easier to understand. The more that images are detachable from ideas the better they fulfill this purpose. Adams also writes that "perhaps the effect of knowing no mathematics is to leave the mind to imagine figures-images-phantoms": even as explanatory devices, images are only inadequate substitutes for mathematics. Adams uses images in this narrowly rhetorical way to make his statement of the dynamic theory of history in *The Education* as scientifically respectable as possible. In the two later essays, where this purpose is even more pervasive, the imagery is still further devitalized. "The figure used for illustration," Adams says in one case, "is immaterial except so far as it limits the nature of"[14] what is being discussed. The result is expression almost wholly lacking in that imaginative quality which more poetic images give most of his major work.

Such is the pattern of development—if indeed it be a "development" —in Adams' use of individual symbols in his work.[15] Yet discussion of individual symbols does not exhaust Adams' use of symbolic entities. Some of his symbols are related to systems of thought, and thus move in the direction of "myth." In *The Life of Albert Gallatin*, for example, an opposition between two places expresses eighteenth-century liberalism's contrast between nature and civilization. Yet these places never become fully developed symbols. Adams treats liberalism as a system of abstract ideas with some power to affect Gallatin's behavior, but he frequently does not emphasize—or even note—its influence, and when he does, he treats the results of this influence as effects of the ideas

[13] Henry Adams, *The Education of Henry Adams*, with an introduction by James Truslow Adams, The Modern Library (New York: Random House, Inc., 1931), p. 489. The following quotation is on pp. 426–427.

[14] Henry Adams, "The Rule of Phase Applied to History," in *The Degradation of the Democratic Dogma*, with an introduction by Brooks Adams (New York: The Macmillan Co., 1919), p. 309.

[15] R. P. Blackmur discusses some personal symbolic expressions in Adams' late life in "Henry Adams: Three Late Moments," *Kenyon Review*, II (Winter, 1940), especially 10–15, 27–29.

rather than as their symbolic expression. By contrast, "A Prayer to the Virgin of Chartres" (written 1898), and the works after it (except *Tahiti*) both depend on the ideas of the dynamic theory of history and embody them in a multitude of symbols. In part this difference is a result of the different relationship Gallatin and Adams have to the two systems. Adams portrays Gallatin's adherence to Rousseauistic ideas as a profound commitment to ideas pervasive in his time but alien and even opposed to his own nature. Adams himself dislikes and disbelieves in them. The dynamic theory of history, however, is described in *The Education* as an organic, though willed, expression of Henry Adams' total experience, a rationalization of his own life in terms of history. Instead of helping to produce a life, as Rousseau's ideas did in the case of Gallatin, the theory is produced by a life. The experiential essence of this life, as it is described in *The Education*, is the process of unity disintegrating into chaos. Repetition of this process eventually generates two symbols, the Virgin and the dynamo, which express and embody its two poles—its beginning in unity and its ending in chaos—as these have appeared in human history. The attempt to connect these symbols is described in *The Education* as generating both it and *Chartres*. Finally, at the end of *The Education*, Adams shows his persona working out a formula for reality, and his and other men's relationship to it, in terms of his own experience, and thereby arriving at a systematic conceptual account of the connection in history between the two symbols. He calls this account "A Dynamic Theory of History." Though Adams does not much like the system, nor believe in it, he does attribute more validity to it than he did to the ideas of Rousseau in *Gallatin*.

Actually, *Gallatin* and *The Education* are not so antithetical as I have made them seem. Many events, places, and people in *Gallatin*—especially the actions which Adams deplores as foolish—have symbolic significance in terms of the Rousseauistic system, both in the life and in the biography, although Adams often fails to show that they do. *The Education*, though it depicts the ideas of the dynamic theory as being the result of conceptualizing symbols generated by experience, was itself shaped by the theory in its abstract form. A system of ideas is important in both works; in both, myth—or a system of symbols—has some significance. Here I am not using "myth" in the most common sense of the term—that expressed in Abrams' definition, for example: "a story . . . once widely believed to be true . . . which served to explain, in terms of the intentions and actions of supernatural beings, why the world is what it is and why things happen as they do." [16] Rather, I am using it in the modern and literary way it is used when W. B. Yeats's system in *A Vision* is called a "myth" or a

[16] Abrams, *Glossary of Literary Terms*, p. 54.

"mythology" (a system of myths). In this usage a myth is simply "the iconography of a world view," [17] as Henry Murray has said. *A Vision* is more a myth (or mythology) in this sense than the dynamic theory of history is because in *A Vision* symbolization is both more complete and more integral to the system. Though none of the poems Yeats bases upon his system present it so fully as *Chartres* and *The Education* do Adams' system, the poems function far more fully in terms of their symbols and less in terms of abstract ideas than do Adams' works. This difference appears again in the last works of the two men. Many of Yeats's last poems are unconnected with the images or abstractions of his system whereas those of Adams' last works which he wrote by choice are new abstract versions of the theory. Adams is therefore less a mythical (or imaginative) writer and always more of an intellectualist than Yeats. Nonetheless, his system does share many of the qualities of myth in the modern literary usage of that term.

The present work consists basically of explications of six of Adams' major works primarily in terms of his pervasive concern with the problem of illusion and reality and his equally pervasive use of symbolism. It emphasizes works in which the symbols are at least partly "poetic." It is also concerned with the systems of ideas which appear in Adams' work and especially with their tendency to become myths. The two chapters entitled "The Ultimate Symbols" consider in a primarily chronological way the major recurrent symbols in all of Adams' work and show how the changes in them parallel shifts in his ideas.

[17] Henry A. Murray, "Introduction to the issue 'Myth and Myth making,'" in *Daedalus: Journal of the American Academy of Arts and Sciences*, LXXXVIII (Spring, 1959), 211–212.

CHAPTER I

THE AMERICAN DEMOCRATIC HERO

In his first book, *The Life of Albert Gallatin*,[1] Adams is concerned with the least known member of that Republican triumverate of Thomas Jefferson, James Madison, and Albert Gallatin which ruled the United States from 1800 to 1816. Gallatin was secretary of the treasury under both Presidents and secretary of state under Madison. To Adams he seemed the ideal American statesman[2] and it is that aspect of his life which Adams stressed in a work he called a "labor of love" because of his admiration for its subject. But he also called it "my prize ox"[3] because of the bulkiness and clumsiness of form which resulted from his literary method: elaborate quotation of sources (some in untranslated French) interspersed with narration and comment.

In such a book, where the author stays so far in the background, it is not surprising that the clear-cut symbols which appear in most of Adams' work should be missing. What *is* surprising is the extent to which Adams, although not wholly intentionally, gave coherence to his compilation by presenting Gallatin's life as one which in most of its aspects was given unity and direction by a system of ideas which Gallatin believed in and tried to realize in action. The core of the system was the belief that man is naturally a virtuous part of a beneficent natural order. It also asserted that individual freedom and weak government are desirable, that the earth should be repossessed by each new generation, and that the most virtuous and best life is one lived close to nature (whether as a farmer or a "noble savage"). Adams first describes the system near the beginning of the book, in reference to Gallatin's associates before his emigration:

[1] Henry Adams, *The Life of Albert Gallatin* (Philadelphia: J. P. Lippincott and Co., 1879). All page references to this work will be found between parentheses in the text.

[2] HA to Samuel Jones Tilden, Jan. 24, 1883, in Henry Adams, *Henry Adams and His Friends: A Collection of His Unpublished Letters*, compiled with a biographical introduction by Harold Dean Cater (Boston: Houghton Mifflin Co., 1947), p. 125; hereafter cited as Cater. The following quotation is on the same page.

[3] HA to James Russell Lowell, May 3, 1880, in Cater, p. 101.

"if not quite followers of Rousseau," he says, they "were still essentially visionaries. . . . They believed in human nature, and believed that human nature when free from social trammels would display nobler qualities and achieve vaster results, not merely in the physical but also in the moral world." Gallatin himself "disliked great cities and the strife of crowded social life. . . . He preferred a wilderness in his youth, and . . . continued in theory to prefer it in his age" (16, 25). Later, Adams suggests that Gallatin believed a life in the wilderness, close to nature, was conducive to physical and moral health (646). As Gallatin grew older, he lost most of his belief in this system. Experience convinced him that its doctrines were largely false and that, even when true, their effectiveness was controlled and limited by circumstances. As a result, he lost much of his drive to realize the doctrines in action. Nonetheless, as Adams presents his life, even his later actions were significantly influenced by one or more aspects of the system.[4] Adams' own emphasis is upon the system's invalidity. He calls its confidence in human nature sublime and makes it clear that he believes in democracy, but he is unsympathetic toward the system as a rationale for that belief. He notes its influence on Gallatin usually to deplore the impracticality of the actions it inspires. When it does seem to have influenced an action he admires, he often fails to note the influence, even though his own documentation seems to make it clear. He does, however, consistently praise Gallatin's democratic and nationalistic ideas, his efforts to realize them in action, and his ability to modify them when experience taught him they were false.

In his account of Gallatin's early life in Switzerland, Adams concludes that neither place, education, family, nor temperament explains why Gallatin accepted the system. Geneva, his birthplace, was the home of Calvinism, the antithesis of the system, and retained much of its religious atmosphere during Gallatin's boyhood there from 1760 to 1780. His family (one of those which controlled the city), though it counted Voltaire as a personal friend, firmly believed in aristocracy. Hence, "Albert certainly never found encouragement for liberal opinions in his own family, unless they may have crept in through the pathway of Voltairean philosophy as mere theory, the ultimate results of which were not foreseen." Gallatin himself was "clear-headed, sober-minded, [and] practical." Adams concludes that his faith must have been created "by some bond of sympathy which can hardly have been anything more than the intellectual movement of his time." It "was the instinct of his time and his associations; the atmosphere of Rousseau and Jefferson" (16, 25).

Nonetheless, Gallatin's earliest—and latest—actions seem to have been profoundly influenced by that bond of sympathy. In 1780, when he was

[4] See critical note 2.

nineteen, two main possibilities of action were open to him, Adams says: to try to improve Geneva or to emigrate. His decision was, secretly and against the wishes of his relations, to leave Geneva with a friend, Henri Serre,[5] and emigrate to America. When Adams comments that Gallatin "turned his back on the past," the appropriateness of the action to the system is clear: according to it the world belongs wholly to each new generation, to fashion as it will, with no obligation to the past. Adams, however, is critical—both of the action and of the means used to effect it. Describing Gallatin as cruel to his family (which, in general, had been kind and helpful to him), Adams asserts the responsibilities of family membership and thus of obligations to the past. He also argues that Gallatin's move was impractical: "there is no reason to suppose that Albert Gallatin's career was more brilliant or more successful in America than with the same efforts and with equal sacrifices it might have been in Europe." Clearly, Adams does not base *his* standards of morality and success upon the system. More important, he explicitly denies that positive idealistic motives based upon the myth played a significant part in the emigration (18). Yet this denial seems contradicted by the significance he attributes to a quarrel which had occurred a few months earlier between Gallatin and a woman in his family. When she suggested that he make a career in the army of a Hessian prince—her personal friend—then fighting the revolutionists in America, Gallatin's reply, "that he would never serve a tyrant," earned him a cuff on the ear. Adams says this incident had "no small weight in determining the young man's course of action" (17–18).

It is also curious that a young and urban European whose ideas were merely part of "the intellectual movement of the time," and who secretly left home and came to America for primarily personal reasons, should, upon arriving, plunge immediately into the wilderness. Again Adams is critical of the impracticality of Gallatin's action:

> Had Gallatin gone at once to New York or Philadelphia and devoted himself to the law, for which he was admirably fitted by nature, had he invested his little patrimony in a city house, in public securities, in almost any property near at hand and easily convertible, there is every reason to suppose that he would have been, financially and politically, in a better position than ever was

[5] Henri Serre, also of Geneva, was a school friend of Gallatin's there, and emigrated with him in 1780. According to Adams he had an "imaginative and poetical character," but "his idea of life and its responsibilities was simply that of the run-away schoolboy." Adams believes the "rude, free life" of the wilderness was even more his ideal than Gallatin's. The two friends were together most of the time until late 1783 or early 1784, when financial problems led Serre to go to Jamaica, "where he died, in 1784, of the West India fever." *Gallatin*, pp. 6, 15, 18, 34, 46.

the case in fact. In following this course he would have had the advantage of treading the path which suited his true tastes and needs.

In Adams' practical view, once Gallatin had made the mistake of leaving Europe, the next best thing for him to have done was to identify himself with some place in America which closely resembled the urban conditions he had left. In explaining why Gallatin did not make this decision, Adams now admits the influence—indeed, the decisive influence—of the system, but does so to deplore it. "Like many other brilliant men," he complains, Gallatin

> would not, and never did, learn to overcome some youthful prejudices; he disliked great cities and the strife of crowded social life . . . . He preferred a wilderness in his youth, and, as will be seen, continued in theory to prefer it in his age. It was the instinct of his time and his associations; the atmosphere of Rousseau and Jefferson; pure theory, combined with shy pride.

Here the system is still "the instinct of his time and his associations," but suddenly it has become important enough to Gallatin to be the major influence in his second critical decision. One wonders that a motivation so secondary in Geneva should become so important in New York (16, 67, 25).

It remained equally important in the wilderness. Disapprovingly, Adams notes that Gallatin and his friend remained all the following summer "buried in this remote wilderness" and returned to civilization only because they ran out of money. Then, after replenishing his purse by teaching French at Harvard, Gallatin again entered the wilderness, as speculator, surveyor, and storekeeper. In 1785 he and his party penetrated as far west as the headwaters of the Big Sandy River on the border of Kentucky and West Virginia. An attempt to settle there was frustrated by an Indian outbreak. Adams observes with satisfaction that "this wild attempt to make his home in an utter solitude one hundred and twenty miles beyond the last house then inhabited on the banks of the Ohio, was obviously impracticable even to Gallatin's mind, without incurring imminent danger of massacre." Here Adams seems both amused and irritated at the folly of his "clear-eyed, sober-headed, practical" young Genevan. Yet many thinkers—and Frederick Jackson Turner is only the best known among them—have believed, as Henry Nash Smith says, that American society has been shaped primarily "by the pull of a vacant continent drawing population westward through the passes of the Alleghenies, across the Mississippi Valley, over the high plains and mountains of the Far West to the Pacific Coast." [6] In these terms, Gallatin's frontier

---

[6] Henry Nash Smith, *Virgin Land: The American West as Symbol and Myth* (Cambridge, Mass.: Harvard University Press, 1950), p. 3.

experience was a participation in the basic experience of American national life. His years in the wilderness were a sort of prolonged initiation ceremony in which his European system of ideas took on a national character and became the ideas of the agricultural, democratic, American land-frontier. In the wilderness what had been "pure theory" was fused with reality, and Albert Gallatin, Genevan liberal, became Albert Gallatin, American democrat (38, 62, 16).

After being forced to leave his farthest outpost on the frontier, Gallatin helped establish another store on the border of Virginia and Pennsylvania and began his gradual emergence from the wilderness into urban life. Adams describes this movement as a kind of retreat, but he also shows that (68) it was the result, first, of an Indian outbreak, then of Gallatin's response to a sense of patriotic duty, and finally of his desire to make his family happy. Moreover, even though New York (the home of his second wife's family) eventually became his permanent residence, he himself always considered his true home to be his second outpost in the wilderness, a farm in Fayette County, Pennsylvania, called "Friendship Hill." It suggested Switzerland in its scenic beauty, Adams says, and describes it in accordance with his own prejudices: "Friendship Hill rises abruptly from the Monongahela, and looks eastward to the Laurel Ridge, picturesque as Serre could have imagined, remote as Rousseau could have wished" (63). As Adams presents it, Gallatin's life could be described as a struggle to leave Geneva and reach "Friendship Hill," a struggle which ended in the compromise of residence in New York City.

Adams says of Gallatin's life during the wilderness period that "there was indeed little at this time of his life, between 1786 and 1788, which could have been greatly enjoyable to him, or which can be entertaining to describe"; there were many trials and "no pleasures that even to a mind naturally disposed, like his, to contentment under narrow circumstances, could compensate for its sacrifices." Perhaps the satisfaction derived from attempting to live in accordance with a profoundly believed body of ideas may have partly compensated for these difficulties. Certainly it did so—with a different system—for Adams' own Puritan ancestors. Later in his own life Adams admired far more impractical actions, based upon what he considered a false view of reality, when he came to write about St. Francis. But here he is unsympathetic (66–67).

Yet he does admit that Gallatin's immediate motive for his initial departure from the wilderness was an interest in national politics: "The constitutional convention sat during the summer of 1787. The Pennsylvania convention, which ratified the Constitution, sat shortly afterwards in the same year. Their proceedings were of a nature to interest Gallatin deeply.... His first appearance in political life naturally followed."

Adams presents Gallatin as immune to the attractions of military life, whether as Hessian mercenary or revolutionary patriot. But politics suited his nature and training, gave him an opportunity for the positive expression of his ideas, and was therefore a powerful enough force to make him leave the wilderness. Personal tragedy also played an important part in his decision. In 1786 both his first wife and his Swiss friend Serre died. Each death turned his thoughts momentarily toward Geneva; once he even expressed a desire to his foster mother to return to Geneva for her sake. From that time on, he ceased trying to realize his ideas directly, as an individual in the wilderness, and sought to realize them indirectly, as a member of American urban society engaged in politics and diplomacy (68).

At the time of Gallatin's entrance into politics, there were two primary contending factions in America.

> Among the commercial and professional citizens of the sea-board towns a strong government was thought necessary to protect their trade and their peace. . . . Among the agricultural and scattered population of the country, where the necessity of police and authority was little felt, and where a strong government was an object of terror and hatred, the more ignorant and the more violent class might perhaps honestly deny the necessity for any national government at all; with the great majority, however, it was somewhat unwillingly conceded that national government was a necessary evil, and that some concessions of power must be made to it; their object was to reduce these concessions to the lowest possible point.

"No one can doubt," Adams continues, "where Mr. Gallatin's sympathies would lie as between the two great social and political theories. The reaction against strong governments and their corruptions had a great part in that general feeling of restlessness and revolt which drew him from the centre of civilization to its outskirts." Again, Adams does not acknowledge any direct influence by the system. Yet this is the clearest connection he makes in the entire book between Gallatin's life on the frontier and his Republican political principles. These principles were consistent, Adams says, with the feeling which had drawn Gallatin to America and into the wilderness (76).

Gallatin's version of these principles differed from that of many other Republicans, including Jefferson, in two respects. First, he interpreted the system more nationalistically than they: he adhered less to the dogma of strict construction (156, 157) and felt more loyalty to the Union than to any particular state (214). Second, he had the ability to act in terms of facts as well as of principles derived from the system. Adams notes that "it is obvious at the outset that the weak point of what may be called the Jeffersonian system lay in its rigidity of rule. That system was . . . a system of doctrinaires, and had the virtues and faults of *a priori* reasoning" (272). But eventually, Adams believes, circumstances forced Jefferson and Gallatin to act in ways which contradicted their principles. The Louisiana Purchase, which flagrantly abused strict construction, and the embargo, which made despots of avowed believers in weak government, are two examples. In these and other cases both men were forced to act in accordance with the Federalist idea that "circumstances must by their nature be stronger and more permanent than men." According to Adams, the two reacted differently to the lesson. Jefferson,

> brought at last face to face with this new political fact which gave the lie to all his theories and hopes . . . felt the solid earth reel under him, and his courage fled. . . . Mr. Gallatin was made of different stuff. In his youth almost as sanguine as Mr. Jefferson, he knew better how to accept defeat and adapt himself to circumstances, how to abandon theory and to move with his generation. (379)

Gallatin never regained his wholehearted belief in his system, though he continued to assert its principles. As head of the board of commissioners which arranged the Treaty of Ghent ending the War of 1812, he was primarily responsible, Adams says, for an agreement done "in the true spirit of Mr. Gallatin's political philosophy and in the fullest sympathy with his old convictions." But in 1816 he refused his old position as secretary of state because, as Adams explains, although he was

> riper, wiser, and infinitely more experienced than in 1800, Gallatin had still lost qualities which, to a politician, were more important than either experience, wisdom, or maturity. He had outgrown the convictions which had made his strength . . . —that sublime confidence in human nature which had given to Mr. Jefferson and his party their single irresistible claim to popular devotion. . . . Gallatin . . . had outgrown the Jeffersonian dogmas. There was no longer any great unrealized conviction on which to build enthusiasm.

Here validity yields to practicality as Adams' principal criterion of value, and practicality finally enables him to see value in Gallatin's system. Convictions, he implies, whether they be true or false, stimulate strength and enthusiasm; hence, their importance to a man of action. Developed in *Chartres* and *The Life of George Cabot Lodge*, this idea will become the principal *human* truth Adams has to teach: that man at his best acts on the basis of ideas which he believes to be true although they are, in fact, illusions. Here Adams does not go so far. But he can see the value to Gallatin even of his false beliefs and the loss to him when he learns they are untrue (547, 559–560).

Instead of his old position, Gallatin accepted an appointment as minister to France. Adams believes that "Mr. Gallatin never was so happy and never so thoroughly in his proper social sphere as when he lived in Paris." In a letter to Jefferson, however, Gallatin himself says, "I thirst for America, and I hope that the time is not distant when I may again see her shores and enjoy the blessings which are found only there." Adams expands this statement, noting that Gallatin "was indeed always possessed with the idea that he would rather be at home, and he averred every year with great regularity that he expected to return in the following summer." Such apparent homesickness Adams dismisses as "a very common if not universal rule among American diplomatists of the active type." This resolution of a seeming inconsistency is made less tenable by Adams' observation that in France "the apostles of legitimacy and the oracles of the Faubourg St. Germain were never favorites with him, and his old republican principles were rather revived than weakened by this contact with the essence of all he had most disliked in his younger and more ardent days." Adams dislikes the influence of the system, but it continues to break out almost in spite of him (564–566).

Another example is his account of Gallatin's return to the United States in 1823. Again Gallatin came of his own volition and again he went to the wilderness, this time to his home at "Friendship Hill." "He sent his younger son [there]," Adams says, "with directions to build a stone house in extension of the brick building he had constructed thirty years before; here he proposed to return with his family and to pass the remainder of his life." This decision provokes Adams' anger. "One of Sir Walter Scott's favorite sayings," he says,

> was that the wisest of our race often reserve the average stock of folly to be all expended upon some one flagrant absurdity. He might have added that when a shrewd and cautious man once commits such a folly there is more than a fair probability of his repeating it. . . . Philosophy might trace such eccentricities to the peculiar structure of individual minds and to *ineradicable habits of thought* [italics added]. Mr. Gallatin had in the pride of youth and the full fervor of fresh enthusiasm committed the folly of burying himself in the wilderness . . . [N]ow, when more than sixty years old, after an active life of constant excitement, with a family of children almost entirely educated in Paris, and a wife who even thirty years before had found the western country intolerable, he proposed to return there and end his life. Had the great wave of western improvement swept New Geneva before it in its course, there might have been an excuse for Mr. Gallatin's determination; but New Geneva remained what he had left it, a beautiful and peaceful mountain valley, where no human being could find other employment than that of cultivating the soil with his own hands. There Mr. Gallatin decided to go, on the extraordinary plea that he could afford to live nowhere else, and the loss of a part of his private income in 1823 only fixed him more firmly in his determination.

It seems clear that Adams believes Gallatin's decision was based in part on the same motives, derived from the system, which decided his earlier venture into the wilderness. This continuity would be even clearer if Adams had made more explicit reference to the system instead of vaguely referring to "ineradicable habits of thought." Such an emphasis might have led him to note that it was at least appropriate that the same European experience which revived Gallatin's political principles should ultimately have led him to reassert the system in the radical and direct form of a second venture into the American wilderness (578–579).

According to Adams, Gallatin's "own preference would have been to take only a leave of absence in 1823, to arrange his affairs and settle his sons in business; then to return himself to Paris." Two letters are used to support this view. In 1822, Gallatin wrote to James Monroe that his position in Paris was "more agreeable than any other *public* [italics added] employment which [I] might fill." Two years later, in 1824, when the family had been at New Geneva for a year, Gallatin wrote a friend in Europe that

> the last seven years I spent in Europe, though not the most useful, were the most pleasant, of my life, both on account of my reception in Geneva, where I found many old and affectionate friends . . . , and from my standing with the first statesmen and men of merit in France and England. Where you do not stand in the way of anybody, instead of collision and envy, you meet with much indulgence if you can fill with credit the place you occupy; and this was a disposition to which I had not been accustomed towards me, and the want of which I now on that account feel, perhaps, more than formerly.

Just a year later, in 1825, he reached the low point of his regard for his life in America: "I believe emigration, when not compulsory, to be always an error" (579, 585, 598, 610).

What Gallatin says is clear enough. Yet a consideration of the circumstances under which the letters were written at least partially modifies their effect. All were written during the two years following his return to America and reflect the depression anyone, especially a man over seventy years of age, would feel on returning from a place where life was relatively easy, free from pressure and conflict, to a situation where he must struggle once again. Even under these circumstances Gallatin did not say that Europe was intrinsically more enjoyable for him than America. He made it clear that his happiness in Europe resulted from the freedom from conflict which he enjoyed there. That freedom was made possible by the success which had crowned his efforts in America. Some of his Genevan friends might have welcomed him in any case, but the reception he received from statesmen in France and England was wholly the result of his position in America. His expression of implied regret for his own emigration is less easily explained; it is significant, however, that it is the only such expression presented in the work.

The effect of these letters is further modified by what Gallatin wrote about his life at "Friendship Hill" after the family returned in 1823. According to Adams "the experiment of living at Friendship Hill did not succeed. Not only was New Geneva an unsuitable place for the advancement of children, but it was beyond question intolerably dull for Mr. Gallatin himself. He made the experiment during one winter, and then abandoned it, as it proved, forever." Yet this is not made clear in the letters Adams quotes. In 1823, for example, Gallatin writes that "although I should have been contented to live and die amongst the Monongahela hills, it must be acknowledged that, beyond the invaluable advantage of health, they afforded either to you or me but few intellectual or physical resources." In 1824 he says, "We are here very retired, which suits me and my sons, but is not so agreeable to the ladies." Five years after leaving, he writes again: "It was an ill-contrived plan to think that the banks of the Monongahela, *where I was perfectly satisfied to live and die in retirement* [italics added], could be borne by the female part of my family or by children brought up at Washington and Paris." In all three of these letters Gallatin expresses his own satisfaction with life at "Friendship Hill." Only in the first letter is there a suggestion of Adams' belief that life there "was ... intolerably dull for Mr. Gallatin" (610–611, 646, 612, 630–631).

Yet the quotations do show that Gallatin was happy in Paris and no more than contented at "Friendship Hill." It is also clear that he became disillusioned with his system. The political aspects of this disillusionment have already been noted. But it went deeper than politics: Gallatin also lost much of his faith in the fundamental tenet of the system—the crux of its opposition to his native Calvinism—its belief in the natural goodness of man. "As to the world," Gallatin wrote to a friend, "I have been, like you, disappointed in the estimate I had formed of the virtue of mankind and of its influence over others." Even here, however, Gallatin expresses only disillusionment, not total disbelief (610).

From 1829, when he retired from politics, until his death, Gallatin's interests were scientific. These interests had begun in 1812, the year he went to France. By this time he had "outgrown the Jeffersonian dogmas," and "his statesmanship had become, what practical statesmanship always has and must become, a mere struggle to deal with concrete facts at the cost of philosophic and *a priori* principles." Hence, Adams says, "there remained no sufficient force, perhaps no sufficient prejudice, to overbalance the natural tendency of Mr. Gallatin's mind towards science and repose." Adams believes that it was partly Gallatin's loss of belief in the system which led him into science. His mind had always had two aspects: an ability to deal empirically with facts, and an intense, creative belief in his system. The latter led him into politics, but when his faith decayed he lost both the desire and strength to struggle for its realization. His mind turned to science, where the emphasis is wholly empirical and inductive—where one starts with facts and works toward a principle (560, 561, 635).

While Gallatin was in Paris his interest in science was probably stimulated by contact with his European scientist friends. According to Adams, his own scientific work, the classification of the groups and families of American Indians, "may be said to have created the science of American ethnology" (645). This final interest has its own relevance to his system and to its national expression. Twice Adams suggests the indirect influence of Jean Jacques Rousseau upon Gallatin (16, 63). In neither case does he mention Rousseau's notion of the "noble savage," but it is perhaps significant that a man partly led to begin his life in America by a body of ideas which included this notion should have ended it by a scientific study of the American Indian. In between lay the concrete reality of his frontier experience, during which he was once in danger of massacre by Indians. Thus, the pattern of European system, the struggle to make American reality conform to the system, and an acceptance of a final compromise, which appeared in Gallatin's search for a home and in his political life, appears again in the direction taken by his interest in science in his old age.

The significance of this book in relationship to Henry Adams' use of symbol and myth in all his work becomes wholly clear only in the light of his later works. Present here is the same basic dichotomy which runs throughout the work: Gallatin's life is depicted as a struggle between illusion and reality, a struggle in which reality came to dominate. But this dichotomy never crystallizes into clear-cut symbols as it does in the later work. Jeffersonian Republicanism and Hamiltonian Federalism are its primary expression; paralleling them is the contrast between the wilderness and the city and, at times, between America and Europe. The closest to true symbols are "Friendship Hill" and New York City, whose opposition suggests Adams' pervasive rejection of nature and acceptance of civilization as the norm for human life. Other key ideas here are less pervasive in his work. For example, here as elsewhere in his early work, Adams rejects illusion for reality, ideas for facts, though he admits that belief even in illusion can be a source of strength. He also rejects the "instinct" which leads to the acceptance of systems of ideas, in this case the "instinct of his time" which led Gallatin to believe in eighteenth-century liberal ideas. Yet he also rejects deductive reason as a means of knowing.

Only empirical reason is acceptable. In his later works, though he continues to believe that it is primarily empirical reason which leads to knowledge of reality, his attitude toward instinct, illusion, and systems of ideas changes. He becomes more sympathetic to all their manifestations, though more favorable to some than to others.

CHAPTER II

THE FAILURE OF DEMOCRACY AS ULTIMATE AUTHORITY

In *Democracy: An American Novel* (1880)[1] Henry Adams again examines the problem of illusion and reality as it relates to American political history. In *Gallatin* his testing of eighteenth-century liberalism in the crucible of American politics revealed that its tenets, including its principal doctrine that man is naturally good, are largely illusions. In *Democracy* he examines the doctrine of American exceptionalism, the assertion that American democratic government is morally superior to other governments. This, too, proves to be an illusion. This theme is expressed through the personal experience of Madeleine Lightfoot Lee, a woman seeking to make her life meaningful after losing her husband and children. In the novel she goes to Washington, D.C., hoping to find in democracy an ideal worthy of the religious devotion accorded it by many of her American contemporaries: she was, Adams says, bent "upon getting to the heart of the great American mystery of democracy and government." A second complicating theme is Mrs. Lee's increase in self-knowledge during her quest. She herself is not aware that such knowledge is a part of her quest until the end of the novel, but the reader is informed of it in the first chapter, when the narrator describes the confusion in Mrs. Lee's motives. She recognizes her desire to be amused and, more importantly, to satisfy her curiosity. But though she also hopes to find strong individuals who will give her a sense of security, Adams says that she "frowned on the idea of seeking for men. What she wished to see, she thought, was . . . the tremendous forces of government, and the machinery of society, at work." Adams suggests that she confused "the force of the engine [of government] . . . with the men who wielded it." He also suggests another motive, of which she was completely unaware: "What she wanted," he says, "was POWER" (10–12).

[1] Henry Adams, *Democracy: An American Novel* (New York: Henry Holt and Co., 1908). All page references to this work will be found between parentheses in the text.

Soon after arriving in Washington, Mrs. Lee visits the Capitol. Washington, as the nation's capital city, and the Capitol building, as the political center of Washington, are primary symbols for working democracy.[2] Mrs. Lee attends several sessions of Congress, frequently accompanied by John Carrington, a Virginia lawyer and former Confederate soldier. Carrington is important in the novel because his point of view seems to coincide most closely with that of Adams himself and because he is involved in the novel's third theme—the necessity of reuniting North and South in order to counter the bad influence of the West on American life. A principal bond drawing the two sections together is their mutual veneration for certain symbols and heroes, especially George Washington.[3] Throughout the novel Washington is used as a "touchstone of national virtue"[4] by Adams and Mrs. Lee. The value each places upon Carrington can be judged by Adams' characterization of him as a "Virginian . . . of the old Washington school," and the comment that Mrs. Lee "trusted in him by instinct. 'He is a type!' said she; 'he is my idea of George Washington at thirty'" (21, 22).[5]

Carrington introduces Mrs. Lee to the antagonist of the novel, Senator Silas P. Ratcliffe. Ratcliffe is a native of New England who went to Illinois after leaving college and was there elected senator and almost nominated for President as a result of his involvement in the antislavery movement. When Mrs. Lee becomes bored by Congress, she decides to study democratic politics by studying him as a representative leader of nineteenth-century democratic government. Re-emphasizing the religious quality of her quest, Adams says that for her Ratcliffe became "the high-priest of American politics; he was charged with the meaning of the mysteries" (36). What she wants to know is "whether America is right or wrong" (75). Her answer comes to depend on whether she can believe

[2] The counter-symbol to Washington, D.C., is Mount Vernon.

[3] Ernest Samuels, *Henry Adams: The Middle Years* (Cambridge, Mass.: Harvard University Press, 1958), p. 77, makes the same point. For historical background, see Ralph Henry Gabriel, *The Course of American Democratic Thought: An Intellectual History since 1815* (New York: The Ronald Press, 1940), pp. 91–94; and Robert E. Spiller, Willard Thorp, Thomas H. Johnson, Henry Seidel Canby, *et al.* (eds.), *Literary History of the United States* (3 vols.; New York: The Macmillan Co., 1948), I, 198–200. The theme of reunion is suggested in C. Vann Woodward, "A Southern Critique for the Gilded Age," in *The Burden of Southern History* (Baton Rouge: Louisiana State University Press, 1960), esp. pp. 123, 126; and developed in Earl N. Harbert (who cites Vann Woodward), "Henry Adams' New England View: A Regional Angle of Vision?" in *Tulane Studies in English*, XVI (1968), esp. 116–117.

[4] Henry Burr Rule, "Irony in the Works of Henry Adams" (Ph.D. dissertation, University of Colorado, 1960), p. 107.

[5] See critical note 3. Adams' association of Carrington and Washington is noted by Vann Woodward, p. 121.

in Ratcliffe. What it will be is foreshadowed by a comparison she makes during their first meeting. She flatters Ratcliffe by comparing his oratory favorably with that of Daniel Webster. Unwittingly, says Adams, she had "here hit on Ratcliffe's weak point; the outline of his head had, in fact, a certain resemblance to that of Webster, and he prided himself upon it, and on a distant relationship to the Expounder of the Constitution" (33-34).[6] There is no suggestion in *Democracy* of Adams' own attitude toward Webster; later, in *The Education*, he characterizes him as a cold man, led by "party discipline and self-interest" to sacrifice moral principle under the pretense of preserving the Union.[7] Mrs. Lee will eventually discover that this is what Ratcliffe did during the Civil War.[8]

These comparisons of Carrington and Ratcliffe to Washington and Webster heighten the antithesis Adams draws between his two chief male characters. Later he will make Washington also the prototype of Robert E. Lee (221) and thus identify Carrington with both as a man led by high principles to participate in a political revolution. Ratcliffe, by contrast, is shown to be a man whose loyalty was determined by self-interest and exploited for that end; he is the symbol and embodiment in the novel of the moral corruption of working democracy. Through this contrast, Adams implies that the best interests of America suffer from its continued division into North and South. The important division, he suggests, is not between former traitors and loyalists, but men who act upon principle and those who act out of self-interest. This moral distinction is the novel's contribution to Reconstruction. The allusions emphasize the point and also extend its application beyond the immediate temporal context of the novel.

Mrs. Lee studies Ratcliffe at private gatherings in her home. In time she receives three significant answers to her question whether working democracy is good or bad. A negative answer is given by Baron Jacobi, Bulgarian minister to the United States, who, possessing a witty and cynical worldly wisdom, is twice compared to Voltaire (109, 204).[9] "In all my experience," he says, "I have found no society which has had elements of corruption like the United States." In a hundred years "the United States will . . . be more corrupt . . . than the Church under Leo X.; more corrupt than France under the Regent!" The most idealistic answer is given by Nathan Gore, of Massachusetts, historian and former United States minister to Spain. "I believe in democracy," he says; "I

---

[6] This comparison appears again in the novel on pp. 57, 58, 102.

[7] Henry Adams, *The Education of Henry Adams*, introduction by James Truslow Adams, The Modern Library (New York: Random House, Inc., 1931), p. 29.

[8] See critical note 4.

[9] See critical note 5.

grant it is an experiment, but it is the only direction society can take that is worth its taking. . . . Every other possible step is backward." Later, Gore makes clear the theoretical basis for his belief: "I have faith; not perhaps in the old dogmas, but in the new ones; faith in human nature; faith in science; faith in the survival of the fittest. Let us be true to our time, Mrs. Lee!" Gore's faith is in Darwinian evolutionism and nine-teenth-century mechanistic science, interpreted in terms of a continuing belief in the Enlightenment's faith in the goodness of human nature. The explicit rejection of this eighteenth-century dogma in *The Life of Albert Gallatin*, together with the view of human nature which appears in the rest of *Democracy*, suggests that Gore does not speak for the author of *Democracy*. Adams' characterization of him as "abominably selfish, colossally egoistic, and a little vain" further substantiates this suggestion, as does his comment, after Gore's explicit profession of belief in Ratcliffe, that "ill-natured people might say that Mr. Gore saw in Senator Ratcliffe a possible Secretary of State"—and therefore a man with power to dispense the diplomatic post Gore has come to Washington to get. When he fails to do so, both his professed faith in Ratcliffe and in democracy disappear. He tells Mrs. Lee that in Washington she "will find nothing but wasted effort and clumsy intrigue" and that for her to try to reform Ratcliffe is a hopeless task (72–73, 77, 78, 43, 59, 200).

What, then, is the significance of Gore's profession of faith? In relation to the novel's main theme, it is a statement of the ultimate democratic ideal and therefore an extreme abstract statement of what Mount Vernon and George Washington symbolize later. Appropriately, it is expressed by a man with the knowledge of a historian and the articulateness of a literary man. Gore acknowledges the orthodoxy of the statement when he asks at its conclusion, "Have I repeated my catechism correctly?" When he adds, "Now oblige me by forgetting it. I should lose my character at home if it got out," his flippancy is not necessarily a sign that he has been insincerely repeating a rote formula, but seems to represent his knowledge that among sophisticated people anyone who believes such ideas is considered naïve. It may be, too, that he is aware of the gap between his ideals and his own actions. Indeed, Adams' characterization of him would seem to be a satirical thrust at the New England character. Puritans have often been satirized for the seeming or real hypocrisy growing out of their belief that one should pursue his calling with diligence while inwardly remaining aloof from the world. Adams' use of the stereotype here enables Gore to perform three important functions in the novel. First, he presents the ideal and reveals in his own person its lack of viability in the late nineteenth century. Even more important, he helps to explain Ratcliffe. As a New Englander, Ratcliffe was born to the same double tradition as Gore, but his upbringing in the West destroyed the ideal side of his nature (as he himself says later in regard to New England's idolization of George Washington). As a result, his great diligence in his calling is completely undirected by any ideals, religious or political. This triumph of absolute pragmatism is accompanied by an enormous energy whose source is Ratcliffe's particular temperament and his complete freedom from all standards except success. Again Gore offers a contrast. His weakness, too, is in part a temperamental matter, but it would also seem to be the consequence of his believing—or thinking he believes—in ideals no longer viable for himself or his society (79).[10]

Jacobi and Gore take opposite views of American exceptionalism. But both agree with Mrs. Lee in identifying Ratcliffe with American democracy. Carrington separates the two. He dislikes and disbelieves in Ratcliffe, though, unlike Jacobi, he bases these attitudes, initially at least, upon specific evidence of the Senator's misconduct in office. Later, his dislike is sharpened by personal jealousy. Yet he reveals the information he has against Ratcliffe to Mrs. Lee only when all other means of stopping their marriage fail. In regard to American democracy, he is not the idealist that Gore at least seems to be, but, unlike Jacobi, he does believe in it enough to believe in the possibility of reform (75). In these attitudes he is more at one with the attitudes of the book as a whole—and therefore, presumably, those of Henry Adams—than any other character.

Mrs. Lee's quest is soon complicated by her realization that both Carrington and Ratcliffe wish to marry her. She favors Ratcliffe because he succeeds in convincing her that he is fundamentally a moral man, who has had to compromise upon occasion for the good of the country and because of the character of the American citizen. By asking her for help he appeals both to her need for self-sacrifice, which she is aware of, and her ambition, which she is not, and thus keeps an advantage over Carrington, despite Mrs. Lee's personal preference for the latter and her continued uneasiness over Ratcliffe's morality.

The second section of the novel begins in chapter 6 with a visit to Mount Vernon, a symbol, like George Washington, of the ideal of American democracy, and ends with the grand ball in chapter 11. Chapter 6 begins with one of the most vivid of Adams' sensuous descriptions, used as an image of the answer to Mrs. Lee's quest. Speaking of Washington, D.C., the antithesis of Mount Vernon, Adams says,

In February the weather became warmer and summer-like. In Virginia there comes often at this season a deceptive gleam of summer, slipping in between heavy storm-clouds of sleet and snow; days and sometimes weeks when the

[10] See critical note 6.

temperature is like June. . . . Then men and women are languid; life seems, as in Italy, sensuous and glowing with colour; . . . the struggle of existence seems to abate; Lent throws its calm shadow over society; and youthful diplomatists, unconscious of their danger, are lured into asking foolish girls to marry them; the blood thaws in the heart and flows out into the veins, like the rills of sparkling water that trickle from every lump of ice or snow, as though all the ice and snow on earth, and all the hardness of heart, all the heresy and schism, all the works of the devil, had yielded to the force of love and to the fresh warmth of innocent, lamblike, confiding virtue. In such a world there should be no guile—but there is a great deal of it notwithstanding. Indeed, at no other season is there so much. This is the moment when the two whited sepulchres at either end of the Avenue reek with the thick atmosphere of bargain and sale. The old is going; the new is coming. Wealth, office, power are at auction. Who bids highest? who hates with most venom? who intrigues with most skill? who has done the dirtiest, the meanest, the darkest, and the most, political work? He shall have his reward.

The dash between "guile" and "but" breaks this Melville-like passage into two separate, but related parts. In the first, the words "deceptive," "seems," "lured," "as though," "should be," and finally "guile" counterpoint the dominant note of sensuous beauty. In the second part, these abstract terms become concrete in the image of "whited sepulchres," whose ugliness both brings the counterpoint of the first part to a climax and suggests that man's guile is more hideous than nature's (113–114). The mention of Lent in the first part also prepares for this image. Both suggest the pervasive religious atmosphere of the book and place it in the context of the Christianity from which the "democratic faith" partially derives. "Whited sepulchres" is Jesus' image of human hypocrisy: "Woe unto you, scribes and Pharisees, for ye are like unto whited sepulchres, which indeed appear beautiful outward, but are within full of dead men's bones, and of all uncleanness." Here in *Democracy* the image suggests the contrast between the moral pretense and the immoral reality of American democracy.

The rest of the chapter presents this contrast through narration as well as imagery, as a journey which Mrs. Lee and her friends take to Mount Vernon. Religious imagery continues to appear, though now general rather than specifically Christian: "In another moment the little steamer had begun her journey, pounding the muddy waters of the Potomac and sending up its small column of smoke as though it were a newly invented incense-burner approaching the temple of the national deity." The tone here is facetious, but the meaning is not. In going to Mount Vernon, the party is visiting the "temple" of the "national deity"; its journey is really a pilgrimage to the principal shrine of the democratic faith. This pilgrimage is an important part of Mrs. Lee's quest; Mount Vernon and George Washington are epitomes of the democratic ideal and are used as touchstones by Mrs. Lee to assess the value of Ratcliffe and the working democracy he represents. The climax of the pilgrimage is a "stylized procession of [the] characters who one by one come forward to declare what the great national symbol [Washington] means to them." [11] Mrs. Lee feels complete rapport with the spirit of the place. "Is not the sense of rest here captivating?" she asks. This rapport suggests the question whether, like Carrington and Ratcliffe, she too might not have some historical or other prototype and thus be more than simply an individual. None is ever mentioned specifically, yet there seems to be evidence of such significance. Ratcliffe, Carrington, and Gore represent the geographical extremities of America, the corrupt West, the essentially moral South, and the combined moralism and self-interestedness of New England respectively. Mrs. Lee, by contrast, is from Philadelphia and has lived in New York most of her life. She tells Carrington at one point that she is half Yankee, and she married a displaced Southerner living in New York. Thus she represents all of America geographically except the West, which is considered socially and morally inferior to the rest of the country. She herself feels that she is "American to the tips of her fingers." This identification appears in her reaction to the charge of Lord Skye, the British ambassador, that Americans are unable to appreciate the subtler beauties of their own country:

> Mrs. Lee resented the charge. America, she maintained, had not worn her feelings threadbare like Europe. She had still her story to tell; she was waiting for her Burns and Scott, her Wordsworth and Byron, her Hogarth and Turner. "You want peaches in the spring," she said. "Give us our thousand years of summer, and then complain, if you please, that our peach is not as mellow as yours."

Adams would seem to suggest that Mrs. Lee's prototype is America itself, at its moral and aesthetic best, that she is America's ideal self, as it were, personified as a woman. [12] In this role she combines the best of the

---

[11] J. C. Levenson, *The Mind and Art of Henry Adams* (Boston: Houghton Mifflin Co., 1957), p. 94. Levenson also says that Mount Vernon is a "backdrop" for this procession. In the novel as a whole Mount Vernon has the same significance as George Washington through association with him. Ratcliffe and Washington, D.C., function similarly as opposite symbols, except that Ratcliffe is only one representative of the many figures whose corruption has, by association, become associated with the city. The "procession" here is discussed fully by Levenson, pp. 94–95, and more briefly by Rule, "Irony in the Works of Henry Adams," pp. 105–106, and Robert A. Hume, *Runaway Star: An Appreciation of Henry Adams* (Ithaca, New York: Cornell University Press, 1952), p. 137.

[12] See critical note 7.

North and South and thus represents the East, suggesting that Ratcliffe, as a New Englander who migrated to the West and became its representative, is America's worst self (119, 132, 5, 126–127).

The analogy between Ratcliffe and Webster does not appear in this visit to Mount Vernon (nor, indeed, again in the novel), but Carrington's likeness to George Washington is remarked again, this time by a person quite different from Madeleine Lee. Victoria Dare, another guest in the party, asks her companion if Mr. Carrington is not "a little your idea of George Washington restored to us in his prime?" (133).

The most extended tribute to Washington is paid by Gore. New Englanders, he says, "never had any liking for Virginia," and Washington liked neither New England nor its people. Nonetheless, he says, "we idolize him. To us he is Morality, Justice, Duty, Truth; half a dozen Roman gods with capital letters. He is austere, solitary, grand; he ought to be deified." Again, the religious nature of the democratic faith appears as Washington is characterized as a national deity. Carrington's only contribution to the discussion is an anecdote demonstrating Washington's honesty and scrupulousness in a money matter; nevertheless, the point is also relevant to the whole of Washington's character. Though the remarks are primarily intended to draw out Ratcliffe, they show that Carrington views Washington as a great man but not a deity.[13] Later he will amplify this opinion—at least by implication—when he tells Sybil Ross (Mrs. Lee's younger sister and companion) that he and the South thought Lee would be their Washington. Again he stands on a common-sense middle ground between the ideal view desired by Mrs. Lee and expressed by Gore, and the complete cynicism of Ratcliffe. The Senator says that as a boy in New England he had been taught Gore's belief that "Washington was a sort of American Jehovah. But the West is a poor school for Reverence. Since coming to Congress I have learned more about General Washington, and have been surprised to find what a narrow base his reputation rests on." His principal objection is that Washington "stood outside of politics. The thing couldn't be done to-day. ... If Washington were President now, he would have to learn our ways or lose his next election." "Our ways" means that "if virtue won't answer our purpose, we must use vice." Challenged by the touchstone of American political purity, Ratcliffe reveals the cynicism and corruption both of himself and of late nineteenth-century American democracy (134–135, 135–136, 140–141).

[13] I owe this characterization of Carrington's views as humanizing Washington to R. P. Blackmur, "The Novels of Henry Adams," *Sewanee Review*, LI (April–June, 1943), 288; and Sister M. Aquinas Healy, "A Study of Non-Rational Elements in the Works of Henry Adams as Centralized in his Attitude toward Women" (Ph.D. dissertation, University of Wisconsin, 1956), p. 158.

In the following two chapters Adams forgoes indirection and describes American democratic government at work. He shows Ratcliffe's success both in bringing the new President under his control and in persuading Mrs. Lee, despite her moral revulsion, to accept his view of the events.

The third section of the novel, extending from chapter 13[14] through the conclusion, begins with Mrs. Lee's discovery that Ratcliffe was once paid $100,000 for pushing a bill through the Senate.[15] Her first reaction is anger: "she was impatient for the moment when she should see him again, and tear off his mask." Here the theme of deception, imaged in the description of Washington, D.C., in February, finally breaks into the action of the novel as Madeleine discovers the corruption behind Ratcliffe's façade. Her second reaction, however, is to be angry at herself. He had never deceived her, she thinks. He had always "openly enough avowed that he knew no code of morals in politics." She realizes that

> she had not known the recesses of her own heart. She had honestly supposed that . . . [her intention of marrying Ratcliffe was] an act of self-sacrifice; and now she saw that in the depths of her soul very different motives had been at work: ambition, thirst for power, restless eagerness to meddle in what did not concern her, blind longing to escape from the torture of watching other women with full lives and satisfied instincts, while her own life was hungry and sad (333, 335–336).

This is the climax of the second theme of the novel and resolves the ambiguity in Mrs. Lee's motives described in the first chapter. Of the five motives given there, her unconscious desire for power has proved altogether too important. Luckily, she thinks, "she had saved herself in time." As for her desire to find strong individuals, she has found Ratcliffe "strong enough to satisfy her," but has failed to find any peace in that strength. Only curiosity, the motive she herself had thought strongest, is fully satisfied. As Ratcliffe defends himself in their final interview, Adams says that Mrs. Lee "felt as though she had got to the heart of politics, so that she could, like a physician with his stethoscope, measure the organic disease." At last she had reached the "heart of the great American mystery." The more she observed Ratcliffe "the surer she was that . . . he talked about virtue and vice as a man who is colour-blind talks about red and green." The figure is medical, but the disease is moral. Madeleine's desire to know whether America is good or bad is answered: American democracy as a working reality is bad. She rejects her Webster-ian suitor in scorn (342, 341, 352, 10, 353).[16]

[14] Actually, chapter 12, but there is no chapter 12 in the edition of *Democracy* I used, due to a misnumbering.

[15] See critical note 8.

[16] See critical note 9.

But though she thereby also rejects working democracy, this does not mean that Mrs. Lee agrees with Jacobi that democracy is potentially worse than other forms of government. What she has found is that it is "nothing more than government of any other kind"—a struggle for power. This realization is the climax of the novel's main theme and again is expressed in terms of deception. For Mrs. Lee, it means the end of a quest which has given her finally neither amusement nor a meaning for her life. "I want to go to Egypt," she says; ". . . democracy has shaken my nerves to pieces. Oh, what rest it would be to live in the Great Pyramid and look out for ever at the polar star!" [17] On leaving Mount Vernon she had used the image of the child crying for the moon and stars to express her longing for a political ideal. Now she uses part of this image once more, again to express her desire for an unchanging absolute able to serve both as a touchstone for perfection and a place of peace and refuge from a corrupt world. [18] George Washington, of course, represents American democracy's closest individual approximation to such an ideal, and, though time has corrupted his political creation, he himself has survived as a human type. Thus it is not surprising that at the end of the novel it is suggested that eventually Mrs. Lee may marry Carrington. Such an alliance would resolve the third theme of the novel by reuniting the North and South. It would also join America's best self with the Washington type and thus give hope of the continuation of the finest aspects of America and the American character. Yet it seems to have no political significance for the future; such higher types of human beings would appear to be cut off from political rule. Mrs. Lee suggests in her final speech to Ratcliffe what Adams also seems to accept, that the West is going to continue to rule America and hence that the worst in the country will rule, for the West, like its representative Ratcliffe, seems to be characterized by a "blind ignorance of morals" and a wholly pragmatic pursuit of power (342, 370, 144, 105).

In breaking with her representative of working democracy, Mrs. Lee, as America's ideal self, also breaks with democratic government. Neither Carrington nor Henry Adams seems to do so, however. Adams' attitude, insofar as it can be identified with that of the book's narrator, is expressed in a passage appearing in almost the exact center of the book, at the

[17] Mrs. Lee's admiration for George Washington and her desire to "look out for ever at the polar star" come together in *The Education*, where Adams writes that "George Washington was a primary, or, if Virginians liked it better, an ultimate relation, like the Pole Star, and amid the endless restless motion of every other visible point in space, he alone remained steady, in the mind of Henry Adams, to the end" (p. 47). By contrast, Adams characterizes himself, in *The Education*, as a "runaway star" (p. 472).

[18] Cf., George Hochfield, *Henry Adams: An Introduction and Interpretation* (New York: Holt, Rinehart and Winston, Inc., 1962), p. 32.

beginning of the second of the two chapters which show Ratcliffe and working democracy if not at their worst at least in the worst light in which they are directly presented in the book. (The ugliness of the "dance of democracy" revealed in these chapters is enhanced by flanking them with the two chapters in the book which present American idealism at its most intense: those about the pilgrimage to Mount Vernon and the ride Carrington and Sybil take through Arlington Cemetery, formerly the residence of Robert E. Lee, whom Carrington says the South believed was to be its Washington.) Adams begins this crucially important passage with the observation that

> Of all titles ever assumed by prince or potentate, the proudest is that of the Roman pontiffs: "Servus servorum Dei"—"Servant of the servants of God." In former days it was not admitted that the devil's servants could by right have any share in government. They were to be shut out, punished, exiled, maimed, and burned. The devil has no servants now; only the people have servants. There may be some mistake about a doctrine which makes the wicked, when a majority, the mouthpiece of God against the virtuous, but the hopes of mankind are staked on it; and if the weak in faith sometimes quail when they see humanity floating in a shoreless ocean, on this plank, which experience and religion long since condemned as rotten, mistake or not, men have thus far floated better by its aid, than the popes ever did with their prettier principle; so that it will be a long time yet before society repents.[19]

The basis for this passage is a contrast between the political principle of the Roman Catholic church and that of democracy regarded as a religion. The popes, Adams says, served people who served God; the leaders of democracy serve all the people. In neither case are people served who serve the devil. In the church the devil's servants were shut out of leadership (and as much as possible out of the community). In a democracy it is not admitted that the devil has servants, for the majority, which rules in a democracy, is considered the spokesman of God and if the wicked be a majority then it must speak for God. The religious context of the passage relates it to the over-all problem of the book, whether democracy is a religious ideal or not. It also enables Adams to push the irony inherent in the democratic principle—that if the majority are evil, then evil should rule—to the point of paradox—that in such a situation evil is good because it is the expression of God. Both logic and religion, therefore—insofar as religion views good and evil, God and the devil, as antithetical—are opposed to the democratic principle. It is also opposed by historical experience, Adams says, meaning apparently that it failed to create an enduring social order in past societies like Athens and Rome. Yet he gives

[19] See critical note 10.

two reasons for accepting democracy. First, he observes (echoing Gore) that mankind has accepted it. Hence there is no constructive alternative in modern life to accepting it. The problem for the individual becomes that of trying to make it work. Second, Adams asserts that "so far" democracy has worked better (apparently in the United States in particular) than the papal principle (171, 181–182).

This view of democracy is both less ideal and less desperate than Gore's. It is not committed to all the nineteenth-century dogmas Gore accepts—one of them the belief that the masses are now raised to a higher level than previously—nor does it require, as Gore does, that belief in democracy be a matter of sheer will. It is not so cynical as Jacobi's view, not because it denies America's potential for corruption but because, by focusing upon a different matter—how well society has got along using the democratic principle as its basis—it has a modicum of hope to offer. It differs from Ratcliffe's view in that while it recognizes the inevitability of evil in democratic government, it does not accept the evil in accepting the government. It is not Mrs. Lee's view because while it rejects democracy as an ideal, it does not reject it as a form of government. It even retains a modicum of that doctrine of American exceptionalism which the intensity of Mrs. Lee's disillusionment leads her to completely reject. It is most like the view of Carrington, who never identifies Ratcliffe with democracy nor thinks of George Washington as a deity. Carrington sees the former as an evil man, the latter as a superlatively good man, but both as men. He never considers democracy an ideal, even at Mount Vernon; presumably, therefore, he views it as human and imperfect, though capable of being improved (as he suggests when he criticizes Ratcliffe for opposing reform movements). His view would seem to be what the novel works toward. Its focus, through Mrs. Lee and her conflict with Ratcliffe, is upon the falsity of the doctrine of American moral exceptionalism and, in general, of the belief that democracy (or any political system) is worthy of religious devotion.[20] But this ironic and sometimes bitter destruction of democracy's ideal pretensions does not prevent Adams, in the above passage and in the person of Carrington, from believing at this time that it has worked well enough to deserve his own continued acceptance.

[20] Cf., Hochfield, *Henry Adams*, p. 27.

CHAPTER III

THE ACCEPTANCE OF NATURE AS ULTIMATE AUTHORITY

Esther : A Novel (1884)[1] is a bridge between the political focus of Adams' early work and his later philosophical emphasis. In both periods he is concerned with philosophical problems, but in the early period these are significant primarily as background for his paramount interest. Throughout his work he seeks for answers to such problems in the relationship between man and nature and particularly in the question of the relative degree of reality and sovereignty possessed by each element in the relationship. In the essays of the 1860's and 1870's the concern with politics itself implies that some degree of reality and sovereignty inheres in man's will and ideas. During the 1870's, however, the essays show a decrease in such faith until in *The Life of Albert Gallatin* "circumstances" are shown to be decisive in determining human events. Mitigated by the moral satire and novelistic form of *Democracy*, this ascription of both reality and sovereignty to nature reaches its climax in the early work in *The History of the United States During the Administrations of Thomas Jefferson and James Madison*, where the "circumstances" of *Gallatin* become natural "forces" which operate mechanically through men to bring about events. After *The History*, nature annexes an even greater share of reality and sovereignty and is conceived of as ultimately chaotic rather than mechanical. Adams' attitude toward man's fate becomes even more pessimistic.

Esther's determinism and its belief in the mechanical operation of nature make it more like *The History* than the later work. Yet it differs from both in two important respects. First, it affirms an optimism toward nature's ruling authority and therefore toward at least the immediate future of man which distinguishes it from all Adams' work after *Gallatin*. There are

[1] Henry Adams, *Esther: A Novel*, by Francis Snow Compton [pseud.], with an introduction by Robert E. Spiller (New York: Scholars' Facsimiles and Reprints, 1938). All page references to this work will be found between parentheses in the text.

37

still ambiguities and uncertainties in Adams' attitude: the basis for optimism is expressed only in terms of a symbol; the story itself is tragic;
and at one point Adams seems to suggest that his optimism grows out of
a more fundamental pessimism. Nevertheless, *Esther* remains the most
hopeful of Adams' major works. Its second unique (or almost unique)
feature is that in it nature is viewed as essentially spiritual rather than
material. Only in "Buddha and Brahma" among Adams' other works
is nature viewed so, and there the material world is not so much spirit-
ualized as made a façade for spirit. Thus *Esther* represents a kind of
spiritual or idealistic interlude in Adams' continuing movement toward
an ever more pervasive naturalism. But it also anticipates the later period.
Between *Gallatin* and *The History*, Adams was primarily concerned with
criticizing the American dream and the liberal system of ideas on which
it rests. After 1890 he shifts away from criticism toward a positive, if
limited, affirmation of his own philosophy of history and its pessimistic
naturalism.[2] This change is a shift of emphasis from practice and even
principles to the conception of reality upon which both practice and principles are based. It is in *Esther*'s concern with this new emphasis that it
represents the beginning of the later period in Adams' work.

The story is of a woman's discovery that she cannot marry a man whose

[2] According to Iredell Jenkins in Dagobert D. Runes (ed.), *The Dictionary of Philosophy* (New York: The Philosophical Library, 1942), p. 205, philosophical "Naturalism"
is defined as "the general philosophical position which has as its fundamental tenet the
proposition that the natural world is the whole of reality. . . . Nature is thus conceived
as self-contained and self-dependent, and from this view spring certain negations. . . .
First, it is denied that nature is derived from or dependent upon any transcendent,
supernatural entities. From this follows the denial that the order of natural events can
be intruded upon. And this in turn entails the denial of freedom, purpose, and transcendent destiny." This is the view which *Gallatin* moves toward and which is fully, if
ambiguously, expressed in *The History*. It is also fully—and explicitly—expressed in the
dynamic theory of history in the later work. It differs from Adams' ultimate view in
ascribing to natural events "order" rather than chaos. I use "pessimistic naturalism" to refer both to the dynamic theory and the final view but not *The History*'s view.

Late nineteenth-century literary naturalism also follows this definition at least to the
extent of asserting "that man belongs entirely to the order of nature and does not have a
soul or any other connection with a religious or spiritual world beyond nature." (M. H.
Abrams, *A Glossary of Literary Terms* [New York: Holt, Rinehart and Winston, 1963],
"Naturalism," p. 76.) The "pessimistic naturalism" of Adams' later work also embodies
the second clause of Abrams' definition of the "philosophical thesis" of naturalism:
"that man is therefore merely a higher order animal whose character and fortunes are
determined by two kinds of natural forces, heredity and environment." For Adams'
relationship to literary naturalism, see John Lydenberg, "Henry Adams and Lincoln
Steffens," *South Atlantic Quarterly*, XLVIII (January, 1949), 42–64, esp. 43, 52–53,
59–60. Lydenberg, however, interprets Adams' later views not in terms of his ultimate
belief in chaos but in terms of the dynamic theory's belief in natural laws and therefore
some degree of order in nature.

ideas she abhors, however much she loves him. Again, a false view of reality is opposed to a truer view, the false view here being identified with the past, the truer, with the present and future. The false view is that of Christian orthodoxy, the truer, that naturalistic view which science is struggling toward. Adams' sympathy with the view of the present and the future is the optimistic element in the book. Intellectually, Esther, the heroine and chief character, agrees with Adams. She rejects orthodox religion as an outworn point-of-view and accepts the validity of the truth science aims at. Her tragedy is that the man she falls in love with is a devout believer in the view she rejects. Thus she is caught between two worlds, unable wholly to accept either, yet forced to choose between them.

Unlike *Democracy*, the focus of *Esther*, as the title suggests, is upon its heroine as much as its subject. In both works the heroine is depicted (as is the Virgin in *Chartres*) as a creature whose deepest need, as a woman, is to give and receive love. In *Democracy* Madeleine's womanliness is depicted from the beginning as being partially destroyed; then Ratcliffe proves morally unworthy of her love; hence her rejection of him is not a denial of her womanly need for love but of woman's subsidiary need for self-sacrifice, motivated by a moral rejection of that direct drive for power which in her has replaced a normal feminine nature. In *Esther*, however, the heroine's womanliness has been awakened fully for the first time and the man she rejects is personally worthy of her love. Hence, the inner as well as outer conflict is greatly intensified. What Esther must do is choose between her womanly need for love and what proves to be her even deeper need for truth.

Adams took the name Esther from Nathaniel Hawthorne's story "Old Esther Dudley,"[3] which concerns a New England woman who remained fanatically loyal to England and the king long after the Revolutionary War has ended; Adams' Esther also has the last name Dudley and is said to be a descendant of the same Puritan family which furnished Hawthorne with his heroine (22). The story and the novel are very different, but they have in common, besides the names of their heroines, a concern with the clash of an incompatible past and present, depicted in each case through the plight of a woman in some way emotionally involved with the past, yet surrounded and confronted by the reality of the present. The allusion also introduces the overtones of national significance in the novel. One of Adams' characters says of Esther that "Miss Dudley is one of the most marked American types I ever saw." The suggestion, lightly made, is that Esther's problem is a national as well as a personal one, that contem-

---

[3] Nathaniel Hawthorne, *The Complete Novels and Selected Tales of Nathaniel Hawthorne*, edited with an introduction by Norman Holmes Pearson, The Modern Library (New York: Random House, Inc., 1937), pp. 982–990.

porary America is involved in as painful a period of transition as was the America Hawthorne was concerned with in his revolutionary tale (26).

In terms of the action of the book Esther's movement toward a decision has four parts: the first three chapters introduce the characters, stress their disagreements about religion, and move toward their common interest in art. Chapters 4 and 5 show two romances growing in the atmosphere of this common interest. Chapters 6 through 8 show these romances under strain and tentatively breaking up; chapters 9 and 10 show them finally destroyed. Symbolically, this movement can be divided into two parts. The first three parts are united by being centered around a recently completed Episcopal church on New York's Fifth Avenue. The last two chapters are even more pervasively dominated by Niagara Falls. Between the two settings (and joining them) is Esther's night journey by railroad from New York, which ends in the morning at the falls. In these terms, as Henry Rule has pointed out,[4] *Esther* has the dichotomous structure based on a duality both of idea and symbol characteristic of Adams' work. The Church is a religious symbol of reality, the falls, a natural symbol of reality, whereas Esther's journey suggests the movement of her thought and action from the temptation to embrace the lesser truth of religion through the confusion which follows rejecting it to her attainment of a fuller truth and her decision to adhere to it despite its cost to her. The conflict of the novel is between the claims of religion and nature as expressions of reality.

But to view the book thus simply—and validly—is to leave out a third element, not so important as religion and nature, but still important. The second part of the book, though it occurs in a church, does not center in it as a religious place but as a building to be decorated with art work. The principal work of art in the section is Petrarch's sonnets, which function in much the same way for the artist as the Church does for the minister Hazard and the falls for Esther. As the church building, church ritual, and especially church doctrines (296) give expression to Hazard's sense of what Adams would later call the infinite; so the story, perhaps the form, and especially the emotions of suffering for love and of hope for eternal peace, which appear in the sonnets, express for Wharton—who, as an artist, "felt rather than talked" (68)—his deepest sense of reality. The Church, the falls, and the sonnets are all not only symbols but the most important of symbols because they embody outwardly and concretely the inner feelings or ideas of the characters about the nature of ultimate reality.

Chapter 1 of the novel is dominated by the Church. The central figure is Stephen Hazard, who four times is referred to as St. Stephen, the first

<hr/>

[4] Henry Burr Rule, "Irony in the Works of Henry Adams" (Ph.D. dissertation, University of Colorado, 1960), pp. 134–135.

Christian martyr.[5] In this book he, too, is martyred for his faith: the allusion both foreshadows his fate and has thematic significance. In chapter 1, however, not his personal life but his sermon and its ideas are central. As spokesman for Christian orthodoxy, he asserts that "behind all thought and matter [exists] only one central idea . . . —I AM!" The ultimate realities are a divine person and His awareness of Himself. Individual human beings have no existence of their own; they "were and are and ever will be only a part of [this] supreme I AM, of which the church is the emblem." Indeed, all beings, all acts, and all thought are but instruments by which this person works "out his unrevealed ends." The conflict between religion and science is therefore meaningless. Though the basic terms here are Cartesian, the sermon expresses what are said to be the "thirteenth-century ideas" of Hazard (8, 7, 104).

The only two members of the audience who are said to understand the sermon react unfavorably. George Strong, a scientist, and his cousin Esther enjoy the service but only as a theatrical performance. Later, Wharton, the artist who is decorating the church, says bitterly, "It *is* a theater. . . . That is what ails our religion" (98). All three suggest that what should be a complex symbol, created by the church building and the service, for a spiritual reality actually has only aesthetic significance— a lesser value. But whereas Esther and Strong can enjoy the church and the service as art, Wharton finds even the art false. "I am sick at heart about our church work," he tells Hazard; "it is a failure. . . . The thing does not belong to our time or feelings" (29). Wharton thinks of himself as being, like Strong and Esther, a part of the world of the present and the future, whereas he calls Hazard medieval (28). The conflict which begins here between the medieval and the modern forms the intellectual context of the book and the background for Esther's personal struggle. But there is some question whether Wharton is really modern. It has been noted that he is "the one figure in the book who can mediate between the centuries"[6]; more important, he is the one figure who can mediate between the two (antithetical) worlds of the book. He can do so because he is a nineteenth-century embodiment of the Renaissance, as Hazard is a nineteenth-century embodiment of the Middle Ages, and Strong, of the modern era—meaning the immediate future as well as present. This identification of Wharton is never pressed very hard, but it seems to follow from several pieces of evidence. First, his name is bracketed with

---

[5] I am indebted for this point to R. P. Blackmur, "The Novels of Henry Adams," *Sewanee Review*, LI (April–June, 1943), 302. The references to St. Stephen in *Esther* are on pp. 13 (two), 17, and 24.

[6] J. C. Levenson, *The Mind and Art of Henry Adams* (Boston: Houghton Mifflin Co., 1957), p. 203.

that of Titian by Mrs. Dyer and Catherine Brooke; more significantly, Esther accuses him of wanting her to paint like Michelangelo, the implication being that Wharton's style resembles that of the Renaissance master. Catherine, seeing him enter the church with Esther one day, imagines she sees Michelangelo and Raphael entering. Wharton himself identifies with Petrarch. Most important, he tells Esther that he had originally wanted to put "beauty of form" in the church but that "only the sternest, strongest types would satisfy the church then. 'It was all I could do to get them down to the thirteenth century!'" (97–98). He seems to mean that he would have liked "to get them down" to the Renaissance. This desire is not contradicted by his statement two paragraphs later that "I would like now, even as it is, to go back to the age of beauty, and put a Madonna in the heart of their church"; like the Renaissance, Wharton is somewhat at home in the medieval as well as the modern world. Presumably he would like to give his Madonna the human "beauty of form" characteristic of Renaissance art, just as later he will anthropomorphize Niagara Falls, symbol of the modern world, in terms of the classical gods the Renaissance delighted in.

Wharton and the spirit of the Renaissance preside over the second section of the novel in chapters 4 and 5. Wharton is directing his workers, including Esther, in completing the paintings that are to decorate the church. Though the setting is within the church, the atmosphere is aesthetic rather than religious. In this atmosphere the pervasive conflict of the book diminishes and a precarious harmony is achieved. In Adams' view art does not make the ultimate claims nor require the ultimate commitments that religion and science do; moreover it has the power (as he will stress in *Chartres*) within its limits to reconcile the irreconcilable. All the characters can participate in this art-world of "religious Bohemianism and acted poetry" (117). Esther's part is to do a painting of the early Christian martyr St. Cecilia (and thereby foreshadow her own form of martyrdom for a different belief). Hazard is a frequent visitor, and Esther's model is Catherine Brooke, a fresh, unsophisticated, young Colorado girl staying with Esther's aunt. Eventually, with Hazard's consent, Esther decides to dress her saint in the green dress Laura wore when Petrarch first saw her. Hazard himself, with Wharton as his model, draws St.Luke opposite St. Cecilia as Petrarch gazing at Esther's Laura. Thus even the Christian decorations in this world become Renaissance portraits. But they also have a personal relevance to the characters. The ability of art to reconcile opposites extends to people as well as their ideas; here it encourages the development of romances between Hazard and Esther, and Wharton and Catherine. These romances are imaged not only by the paintings but also by the characters' united interest in Petrarch's sonnets.

Wharton has long considered Petrarch his poet; years earlier, when he and Hazard were students in France, they had translated a number of the sonnets. Now Hazard begins "to think that he [is] himself Petrarch" and Esther, his Laura, as they paint together and recite lines from the sonnets (115).

It is these sonnets and not the thirteenth-century paintings Wharton is forced to paint which form the real center of the second section of the book. That the poems of a poet often called the first Renaissance man should be favorites with Wharton fits his symbolic role in the novel; but when Hazard points out that Petrarch was "a bit of a churchman" (107), he not only justifies his own liking for them in terms of his symbolic function but reminds the reader of the dual and therefore mediatory role both of the Renaissance and of Wharton. Hazard's observation also helps to justify his own connivance in the transformation of church paintings depicting Christian saints dedicated to the love of God to paintings depicting—Renaissance-like—a man and woman dedicated to love for one another. The sonnets are also very useful to the lovers. All four of them can appreciate their subject matter and, to some extent, their aesthetic appeal. They also make it possible to talk about love without being personal. Yet though the sonnets thus provide a medium in which the two romances can flourish, they also foreshadow their ultimate destruction. The love of Petrarch and Laura was unconsummated, and so will be that of the four characters in *Esther*. The two complete sonnets and four lines of a third which appear in the novel emphasize this aspect of the poems. The two complete sonnets are among those Petrarch wrote after Laura's death, when his unhappiness was most intense. In the one that Esther translates Petrarch tells a bird mourning summer's end and its separation from its mate that his own sorrow is much greater than that of the bird because, while spring may see it reunited with its love, the poet has no such hope. In Hazard's sonnet, the poet, at the end of his life, mourns that he has wasted his life in loving Laura. Esther's sonnet seems to foreshadow her own feelings after she rejects Hazard; his perhaps suggests his rationalizations after that rejection. Only the fragment of the third sonnet approximates the atmosphere of the lovers' "ecclesiastical idyll."[7] Hazard tells Esther that after Petrarch saw Laura in church he "wrote to her face something like this: 'As sight of God is the eternal

---

[7] The numbers of the full sonnets are CCCLIII and CCCLXV. The fragment is CXCI. In *Esther* lines from the last appear on pp. 108, 115, 287–288. Blackmur, "The Novels of Henry Adams," pp. 301–302; and Ernest Samuels, *Henry Adams: The Middle Years* (Cambridge, Mass.: Harvard University Press, 1958), pp. 247–248, discuss Adams' use of Petrarch and see the lovers' concern with his sonnets as a fore-shadowing of their own eventual estrangement.

life, / Nor more we ask, nor more to wish we dare, / So, lady, sight of thee,' and so on, or words to that effect" (107–108). Yet this fragment contains the elements which will destroy the relationship of Hazard and Esther: Esther's disbelief in Christianity and her realization that to be Hazard's wife she must become a part of the Church. Her struggle to believe is her crucial struggle in the book, for on its success or failure hangs her own personal happiness.

Thus the disunity and suffering of parts three and four of *Esther* lie implicit in the very midst of the unity and happiness of part two. Adams warns that such unity is both transitory and unreal: the idyll, he says, was "blind and deaf to the realities of life." The world of art, despite its charm, is an unreal world, an escape from life, and the unity and happiness it provides are illusory and fleeting (101).

In chapter 6, which begins part three of the novel, the bubble bursts: Wharton's estranged, harridan of a wife appears, and Esther's father dies. In the midst of Esther's grief, Hazard declares his love and they become engaged. But Esther's happiness is brief; it ends in church the following morning as she realizes anew her dislike for the Church and her disbelief in its doctrines. She also realizes that Hazard "believes in his church more than he does in me. If I can't believe in it, he will have to give me up." Hazard himself has made the match, despite parish criticism, because of his love for Esther and because "his lifelong faith, that all human energies belonged to the church, was on trial. . . . [If] it broke down in a test so supreme as that of marriage, the blow would go far to prostrate him forever." The stage is set for the struggle which now becomes the principal subject of the rest of the novel. Hazard's struggle is to marry Esther as the prelude to converting her, Esther's, to learn to believe in Christianity or else find the strength to reject her lover. In this part the Church as a religious entity is again dominant, but the emphasis is upon its theology rather than its ritual and it is only briefly important as setting. Indeed, symbolism has less importance in this part of the book than in any of the others. The focus is upon argument (174, 209).

Esther repeatedly turns for help to her paleontologist cousin, George Strong, a Darwinian and a religious skeptic, "who looked at churches very much as he would have looked at a layer of extinct oysters in a buried mud-bank." Strong's sense of the irreconcilability of religion and science is as emphatic as Esther's and Wharton's; his putting this sense in a historical context, the same; and his commitment to science, as profound; but he is far more articulate about his beliefs than either of his friends. Yet he refuses to help Esther and does all he can to help Hazard. His reasons are not altogether clear. In one passage, he is said to believe that Esther's influence will inevitably draw Hazard "away from his old forms of belief." Later, he is said to believe that it is "as easy to believe one thing as another." In both passages he rejects religion, but in the first he seems to accept science as a system of belief, while in the second his view seems to be that of the complete skeptic, to whom science reveals the invalidity of all beliefs. Therefore, it makes no difference what one believes, and Esther may as well accept Hazard's ideas as any others. The difference between these two attitudes perhaps suggests the similar doubleness in Henry Adams' own later beliefs. On the one hand, Adams developed his dynamic theory of history. On the other, he was a complete skeptic except for his belief in chaos. In his case, the latter view was his final view, the former, his "working" view. There is no such resolution here, yet it should be noted that only once in the novel is Strong's position said to be complete skepticism. Generally, unlike the later Adams, he is committed to the scientific world-view, though he thinks of this as a changing and progressing position (219, 192, 220, 72, 272–273).

The fourth part of the book begins when Esther breaks off her engagement, and her aunt, who always opposed it, hustles both girls off to Niagara Falls. As the train speeds through the night, Esther, alone in her berth, finds her solitary thoughts a burden. "Never again," Adams has her reflect,

> could she go back to the old life, but like a young bird that has lost its mate, she must fly on through the gloom till its end. Unluckily all her thoughts brought her back to Hazard. Even this sense of resembling a bird that flies, it knows not where, recalled to her the sonnet of Petrarch which she had once translated for him, and which, since then, had been always on his lips, although she had never dreamed that it could have such meaning to her. Long after she had established herself in her berth, solitary and wakeful, the verses made rhythm with the beat of the car-wheels:

> "Vago augelleto che cantando vai!" (246)

Here, at the beginning of the final section of the novel, the Petrarchan idyll reappears, just as the church appeared in part two. In both cases the effect is at once to unify the novel and to emphasize the contrast between its parts. The disunity fostered by the Church as a religious symbol in part one became unity when the church building became the scene of aesthetic activity in part two. Here in part four that unity again becomes disunity as the tragic implications of the sonnet Esther translated begin to be realized in her own life.

The comparison of Esther to a lonely bird is a recurrent image in the novel.[8] Wharton, maintaining that Esther has a soul while in Catherine's eyes there is "only earth," says, "A soul is like a bird, and needs a sharp

[8] See critical note 11.

tap on its shell to open it." The death of Esther's father and her broken engagement are the taps which bring that soul to life. Indeed, the novel can be looked upon as an account of the birth of Esther's soul. Moreover, as the American "national type," she is also the contemporary American soul, and Adams may be suggesting that in this novel its birth is also being dramatized. In any case, Adams says that, after her father's death, Esther's sense of being alone made her "dizzy, as though she were a solitary bird flying through mid-air." At the same time Hazard sees her as "like a wandering soul, lost in infinite space, but still floating on, with her quiet air of confidence as though she were a part of nature itself." Earlier, Wharton sees her as a "yacht in mid-ocean." All these images portray Esther as alone amidst the vastness of an indifferent reality. This is like the view of all men's relationship to reality which appears in *The Education of Henry Adams*. There Adams sees reality as nature, and nature as an infinite vastness of space containing forces eternally alone except when absorbing or being absorbed by the other forces with which they are continually colliding. Here the picture is similar except that it is drawn in much brighter colors and not so fully intellectualized (77, 28, 157, 155, 27).

This section begins with Esther's discovery that for her Niagara Falls is the symbol of that new world which mankind is entering. On the first morning after her arrival at Niagara she feels a "sense of new life" in the presence of the falls. Adams writes that "she had already taken a fancy to this tremendous, rushing, roaring companion. . . . "

> To brush her hair while such a confidant looked on and asked questions, was more than Pallas Athene herself could do, though she looked out forever from the windows of her Acropolis over the Blue Aegean. The sea is capricious, fickle, angry, fawning, violent, savage and wanton; it caresses and raves in a breath, and has its moods of silence, but Esther's huge playmate rambled on with its story, in the same steady voice, never shrill or angry, never silent or degraded by a sign of human failings, and yet so frank and sympathetic that she had no choice but to like it. (257-258)

The falls is a symbol of eternity, infinity, and omnipotence, and its story is one aspect of ultimate reality. Yet it is not the final symbol for reality—or even a typical symbol, for Adams says that "eternity, infinity, and omnipotence . . . come rarely in such a humor." Apparently his comparison of the falls with the ocean is intended to suggest the difference between the "humor" of the falls and the "humor" of a more representative, or even the most representative, symbol of eternity, infinity, and omnipotence.[9] For Athene is the Greek goddess of wisdom and may,

[9] Adams' characterization of the ocean suggests that multiverse of chaos and contradiction which appears in *The Education*, and of which man is a part. Dennis S. R. Welland,

therefore, represent absolute wisdom in communion with the ultimate and eternal reality of the sea, as Esther represents the relative wisdom of a new world in historical time in communion with the symbol of that world.[10] Such an interpretation would make the basic symbols of the book the sea and art—ultimate reality and the essence of man—with the Church and the falls being symbols from history of man's sense of the relationship between that essence and reality. The definitive theme of the book would then be the eruption of ultimate reality in the midst of human life. Not Esther's choice, but her tragic dilemma would be the focus of the book. The contradiction within herself between the desire for love and the desire for truth would be a human mirror of the absolute contradictoriness of reality. Viewed from this perspective the book suggests that tragedy is the essence of man's relationship to reality and that the comedy of the new world symbolized by the falls is finally as transient an interlude as the ecclesiastical idyll at the center of the novel. Such ideas look forward to *The Education of Henry Adams* and the dynamic theory of history. Yet if Adams had wanted the emphasis of *Esther* to be upon this larger perspective, he could have written it so. The book he did write neither introduces a character who expresses such ideas nor makes use of an omniscient narrator as *Democracy* does. At that, this passage comes the closest of anything in *Esther* to the passage in *Democracy* where Adams seems to express his own views. But whereas there he spoke out directly and literally in a way that seems to relate his views to those of Carrington, here he interweaves his comments with his account of Esther's feelings about the falls, often speaks indirectly through symbols, and does not give his ideas to any actual character. Thus the conclusive view of the book remains largely unstated. Apparently Adams wished the focus of the novel to be not upon the sea and man's relationship to eternity but upon the falls and man's movement in time, not upon the divine Athene and her absolute wisdom but upon the human Esther, her relative wisdom, and its tragic consequences in her own life (260).

The sea, Adams says, "is capricious, fickle, angry, fawning, violent, savage, and wanton," while the falls is "steady," "never shrill or angry." Both symbols are from nature, yet both are characterized in a human way. The sea apparently has all the qualities of humanity; the falls has no "sign of human failings" but only of human virtues. It is completely frank

---

"Henry Adams as Novelist," *Renaissance and Modern Studies*, III (1959), 38, notes that sea imagery occurs during Esther's night journey to Niagara, where it suggests a place where there is nothing "between man and the elements."

[10] Sister M. Aquinas Healy, "A Study of Non-Rational Elements in the Works of Henry Adams as Centralized in his Attitude toward Women" (Ph.D. dissertation, University of Wisconsin, 1956), pp. 192–193, and Rule, "Irony in the Works of Henry Adams," p. 133, equate Esther and Pallas Athene.

in the story it has to tell and represents nature in an attitude of sympathy toward men. It promises much for the new world that such qualities should characterize its symbol. Esther, understandably, is moved to like the human character suggested by the falls. Indeed, Adams writes that

> she fell in love with the cataract and turned to it as a confidant, not because of its beauty or power, but because it seemed to tell her a story which she longed to understand. "I think I do understand it," she said to herself . . . . She felt tears roll down her face as she listened to the voice of the waters and knew that they were telling her a different secret from any that Hazard could ever hear. "He will think it is the church talking!" Sad as she was, she smiled as she thought that it was Sunday morning, and a ludicrous contrast flashed on her mind between the decorations of St. John's, with its parterre [sic] of nineteenth century bonnets, and the huge church which was thundering its gospel under her eyes. (258-259)

Again the truth symbolized by the falls is characterized as the story which its falling water suggests. Now Esther believes she understands this story, though apparently her understanding is more emotional than intellectual, for she does not try to explain its meaning. But she does make clear the superiority of the falls to the Church as a symbol of reality. The description of her experience at Niagara thus moves from a comparison of the falls with the ocean as the basic symbol of reality to a comparison with the Church as an outworn symbol of reality. The key phrase here is the "ludicrous contrast" Esther feels between the fashionable show performed by Hazard and his audience, and the reality before her. For to her the grandeur of the falls is not a mere show but a continuous proclamation of truth. In the presence of this proclamation, she is not an audience but a participant; in her the proclamation becomes revelation and she and the falls become one. Several years later, Adams would write of the change from Romanesque to Gothic architecture in Chartres cathedral that "of a sudden, between the portal and the shrine, the infinite rises into a new expression, always a rare and excellent miracle in thought." [11] This is what has happened in Esther's mind. She has found a new symbol of absolute authority and hence become the votary of a new world-view, thereby simultaneously achieving release and rebirth. She has also found a source of strength which will enable her decisively to choose truth before love and thus reject Hazard. [12]

Her view of the falls is contrasted with the views of her friends in the course of a walk they take together. Wharton, the artist, imagines "what the Greeks would have done with it! . . . They would have set Zeus in a

[11] Henry Adams, *Mont-Saint-Michel and Chartres*, with an introduction by Ralph Adams Cram (Boston: Houghton Mifflin Co., 1933), p. 106.

[12] See critical note 12.

throne on Table Rock, firing away his lightnings at Prometheus under the fall." Esther's restrained comment that "a woman feels most the kind of human life in it" receives a more profane echo in Strong's comment, "A big, rollicking, Newfoundland dog sort of humanity." The likeness between their comments suggests an affinity between Esther and Strong, but it also suggests that Strong's reaction to the falls is perhaps more superficial than Esther's. "You are all wrong," Catherine says. "The fall is a woman, and she is as self-conscious this morning as if she were at church." At this Esther breaks out vehemently, "'It is not a woman! It is a man. . . . No woman ever had a voice like that!' She felt hurt that her cataract should be treated as a self-conscious woman" (266–267).

Taken in conjunction with Esther's idea of how Hazard would react to the falls (which later proves correct [287]), this scene resembles the visit to Mount Vernon in *Democracy* in that each of the principals reveals his own nature by his comments upon one profound symbol. Thus revealed, the characters seem to form a sort of hierarchy of maturity, with Catherine at the bottom and Esther at the top. Throughout the book, Hazard, Strong, and especially Wharton see Catherine as the simplest person of their group and the closest to nature.[13] Yet she herself rebels against being simple and natural. She wants to be an individual human being, not a part of nature, and the first step in being so is to become conscious of herself as a particular person. Thus she admires self-consciousness. For Hazard, self-consciousness is the essence of reality, as he says in his sermon at the beginning of the book. This is not the same self-consciousness that Catherine admires, however. It is self-consciousness projected onto ultimate reality conceived as a superhuman but anthropomorphic being called God. Wharton has passed beyond self-consciousness. He dislikes the quality and criticizes Catherine for liking it. He wishes, he tells her, that she had never left her Colorado prairie, where she had the beauty and charm of nature, and come to the East, where she is sure to become self-conscious. Nonetheless, he perceives that it is Esther, a part of the self-conscious, sophisticated city, who has a soul, at least potentially. A soul to him means a spiritual entity which transcends the personal self. He has such a soul, he believes, gained from suffering. Yet he never conceives of the new world which he realizes he and the rest of mankind are entering in any new way, but, like Renaissance man, only in terms of classical naturism or medieval self-consciousness. On the one hand, he sees the next world as a time when Greek paganism will return; on the other, he speaks of the soul and of Paradise (though, nineteenth-century-like, he calls it Nirvana), which—like his poet Petrarch—he believes is to see what he calls God. Significantly, he has never been able to paint Esther,

[13] See critical note 13.

though he recognizes that she belongs to that new world which he thinks he understands.[14]

The highest place on this hierarchy of maturity must be shared by Esther and Strong. Strong has become a part of the new world by means of science, the new world's intellectual discipline and expression. Self-consciousness seems never to have been a problem for him; whatever awareness of self he has, has been absorbed by his effort to make science truer. Hazard and Wharton have partly grown out of self-consciousness too, Hazard by making it the essential quality of the deity he identifies himself with, Wharton, through his art; but neither way is so effective as science. When the novel begins, Esther is very much aware of self. Wharton asserts that she, unlike Catherine, has a soul, but she denies it, whereupon he says that perhaps it has not yet been awakened. The death of her father and her problems with Hazard bring her "soul" to painful life, and she finds relief from self-consciousness in Niagara Falls as a symbol. At the beginning of the novel she is quite far from the stage of maturity represented by Strong. Indeed, she never becomes unaware of self, as Strong is, but always loathes it. Her final reason for rejecting Christianity is that it is all "personal and selfish." Strong has apparently never felt such a passion. Both in her passionate rejection of self and in her inability wholly to escape from the sense of self Esther is closer to Wharton than to Strong. Yet, in her emotional rapport with the falls she seems to pass beyond Strong, to grasp emotionally the whole of the truth which he and science struggle for intellectually and, therefore, gain only piece-meal.[15] Thus, although through most of the book Strong's is the dominant personality, this dominance grows steadily less as he tries to persuade Esther to accept Hazard and the Church. In order to keep her own soul she has to overcome him as well as Hazard. At the end of the book, when she rejects both men, Adams says that "the peace of despair" reigned over the room; this peace is the peace of her mastery over the scientist as well as the minister. More than any other character in the novel, Esther seems,

---

[14] It is worthy of note, though it may well be reading too much of the later Adams into *Esther*, that Wharton is unable either to paint innocent naturalness or to marry its embodiment in Catherine. In the same manner the Renaissance longed to regain the innocent naturalness of paganism, but, according to Adams in *Chartres*, failed to do so. He characterizes the Renaissance there (*Chartres*, pp. 66–67) by comparing the north tower of Chartres to Diane de Poitiers as an old woman trying to seem young. Similarly, what Wharton wants is Catherine and innocence; what he has is his harridan of a wife and the sadness of experience. This interpretation has the value of giving thematic (though not structural) significance to the seemingly unjustified (cf., Rule, "Irony in the Works of Henry Adams," p. 134, n. 79) melodramatic appearance of the wife at the end of chapter 5.

[15] See critical note 14.

by the end of the book, to have possession of the new world and its truth, as symbolized by the falls (297, 302).

The last struggle between Esther and Strong before her final interview with Hazard demonstrates her increasing mastery. She and Strong have separated from the others and gone off on a walk by themselves. Here Esther makes her final attempt to get Strong to state what is at once his own belief and the general attitude of science toward religion. He admits that he does not believe in a personal God or in future rewards and punishments, but says that "there is evidence amounting to strong probability, of the existence of two things . . . mind and matter. . . . No one ever took up this doctrine," he claims, "who could help himself," but Adams notes that he "wanted to defend his opinions, and it became irksome to go on making out the strongest case he could against himself." Strong goes on to say, "If our minds could get hold of one abstract truth, they would be immortal so far as that truth is concerned. My trouble is to find out how we can get hold of the truth at all." When Esther is puzzled by this, he explains further: "Hazard and I and every one else agree that thought is eternal.[16] If you can get hold of one true thought, you are immortal as far as that thought goes. The only difficulty is that every fellow thinks his thought the true one." When Esther cannot understand how a true thought can make one immortal, Strong explains, "Because then the truth is a part of you!" He continues by arguing that

> we may some day catch an abstract truth by the tail, and then we shall have our religion and immortality. We have got far more than half way. Infinity is infinitely more intelligible to you than you are to a sponge. If the soul of a sponge can grow to be the soul of a Darwin, why may we not all grow up to abstract truth? (269–273)

Here Strong is still trying to persuade Esther to accept Hazard's beliefs and is, therefore, not stating his own ideas. Yet some of these are a part of his argument. He appears to be sincere when he says earlier in the book that "science alone is truth" (72), but he also seems to believe, as he suggests here, that such truth is a gradual and progressive revelation through continuing research and experiment. Thus, when he tells Esther that "Hazard wants you to believe in his [abstract truth], and I don't want you to believe in mine, because I've not got one which I believe in

---

[16] Strong's assertion of the immortality of thought (and the interest in Indian thought implied in Wharton's interest in Nirvana) receives its fullest development in Adams' work "Buddha and Brahma" (1891), where thought as reality is contrasted with the illusion (Maya) of the material world. There, however, it is even more difficult than in *Esther* to decide what Adams' view is. It seems to me that he is writing as if the idealist view were true, but without believing it.

myself" (272), he is being partly sincere, because he has no absolute commitment to any system of thought. His references to Darwin, however, and the fact that another character in the book calls him a "full-fledged German Darwinist" (207; cf. 183, 273, 219) suggest that he accepts Darwinism as a contemporary and tentative synthesis of scientific knowledge.

The tentative character of his belief may help to explain why Adams does not let him be more explicit about his views here in the novel. Adams does not want the struggle to become simply one between contemporary science and orthodox Christianity. Rather, he wants Esther to struggle by herself to find an intellectual expression for her emotional conviction that such religion is false. He also wants her to be convinced by a direct intuitive or emotional contact with reality, symbolized by the waterfall, not by reality as refracted intellectually through a theory. Therefore, it is not Strong who gives the truth of the modern and future world to Esther. Yet it is he and his arguments that enable her to find the answer to her problem. His assertion that possession of truth makes an individual immortal evokes an unexpected reply: "Does your idea mean," she asks, "that the next world is a sort of great reservoir of truth, and that what is true in us just pours into it like raindrops?" Here, Strong's idea and the falls have been fused by Esther's imagination into a figure of speech which completes her decision to reject Hazard. In her image the falls atomizes the solid mass of the Niagara River into an infinite number of individual water drops; similarly, among human beings, existing in time, the wholeness of absolute truth exists in fragments possessed by individual minds. As the drops of water that make up the falls recombine in the reservoir at its foot, so the bits of truth in individuals' minds are recombined when the individual human being at death passes out of time into eternity. From the point of view of eternity, of course, individuals who know something of truth are to that extent always a part of the whole of truth. Thus, it is from the temporal view that Esther's figure of speech is meaningful. But from either view immortality hinges upon the possession of truth, and Esther realizes that her decision, insofar as she believes in the validity of her ideas, is between Hazard and what Christianity would call her own salvation. That she must reject Hazard and Christianity to gain that salvation is an irony which provides much of the scene's vitality. When Esther says finally of her insight that "I wonder whether that may not be what Niagara has been telling me!" she both relates the insight to her previous sense of the falls and makes it explicitly the conclusive expression of that sense (273–274).[17]

Two days after this struggle with Strong, while Esther is making a

[17] See critical note 15.

sketch of the falls from her window, Hazard arrives. Criticizing her work, he tells her:

"What you want to get into your picture . . . is the air, which the fall has, of being something final. You can't go beyond Niagara. . . . Whenever I come here, I find myself repeating our sonnet: 'Siccome eterna vita e veder dio'; for the sight of it suggests eternity and infinite power." Then suddenly putting down the drawing, and looking up to her face, . . . he said: "Do you know, I feel now for the first time the beauty of the next two verses:

'So, lady, sight of you, in my despair,
Brings paradise to this brief life and frail.'"

Just as Esther predicted, Hazard believes that Niagara tells the same story as the Church: he sees the falls as the greatest symbol of the Christian God. In his way as sensitive to the symbol as Esther, he tries to use this mutual sensitivity to help his suit. With the same purpose he also introduces the atmosphere in which their love began by quoting additional lines from the Petrarchan fragment which epitomized the unifying aesthetic and amorous atmosphere of the novel's second part. Finally, he tries to tie the waterfall, Petrarch, the Church, God, and his and her love together, and, by her responsiveness to nature, art, and himself, to persuade her to accept orthodox Christianity and their marriage (287-288).

But Esther too has made up her mind. After a preliminary skirmish she tells him, in plain terms, her objections to the Church. She found, she says, that she "could not enter a church without a feeling of—of hostility. . . . I felt as though it were part of a different world." Here, once more, the primary theme of the novel is introduced; indeed, it is here that it reaches its climax. "I never saw you conduct a service," Esther goes on, "without feeling as though you were a priest in a Pagan temple, centuries apart from me. At any moment I half expected to see you bring out a goat or a ram and sacrifice it on the high altar." Early in the book, Wharton had said that Esther belonged "to the next world . . . when paganism will come again and we can give a divinity to every waterfall." [18] Now Esther makes it clear that, though she has found a divinity in a waterfall, she does not consider it or her worship of it as pagan. To her it is Hazard and his church service, especially its central emphasis upon a bloody

[18] In the first chapter Strong (p. 21; noted by Samuels, *Henry Adams*, p. 239) answers Hazard's query about his sermon's effect on the "Pagans" by saying, "I took with me the sternest little Pagan I know, my cousin, Esther Dudley." Both men appear to identify "Pagan" with "heathen," which both use earlier in contrast to "the orthodox." Both seem to mean by "Pagan" simply an unbeliever in Christianity. It is significant that Strong only uses the word once and then in response to Hazard's use of the term. Wharton, who does not capitalize the term, means specifically some kind of nature worship.

sacrifice, which seem pagan. To Wharton, viewing the new world in Renaissance terms as a return to a pre-Christian, premedieval, point of view, "pagan" is a term of praise. Esther, however, sees the movement of thought as evolutionary. For her, "pagan" is a term of dispraise, and in using it she brackets Christianity with the paganism it displaced as outmoded views of reality (295, 296, 28–29).[19]

When Hazard counters by saying that the truths behind the ceremonies are more important than the ceremonies themselves, Esther replies that she could get used to the ceremonies, "but the doctrines are more Pagan than the ceremonies." "It must be," she says, again taking up the main theme of the book, "that we are in a new world now, for I can see nothing spiritual about the church. It is all personal and selfish. What difference does it make to me whether I worship one person, or three persons, or three hundred, or three thousand. I can't understand how you worship any person at all. . . . I despise and loathe myself," she adds, "and yet you thrust self at me from every corner of the church as though I loved and admired it. All religion does nothing but pursue me with self even into the next world." Finally, she asserts again that the Church is not "really spiritual" but cries "'flesh—flesh—flesh,' at every corner." The "resurrection of the body" she finds "a shocking idea." Here, as in her conversation with Hazard after the death of her father, Esther sees a conflict between spirit and matter and desires the spiritual. But now she asserts that the Church defines spirit in a way inadequate to her own sense of spirituality. Her argument makes three related accusations: the Church is not truly spiritual, but personal, selfish, and fleshly. It views ultimate reality as a person (or three persons) whose essence is His own consciousness of Himself (as Hazard said in his sermon) and whose primary concern, she implies, is His own glory. The highest reach of this selfish person's greatness, she implies, is that He once assumed flesh on earth and retained it even when He returned to His own place of abode. His Church offers man a similar personal and fleshly immortality, and makes its achievement his highest duty (296–298).

Hazard replies to these objections by saying that they are poor and ignorant, "made by men like . . . George Strong . . . who know nothing of the church or its doctrines or its history." Here would seem to be the key to the problem of who, if anyone, speaks for Adams in the novel. Though practically, in regard to the engagement, Mrs. Murray seems to do so, as a believer in Christianity she cannot, any more than Hazard

[19] Most critics approvingly quote Wharton's statement that Esther represents a coming paganism. Healy, "A Study of Non-Rational Elements in Works of Adams," pp. 192–194, presents the fullest discussion of this view, relating it to Esther's living by instinct or feeling rather than reason.

can. It has been noted that Strong has much the same role in this book as Carrington does in *Democracy*, and several critics have pointed out that though Strong seems to be modeled after Clarence King he also has some of Adams' physical characteristics.[20] Strong's weakness as a candidate is that much of the time he plays the role of devil's (Jehovah's?) advocate. Hazard's accusation demonstrates just how much of the time he does this, since Esther never heard the arguments she has used nor anything like them from Strong, even after Hazard specifically urged him to present the "whole Agnostic creed" to her. It becomes clear at this point that Strong was always making the strongest case he could for Hazard's position and that Esther has spoken here not only for herself but for Strong (at least, for Strong's essence, what Wharton would call his "soul"), for Niagara, and for the modern and future world, whose sense of the infinite the falls symbolizes. Yet she does not seem to speak for Henry Adams, whose sense of ultimate reality, while expressed by a natural symbol, appears to be embodied not in the falls but in the ocean. Adams seems to look beyond the optimism of the present and future to the tragic contradictoriness of ultimate reality and its expression in Esther's life (298–299, 223).

Finally Hazard, in desperation, plays what he believes to be his trump card. He asks Esther one more question. "If you answer it against me," he says, "I will go away, and never annoy you again. . . . You say the idea of the resurrection is shocking to you. Can you, without feeling still more shocked, think of a future existence where you will not meet once more father or mother, husband or children? surely the natural instincts of your sex must save you from such a creed!" This question goes to the heart of all Esther has been objecting to in the Church, and this time she replies with the full force of her dislike. "Why," she asks Hazard, "must the church always appeal to my weakness and never to my strength! I ask for spiritual life and you send me back to my flesh and blood as though I were a tigress you are sending back to her cubs" (299). Esther has said that it is the "human life" in the falls that appeals to her. In this final reply to Hazard she reveals the distinction she draws between the superior humanity in herself (her "strength") which responds to the falls, and the inferior flesh and blood humanity ("her weakness") which the Church appeals to. Church and falls both appeal to what is human in man; he would not respond to them if they did not. But they appeal to different aspects of his humanity. Esther rejects the Church's appeal to the personal, selfish, and fleshly in her and longs for a spirituality which will destroy

[20] Robert E. Spiller, Introduction to *Esther* edition used in this text, p. ix. For Strong as partially self-characterization, see, for example, Levenson, *The Mind and Art of Henry Adams*, p. 201.

her self and her flesh, and absorb her into a suprapersonal, wholly spiritual reality. Niagara Falls, an impersonal natural symbol, to her suggests such a spirituality, one which will transcend that suggested by the Christian symbol as the Church once transcended the symbol that preceded it.

At this point Strong enters the room. As he "stepped between" the two former lovers, "a momentary silence followed, when not a sound was heard except the low thunder of the falling waters" (300). Thus the end of Esther's struggle is punctuated by the arrival of the new world in the person of Strong and by the thundering voice of its deity. In the mortification and bitterness of defeat Hazard's sublimated glorification of self-consciousness breaks down. Earlier, Adams had written of Hazard's thoughts when he feared that he might lose Esther that "the danger of disappointment and defeat roused in him the instinct of martyrdom. He was sure that all mankind would suffer if he failed to get the particular wife he wanted. 'It is not a selfish struggle,' he thought. 'It is a human soul I am trying to save'" (254). Now the personal, selfish, and fleshly qualities suggested by these reflections erupt into inquisitorial violence as Hazard turns on the friend who has tried to help him and accuses him of having wooed Esther for himself. His reason for doing so, insofar as he has a conscious reason, would seem to be his belief that it is Strong who has furnished Esther with the arguments she has just used in rejecting him. The strength of his conviction suggest that these were among the strongest arguments Strong used in the all-night discussions about religion which the two friends are said (11–12) to have engaged in. Here, Strong's only reply to Hazard's accusation is to admit that after seeing her fight the minister's "persecution, I would give any chance I have of salvation if she would marry me," though he adds that "she won't." When Hazard leaves, Adams says that there "was peace, but the peace of despair." The new world and its truth have conquered. But the past has claimed Esther's heart as the price of her spiritual victory. When Strong proposes marriage, she replies, "But George, I don't love you, I love him" (301–302).[21]

The emphasis of the novel is upon the tragic consequences for Esther and Hazard of the struggle between a vital expression of truth and an outworn view. As usual in Adams' work, the two basic elements are antithetical and irreconcilable. As in *Chartres*, art is a means of reconciling or at least escaping their conflict. But here, as there, its effect is only

---

[21] In *Chartres* (p. 196), Adams would write that "the scientific mind is atrophied, and suffers under inherited cerebral weakness when it comes in contact with the eternal woman." Here the scientist eventually falls in love; it is the eternal woman who cannot love the scientist.

momentary. Adams in *Chartres* and his characters in *Esther* care more for truth than for beauty, and thus are forced to look for answers to their problems, not in art, but in that arena where illusion and reality, religion and the truth which science struggles toward, wage what Adams views as inevitable and irreconcilable warfare.

CHAPTER IV

AMERICA DISCOVERS ITS NATIONAL IDENTITY

In his *History of the United States During the Administrations of Thomas Jefferson and James Madison* (1889–1891)[1] Henry Adams gives final expression to his concern with the relationship between illusion and reality in American political history. He describes the crystallization of American national identity between 1800 and 1817.[2] In those years America became a unit in political organization and national character. Politically, it became a "democratic nationality," a democracy rather than an aristocracy, a nation rather than a confederation. At the same time, "intelligence, rapidity, and mildness" became the distinctive personal traits of its people. Adams considers personal identity the more important of the two aspects, yet he treats it directly and systematically only in the first and last chapters. His most pervasive concern is with the emergence of the national political identity.[3] As the phrase "democratic nationality" suggests, he emphasizes "nationality" more than

---

[1] The first trade edition of Adams' history was published in four parts by Charles Scribner's Sons between 1889 and 1891. In the first English edition, published by G. P. Putnam's Sons in 1891–1892, and in the American edition (published by Charles Scribner's Sons) of 1921, these four parts are given the single title, *History of the United States During the Administrations of Thomas Jefferson and James Madison*. In the first trade edition, the four parts, on the spine of the volumes, are numbered consecutively from Roman numeral "I" to "IX." For convenience in footnoting, therefore, even though I have used the original trade edition here, I have considered the four parts as one work with the later title and used the consecutive volume numbering given on the spines of the individual volumes. All page references to this work in this chapter will be found between parentheses in the text. References in other chapters are given the following form: Henry Adams, *The History of the United States During the Administrations of Thomas Jefferson and James Madison* (9 vols.; New York: Charles Scribner's Sons, 1889–1891).

[2] See critical note 16.

[3] See critical note 17.

"democratic," though here too (as will be shown) he believes that the subordinate element is finally the more important (III, 20; IX, 240).

This political identity he describes as emerging through a process which separated false ideas from true ones. Between 1800 and 1816 the electorate gave the proponents of one conception of what America's identity should be the opportunity to put their ideas into practice. Adams shows how the interaction between these ideas and circumstances separated what was valid in them from what was invalid. His test for validity is pragmatic: an idea which proves practicable is valid.[4] Practicability depends ultimately upon whether an idea is harmonious with the historical pattern Adams believes is produced by the interaction of primarily nonhuman natural forces. Thus America did not create its political identity; it discovered it by discovering its place in the mechanical movement of history. This determinism—and Adams' touchstone for distinguishing between illusion and reality—is made explicit in a passage concerned with the confused political alignments which followed the Spanish revolt against Napoleon in 1808. "The workings of human development," he says,

> were never more strikingly shown than in the helplessness with which the strongest political and social forces in the world followed or resisted at haphazard the necessities of a movement which they could not control or comprehend. Spain, France, Germany, England, were swept into a vast and bloody torrent which dragged America, from Montreal to Valparaiso, slowly into its movement; while the familiar figures of famous men . . . were borne away by the stream . . . ; each blind to everything but a selfish interest, and all helping more or less unconsciously to reach the new level which society was obliged to seek.

Here (as in *Esther*) individuals are a relatively helpless part of an inevitable movement toward new stages of development.[5] This does not mean that individuals (and groups) cannot make choices which run counter to the stream. If an individual be a person in authority, he may contain or even reverse the historical movement. Thus Napoleon's "*coup d'état* . . . in 1799 forced both France and England back on their steps." But such reversals are never more than momentary. Eventually, the inhibiting force is overcome, the movement of the stream accelerates until its accumulated force is spent, and it then resumes its normal pace (IV, 301–302, 300).

The forces which move history are not sensuously apprehensible. Success and failure, however, are so, and enduring success is the final test

[4] Cf., J. C. Levenson, *The Mind and Art of Henry Adams* (Boston: Houghton Mifflin Co., 1957), pp. 130–131.

[5] See critical note 18.

in *The History* of whether ideas and actions are in harmony with the pattern determined by these nonhuman forces. Also sensible to an extent is the greater energy developed by ideas and actions which succeed. Adams' necessitarian world is also the "bloody arena" of the Darwinians. This is clear when he observes that General William Henry Harrison's

> account of Indian affairs offered an illustration of the law accepted by all historians in theory, but adopted by none in practice; which former ages called "fate," and metaphysicians called "necessity," but which modern science has refined into the "survival of the fittest." No acid ever worked more mechanically on a vegetable fibre than the white man acted on the Indian.

Adams' point is that the three terms describe the same phenomenon and are therefore equivalent. Yet, though he does not say so, his account of the phenomenon as a purely mechanical process suggests that the machine is actually a better model for reality than the organism and hence that what he calls the metaphysicians' term—"necessity"—is probably more basic than the biologists' term. More important, it suggests that the laws of physics are a better description of reality (the totality of those forces which make history) than those of biology. The Darwinian terms do suggest, however, Adams' belief that the clearest manifestation of a group's harmony with the pattern of forces in its time is its ability to arouse and sustain the most concentrated, intense, and effective form of human energy —military force. *The History* shows that even though democratic America was in the vanguard of the mechanical movement of history, its position was of merely potential value until it was able to give its energies effective military expression (IV, 289; VI, 69).

The second most important expression of energy is science—specifically the ability to create new technology. Adams believed that America's physical isolation made it unnecessary for it to emulate the military state which the propinquity of dangerous rivals made necessary in Europe. Nonetheless, it is only through science, he believes, that America has a chance of being successful without war. The chance seems to him a very slight one, but that he will grant it at all shows how important he believes science is for national success. The most significant example of this belief in *The History* is his assertion that Robert Fulton's steamboat voyage in 1807 was the beginning of a new era in American history.

Opposed to energy is theory. Adams asserts that ideals, constitutions, laws, and policies have no energy in and of themselves (though ideals and constitutions, at least, may inspire energy[6]). They are not practicable

[6] Many critics note the importance of Adams' "Centennial Oration" in his and Henry Cabot Lodge's review of Hermann Eduard Von Holst's *The Constitutional and Political History of the United States*, in *North American Review*, CXXIII (Oct., 1876), 328–361, to the theme of national development in *The History*. But only Charles

unless they are supported by military—or possibly scientific—force or unless the energy they inspire can be expressed in such force. Nor has diplomacy, the attempt to achieve ends by intellectual rather than military means, any chance of success unless it is supported by the possibility of military force.

Yet the practicability of energy is finally dependent upon its being in harmony with the mechanical movement of history. Napoleon failed, despite his enormous military and personal energy, because he was opposed to "the new level which society was obliged to seek" in his time. This level was political democracy, "the coming popular movement throughout the world." Moral leadership of this movement belonged naturally to the United States, its spearhead and culmination. Adams believes it was inevitable that America would become "a democratic ocean," the final state of human society. Yet the Americans of 1800 believed they had the power to create their own future. In *The History*, as in *Gallatin*, this is the chief illusion which concerns Adams, but whereas in the earlier work Gallatin himself learned the lesson that circumstances are stronger than men, here only Adams—and perhaps the reader—permanently learns it. Most Americans in 1800 believed they were creating the future in terms of the ideals which together make up what Adams calls the American democratic or liberal dream.[7] Noting the contradictory opinions of the American held by European travelers in the eighteenth century—that he was both a sordid moneygrubber and the victim of fantastic ideas—Adams observes that "even on his practical and sordid side, the American might easily have been represented as a victim to illusion": he dreams of a country embracing the continent and covered with rich farms and beautiful cities. But his dream has another and more ideal aspect:

> Every American, from Jefferson and Gallatin down to the poorest squatter, seemed to nourish an idea that he was doing what he could to overthrow the tyranny which the past had fastened on the human mind . . . [and] working for the overthrow of tyranny, aristocracy, hereditary privilege, and priesthood, wherever they existed.

On its positive side, this aspect of the dream asserted that "the next

---

Andrew Vandersee, "The Political Attitudes of Henry Adams" (Ph.D. dissertation, UCLA, 1964), pp. 88–90, 229–234, has noted the new pragmatic basis for Adams' veneration of the Constitution in the review and his further departure from "his own earlier fetish notions of the Constitution as absolute sovereign" (p. 234) by the time he wrote *The History*.

[7] The fullest account of the dream is in George Hochfield, *Henry Adams: An Introduction and Interpretation* (New York: Holt, Rinehart and Winston, Inc., 1962), pp. 56–62.

necessity of human progress was to lift the average man upon an intellectual and social level with the most favored." Freedom itself would do
this, for, once freed, the average man would "become more virtuous and
enlightened, by mere process of growth, without church or paternal
authority." These two aspects of the dream are the foundation of the
identity which Adams believes America discovered in this period. The
ideal aspect is the basis for the democratic movement: the desire to free
the individual from external authority and to make the will of a majority
of the people sovereign in the country. The material aspect is the basis
for the national movement: the desire to have a union rather than a collection of states. Dream and identity both have as their essence a free people
ruling a united continent (IV, 302; III, 81; IX, 225; I, 172, 175–176,
158, 159).

Not all Americans accepted the dream. "The rich for a long time stood
aloof . . . between them and the American democrat was a gulf." To
Federalists and other conservatives the democratic aspect of the dream
was anathema. Holding the biblical view that man was by nature prone
to do evil, they asserted the need for an authoritarian Church and State
to restrain him. Despite the size of this group Adams identifies Americans
with the dream. For the American, he says, "his dream was his whole
existence." The poor were especially convinced. After portraying the
American as offering "to the rich as to the poor" a share in "these
unimaginable stores of wealth and power!" Adams notes that "the poor
came, and from them were seldom heard complaints of deception or delusion. Within a moment, by the mere contact of a moral atmosphere, they
saw the gold and jewels, the summer cornfields and the glowing continent."
It is primarily through the masses of the people, therefore, and through
the pressure which they have exerted upon society that the forces of
history have moved America steadily toward political democracy (I,
173–174).

Yet Adams warns that it is difficult to assess the precise influence
actually exerted by the dream upon government policy, in part because
of the vagueness which was the result of its being the expression of the
inarticulate masses. "The people themselves . . .," he says, "could not
have expressed their finer instincts had they tried, and might not have
recognized them if expressed by others." Most of them, however, felt, as
Adams does, that Thomas Jefferson came closest to giving their dream full
expression. Adams warns that, because Jefferson dreaded the "reputation
as a visionary" given him by his enemies, his writings may be searched
from beginning to end "without revealing the whole measure of the
man, far less of the movement." But it was clear that in 1800 Jefferson
hoped to establish "a democratic republic, with the sciences for an

intellectual field, and physical and moral advancement keeping pace with their advance" (I, 177–179).

In its essentials, both the dream and Jefferson's expression of it are the same liberal system of ideas which Adams described as motivating Albert Gallatin in *The Life of Albert Gallatin*, although there he did not call it a dream but "pure theory" and "the prejudice of his time." As the word "theory" suggests, the system was presented there as a body of ideas. The phrase "prejudice of his time" suggests that the system was also an emotional bias. Together, prejudice and theory, emotion and idea, tended to generate an image of man in a perfect society. In *The History* there is a similar combination of ideas and emotions, expressed in the symbols of the democratic dream. But now the symbol is viewed as preceding the idea. In the biography Gallatin, as an educated member of the *bourgeoisie*, was presented as accepting the system as a body of ideas in harmony with an emotional bias. In *The History* those who are motivated by the dream are presented as being affected less by an idea than by an image and the emotion it generates. Thus Jefferson, in *The History*, gives rational expression to something which is basically not intellectual. (The term "dream" stresses this pre-eminence of emotion and image.) The dream is also represented as less personal and less universal in *The History* than it was in *Gallatin*. In the latter, although it found expression in national and Jeffersonian terms when Gallatin entered politics, it was presented as primarily his personal version of the liberal system of the Enlightenment. In *The History* (I, 176–177) Jefferson's similarly derived ideas are viewed —as are Gallatin's—as the expression of the national American dream.

But there is an important difference between the two men's application of the dream. In both works, Adams says that Gallatin's chief allegiance was to the United States; Jefferson's, to all mankind or to Virginia and the South. Both of the latter's loyalties, Adams asserts, limited his effectiveness as a national leader; they also blinded him to the nationalizing aspect of the dream. Not until twenty years after his inauguration, Adams says, did Jefferson doubt his belief that centralization was antithetical to democracy, and "even then he did not admit a mistake. In the tendency to centralization he still saw no democratic instinct, but only the influence of monarchical Federalists." It was at this point that Jeffersonianism ceased to be an adequate expression of the dream. While giving even excessive expression to the democratic instinct, it gave none to the national instinct. It was the moderate Federalists who gave full expression to the latter aspect of the dream—even though, as conservatives, their opposition to democracy made them antagonists of the dream's more fundamental aspect. During Madison's administration the "war" Republicans would aggressively represent both aspects, under but Jefferson (when even many Federalists deserted the national cause) it was the moderate Federalist John Marshall who, as chief justice of the Supreme Court, gave deliberate expression to the national instinct in government: Marshall, Adams says, "was bent on enlarging the powers of government in the interests of justice and nationality." Jefferson, by contrast, was "bent on restricting the powers of the national government in the interests of human liberty" (I, 210, 192).

There was one state, even in 1800, which believed in both democracy and centralization—and thus served as type and model of what the nation would become (III, 366). Pennsylvania, Adams says, was "the only true democratic community then existing in the eastern States." Yet

> the value of Pennsylvania to the Union lay not so much in the democratic spirit of society as in the rapidity with which it turned to national objects . . . . Too thoroughly democratic to fear democracy, and too much nationalized to dread nationality, Pennsylvania became the ideal American State, easy, tolerant, and contented (I, 114–115).

Pennsylvania's democracy was of a purer and more complete sort, Adams says, than that of Virginia (I, 114, 211, 209). Its notion of nationality was based on confidence in a strong, popularly elected central government, and, therefore, by the dream's standards, was of a purer sort than that of the Federalists. Its anticipation of the national identity crystallizing in this period gave Pennsylvania great influence: "In every . . . issue that concerned the Union," Adams says, "the voice which spoke in most potent tones was that of Pennsylvania." If it had cared for "power and patronage," he implies, its pattern of democratic nationality might have prevailed in the nation much sooner. Instead, it cared only for its interests and, therefore, Virginia, which sacrificed interest to its "passion for political power," ruled. The national identity worked itself out, first in conflicts between Virginians and Federalists for power, then between the theories of the successful Virginians and the necessities of history (I, 114, 115; V, 20).

As democrats (albeit imperfect ones) the Virginians were in harmony with the movement of history and therefore successful: "The mass of Americans," Adams writes of Jefferson's first term, "had become democratic in thought as well as act . . . . As a democrat, Jefferson's social success was sweeping and final." But as decentralists he and his friends were failures. The movement toward nationality, begun by the Federalists, continued throughout the twenty-four years of Republican leadership despite its avowed hatred for centralization. Here is the crucial aspect of the period for Henry Adams' thesis that circumstances are stronger than men and hence that America discovered rather than created its identity.

Repeatedly, the states' rights principles of the Virginia and Kentucky Resolutions were violated by Jefferson and Madison under the pressure of circumstances tending toward centralization. This process was complicated, Adams says, by the personal qualities of the two men. Necessity was partially responsible for the violations—the necessities of war in 1812–1813, for example—but Jefferson's love for power, his overconfidence in himself and his supporters, his fear of losing popularity, his evasion of unwanted responsibility, and his inability to modify his ideas in the face of facts, facilitated the mechanical pattern of events and prevented his making as effective a stand against the national movement as Napoleon, for example, did against the democratic movement (II, 76).

The three most important triumphs of nationality during Jefferson's administration were also the three most important failures of Jefferson's principles and character: the Louisiana Purchase, which Adams describes primarily as a failure of Jefferson's principles; the unsuccessful attempt to control John Marshall and the Supreme Court by impeaching Justice Samuel Chase; and the disaster of the embargo. The purchase of Louisiana added an enormous tract of land to the United States and established de facto constitutional interpretations that greatly expanded the powers of the central government; the failure of the impeachment freed the judiciary, under Marshall's leadership, to expand the powers of the central government; while the embargo provoked a violent reaction against Jefferson and his policies. In each case Jefferson assisted rather than inhibited the national movement. Adams' criticism of him is severe, not primarily for the ideals which motivated him in the last two instances, not for the deeds themselves, not even for the violation of his principles when Adams can see that the pressure of necessity was primarily responsible for the violation. For Adams is sympathetic to the democratic dream throughout The History—though his faith in it is very limited—and, basically, to Jefferson as its spokesman. What he condemns Jefferson for is his repeated sacrifice of principle in situations where Adams can see little or no necessity for his doing so and hence can explain the sacrifice only as a moral failure. Thus in regard to the Louisiana Purchase, Adams' ironic but sympathetic awareness of the incompatibility of Jefferson's principles with the particular circumstances involved gives way to contempt when Jefferson yields to his friends' fears and fails to carry through his belief that a constitutional amendment is needed to make the act legal. Similarly, he condemns Jefferson for failing to provide the leadership that might have led to a better choice than John Randolph for the prosecution of the Republican cause in the impeachment of Chase. His most acidulous remarks, however, concern Jefferson's abandonment of presidential leadership in his last months in office on the grounds that he did not wish to tie Madison's hands, while at the same time he covertly sought to avoid personal humiliation by delaying repeal of the embargo—which had clearly failed—until Madison would have to take the responsibility.

The failure of Jefferson's policies and the public's reaction against them led to the emergence of a new party, calling itself Republican but favoring energy in government. With Madison's co-operation it led the country into the War of 1812, partly in the hope of strengthening the national movement. The irony of such motives leads Adams to make one of the most trenchant statements in *The History* of his deterministic thesis:

> Only with difficulty could history offer a better example of its processes than when it showed Madison, Gallatin, Macon, Monroe, and Jefferson joining to create a mercenary army and a great national debt, for no other attainable object than that which had guided Alexander Hamilton and the Federalists toward the establishment of a strong government fifteen years before.

The war had the nationalizing effect its supporters hoped it would. The belief of Timothy Pickering's antidemocratic ultra-Federalists that democratic government would inevitably collapse in such a crisis proved false, as "the silent undercurrent" of democratic national feeling "tended to grow in strength precisely as it encountered most resistance from events." On the other side, many Republicans appeared to be thinking in national terms. Madison's annual message of 1815, for example, "seemed to prove . . . that [his] views and wishes lay in the direction of strong government." Jefferson and his antinationalist followers had found, Adams says, whether they admitted it or not, that there was a "national instinct" as strong as the "democratic instinct" and in harmony with it. Thus at the war's end, both democracy and nationality had triumphed (VI, 418; VII, 69; IX, 105, 187; I, 183).

But it was an incomplete victory. The progress of the democratic movement was inhibited not only by continued conservative opposition but by certain Republican policies growing out of the South's greed for Florida. Nor had the national movement progressed as far as the war Republicans had hoped. The Hartford Convention was stifled only by Jackson's victory at New Orleans and the end of the war. Even the people, though more patriotic than the leaders, had taken a long time to support the war and then had done so only under the "pressure of circumstances." And Madison, despite his annual message, as the last official act of his administration vetoed an internal improvements bill, on the ground that it violated the old Republican principle of strict construction. Adams comments wryly that every one who looked at the Constitution as an instrument . . . to be employed for the first time, must have admitted that Madison was right. . . . Unfortunately, . . . sixteen years had affected national character; and although precedents might not bind Congress or Executive, they marked the movement of society.

Madison's veto was a futile attempt to reverse history. By 1814, the outlines of a national identity had become clear: "The character of people and government was formed; the lines of their activity were fixed." Henceforth the United States would be a democratic nationality (VII, 67; IX, 152, 153, 195).

Yet Adams expresses no certainty that such unity ensures progress. The dream asserts the inevitability of progress once the individual is free; but Adams begins his final chapter by warning that "the laws of human progress [are] matter not for dogmatic faith, but for study." He considers the problem as twofold: (1) will the nation progress? (2) will the individual progress? In the end, of course, the nonhuman forces of history will decide the answers, but Adams tries to discern signs of the future. The uniqueness of America's size makes the history of other countries nearly useless as a guide to its future, he believes, but he chastens excessive optimism by noting that such progress as the world has known has hitherto been coupled with the "clashing interests and incessant wars" of small states and that "the few examples offered by history of great political societies, relieved from external competition or rivalry, [are] not commonly thought encouraging." He is no more encouraging about individual progress. That national progress depends upon individual progress was demonstrated, he believes, as early as the Louisiana Purchase. Jefferson's abandonment at that time of his principles of limited government proved that "the hopes of humanity lay thenceforward, not in attempting to restrain the government from doing whatever the majority should think necessary, but in raising the people themselves till they should think nothing necessary but what was good." But Adams sees few signs that such progress is going on; American life in 1806 seems to him to offer "no evidence that the human being, any more than the ant and bee, was conscious of a higher destiny, or was even mechanically developing into a more efficient animal" (IX, 219, 219, 220; II, 130; III, 212).

The War of 1812 provided a partially encouraging answer to his question, "What would happen when society should be put to some violent test?" The war was fought "by a relatively small number of individuals," but their success seemed to Adams extraordinary. Americans showed that they could develop the military energy to fight effectively a nation which was soon to prove itself the chief military power of the world. Yet Adams saw much in postwar America that argued weakness. In 1812 Congress was publicly condemned for slightly raising its salaries, despite the "popular admission that the Fourteenth Congress, for ability, energy, and usefulness, never had a superior." Adams' interpretation is that the people were expressing their resentment of the superiority of the men they had elected under the duress of war, that normally the people disliked being "represented by something nobler, wiser, and purer than their own average honor, wisdom, and purity." He fears the possibility that the pressure of social uniformity might also stifle anything exceptional in the American individual and predicts that "if at any time American character should change, it might . . . become sluggish . . . . The inertia of several hundred million people, all formed in a similar social mould, was as likely to stifle energy as to stimulate evolution." In *Democracy* it was the stunted development of Americans that led Madeleine Lee to go to Washington in hopes of finding fully developed human beings; later this lack of development will be the basis for Adams' own complete loss of faith in democracy even as a social principle. At the end of *The History* he is not so pessimistic about the national character in 1817 but neither is he optimistic. The most striking quality of his remarks are their ambiguity: "That the individual should rise to a higher order either of intelligence or morality than had existed in former ages," he says,

> was not to be expected, for the United States offered less field for the development of individuality than had been offered by older and smaller societies. The chief function of the American Union was to raise the average standard of popular intelligence and well-being, and at the close of the War of 1812 the superior average intelligence of Americans was so far admitted that Yankee acuteness, or smartness, became a national reproach; but much doubt remained whether the intelligence belonged to a high order, or proved a high morality. . . . American morality was such as suited a people so endowed, and was high when compared with the morality of many older societies; but, like American intelligence, it discouraged excess. . . . Like the character of the popular inventions, the character of the morals corresponded to the wants of a growing democratic society; but time alone could decide whether it would result in a high or low national ideal. (III, 213; IX, 81, 138, 135, 241, 237)

At the end of *The History*, Adams returns to this question of national ideals.[8] "What ideals were to ennoble it?" he asks of the United States. "What object, besides physical content, must a democratic continent aspire to attain?" By failing to mention his belief that a successful ideal must be in harmony with the natural forces that move history, Adams

[8] The fullest discussion of Adams' early ideals and their importance to him is in *ibid.*, pp. 5–9, 13–15.

implies that ideals have an intrinsic as well as an instrumental value. If sincerely believed in, a high ideal ennobles human life, by which Adams seems to mean that it gives life dignity and meaning, provides motivation for action (as in *Gallatin*), and serves as a standard for personal judgments (as in *Democracy* and *Esther*). Another omission is equally significant. In the first volume of *The History* Adams described the democratic dream as *the* American ideal. In raising the question of ideals again at the end of the work without mentioning the dream, he suggests that it has become inadequate.[9] For one thing, it points to no object besides physical contentment, a goal Adams clearly does not believe is based upon an ideal which produces moral progress. The dream asserts that such progress inevitably accompanies physical and mental development. By implication, Adams also denies this aspect of the dream. What Adams wants is a modern equivalent of the medieval City of God which would be in harmony with the forces of history and the American character. But he has no such ideal to suggest himself nor seems to think it can be known by others at the time he is writing: "For the treatment of such questions," he says, "history required another century of experience" (IX, 242).

The ambiguity in his final position can be diminished by studying *The History*'s four symbols, one of which appears first in Volume IV, the others, only in the final chapter of the work, as part of Adams' summing up. Here one is dealing with subtleties, yet the influence of the dream, except in Volume I, is also a subtlety and rarely mentioned specifically. The forces which Adams believes are the prime movers of history are not mentioned much more often. The work focuses upon the ideas and actions of people—material which documents make relatively easy to obtain and prove. The dominance of such material is justified by Adams' conception at this time of the task of the historian: to "state facts in their sequence." Dreams, forces, and symbols are largely inferences from such facts. Nonetheless, to understand *The History* it is essential to understand its symbols. They are derived from certain nonsymbolic material things which Adams views as embodiments of the ideas he is chiefly concerned with. In the case of the two major symbols—the flag and the ocean—he chooses two things whose existence and significance transcend the particular time and place he is writing about. In the case of the two subordinate symbols—the steamboat and the schooner—the things are products of a particular time and place and of great practical significance to it. The implications of this difference are significant—the major symbols suggest that the fundamental tension which together they embody is of universal significance; the two minor symbols suggest the particular form this tension takes in early nineteenth-century America.

[9] Cf., *ibid.*, p. 86.

The latter symbols are also personal creations (as symbols) of Henry Adams, while the flag and the ocean are traditional symbols. All four, however, serve to vivify and concretize the interpretive statements Adams makes in his objective work. They also have another, even more important function. In 1895 Adams wrote to his brother Brooks, "I have deliberately and systematically effaced myself, even in my own history. I can conceive of nothing but harm, to our society, from the expression of its logical conclusions."[10] The symbols seem to suggest at least part of what Adams did not wish to state (III, 45).

The flag means basically what it does outside *The History*: it is the symbol of a nation. Usually it appears in official documents; over half of its appearances are in passages quoted from official statements by Napoleon.[11] In these statements it stands for something more complex, a concept of what a nation is: an effectively independent national sovereignty. The flag implies that a country *is* a nation, that it has the desire and ability to prevent violations of its right to independent action. "To insult a merchant vessel carrying the flag of any Power," Napoleon says, "is to make an incursion into a village or a colony belonging to that Power" (V, 137). "I consider the flag of a nation as a part of herself; she must be able to carry it everywhere, or she is not free." Napoleon considered a country which permitted such violations, whether of its territory or its ships, denationalized and hence fair prey: "That nation which does not make her flag respected is not a nation in my eyes" (V, 398). Adams himself uses the symbol sparingly in this explicit way. He does speak of "States like Denmark, Portugal, and Spain, whose flags had ceased to exist" (IV, 126), meaning that those states had ceased to function as independent national sovereignties. He also says that the young war Republicans wanted to carry "the American flag to Mobile and Key West" (VI, 123; see also V, 423). But the main use of the flag, aside from the decrees of Napoleon, is in connection with the War of 1812, when the surrender of a ship is signified by the striking of its flag (VII, 127). The explicit symbolic meaning of the flag, as expressed through

---

[10] HA to Brooks Adams, June 5, 1895, in Henry Adams, *Letters of Henry Adams, 1892–1918*, ed. Worthington Chauncey Ford (Boston: Houghton Mifflin Co., 1938), p. 70. Quoted in Edward Allan Chalfant, "Henry Adams and History" (Ph.D. dissertation, University of Pennsylvania, 1954), p. 169. Sister M. Aquinas Healy, "A Study of Non-Rational Elements in the Works of Henry Adams as Centralized in his Attitude toward Women" (Ph.D. dissertation, University of Wisconsin, 1956), pp. 631–633, discusses the use of metaphor and symbol in *The History*.

[11] The flag is used as a symbol in the following passages (those by Napoleon are indicated by a parenthesized *N*): IV, 28, 109(N), 110(N), 126(N), 295(N); V, 137(N), 245(N), 307, 384(N), 392(N), 397(N), 398(N), 399(N); VI, 26, 48, 123, 135, 213, 222, 249(N), 253(N).

Napoleon earlier, gives this action in the later volumes a depth of symbolic significance it would otherwise lack. It makes the sea battles more explicitly a microcosm of the entire war.

It is appropriate that this symbol should appear most often and most significantly in quotations from Napoleon. One of the fundamental differences which Adams points out between America and Europe is the military energy which all European nations must have in order to survive (IX, 222). Such energy is possessed only by extremely unified countries with autocratic governments. Europe is also said to differ from America in emphasizing individuals rather than society, again largely because of military necessity. The definitive expression of individualism is the hero, whose natural field of action, Adams says, is war (IX, 223). Napoleon's dictatorial rule was a nineteenth-century epitome of such concentrated government and military energy; he himself was an epitome of the European military hero, an ultimate human expression of France and an incarnation of its flag.[12] In a phrase which represents the extreme of the meaning he gives to the flag, Napoleon demands that all nations do what he does (or purports to do) and "maintain the religion of their flag" (V, 397)—elevate, that is, national loyalty to the level of religious devotion and make the flag the supreme object of veneration.

In the United States, by contrast with Europe, it became increasingly clear, Adams says, that "war counted for little; the hero for less; on the people alone the eye could permanently rest." Since society was more important than the individual or the government, the latter constantly tended toward decentralization. Jefferson, as spokesman for the democratic dream, gave expression to an extreme but widely popular version of these American tendencies and therefore represented a view antithetical to that of Napoleon. Himself more an expression of the energy of society than a source of energy, Jefferson (and the dream) denied that the "religion of [the] flag" was either desirable or necessary. He believed that through decentralization of political energy and commercial rather than military methods America could both succeed as a nation and preserve a maximum of individual liberty. Adams shows how, under Jefferson and Madison, the practical necessities of the "bloody arena" drew the United States "slowly toward the European standard of true political sovereignty,"

---

[12] Heroes were not necessarily perfect in their role. How far they could fall short of its requirements is suggested when Adams says that "the sale of Louisiana was the turning-point in Napoleon's career; no true Frenchman forgave it." It was "a second betrayal of France" (II, 39). See also his initial characterization of Napoleon (I, 334–335). What the hero *must* have is the charisma which Napoleon had but Talleyrand, for example, lacked, although Adams considers him a great man and much more deeply dedicated to France than his master (I, 335–336).

even forcing it into a war, but the final result, Adams believed, would be a compromise between the dream and European practice. This American concern to permit only as much governmental sovereignty as necessity required means that the best symbol for America and its goals is not the flag (appropriate though it is to the national movement and its ultimate expression in a centralized government) but something which will emphasize the democratic movement and its individualism (IX, 224; V, 397; IV, 289; IX, 221).

Adams' symbol is the ocean,[13] the most important symbol in *The History*, even though it appears only once as an explicit symbol. In various nonsymbolic passages he suggests a relationship between the ocean and democracy. As "an element open to all," he says, "the ocean was the only open field for competition among nations." Internationally the ocean is the great democratizing influence upon nations because "Americans [and, presumably, other nationalities as well] enjoyed there no natural or artificial advantages." This would seem to be one of the "several reasons" he mentions, without listing them, why "the sloop battles and cruises afforded one of the best relative tests of American character and skill among all that were furnished in the early period of the national history." In the final chapter of *The History*, he makes the ocean an explicit symbol of democracy in the extended metaphor which concludes his contrast between European and American history. "Travellers in Switzerland," he says,

> who stepped across the Rhine where it flowed from its glacier could follow its course among mediaeval towns and feudal ruins, until it became a highway for modern industry, and at last arrived at a permanent equilibrium in the ocean.

[13] Adams' use of the ocean as a symbol in *The History* has been pointed out previously. Edwin C. Rozwenc, "Henry Adams and the Federalists," in *Teachers of History: Essays in Honor of Laurence Bradford Packard*, ed. H. Stuart Hughes (Ithaca, N.Y.: Cornell University Press, 1954), p. 143, describes the democratic ocean as being like the Gulf Stream, with all the forces part of a "current system." Chalfant, "Henry Adams and History," p. 211, says that the ocean is "total democracy, in the United States, then everywhere." Robert M. Bunker, "The Idea of Failure in Henry Adams, Charles Sanders Pierce, and Mark Twain" (Ph.D. dissertation, University of New Mexico, 1955), pp. 85–86, relates the ocean in *The History* to its use in "The Rule of Phase Applied to History." Healy, "A Study of Non-Rational Elements in the Works of Adams," p. 631, says that "the ocean is the major symbol of democracy itself." John Brunner, "Henry Adams: His Decline and Fall" (Ph. D. dissertation, UCLA, 1956), says that the ocean suggests that democracy was "the final equilibrium of the evolution of government" (p. 51) and "the final goal of social development" (p. 69). Ernest Samuels, *Henry Adams: The Middle Years* (Cambridge, Mass.: Harvard University Press, 1958), pp. 358–360, connects Adams' use of it with that of Herbert Spencer in his *First Principles* and "Fiske's commentary in the *Outlines of Cosmic Philosophy*." (See critical note 19.)

American history followed the same course. With prehistoric glaciers and med-iaeval feudalism the story had little to do; but from the moment it came within sight of the ocean it acquired interest almost painful. A child could find his way in a river-valley, and a hoy could float on the waters of Holland; but science alone could sound the depths of the ocean, measure its currents, foretell its storms, or fix its relations to the system of Nature. In a democratic ocean science could see something ultimate. Man could go no further. The atom might move, but the general equilibrium could not change.

This passage and the ocean metaphor clarify and emphasize Adams' doubts earlier in this final chapter that the democratic movement, espe-cially in America, is a movement of progress. If man can go no further than the democratic ocean, clearly evolution will stop once America becomes wholly democratic. Moreover, the ocean does not move in a direction; there is no place for it to move to. Its only movement is the cyclical movement of its tides. Once man has arrived on (or in) the ocean of democracy, he too will be incapable of progressive movement.[14] Thus the "new level which society was obliged to seek" in this era is the last it will seek: democracy is the end of history (VII, 319; IX, 227, 227–228; VIII, 185; IX, 225; IV, 302).

The primary theme of *The History* is the struggle of the democratic and national movements in America toward the unity and harmony of the democratic nationality which the country had arrived at by 1815. Later, in *The Education*, Adams will again depict the history of the United States in terms of a comparable duality (though not using the same symbols) and see the relationship as one of conflict. Again, the democratic movement will seem to him the stronger, but then he will interpret its meaning and the significance of its strength. "All one's life," he will write,

> one had struggled for unity, and unity had always won. The National Govern-ment and the national unity had overcome every resistance . . . ; yet the greater the unity and the momentum, the worse became the complexity and the fric-tion. . . . The multiplicity of unity had steadily increased, was increasing, and threatened to increase beyond reason.[15]

In terms of *The Education* the democratic movement in *The History* is a movement toward chaos.[16] But is there evidence of such a view in *The*

[14] See critical note 19.

[15] Henry Adams, *The Education of Henry Adams*, introduction by James Truslow Adams, The Modern Library (New York: Random House Inc., 1931), p. 398.

[16] Samuels, *The Middle Years*, p. 369, says that, in *The History*, "No single term recurs more often than 'chaos.'" Vandersee, "The Political Attitudes," p. 206, sees the "circumstances" of *Gallatin* as becoming chaos in *The History*: "An important part of the definition of democracy was chaos. And the American democracy was one fragment of a dizzily chaotic world." (On p. 210 n. 19 he also cites p. 369 of Samuels.) Neither writer specifically equates the ocean symbol with chaos.

History? The work is presented in terms of that dichotomizing view of experience which appears in all of Adams' books and provides the fundamental key to their meaning (as well as helping to create their dramatic intensity). In *The History* the tension between these dichotomies—man vs. nature; theory vs. energy; Federalist vs. Republican; America vs. Europe; and so on—has, in most cases, decreased by the end of the work. Thus the seeming fusion of democracy and nationalism in the American identity is only an extreme example of a phenomenon characteristic of the era (III, 20).

But there is an implicit dichotomy among those dichotomies that are not said to have diminished which suggests the possibility of the kind of conflict described in *The Education* and hence a fundamental irreconcilability between the flag and ocean. Describing the reaction against Jefferson's system as part of a rhythmic pattern in American development, Adams observes that

> after the Declaration of Independence twelve years had been needed to create an efficient Constitution; another twelve years of energy brought a reaction against the government then created; a third period of twelve years was ending in a sweep toward still greater energy; and already a child could calculate the result of a few more such returns.

In this passage American history is viewed as alternating between periods of maximum and minimum energy, but its ultimate movement is said to be toward greater energy. Yet, in the passage cited earlier, the river of American history is said to be moving toward equilibrium in the democratic ocean of minimum energy. The national and democratic movements would thus seem to be unalterably opposed. Together, the two passages suggest that the increasingly energetic unity of the national movement is like the increasing momentum of a river as it nears the ocean and thus that soon its energy, unity, and progress will disappear in the stability of the ocean of democracy. The difference between this situation and that in *The Education* is that there the centrifugal movement is one of an uncontrollable maximum of energy destroying the centripetal movement by explosion; in *The History*, the centrifugal movement is one of uncontrolled minimum energy also destroying the centripetal movement but doing so by absorbing and dissipating its force. In both cases the stronger democratic, centrifugal movement opposes unity and eventually produces chaos (VI, 123).

The first subordinate symbol of *The History* is the steamboat.[17]

---

[17] Levenson, *The Mind and Art of Henry Adams*, pp. 137–139 (see also p. 299), makes the steamboat a more complex symbol than I do, but also sees it as opposing the "centrifugal forces in . . . American society."

Given Adams' emphasis on America's antipathy toward war, together with his belief that science is the only possible alternative to war as a means of creating and preserving a society, it is appropriate that this "most striking success" in the application of science in nineteenth-century America should be one of his primary symbols. The peculiarly American character of the steamboat is suggested when he says of four American authors and politicians that "they were the product of influences as peculiar to the country as those which produced Fulton and his steamboat." The steamboat's importance lay in its usefulness in developing America's internal resources. It was "the most efficient instrument yet conceived for developing such a country." Though few contemporaries recognized it, Adams says,

> the 17th of August, 1807, [marked] the beginning of a new era in America,— a date which separated the colonial from the independent stage of growth; for on that day, at one o'clock in the afternoon, the steamboat "Clermont," with Robert Fulton in command, started on her first voyage. . . . The problem of steam navigation, so far as it applied to rivers and harbors was settled, and for the first time America could consider herself mistress of her vast resources.

In making possible the development of these resources by connecting previously isolated parts of the country, the steamboat contributed to that national unity and strength symbolized by the flag. Since it plied inland waterways, it actually functioned within the land area embraced by the flag rather than on the ocean. Adams seems to imply the symbolic strengthening of the centripetal flag at the expense of the centrifugal ocean which this fact suggests when he says that "the invention of the steamboat counterbalanced ocean commerce" (IX, 236, 213, 173; IV, 134–135; IX, 221).

The symbol which embodies the opposite tendency in American life is the schooner,[18] a uniquely American creation built during the War of 1812 for use as a privateer: "No people, in the course of a thousand years of rivalry on the ocean," Adams says, "had invented or had known how to sail a Yankee schooner." By the close of the war it was probably the "most efficient vessel afloat" and had, he asserts, "contributed more than the regular navy to bring about a disposition for peace in the British classes most responsible for the war" (VII, 320, 316, 331). He himself juxtaposes it with the steamboat. The latter, he says, was the "most

[18] Healy, "A Study of Non-Rational Elements in the Works of Adams," p. 631, calls "the American privateer . . . a symbol of the young Republic." Levenson, *The Mind and Art of Henry Adams*, p. 180, says that "by the conclusion of the entire work, the American sailing ship has become the symbol of the American divergence from the European pattern."

striking success" in the application of science, but it did not "offer the best example of popular characteristics . . . . The fast-sailing schooner . . . best illustrated the character of the people" (IX, 236). "Such literature and art as [Americans] produced, showed qualities akin to those which produced the swift-sailing schooner" (IX, 218). As the ocean is Adams' symbol for American society, so the schooner is his symbol for the American individual. Thus when he discusses the chief qualities of that individual in the final chapter of *The History*, he is presumably also discussing the qualities of its most representative creation. "The traits of intelligence, rapidity, and mildness," he says, "seemed fixed in the national character as early as 1817" (IX, 240–241). By "mildness" he means that "antipathy to war" which he calls the "first . . . political trait" of the American people (IX, 226). The privateer, unlike naval vessels, was built to flee rather than to fight, and, if caught, always tried to escape. The steamboat is an even more peaceful vessel, but reflects no actual antipathy to fighting. The schooner is also built lightly in order to give it the speed necessary to escape; it reflects the rapidity Adams sees in the national character. The slower moving steamboat has much less of this quality. The intelligence Adams mentions as the third quality of American national character seems as exemplified in the steamboat as in the schooner unless the particular kind of intelligence he means is examined. He characterizes American intelligence as quick and shrewd (IX, 218, 237). Perhaps the schooner also shows more evidence of such intelligence than the steamboat. This is particularly true when intelligence is coupled with that "keen sense of form and style" (IX, 216) which Adams sees as the common characteristic of Americans. Probably this sense is revealed more clearly in the schooner, "a creation as beautiful as it was practical" (VII, 319), than in the more exclusively practical steamboat.

A fourth characteristic of the schooner-privateer which does not appear in Adams' list suggests another primary way in which it differs from the steamboat. Whereas the steamboat assists and symbolizes the national movement, the privateer expresses the democratic movement and its concern with the free individual. The privateer was involved in wholly private enterprise. Although Adams begins by emphasizing its contribution to the American cause, he concludes by emphasizing the disharmony between the private economic aims it represented and the public aim of the war (VII, 333–335, 337; VIII, 194). Ultimately, the privateer was as much a private exploitation of the war as a contribution to it. If this fact about the privateer expresses an aspect of the national character—and why make the privateer a symbol if so important a fact about it were untypical?—it suggests a strong tendency for American individualism to be contrary to the interests of society as a whole.[19] Thus, again, when the two aspects of the democratic dream are treated separately, as symbols, they manifest a fundamental opposition, and the possibility of renewed conflict between them is implied. And again it is clear that the stronger force is the centrifugal or democratic force. In *The Education* Adams will emphasize what he calls there the anarchic nature of the American character and suggest that finally it is the dominant tendency in all human character and in reality in general. In *The History* he stops at suggesting that the typical American is primarily an individualist and tends to pursue his own aims rather than contribute to the social whole.

Thus the symbols in *The History*, though they occur only occasionally, prove upon examination to be of great importance. They fuse its theme and Adams' attitude toward the theme into images which suggest unstated meanings. Principally, they imply that the identity America discovered between 1800 and 1815 was a highly unstable, momentary equilibrium between antithetical forces which might bring about a social state in which the inertness of society would stifle the growth of the individual while his isolation would prevent any social unity. This meaning is relevant to Adams' concern with illusion and reality as it appears in *The History*. On the explicit level, the interaction of human action and natural forces separates what is true in the former from what is false; the result is an American identity. The symbols do not deny this meaning but they do extend it by implying that one of the two forces combined in the democratic nationality of America is an illusion, in the sense of not being permanently practicable. For, if the increasing energy and unity of America is that of a river gathering momentum in its plunge toward the ocean, then the centripetal national movement is ultimately an illusion and the centrifugal democratic movement, the only reality. Such a conclusion looks forward to the future direction and character of Adams' thought. In the final chapters of *The History*, therefore, Adams has begun to explore his pervasive theme, primarily through symbolism, on a profounder level than he did at the beginning of the work, a level which leads directly to his dynamic theory of history and the works based upon it.

[19] The difference between this American individualism and that of Europe is that European individualism is produced by military necessity and is subordinate to the creation or preservation of political unity. Danger produces the individual creator or savior of society. American individualism results from the absence of military necessity and is stronger than the political unity symbolized by the flag. In America security produces an individual who defies or exploits society in order to realize purely personal ends.

CHAPTER V

PESSIMISTIC NATURALISM AND THE CHILDHOOD OF MAN

A Theory of Chaos

In *Mont-Saint-Michel and Chartres* (1904, 1913)[1] and the works which follow it, Adams presents his final answers to the problems of illusion and reality. These answers have a fundamental unity derived from Adams' commitment after 1890 to pessimistic naturalism. His position appears most clearly and emphatically in *The Education of Henry Adams* (1907, 1918): "Chaos," he says, is "the law of nature; Order [is] the dream of man."[2] "In essence," history is "incoherent and immoral"; hence no theory, either of reality or of history, can be absolute truth. Even his own dynamic theory of history is an illusion. Yet, because it satisfies his human need to order his knowledge and experience,[3] it is useful to him. In *The Education* he says that *Chartres* and *The Education* were written to establish the two critical "points of relation" in the theory, the point when man thought of himself as "a unit in a unified universe,"[4] and that when he realized he was actually a fragment of a chaotic multiverse.

---

[1] Henry Adams, *Mont-Saint-Michel and Chartres*, with an introduction by Ralph Adams Cram (Boston: Houghton Mifflin Co., 1933). All page references to this work will be found between parentheses in the text. Both this work and *The Education* appeared originally in limited, privately printed editions and only much later as regularly published works; hence the double dates for both books.

[2] Henry Adams, *The Education of Henry Adams*, introduction by James Truslow Adams, The Modern Library (New York: Random House, Inc., 1931), p. 451. The following quotation is on p. 301.

[3] References in this and following chapters to the theory in general or as it appears in "The Rule of Phase Applied to History" or "A Letter to American Teachers of History" are not capitalized. Capitals indicate that the reference is to the theory as it appears in *Chartres* and *The Education*. When there is any doubt or any possibility of confusion (as in this paragraph) lower case letters are used. For a discussion of the unity of the various versions of the theory, see Appendix I.

[4] *The Education*, p. 435.

In this view the dynamic theory, although first promulgated systematically in *The Education*, is equally integral to *Chartres*. Recent scholarship suggests that Adams developed the theory—indeed, decided to write *The Education*—only after writing at least the first version of *Chartres*.[5] Like other writers he seems to have discovered what he had to say partly in the process of saying it.

In the version of the theory which appears in *Chartres* and *The Education* (hereafter referred to as the Dynamic Theory of History) nature is described as a chaos of anarchic forces.[6] Man is one of these forces.[7] His motion in time (like that of the others) is determined by the motion of the sum of all forces.[8] His basic characteristic is also the same as that of every force: he seeks power—i.e., he seeks to grow by absorbing other forces.[9] But in one respect man is unique: he perceives reality not as the chaos it is but as a unity,[10] which he tries to perfect by his own efforts.[11] This illusion is innate in all human beings, but is stronger in the woman than in the man.[12] In periods when human energy is at a maximum and the illusion of unity is most intense, the woman and her use of feeling to comprehend and deal with reality dominates the man and his reason.[13] Religion, the ultimate expression[14] of human illusion,[15] and art—both, in essence, expressions of emotion[16]—reach their height in such periods. Humanity worships unity personified as a goddess who is adored for the sexual force she embodies.[17] The Middle Ages represented the last great upsurge of the illusion of unity.[18] With the Renaissance the man, reason, science, and technology permanently triumphed over the woman, feeling, religion, and art.[19] Reason itself became increasingly inductive rather than deductive[20]; eventually this empiricism led to the discovery that nature was multiplicity.[21] Yet so strong is man's sense of unity that it continued to dominate even science to the end of the nineteenth century.[22]

The growth of science, reason, and multiplicity at the expense of religion, feeling, and unity has been accompanied socially by a parallel

[5] Ernest Samuels, *Henry Adams: The Major Phase* (Cambridge, Mass.: Harvard University Press, 1964), pp. 254, 307, 312. J. C. Levenson, *The Mind and Art of Henry Adams* (Boston: Houghton Mifflin Co., 1957), pp. 354–355. See critical note 20.

[6] See critical note 21. The Dynamic Theory as presented in this paragraph appears in *Chartres* as a whole, in chapters 33 and 34 of *The Education*, and on pp. 458–459 of the latter (with a few citations from chapter 25 which clarify and develop the material on pp. 458–459, as explained in critical note 28).

[7] See critical note 22.   [8] See critical note 23.   [9] See critical note 24.
[10] See critical note 25.   [11] See critical note 26.   [12] See critical note 27.
[13] See critical note 28.   [14] See critical note 29.   [15] See critical note 30.
[16] See critical note 31.   [17] See critical note 32.   [18] See critical note 33.
[19] See critical note 34.   [20] See critical note 35.   [21] See critical note 36.
[22] See critical note 37.

growth in individualism at the expense of a sense of community. In the twentieth century, human society—homogeneous in its early phases—is moving toward anarchy.[23] Man no longer views himself as a participant in an organic universe (and therefore an organic church and state) but as an isolated atom, "responsible only to himself" (367). The same movement from unity to multiplicity occurs in the life of individual men. Childhood is the period of strength and illusion; age, of weakness and a sense of reality.[24] The degree of strength and of weakness depends upon the temperament of the individual, the nature of his experience, and the historical period in which he lives. In the twentieth century, the period of illusion tends to be brief. In *The Education* Adams presents himself as a representative nineteenth-century man to whom age has brought an understanding of the twentieth-century mind and therefore of reality. As Everyman[25] grown old, he has entered into the ultimate knowledge which heralds his own death and may herald that of his race. It is this representative quality in his life which gives Adams what belief he has in the earlier versions of his dynamic theory—an avowed rationalization of history in terms of his own life,[26] writ, as Ralph Waldo Emerson advised, in "colossal cypher" and thereby ostensibly transformed into the life of Everyman.

THE PERVASIVE DICHOTOMY

The correspondence between any man and Everyman is the source of the basic structural device of *Chartres*, the contrast between the child and the old man.[27] The child has strength and lives by feeling; the old man is weak and lives by reason. The child believes reality is unity; the old man knows it is multiplicity. As its subtitle, "A Study of Thirteenth-Century Unity," suggests, *Chartres* concerns the child's world; *The Education*, "A Study in Twentieth-Century Multiplicity," explores the world of the old man.[28] Yet both have the same point of view—the truth which only the old man knows. In *The Education*, the coincidence between this point of view and the period being discussed makes the reality of chaos omnipresent throughout the book. The young men who make up the intended audience,[29] the age they live in, and Adams' appeal to them primarily through their (empirical) reason accentuate this emphasis. Their youth and its tendency to illusion only provide him with the opportunity and motive for bringing them to maturity by destroying their illusion of

---

[23] See critical note 38. [24] See critical note 39.
[25] See chapter 6 of the present work, p. 130.
[26] *The Education*, p. 472. [27] See critical note 40.
[28] *The Education*, p. 435. [29] *Ibid.*, Preface, p. x.

unity and thereby giving them the knowledge of multiplicity required for effective action in the twentieth century. In *Chartres* Adams' purpose is more complex. He wants his audience to know the truth, but he also wants it to know—and to experience—man's illusion of unity.[30] The point of view is also that of the old man, but now the period being presented is one when the child's point of view prevailed. This view is emphasized by the nature of the supposed audience—young women[31]— whom Adams addresses primarily through their feelings. Only the fact that they are twentieth-century girls reinforces the twentieth-century point of view. Hence in *Chartres* the old man's sense of reality tends to be balanced by the child's illusion.

A parallel contrast in the two books appears in their use of time. Both are historical:[32] time and its linear movement are the basis of the form and meaning of each. *The Education* is an account of a life which was a series of disillusionments, a cumulative realization that unity is real only as the human mode of perception. Time is the medium in which this process occurs; it is also frequently the agent through which the unreality of unity is demonstrated. The movement of time is therefore emphasized. *Chartres*, too, is ultimately dominated by the fact that time moves and in its movement destroys unity. But here Adams is presenting a period when man's sense of unity was strongest and he achieved a large measure of intellectual and imaginative unity. To convey the fullest sense of that unity, the flow of time is muted (as is the presence of multiplicity). This is done partly by handling time in blocks, by centuries instead of by years. But even these blocks are partially fused by being all part of the child's world and thus sharing the child's belief in unity. The result is the re-creation, in all its "intense fragility," of a perfect moment in history, varying in mood but true to a single ideal, delicately suspended amidst the chaos of reality and the disintegrating movement of time.

The sense of balance is enhanced by setting the unity of the medieval world against the twentieth-century narrator and audience and thereby creating tension through contrast rather than a sense of time's flow. This contrast and tension are sharpened by the fullness with which Adams objectifies each world. By presenting his vivid account of medieval life, thought, and art as if it were being told to a niece by a twentieth-century "uncle" on a journey, he dramatically juxtaposes the medieval world as an

---

[30] *Chartres*. On p. 106, the uncle tells the niece that their purpose is "to feel Gothic art." On p. 195, he makes it clear that the Virgin was a work of art, and on p. 224, he suggests that society, as a group of human beings unified to some extent by commonly held ideals, is a work of art.

[31] *Chartres*, pp. xiii–xiv.

[32] See critical note 41.

epitome of man's childhood and its illusions with the constant, physical presence of an epitome of the old man's world and its wisdom. The somewhat less physical presence of a twentieth-century niece as the old man's auditor enhances this balance. But she has another—and more important —function. As a woman she represents what Adams calls "the eternal woman" and thus "unites the ages." As a young woman she is both naturally sympathetic to the child's world and, to some extent, still a part of it. As a twentieth-century girl she is also a part of the old man's world. This dual aspect makes her an ideal person to appreciate fully both the beauty of man's childhood beliefs and the horror of his discovery that they are illusions.

During most of the book, however, this function is only implicit. Usually she is a silent listener, whose presence, though continuous for the uncle, is not explicit enough to be so for the reader (196, 284). What he is generally aware of is a tissue of subject and attitude in which the child's world and the old man's point of view are sometimes juxtaposed, sometimes fused. The result is not the bitter irony of *The Education* but an irony permeated by intense nostalgia.[33] The uncle is Everyman grown old, looking back, from a position of disillusionment, with affection and homesickness to the illusory world of childhood. His love for this world is a grandfather's love for children, and his nostalgia in writing of it, a grandfather's yearning for the vanished joys and illusions of his own childhood. This mood tends toward tragic intensity because of the uncle's constant awareness of the chasm which separates the child's world from reality. Sporadically, he reveals this chasm to his auditor by first making an exalted statement in praise of something believed in by the child and then abruptly revealing its falsity. This device both reminds the niece (and reader) of what time, maturity, and knowledge have taken from man and, more important, suggests the constant presence of multiplicity even in the child's world.

The balance Adams achieves by objectifying the book's point of view in these characters and juxtaposing them with its subject matter is further enhanced by his principal narrative device—the journey. Actually, there are two journeys, the first a physical journey in space along the "architectural highway" from Mont-Saint-Michel to Chartres. This device has a particular appropriateness to the subject of *Chartres*, for in the Middle Ages "the passion for pilgrimages," the uncle says, "was universal . . . . For at least a thousand years it was [our ancestors'] chief delight, and is not yet extinct." The final phrase implies what the uncle makes explicit elsewhere when he calls his and the niece's journey a "pilgrimage." In his letters Henry Adams sometimes distinguishes between "pilgrims,"

[33] See critical note 42.

whose journeys were motivated by an idea, and "tourists," their modern, degenerate descendants, who lack religious or intellectual purpose and are motivated only by curiosity or ennui.[34] In *Chartres* the uncle uses both terms and treats them as synonyms. Yet his tourists do have a purpose, albeit not a religious one. They wish "to feel Gothic art"; thus they are "pilgrims of art" (46, 16, 195, 106, 191).

The easy part of their pilgrimage is the physical journey. More difficult is the journey in time. Yet to know what the church door of Mont-Saint-Michel meant to its builders, "one needs to be eight centuries old" and "even then one must still learn to feel it." To grow thus "prematurely young," one must be able to return, in imagination, to humanity's child-hood. Here the return is to the Middle Ages. But the uncle points out that the ideas and symbols of that period were also characteristic of Every-man's youth as a whole. Basic was the belief in unity; pervasive also was the worship of a woman goddess; recurrent too was the glorification of passionate love. Thus, in telling the story of Tristan and Isolde, the uncle notes that "behind the Welsh Tristan, . . . critics detect a far more ancient figure . . . . King Marc was a tribal chief of the Stone Age. . . . Tristan's weapons were the bow and stone knife" (2, 217).

The basic organization of *Chartres* is a threefold temporal division into the eleventh, twelfth, and thirteenth centuries, marked by two stops in the spatial journey, at Mont-Saint-Michel and at Chartres, and a contin-uation, intellectually, to a third stop at the philosophical church of St. Thomas Aquinas. This imaginative temporal journey parallels the physical spatial journey, but the two never meet. Indeed, there tends to be a tension between the two. Though the temporal journey is divided into three parts, the continuity of the spatial journey tends to draw all three centuries into a single temporal unit and thereby reinforce the balance between the child's world and the old man's twentieth-century perspective. At the beginning of the book the uncle says of the temporal journey that "one can do it, as one can play with children." Later, however, he says that "it may be that not one tourist in a hundred—perhaps not one in a thou-sand of the English-speaking race—does feel [medieval art], or can feel it even when explained to him." The uncle would seem to be prevaricating at the beginning of *Chartres* for fear of losing nieces who could make the journey but might lose heart before they began if they knew how few were qualified. In any event, in his initial remarks he makes use of William Wordsworth's Immortality Ode to assert that "one can still have sight of that immortal sea which brought us hither from the twelfth century; one can

[34] HA to John Hay, Sept. 7, 1895, in Henry Adams, *Henry Adams and His Friends: A Collection of His Unpublished Letters*, compiled with a biographical introduction by Harold Dean Cater (Boston: Houghton Mifflin Co., 1947), p. 347.

even travel thither and see the children sporting on the shore." In saying here that modern man may imaginatively recapture his racial past, the uncle is making a cuckoo-like use of Wordsworth's ocean symbol. Wordsworth wrote that " . . . in a season of calm weather / Though inland far we be, / Our souls have sight of that immortal sea / Which brought us hither, / Can in a moment travel thither, / And see the children sport upon the shore." This ocean is an all-embracing, all-pervading spiritual reality. In *Chartres* the sea is the natural multiverse of blind force of the Dynamic Theory.[35] Yet at this point neither niece nor reader knows enough to be aware of the discrepancy. Only in the light of the book as a whole does it become clear that here, on its second page, the uncle is beginning that ironic shifting between the beauty of the child's world and the horror of reality which pervades *Chartres* (2, 129, 2).

Soon afterwards Wordsworth's poem is again alluded to, though now the focus is upon the children found upon the medieval shore. The uncle describes himself—and Henry Adams—in noting

> the fanatical conviction of the Gothic enthusiast, to whom the twelfth century means exuberant youth, the eternal child of Wordsworth, over whom its immortality broods like the day; it is so simple and yet so complicated; it sees so much and so little; it loves so many toys and cares for so few necessities; its youth is so young, its age so old, and its youthful yearning for old thought is so disconcerting, like the mysterious senility of the baby that
>
> > Deaf and silent, reads the eternal deep
> > Haunted forever by the eternal mind.
>
> One need not take it more seriously than one takes the baby itself. Our amusement is to play with it, and to catch its meaning in its smile.

Here the equation of the uncle's child with Wordsworth's child is specific. The disparity between Wordsworth's traditional use of the image and the uncle's passage is the source of the latter's series of paradoxes. The Dynamic Theory makes their meaning clear. According to the theory, the immortality which broods over Wordsworth's child is not the personal immortality of the soul, but the nonhuman immortality of energy in the multiverse. In Wordsworth the child is simple because it is whole, fresh from the hand of ultimate wholeness; it is complex because it is profound, fresh from the heart of ultimate reality. According to the theory the child is simple because it is ignorant and has the strength to shut out the truth and see reality as it wishes. It is complicated because, on the foundation of its basically simple view of a universe, it erects immensely complicated systems of architecture and thought. It sees much in terms of its false

[35] See critical note 43.

idea of reality, yet little of reality itself. As a result (and here the uncle has departed completely from Wordsworth), it loves illusions much and cares little for what it fails to recognize are necessities. The child's yearning for old thought may be the medieval desire for authority; it may also be his aspiration toward maturity, always disconcerting to grandfathers (though the young Wordsworth also found it so) who have outgrown that aspiration in attaining it and instead yearn for youth. The quotation from Wordsworth suggests that the child is especially close and sensitive to the divine mind. The theory agrees that the medieval child was haunted by the "eternal," but it would assert that this awareness was man's projection of his innate belief in unity onto the multiverse. It would also assert that the child was haunted by another, more valid sense of the eternal, which he personified as Satan, but which Adams calls the multiplicity of reality, always present behind the veil of illusion. Finally, whereas Wordsworth treats the child with the utmost seriousness, the uncle would not have the niece take the medieval child with any more seriousness than one takes a baby[36]—since both lack the wisdom of maturity— and suggests that the best way to understand either is to catch its meaning in its smile (Chartres cathedral here being compared to a smile). The happy, simple, ignorant child; the unhappy, complex, wise old man: these are the uncle's antitheses, ironically set off by Wordsworth's glorification of the child as the repository of all wisdom (87–88).

This contrast is Adams' symbolic way of presenting, at the beginning of *Chartres*, its fundamental problem. At the end of the book he presents it directly and rationally. The problem of *Chartres* (and of *The Education*) is what the uncle calls "the oldest problem of philosophy, religion, and science," "the attempt to bridge the chasm between multiplicity and unity," "to connect the two." In *Chartres* the problem is shown to be fundamental not only for all of Adams' medieval characters, but also for twentieth-century scientists and for the uncle. It is presented as the problem of which is the most valid point of view, the old man's or the child's, and what is the relationship between them. The child always answered the question as he did in the Middle Ages: "The Church had committed itself to the dogma that order and unity were the ultimate truth . . . and society supported her." Moreover, "good was order, law, unity. Evil was disorder, anarchy, multiplicity." Connecting unity and multiplicity meant transforming the latter into the former, a creative process. The ultimate possibility of unity for man was his achievement of oneness with God, the divine unity, after death. The earthly road to this unity always ran through the Church, though different centuries traveled it by various means: the eleventh century by force; the twelfth, by love;

[36] See critical note 43.

the thirteenth, by reason. In the twentieth century, the uncle says, society still, for practical reasons, acts as if unity were reality. But "science hesitates, more visibly than the Church ever did, to decide once for all whether unity or diversity is ultimate law; whether order or chaos is the governing rule of the universe, if universe there is; whether anything, except phenomena, exists." Henry Adams seems not to hesitate. As the subtitle of *The Education*, "A Study of Twentieth-Century Multiplicity," suggests, Adams believes that multiplicity is real, and that connecting unity and multiplicity is a destructive process.[37] Yet only the old man sees this truth; the child, living in illusion, believed that unity was alone real and lasting (299, 319, 364–365, 364, 288).

The opening paragraph of *Chartres* evokes its fundamental dichotomy. The Archangel Michael, standing on the summit of the tower that crowned his church, stood "for Church and State [i.e., all humanity], and both militant. He is the conqueror of Satan. . . . Therefore," the uncle says, "you find him" next to the ocean. St. Michael and his church symbolize humanity, its sense of unity personified as God, and religion as the ultimate means of connecting unity and multiplicity. The ocean symbolizes nature,[38] its multiplicity—personified as Satan—and disintegration as the ultimate method of connecting unity and multiplicity. In the following paragraph the uncle contrasts the ocean setting of the church, which, because it is eternal, twentieth-century tourists "can understand and feel" as well as men of any period, with the church door, which, because it was created by man, is bound by time and transcience and requires historical imagination in order to be understood and felt. The uncle immediately focuses the niece's attention upon the church because it is the supreme expression in act of the child's attempt to transform multiplicity into unity: it "expressed [both] the deepest [emotion] man ever felt—the struggle of his own littleness to grasp the infinite [and his] own unsatisfied, incomplete, overstrained effort . . . to rival the energy, intelligence, and purpose of God." This emotion and this ambition have also been expressed in other human creations. All of them contrast with the ocean, the symbol of nature. Adams views the church as the primary symbol of man in the Middle Ages; he also makes it the primary symbol of *Chartres*, as the title suggests.[39] The three centuries of his medieval triptych he pre-

---

[37] See critical note 44.

[38] See chapters 6 (pp. 135–138) and 8 (pp. 209–210, et al.) of the present text; John Brunner, "Henry Adams: His Decline and Fall" (Ph.D. dissertation, UCLA, 1956), p. 217, says of this passage that St. Michael "towered high above his abbey church on the sacred Mount in Peril of the Sea, suggesting through his symbolic connotations the tides of social concentration that were sweeping the eleventh-century world to a high-water mark of instinct."

[39] As noted in John P. McIntyre, "Henry Adams and the Unity of Chartres," in *Twentieth Century Literature*, VII (Jan., 1962), 164.

sents in terms of Mont-Saint-Michel, Chartres, and the philosophical church of St. Thomas Aquinas (1, 2, 104).

These three examples of the "Church Architectural" also serve as one of the two principal unifying devices in the book (the other being the persons of the uncle and the niece). They assist in creating that balance Adams tries to maintain between the flow of time and the unity of his medieval moment. The uncle's epitomizing of each century in a church is his principal means of making the reader's sense of time one of century-long blocks. Even this division is not absolute: neither church (nor St. Thomas' thought, in a sense [348]) was built in a single century. Moreover, the artists of later centuries tried to remain as true as they could within the limits of their own styles to the original work. As a result, the churches overlap the centuries they epitomize; the century divisions are weakened; and the churches, instead of being contained by time, become independent of it and even tend to contain it. The balance thus achieved between time's movement and the church contributes to the book's pervasive balance between the ocean's movement and the church's stasis, the point of view of the old man and that of the child.

UNITY IN FEELING

The pilgrimage begins at Mont-Saint-Michel in Normandy. The uncle presents the spatial trip there as being also a temporal trip to the childhood home of his and the niece's Norman ancestors. He finds the setting "familiar [and] homelike," the church, initially, a place of "repose," its Romanesque arch, a "cradle of rest." "Cradle" epitomizes the pervading tone of homesickness. But immediately the uncle destroys the human illusion, born of desire, with the reality—as he will do throughout the book: the Roman arch, he says, is perhaps "the most unreposeful thought ever put into architectural form." The child it expresses was the eleventh-century masculine warrior of the Church Militant, worshipping God and the Archangel Michael to the exclusion of the Virgin and Christ. As the uncle presents them, both God and Michael were human creations, projections and objectifications of eleventh-century man's profoundest feelings and ideas, which, once created, inspired their creators to perform deeds of military valor, build churches like Mont-Saint-Michel, and write poems like the "Song of Roland"—all expressions of the military ideal (3, 7, 8).

Religious figures and works of art were also "social symbol[s]" expressing their society. In the uncle's account of the eleventh century, he emphasizes the church, the work of art, rather than the inspiring deities, God and St. Michael, but both the art and the deities are said to be "an assertion of God and Man in a bolder, stronger, closer union than ever was expressed by other art." Against this union Satan waged constant war, and the uncle ultimately decides that it was Satan who was the victor. At that point the uncle evokes for the first time the tone of anguish which grows steadily stronger as the book moves on: "Nothing," he says, "is sadder than the catastrophe of Gothic art, religion, and hope" (67, 45).

After many more miles along the architectural highway, uncle and niece arrive at the twelfth century—"the most perfect moment of art and feeling in the thousand years of pure and confident Christanity"—and at Chartres, the church that "fills our ideal." Here is the moment of the "church triumphant," the heart of *Chartres*, and "the object of our pilgrimage." Continuing the dominant image of the book, the uncle calls the period (which he dates from 1115 to 1215) by its architectural name, the Transition. To its combined use of the round Romanesque and the pointed Gothic arch, he attributes symbolic significance, calling the former masculine, the latter, feminine.[40] He says that the period was one of delicate balance between these opposites, but in his own talk the masculine and logical serve simply as a foil to show the dominance of woman and love. "Perhaps," he says, "the passion of love was more serious than that of religion, and gave to religion the deepest emotion, and the most complicated one, which society knew." The kind of unity created by this emphasis was very different from that of the previous century. It had hoped to unite men by force; the twelfth century sought to attain the same end by love. Now the struggle was between men attempting to win a woman's favor. Socially, this change marked a shift in emphasis from converting pagans abroad to alleviating anarchy at home (330, 87, 33, 216).

"The last and highest moment" of the Transition "is seen at Chartres," built by men inspired by the Virgin Mary, the "social ideal" of the time, as Mont-Saint-Michel had been inspired by St. Michael—though now the uncle emphasizes the deity rather than the cathedral. As in the case of Michael, a man-made religious symbol of an "ideal of human perfection" became a commanding influence in the lives of its creators. The uncle's principal purpose is to show how immediately and pervasively the Virgin influenced almost every person and activity of the time. This influence was far greater than Michael ever exerted. Indeed, the uncle says the Virgin was "the most intensely and the most widely and the most personally felt, of all characters, divine or human or imaginary, that ever existed among men." As he presents her,[41] the negative source of her power was the fear and hatred human beings had for law, and their belief that she alone represented a power outside law. The Trinity was divine justice; "the Mother alone was human, imperfect, and could love." She could understand, as it

---

[40] Brunner, "Henry Adams: His Decline and Fall," pp. 218, 240, notes both this meaning for the arches and their later meaning in the book (*Chartres*, pp. 317, 297).

[41] See critical note 45.

could not, that men are "irregular, exceptional," and unfitted for systems of law; hence she judged them solely by their love for her. This view of her, which, contrary to orthodox belief, saw her, not as having atoned for Eve's disobedience but as succeeding where Eve failed, was, the uncle says, in origin a popular belief, forced by the people upon an unwilling clergy, and hence "in substance a separate religion." In the twelfth century it became so powerful that the Virgin absorbed the Trinity, which became simply her child (318, 200, 249, 254–255, 261, 259).

The belief that she and her rule of favor were above law was an assertion that a human being, acting as an anarchist (as if his ultimate responsibility were to himself), overruled God in His own universe. It is significant that this human being is a woman. In *The Education* Adams views woman's maternity as the source of the only lasting continuity in human history, the biological continuity of the race, and as the profoundest source of that sense of unity which distinguishes man from other forces in the multiverse. To deify an ideal mother is therefore to deify the source both of man's life and of his identity. When man's energy is at its greatest, he worships a mother goddess. This fact explains why the worship of the Virgin, the "last and greatest" of these goddesses, has lasted so long and why, "to this day," she remains "the strongest symbol with which the Church can conjure" (196, 250).

Actually this divine mother was the creation of man's imagination and real only there. Her dependence upon her creator is presented in one of the most charming passages in *Chartres*. Addressing the niece as directly as he does anywhere in the book, the uncle says of Chartres that,

> To us, it is a child's fancy; a toyhouse to please the Queen of Heaven—to please her so much that she would be happy in it—to charm her till she smiled. . . . This church was built for her in this spirit of simple-minded, practical, utilitarian faith—in this singleness of thought, exactly as a little girl sets up a doll-house for her favourite blonde doll. Unless you [i.e., the niece] can go back to your dolls, you are out of place here. If you can go back to them, and get rid for one small hour of the weight of custom, you shall see Chartres in glory.

The Virgin has been transformed from all-powerful queen to a child's doll. The key to the change lies in the phrase "to us," meaning the uncle and the niece. The change is a shift in perspective from the twelfth to the twentieth century. The twelfth-century child's sense of the divine mother is that of a human personality, omnipotent and omnipresent, enfolding him and the whole universe in her loving arms. He sees her as perhaps a child always sees its mother, only on an enormously magnified scale. But here the perspective has suddenly become that of the twentieth-century old man, who sees the Virgin as a humanly created doll. To understand the Virgin, the niece must be able in imagination to go back to her dolls; she must become "prematurely young" again (88–89).

This is the most explicit juxtaposition in *Chartres* of the uncle's auditor and the principal subject of his "talk." It is also the point at which Henry Adams makes it clear that the uncle's presentation of the twelfth-century Virgin is primarily intended for a twentieth-century young woman, young enough to remember her dolls, old enough to have the emotions of a woman. In *The Education* Adams will show young men of the twentieth century an age in which their plans and lives must finally be failures; here he shows a young woman of the century what an age was like which saw life as she instinctively tends to see it and what the result of such a view was. Ultimately, he is showing her how successful the woman's effort to unify the race has been and what relation her attempt has to the reality of the multiverse.

He wants to do this primarily in terms of feeling rather than understanding. Uncle and niece have come to Europe to "feel Gothic art" and only secondarily to understand it, and for them the Virgin as well as Chartres is art. The difficult problem is that, according to the Dynamic Theory, the modern mind functions in terms of understanding, not of feeling. It is a "scientific mind" and therefore "atrophied," having "lost much of its taste for poetry . . . , for colour and line, . . . for war and worship, wine and women." All this is a natural concomitant of old age. Twentieth-century tourists are Everyman grown old; they must expect such enfeeblement: "society has no right to feel it as a moral reproach to be told that it has reached an age when it can no longer depend, as in childhood, on its taste, or smell, or sight, or hearing, or memory." Most tourists cannot feel; they must be content to study. The few who can feel, however, should trust their feelings about the child's world more than the historian's or archeologist's understanding. The uncle's purpose is to increase the intensity of that feeling as much as possible. Ultimately he hopes to increase it enough to project the niece into an imaginative vision of the Virgin (106, 196, 29, 138).

He makes four preliminary efforts to do this (106, 137, 143, 147) before his first large-scale effort at the end of chapter 9. There he says of the Virgin that one sees her personal presence on every side. Any one can feel it who will only consent to feel like a child. "Sitting here any Sunday afternoon, while the voices of the children of the mâitrise are chanting in the choir"

> —your mind held in the grasp of the strong lines and shadows of the architecture; your eyes flooded with the autumn tones of the glass; your ears drowned with the purity of the voices; one sense reacting upon another until sensation reaches the limit of its range—you, or any other lost soul, could, if you cared

to look and listen, feel a sense beyond the human ready to reveal a sense divine that would make that world once more intelligible, and would bring the Virgin to life again, in all the depths of feeling which she shows here—in lines, vaults, chapels, colours, legends, chants—more eloquent than the prayer-book, and more beautiful than the autumn sunlight.

The primary function of the cathedral is clear: together with the church service, it evokes the deity which inspired it. But that deity can only be known by feeling, and only a child can feel it, for only a child can re-enter the religious world. Moreover, even at this penultimate moment in the evocation, the elegiac note in *Chartres* appears: the sunlight shining through the stained-glass windows is not that of spring and morning—symbolically appropriate to the freshness of the child's world—but the light of late afternoon and autumn, suggesting the old man's sadness and nostalgia as he evokes the lost world of childhood (176-177).

This passage prepares for the final and complete evocation in the last chapter of the section on Chartres.[42] Uncle and niece enter "The Court of the Queen of Heaven" and kneel at Mass—first as tourists, then as twelfth-century participants—before a window depicting the Virgin of Majesty. When Mass is ended, and

we . . . lift our eyes . . . we see, far above the high altar, high over all the agita-tion of prayer, the passion of politics, the anguish of suffering, the terrors of sin, only the figure of the Virgin in majesty, looking down on her people, crowned, throned, glorified, with the infant Christ on her knees. . . . There she actually is—not in symbol or in fancy, but in person, descending on her errands of mercy and listening to each one of us, . . . or satisfying our prayers merely by her presence which calms our excitement as that of a mother calms her child.

The next paragraph abruptly returns to the twentieth-century point of view. "It was very childlike, very foolish, very beautiful, and very true—as art, at least." Never again in the book will the twelfth century be so intensely evoked, for "when we rise from our knees now," the uncle says, "we have finished our pilgrimage." Then, in the final sentence of the chapter, he brings the book's mood of mingled longing and despair to a

[42] Charles Anderson, *American Literary Masters* (New York: Holt, Rinehart and Winston, Inc., 1965), p. 339, brilliantly illuminates this climax (noted earlier by Levenson, *The Mind and Art of Henry Adams*, pp. 267-269) and its relationship to the whole form and purpose of the first half of *Chartres* in observing that here the uncle and niece achieve their avowed purpose of learning to feel the Gothic art by becoming children again. Anderson observes that their momentary attainment of complete identi-fication with medieval man is marked by a momentary shift in the uncle's use of tense from the past to the present, a change which also helps to accentuate the disillusionment of the final paragraph of the chapter, where the uncle returns to the past tense.

climax. The ultimate futility of the vision he has evoked, the despair which lies behind its beauty, is revealed as he announces the disappearance of the faith which had once created and sustained it:

> For seven hundred years Chartres has seen pilgrims, coming and going more or less like us, and will perhaps see them for another seven hundred years; but we shall see it no more, and can safely leave the Virgin in her majesty, with her three great prophets on either hand, as calm and confident in their own strength and in God's providence as they were when Saint Louis was born, but looking down from a deserted heaven, into an empty church, on a dead faith. (178, 192, 194, 195)

This is the emotional climax of *Chartres*—and of its contrast between the child's world and the old man's point of view. Yet it is but one of many points at which the fusion of the two breaks down and the twentieth-century view appears. Skepticism, indeed, was not wholly lacking in the twelfth century, though opposed by faith, the Church, and the sheer investment men had made in that faith. But such contemporary skepticism has little or no part in the uncle's account of the Virgin of Chartres. The skepticism which does appear is that of the twentieth-century old man. Usually this is fused with the uncle's account of the child's world, but occasionally he goes beyond description and states his own views. The best example is this conclusion to his evocation of Mary; another is his comment, when describing Mary as a means of escape from divine justice, that, without her, "man had no hope except in atheism, and for atheism the world was not ready" (250).

At the end of his discussion of Chartres, the uncle says that, "we have finished our pilgrimage. We have done with Chartres." The title of the book, *Mont-Saint-Michel and Chartres*, also suggests that Chartres is its terminal point. Yet this point occurs at the middle of the book! What happens is that, though the uncle goes on talking, the physical journey stops at its high point. This device divides the book into two parts[43] and thereby emphasizes its dominance by the twelfth century, Chartres, and the Virgin. In the first paragraph of the second half of the book, the uncle gives one reason why he makes Chartres the end of the journey: "After worshipping at the shrines of Saint Michael on his Mount and of the Virgin at Chartres . . . all later Gothic art comes naturally, and no new thought disturbs the perfected form." But there is another reason: at the thirteenth-century church of Amiens "emotion is trained in school"; instead of feeling, reason and the "architect's compass" rule. The importance of the thirteenth-century church in the book is as a structural device for the exposition of what *is* vital in the century, scholastic thought, and especially the thought of St. Thomas Aquinas (195, 196, 318, 115).

[43] See critical note 46.

The last half of *Chartres* is not entirely concerned with the thirteenth century, however, or with reason. More than half of it concerns the twelfth century. But the uncle's approach to his material changes. In the first half of the book he tried to make the audience feel the medieval art, though this required a good deal of explanation. In the second half, though there continues to be much appeal to feeling, his emphasis is on helping the audience to understand. He suggests this change in the opening paragraph of the second part:

> The twelfth and thirteenth centuries, studied in the pure light of political economy, are insane. The scientific mind . . . suffers under inherited cerebral weakness, when it comes in contact with the eternal woman. . . . Very rarely one lingers, with a mild sympathy. . . . Still more rarely, owing to some revival of archaic instincts, he rediscovers the woman. This is perhaps the mark of the artist alone, and his solitary privilege. The rest of us cannot feel; we can only study.

The confidence which led the uncle to assert at the beginning of the book that anyone could make the journey in time seems to have disappeared. Perhaps he is being more realistic or—more likely—more frank. In any case, the second half of the book moves toward a rational climax, as the first half moved toward an emotional climax. The pilgrimage of feeling reached its high point in the evocation of the Virgin and of the twentieth century's loss of faith in her; the effort to understand reaches its climax in an exposition of the thought of St. Thomas Aquinas and the twentieth century's loss of faith in it (196).

The first subject of study is the biological and social background for the Virgin's pre-eminence in the twelfth century. "The study of Our Lady," the uncle says, "as shown by the art of Chartres, leads directly back to Eve, and lays bare the whole subject of sex." The Virgin and Eve are one; both are the eternal woman, whose essence is the force she embodies, sex or reproduction. To study the Virgin one must study this force as it appears in human beings and in nature as a whole, where one discovers that "Nature regards the female as the essential, the male as the superfluity of her world." The twelfth-century role of the Virgin was not anomalous but in harmony with nature. It was also harmonious with twelfth-century French society, which "showed a taste for Eves"; everywhere "the superiority of the woman was . . . a fact." The social consequences of this position were very different from those when men are dominant. Woman, too, struggles for power, but, whereas man's struggle is self-assertive and therefore socially disruptive, woman struggles to secure a social state which embodies her belief in unity and provides conditions in which she can exercise her primary traits of love and grace and perform her essential function of motherhood. Like the Virgin she struggles for power primarily by inspiring love in men. In the twelfth century, the uncle says, her efforts resulted, among the aristocracy, in a school called the "Court of Love" and a code of law called "courteous love." Its discipline of manners was the courtly counterpart of the Virgin's discipline of morals: both "insisted on teaching and enforcing an ideal that contradicted the realities." The realities were the "emancipated man" and the social chaos he fomented; the ideal was love and the social unity it created. The ideal was also expressed in a body of literature which suggests that "perhaps the passion of love was more serious than that of religion."

> The poets of "courteous love" showed as little interest in religion as the poets of the eleventh century had shown for it in their poems of war. . . . The true knight of courtesy made nothing of defying the torments of hell, as he defied the lance of a rival . . . ; the perfect, gentle, courteous lover thought of nothing but his love. Whether the object of his love were Nicolette of Beaucaire or Blanche of Castille, Mary of Champagne or Mary of Chartres, was a detail which did not affect the devotion of his worship. (196, 200, 197, 211, 216, 232–233)

The relationship between the first and second sections of the discussion of the twelfth century is therefore partly that of image and idea. The first section describes Chartres as a basis for evoking the Virgin; the second seeks to show the social and, partly, the biological background for the worship of the Virgin. But the uncle is also interested in the code of courteous love itself, a social formulation of the ideal formulated in religious terms by the cult of the Virgin. The primary artistic symbol of the latter was Chartres cathedral; that of the former is the literature of courteous love. These parallels help to tie the two sections together. (Fundamentally, of course, they are tied together by the time in which the two phenomena occurred and by their common emphasis on love and woman.) They are also connected by the fact that the same great ladies of the court who promulgated the code of courteous love and presided at the Courts of Love had an important influence on the art of Chartres. Because they too were queens, they "knew better than the Saints what would suit the Virgin." The final chapter of the second section also helps tie the sections together, for, after discussing courteous love, Adams returns to a discussion of the literature of Mary, "Les Miracles de Notre Dame," thereby clearly indicating his dominant interest in the Virgin throughout the section (162).

Finally, the two sections are tied together by their common use of the rose as a symbol both for the Virgin and for the love-object of the courteous lover. "Even twentieth-century eyes," the uncle says, "can see [at Chartres] that the rose [motif] . . . dominates everything, and gives character to the whole church." The architect "concentrated his whole energy on the rose [window], because the Virgin has told him that the rose symbolized herself." Unlike most of the symbols in *Chartres* the rose was a pervasive symbol in the Middle Ages. As a secular symbol its most important appearance in *Chartres* is in connection with the "Roman de la Rose" of William of Lorris. In that poem, the uncle says, "the Rose is any feminine ideal of beauty, intelligence, purity, or grace—always culminating in the Virgin." "The simple action [of the poem] . . . owes its slight interest only to the constant effort of the dreamer to attain his ideal—the Rose— and owes its charm chiefly to the constant disappointment and final defeat." The uncle here could be characterizing his own "talk" about the twelfth century as a child living in humanity's dream of unity and trying to attain that unity through love, "talk" whose charm is ultimately that of the child's inevitable disappointment, the charm of a vanished ideal. The resemblance is made even more marked when the uncle notes that "an undertone of sadness runs through [the poem], felt already in the picture of Time which foreshadows the end of Love—the Rose—and her court, and with it the end of hope." The undertone of sadness runs just as constantly through *Chartres*. Moreover, one of Henry Adams' principal artistic problems is how to strike a balance between a suspension of time and a sense of its movement. Time stops as the Virgin is evoked and love reaches an epiphany, but only for a moment. Then time begins again and "takes my love away," whether it be the Rose of William of Lorris or the Virgin Mary. The end of love is the end of hope and the beginning of irony and, after the bitterness has passed, of nostalgia, the dominant note in the *Chartres* (111, 110, 246, 247).

The ostensible reference, however, is to the end of the twelfth century, the end of the dominance of the woman and love. After the death of William of Lorris, John of Meung continued his poem with a cynical attitude toward his predecessor's ideal:

> Between the death of William of Lorris and the advent of John of Meung, a short half-century (1250–1300), the Woman and the Rose became bankrupt. Satire took the place of worship. Man, with his usual monkey-like malice, took pleasure in pulling down what he had built up. . . . The world had still a long march to make from the Rose of Queen Blanche to the guillotine of Madame du Barry; but the "Roman de la Rose" made epoch. For the first time since Constantine proclaimed the reign of Christ, a thousand years, or so, before Philip the Fair dethroned Him, the deepest expression of social feeling ended with the word: Despair.

This passage closes the description of the twelfth century's social ideal on the same note of despair and nostalgia with which the evocation of its religious ideal had ended. But the rose and the woman also mean the

Virgin; the passage is therefore a less emotional, more analytic conclusion to both sections. In it there is no stark opposition between the child and the old man; the emphasis is upon explanation, and the old man is clearly dominant throughout. Yet the tone of elegy is also present and grows stronger at the end of the paragraph as the old man, from a twentieth-century perspective, both looks back to the twelfth century and, from there, forward to the death of the rose in the eighteenth century. For, it was the guillotine of the French Revolution—precursor of the dynamo as a symbol for a scientific era—which, according to the uncle, finally destroyed the dream of organic social unity through love and opened the way to social chaos. The rose was also the last great illusion protecting man from the multiverse; and its destruction enabled him to move with greatly accelerated rapidity toward full knowledge of the chaos of reality (248).

Conflict and Unity in Thought

The final section of *Chartres* (chapters 14 through 16) moves several steps closer to the full revelation of that reality in *The Education*. Adams is concerned with the philosophical expression of medieval unity and the philosophical means of merging unity and multiplicity. The first chapter concerns the philosophical conflict of the early and middle twelfth century; the second, the dominant philosophy of the later Transition; the third, St. Thomas Aquinas and the thirteenth century. This section is distinctive in its emphasis on conflict, which, though important, was kept subordinate to unity in the first two sections. Here the first chapter is wholly concerned with conflict, and the last two chapters, though individually not primarily concerned with it, are, when taken together, the final expression of the ultimate conflict of the book, the antithesis between the child and the old man. This emphasis arises, in part, from the uncle's interest in the transition from the twelfth to the thirteenth centuries; the single chapter on the thirteenth century has much the same emphasis on unity as have the early sections. Yet the very fact that the transitional chapters (and they are not simply that) emphasize conflict so much suggests that the change from the twelfth to the thirteenth century was a more significant and difficult change than that from the eleventh to the twelfth century. In terms of the Dynamic Theory this is certainly true. Both earlier centuries emphasized feeling, whereas the thirteenth century emphasizes reason and thus marks the beginning of the transition from humanity's religious childhood to its scientific old age.

The conflict itself involved two basic problems. The first was that of demonstrating logically that unity was real. "The schools knew," the uncle says, "that their society hung for life on the demonstration that

God, the ultimate universal, was the reality, out of which all other universal truths or realities sprang." This problem also had two aspects: whether there are universal truths or realities at all—whether *any* unities are real —and whether God, the supposed ultimate unity and source of all other unity, is real. The second problem was the nature of the relationship between the universal and the particular, God and nature, unity and multiplicity, "the oldest problem," says the uncle, "of philosophy, religion, and science." If a universe exists, created and ruled by a divine unity and a single, all-embracing law, then creator and creation, form and content, are necessarily connected. The question is how. According to the uncle this has always been the ultimate philosophical problem. It is avowedly the problem Henry Adams is chiefly concerned with, both here and in *The Education*. In these final chapters the uncle presents three (or four) philosophical methods of solving the medieval version of the problem in terms of two fundamental conflicts. First, the conflict between two (or three) rational means, realism and nominalism (and conceptualism); second, the conflict between all these rational means, collectively called scholasticism, and mysticism, an emotional means of knowing the unity of God and of merging multiplicity in unity (289, 299).

The first chapter, "Abélard," presents all four methods struggling for dominance in the early twelfth century. The struggle begins with the arrival of Abélard in Paris, an event contemporaneous with the First Crusade. Abélard is presented as a warrior as well as a philosopher; his antagonist was William of Champeaux. "In these scholastic tournaments," the uncle says, "the two champions started from opposite points:—one, from the ultimate substance, God—the universal . . . ;—the other from the individual. . . . The first champion—William in this instance—assumed that the universal was a real thing; and for that reason he was called a realist. His opponent—Abélard—held that the universal was only nominally real; and on that account he was called a nominalist." The chief problem of each side was to connect what it assumed with what it did not. Realism had to connect God (the universal, unity) with the individual (the particular, multiplicity); nominalism, the individual with God. In so doing, realism, according to the uncle, led to the assertion that "all energy at last becomes identical with the ultimate substance, God Himself." "This is pantheism," the uncle imagines Abélard as saying and then adds that "realism, when pressed, always led to pantheism." Abélard's objection was fatal to William's argument because pantheism is necessarily a heresy: "If God is the only energy, human free will merges in God's free will; the Church ceases to have a reason for existence; man cannot be held responsible for his own acts, either to the Church or to the State" (291, 296–297).

Abélard agreed with William at an earlier point in their hypothetical debate that form is a divine concept. When asked whether he believed this concept was "a reality or not," Abélard seems to have refused to answer, but the uncle supposes him to have taken the view of "pure nominalism" and answered that the concept was not real. This answer would have forced Abélard into a position as heretical as that of William. "You suppose yourself to exist," the uncle imagines William as saying,

> but you have no means of knowing God; therefore, to you God does not exist except as an echo of your ignorance; and . . . the Church does not exist except as your concept of certain individuals, whom you cannot regard as a unity, and who suppose themselves to believe in a Trinity which exists only as a sound, or a symbol. . . . It is only too clear that you are a materialist.

The uncle says that Abélard might have answered, as the Church often did, that the concept was real, but asserts his own belief that the human concept is "the flimsiest bridge of all" for the chasm between multiplicity and unity, "unless somewhere, within or beyond it, an energy not individual is hidden; and in that case the old question instantly reappears: What is that energy?" If the answer is God, this leads directly to pantheism again. "Narrow and dangerous," says the uncle, "was the border-line always between pantheism and materialism, and the chief interest of the schools was in finding fault with each other's paths" (297–299, 358).

Abélard at this time succeeded in pushing William into a position where he had to change his doctrine to avoid the charge of pantheism. Soon thereafter, William "received his reward . . .—a bishopric." For the Church continued—necessarily, the uncle believes—to maintain the realist position: "realism was the Roman arch—the only possible foundation for any Church; because it assumed unity, and any other scheme was compelled to prove it, for a starting-point." Thus, in the uncle's view, the Church's position is ultimately always pantheistic. It was so at the time of the First Crusade, he says. Hence Abélard's victory proved to be only momentary. Bishop William joined forces with Bernard of Clairvaux, who opposed all scholasticism, believing "that because dialectics [or reason] led wrong, therefore faith [or feeling] led right." Bernard's success in having Abélard's works condemned by a council and the Pope proved to be a victory not only over Abélard but over all scholasticism and opened the way for the dominance of thought in the next seventy-five years by the opponents of reason, principally the mystics. Though a personal victory over Abélard, it was a victory necessary for the survival of the Church— and of the medieval child. For although William of Champeaux was a scholastic philosopher and St. Bernard, a mystic, both started with a belief in unity. In this they were at one with the Church. Abélard, however, *as the uncle presents him*, was a man of reason who started with a belief in multiplicity rather than unity. In both respects he heralded the end of humanity's childhood and the advent of its maturity. Intellectually, he is the first (and only) human representative in the book of multiplicity or Satan. Yet his relationship with Héloïse is one of the famous love affairs of history. Thus, intellectually he is the villain of *Chartres*; but in feeling he shares its highest ideal. No other figure in the work is so complex (299, 297, 311).

In the next chapter, the uncle examines twelfth-century mysticism. He begins with a definition:

> In essence, religion was love; in no case was it logic. Reason can reach nothing except through the senses; God, by essence, cannot be reached through the senses; if He is to be known at all, He must be known by contact of spirit with spirit . . . ; directly; by emotion; . . . by absorption of our existence in His.

Thus scholasticism's emphasis on logic made it alien to the true spirit of religion, while the twelfth century's emphasis on love helped to make it "the most perfect moment of art and feeling in the thousand years of pure and perfect Christianity." It is especially the mystic who sees the divine unity as love and seeks to become one with it. He is the essential religious person and the human climax of the twelfth century's perfection. In terms of the Dynamic Theory, he is also the supreme embodiment of the child. The highest ideal ever expressed by the child was the Virgin; St. Francis of Assisi was the child itself,[44] as the uncle suggests when he calls him "the ideal mystic saint of Western Europe." In Christian terms, there "was reincarnated in Assisi" the Christ who said, "Whosoever shall not receive the kingdom of God as a little child, he shall not enter therein." The difference between Francis and the Virgin can be measured by comparing Francis' vision of unity with hers. She was human, the uncle says; seeing disunity, she sought by the love she felt and inspired to draw irregular, exceptional, and outlawed humanity into greater unity. But "Francis was elementary nature itself"; he saw all men and all nature—organic and inorganic forms alike—as already wholly united in God and therefore in complete sympathy with one another, with himself, and with God. He "saw God in nature, if he did not see nature in God; as the builders of Chartres saw the Virgin in their apse." And as the builders strove to make Chartres an architectural embodiment of the Virgin, so Francis saw nature as the architectural expression—the church—of God. This belief, the uncle says, is "the simplest and most childlike form of pantheism." It

---

[44] McIntyre points out ("Henry Adams and the Unity of Chartres," p. 164) that St. Francis "epitomizes the naïveté and intensity of Adams' childlike ideal."

received expression in Francis' life and also in his poem, the "Chant (or Song) of the Sun." Both are expressions of man's primal beginnings. The poem's content, the uncle says, was "probably the first" "word of religion"; its art "seems to go back to the cave-dwellers and the age of stone." According to the uncle's paraphrase, Francis says to God in the poem that "we are all varying forms of the same ultimate energy; shifting symbols of the same absolute unity; but our only unity, beneath you, is nature, not law!" He thanks God, therefore, not for the Church but "our mother Earth." On his deathbed he added a stanza "of gratitude for 'our sister death,' the long-sought, never-found sister of the schoolmen, who solved all philosophy and merged multiplicity in unity." To Francis death seemed simply the means whereby man passed from loving God in the unity of nature to loving Him in the spiritual essence of that unity (321, 330, 329, 334, 339, 340–341, 341).

The intensity of this vision did not mean that Francis saw no multiplicity. On the contrary, he saw his life as a crusade and the scholastic philosopher as his chief enemy. "Satan was logic." But his attempt to destroy the pride of human reason failed. Even before his death his own order had begun to yield to the growing emphasis upon reason and scholasticism. The Church, seeking, as always, to satisfy the needs of all men and all times, turned to the new method of seeking God as well as the old (331).

Ultimately, the uncle believes, these are the only two roads man can follow if one "starts by taking for granted that there is an object to be reached at the end of his journey. . . . The two poles of social and political philosophy seem necessarily to be organization or anarchy; man's intellect or the forces of nature." He believes that Francis' embrace of nature and contempt and hatred for intellect amounted to an unwitting embrace of nature's multiplicity. When he says that "Francis, acting only for himself, could throw caution aside and trust implicitly in God, like the children who went on crusade," he means—in terms of the Dynamic Theory— that Francis was actually trusting his own personal emotions or intuition. Francis, like the Virgin, was an anarchist acting out the promptings of his own nature, regardless of the dictates of law, human or divine. The consequences of such anarchism are suggested when the uncle compares Francis' self-trust with that of "the children who went on crusade." The twentieth-century grandfather dearly loves the child throughout *Chartres*, and this love reaches one of its climactic expressions in this chapter. Explicit irony is at a minimum; even the elegiac tone is muted, subordinated to a pervasive lyric joyfulness. This phrase is the one great exception. For surely Henry Adams remembered as he wrote it the tragic end of most of the children who went on the Children's Crusade: robbery; rape; slavery;

death from fatigue, heat, drowning, disease, and want—these were the fates suffered by those other children who, like St. Francis, threw caution aside and trusted implicitly in God (339, 337).[45]

But the uncle does not believe that the other "pole . . . of social and political philosophy" was successful either. After "five hundred years had been devoted" to trying out both, he says,

society declared both to be failures. [But] perhaps both may some day be revived. . . . [Hence] until mankind finally settles to a certainty where it means to go, or whether it means to go anywhere—what its object is, or whether it has an object—Saint Francis may still prove to have been its ultimate expression. In that case, . . . the "Cantico del Sole" . . . will be the last word of religion, as it was probably its first.

The uncle is generous to both sides, but, according to his own definition, religion is love and, therefore, essentially mystical. If a divine unity *is* the true goal of man's journey, Francis, not the schoolmen, is its "ultimate expression." Yet even if "Chaos [is] the law of nature; Order [but] the dream of man," Francis may still be the ultimate expression of humanity, in the sense that he is the most complete embodiment of man's essence, his sense of unity. In the religious view, Francis represents the closest approximation ever made by man to the divinity that underlies the universe. In Adams' view he is the ultimate expression of Everyman as the Don Quixote of the multiverse, to whom the uncle here plays a sympathetic but incredulous companion (339–340).

The thirteenth century marked the triumph of scholasticism and logic. This triumph coincided architecturally with the end of the transition between the Romanesque and Gothic styles: "The pointed arch revelled at Rheims and the Gothic architects reached perfection at Amiens just as Francis died at Assisi and Thomas was born at Aquino." The Transition's balance between emotion and reason ended; "emotion [was now] trained in school."[46] In this century of intellect "Thomas Aquinas reigns." The uncle suggests the difference between Thomas and Francis when he says that "Francis of Assisi was not more archaic and cave-dweller than Thomas of Aquino was modern and scientific." Francis faces backward toward the childhood of man; St. Thomas faces forward toward man's old age. Yet there are also important likenesses between Francis and Thomas which make them both part of the Middle Ages and distinguish them from twentieth-century man. Together, their lifetimes spanned only eighty-eight years, Francis living from 1186 to 1226, Aquinas from 1224 to 1274. More importantly, both saw reality as a divine unity and made the effort

45 [Joseph François Michaud] *Michaud's History of the Crusades*, translated by W. Robson (3 vols.; London: George Routledge and Co., 1852), III, 441–446.

46 See critical note 47.

to attain this reality the mainspring of their lives: neither was as close to the twentieth century and its belief in multiplicity as Abélard. Viewed in this way, Francis is still the final and perfect expression of the eternal child and Abélard, an initial expression of the old man; but now Thomas represents the Church's middle road between the mysticism of the one and the nominalism of the other. Francis Bacon, the key figure (according to the Dynamic Theory) for the beginning of the scientific period, rejected both mysticism and logic as means to truth, but, according to the uncle, his view of reality led ultimately to one that was closer to Abélard's than either Francis' or Thomas'. Thus the old man and St. Thomas are not at all identified, and constantly throughout this last chapter the uncle criticizes St. Thomas' thought in terms of the old man's point of view. Nonetheless, the century in which Thomas and scholasticism reigned was the first in which reason dominated faith and therefore the first which clearly pointed toward the twentieth century (342, 318, 358).[47]

The uncle presents St. Thomas' thought as he presented Mont-Saint-Michel and Chartres, the Virgin, and the code of courteous love—as a work of art: "For us, these great theologians were also architects who undertook to build a Church Intellectual, corresponding bit by bit to the Church Administrative, both expressing—and expressed by—the Church Architectural." The church they expressed was not the "eleventh-century Romanesque church of Saint Michael" nor "the twelfth-century Transition Church of the Virgin," but "the thirteenth-century Gothic Cathedral of the Trinity" in which the other two "merged and ended." Specifically, Thomas' theology is the intellectual counterpart of Amiens (and Beauvais). His was a philosophical as theirs was an architectural attempt to merge multiplicity in unity (344, 346).

Three key problems in the uncle's interpretation of St. Thomas need to be examined for the light they throw on the interaction between the child and the old man and the problem of merging multiplicity in unity: Thomas' proof of God's existence, his explanation of the creation of multiplicity out of unity, and his explanation of free will. The foundation of Thomas' church is God, the divine unity, and His active presence in His creation, the multiplicity of nature and man. According to the uncle's paraphrase of Thomas, "God must be a concrete thing, not a human thought. God must be proved by the senses like any other concrete thing."[48] After showing how this assertion differs from the beliefs of the mystics, the uncle gives Thomas' proof:

[47] An analysis of Adams' attitude toward the four men he is principally concerned with in the three chapters of the fourth section of *Chartres* appears in chapter 7 of the present text, pp. 170–172. See also critical note 65.

[48] Brunner points out ("Henry Adams: His Decline and Fall," pp. 255–256) that in thus attempting to prove God's existence, rather than assuming it, as the realists did,

"I see motion," said Thomas: "I infer a motor!" . . . The average mechanic stated it differently. "I see motion," he admitted: "I infer energy. I see motion everywhere; I infer energy everywhere." Saint Thomas barred this door to materialism by adding: "I see motion; I cannot infer an infinite series of motors: I can only infer, somewhere at the end of the series, an intelligent, fixed motor." The average modern mechanic might not dissent but would certainly hesitate. "No doubt!" he might say; "we can conduct our works as well on that as on any other theory, or as we could on no theory at all; but, if you offer it as proof, we can only say that we have not yet reduced all motion to one source or all energies to one law, much less to one act of creation, although we have tried our best. . . . In fact, if you are aiming to convince me, I will tell you flatly that I know only the multiple, and have no use for unity at all."

In the thirteenth century men did not depend so much as now on actual experiment, but the nominalist said in effect the same thing. Unity to him was a pure concept. (346, 347–348)

In these passages, the uncle, instead of criticizing the child's point of view himself, makes a twentieth-century "mechanic" the mouthpiece of the old man's point of view, thereby freeing himself to comment on both views. The mechanic, whose twentieth-century view the uncle connects with medieval nominalism (and therefore with Abélard), cannot see any necessity for accepting Thomas' logical inference that motion (or multiplicity) implies a single, fixed motor (or unity) which creates the motion. Indeed, he cannot see any convincing reason why he should go beyond multiplicity at all. He knows the reality of phenomena from experience; logical inferences may be valid as logic, but they are not proof. Just as the Church Intellectual and the Church Architectural imply "not one architect, but myriads, and not one fixed, intelligent architect at the end of the series, but a vanishing vista without a beginning at any definite moment," so the creations of nature may just as well imply not one creator but myriads. As far as he is concerned, there is only an infinite and eternal multiplicity (348).

In his attempt to connect unity and multiplicity, Thomas is concerned, like the realists, with the creation of multiplicity out of unity, though, unlike them, he first tries to prove the existence of a divine unity. Having

---

Aquinas was taking the nominalist position (see *Chartres*, p. 297). "Such beginnings," Brunner says, "in Adams' opinion always ended in materialism; yet Saint Thomas somehow managed to avoid this usual consequence by flatly postulating at the end of his series of mechanisms an 'intelligent, fixed motor' . . . . In this, Thomas was relying on a realistic divination not far different from that of Saint Francis." That is, though Aquinas did not assume God's existence, his postulation, in order to prove that point, of a "prime motor" was equivalent to such an assumption. See also critical note 48.

done that, he asserts that "whatever has form is created, and whatever is created takes form directly from the will of God, which is also his act. The intermediate universals—the secondary causes—vanish as causes; they are, at most, sequences or relations; all merge in one universal act of will." "The only true cause is God. . . . The whole universe is . . . a simple emanation from" Him, and, though every individual was a special creation, all acts of creation took place simultaneously. The uncle concludes that "the famous junction, then, is made!—that celebrated fusion of the universal with the individual, of unity with multiplicity, of God and nature, which had broken the neck of every philosophy ever invented . . . was accomplished." Thomas "had merely to assert the fact: 'It is so! it cannot be otherwise!'" It is unlike the uncle to be satisfied with an assertion; thus, one may infer that the old man is not convinced (351, 354, 355).

In explaining the mechanics of individualization in creation, Thomas followed his masters, Aristotle and Albert the Great, in believing that form or soul is individualized by matter. He says that "'division occurs in substances in ratio of quantity, as Aristotle says in his "Physics." And so dimensional quantity is a principle of individuation.'" The uncle comments on the problem this view involves:

> Humanity had a form common to itself, which made it what it was. By some means this form was associated with matter; in fact, matter was only known as associated with form. If, then, God, by an instantaneous act, created matter and gave it form according to the dimensions of the matter, innocent ignorance might infer that there was, in the act of God, one world-soul and one world-matter, which He united in different proportions to make men and things.

That is, men's distinctiveness of form is nothing more than the result of the similar quantity of matter required to make any individual human being. There is no essential human form apart from form's combination with matter, and, if human beings differed radically in the quantity of matter they contained, there would be no distinctively human form at all. "Such a doctrine was fatal to the Church," the uncle says, because it made all nature—and man—share the same soul, and therefore made everything divine. So Thomas vigorously denied "the idea that intellect was one and the same for all men, differing only with the quantity of matter it accompanied." To the uncle this seems a direct contradiction of Thomas' own stated position. Insofar as he can understand it, "Thomas's doctrine of matter and form . . . seems frank pantheism." Thomas' system, like all realism—and like the mysticism of St. Francis—seems to the uncle a form of heresy (355–357).

Another problem is free will. Perfect freedom, said Thomas, existed in God's will before the act of creation. He chose of His own free will to create the reality which now exists and which expresses His own harmony, unity, and order. (Thomas did not deny the seeming discords and evils in reality, but "claimed that they might be [only] incidents, and that the admitted unity might even prove their beneficence," though he offered no proof.) In such a world man must be a free agent; otherwise "the Church was a fraud." For "if God was the sole and immediate cause and support of everything in His creation, God was also the cause of its defects, and could not—being Justice and Goodness in essence—hold man responsible for His own omissions." Yet "experience proved that man's power of choice in action was very far from absolute, and logic seemed to require that every choice should have some predetermining cause which decided the will to act. Science affirmed that choice was not free—could not be free—without abandoning the unity of force and the foundation of law." The uncle uses modern terms in summarizing Thomas' "scientific" solution to the problem:

> By the term God, is meant a prime motor which supplies all energy to the universe, and acts directly on man as well as on all other creatures, moving him as a mechanical motor might do; but man, being specially provided with an organism more complex than the organisms of other creatures, enjoys an exceptional capacity for reflex action—a power of reflection—which enables him within certain limits to choose between paths; and this singular capacity is called free choice or free will. Of course, the reflection is not choice, and though a man's mind reflected as perfectly as the facets of a lighthouse lantern, it would never reach a choice without an energy which impels it to act. (366, 363, 367, 368)

That energy is God. Thus man does not really act by himself; God acts through him in everything that he does. Again, the uncle finds Thomas' system pantheistic.[49]

But now the uncle notes that "science, too, . . . has till very recently been wholly pantheistic. Avowedly science has aimed at nothing but the reduction of multiplicity to unity, and has excommunicated, as though it were itself a Church, any one who doubted or disputed its object, its method, or its results." The uncle believes (and the Dynamic Theory asserts) that the true metaphysical position of science, as the pursuit of truth by empirical means, is with materialism and nominalism. At the end of the chapter he describes how, in the twentieth century, science is beginning to discover this fact. Returning to the architectural analogy, he stresses once more both how modern and how antiquated the thought of St. Thomas is. "Both the 'Summa Theologiae' and Beauvais Cathedral were excessively modern, scientific, and technical," he says. But "the despotic

---

[49] See critical note 48.

central idea"—"both in the thought and the building"—"was that of organic unity." "From that time" to the twentieth century, "the universe has steadily become more complex and less reducible to a central control. . . . Modern science, like modern art, tends, in practice, to drop the dogma of organic unity." "The trouble," the uncle concludes, "was not in the art or the method or the structure, but in the universe itself which presented different aspects as man moved" (371, 374–375, 375, 377).

Here at the end of the uncle's discussion of medieval philosophy, as at the end of his discussion of Mont-Saint-Michel and Chartres, the seeming suspension of time ends and its destructive movement is described. But now the reader's renewed sense of that movement does not come with a shock, as it did at the end of the evocation of the Virgin. The presentation of St. Thomas' system is accompanied from the first by twentieth-century criticism. The effect of the final pages is, therefore, simply one of conclusion. This is appropriate to the emphasis on a rational instead of an emotional method of presentation in the second half of the book. It is also appropriate for the end of a book which tries to achieve a balance between giving a sense of a suspended moment in time and a sense of time's constant movement. In the last paragraph the uncle returns to the dominant church image and presents his final interpretation of its meaning. "Granted a Church," he says, "Saint Thomas's Church was the most expressive that man has made, and the great Gothic cathedrals were its most complete expression." In essence what the cathedral suggests is

> the visible effort to throw off a visible strain . . . . [It] never let[s] us forget that Faith alone supports it, and that, if Faith fails, Heaven is lost. . . . The equilibrium is visibly delicate beyond the line of safety; danger lurks in every stone. . . . All [the] haunting nightmares of the Church are expressed as strongly by the Gothic cathedral as though it had been the cry of human suffering, and as no emotion had ever been expressed before or is likely to find expression again.

This passage does not emphasize the movement of time, but it does emphasize that sense of the instability and transcience of man and all his creations which results from that movement. The use of the church image here is its fourth and final use in *Chartres*, in the course of which it has had a growth comparable to that of a tree. At first it was the massive solidity and grandeur of Mont-Saint-Michel. Then it flowered into the lyric charm of Chartres. In the thirteenth century its own life was beginning to die, and it became the seed of a new kind of world. Finally, the image is used here to sum up the significance of all three forms. For, though the uncle is speaking of the thirteenth-century Gothic cathedral, the aspiration and anguish which he perceives in it are also part of his twentieth-century view of the image as a whole.[50] In this use of it he sums up his understanding of the child's view of reality (377).

The image also sums up the uncle's understanding of the innately human view of reality. In a world of chaotic forces, man—and only man —sees unity. Because reality and this sense of unity are in perpetual contradiction, he lives in constant suffering, which leads him to cry out for relief and to seek ways of ending the contradiction by transforming multiplicity into unity. The highest expressions of this anguish and hope are art and religion. The greatest of all works of art is the medieval church, whose massive transformation of multiplicity into unity is a symbolic embodiment of religion's promise that human suffering is temporary and that after death man will find eternal happiness. Because the human sense of unity centers in woman, the greatest of all churches is Chartres, home of the Virgin, the highest ideal humanity has ever had. Man is a child crying in the night, who, in his most perfect dream, is comforted by a divine mother with the promise that he will spend eternity with her in a place where he will suffer no more. But one day man awakes to realize that the divine mother is only a dream and that no one hears his cries. Childhood ends and maturity begins. Man gives up religion for science and cares less for art and more for technology. He relies less upon his emotions and more upon his reason, and turns from his inner sense of unity to the outer world of multiplicity. He still seeks peace and harmony, but expects to find them only in his earthly life and only partially. By thought and experiment he tries to turn the chaos of nature against itself and make it serve his desire for unity. But here, too (as *The Education* will show), his efforts are futile. Seeking power to create the unity of a civilization out of nature's multiplicity, he competes with other men as well as with nature. With his science he creates weapons of destruction which continuing competition and the breakdown of morality will lead him to use against his rivals. Eventually he may destroy himself.

Yet man is not responsible for his fate. His history is that of a tide in the ocean of the multiverse, its rhythm, one of slow rise, break, and quick destruction. The movement of time must destroy him as inevitably as it awakened him from childhood. Thus when the uncle turns to the niece in the last sentence of *Chartres* and says of the Gothic church, "You can read out of it whatever else pleases your youth and confidence; to me, this is all," he is not only completing the frame structure of the book—he would also seem to be saying that the niece's youth and confidence are anachronistic follies if they lead her to find material for hope here in the church, the symbol of man. Certainly this is the conclusion one has to

[50] See *Chartres*, pp. 45, 87–88, 97, for other examples of Adams' use of "Gothic" as a synonym for "medieval."

make in the light of the Dynamic Theory of History. In this light, the suggestion of youth and confidence is nothing but a sop thrown to an audience incapable of accepting the full force of the old man's wisdom. Yet no man lives wholly in terms of his system, and Henry Adams allowed himself an intellectual escape-hatch from his. If history is incoherent, the coherence of the Dynamic Theory means that it is finally invalid. Thus the uncle may turn to the niece because, if there is a hope for man, it may seem to him to lie, as always, with the woman. Or his final statement may simply be his offering to that unknown God whom the Athenians [51] also honored lest their pantheon be incomplete (377).

The Ultimate Symbol of Illusion

In terms of the future, possibility is all that remains for man. *Chartres* however, is rooted not in possibility nor in Adams' ultimate position, but in the Dynamic Theory of History and its despair. Yet even this orientation offers something to twentieth-century man. He is not wholly caught between the child's faded illusion and the old man's approaching death. What remains is art, and the uncle says specifically that he and the niece are "pilgrims of art." The problem of the Dynamic Theory of History— the oldest problem of religion, science, and philosophy—is that of connecting unity and multiplicity. The child's religion merged multiplicity in unity, but this was illusion; the old man's science dissolves unity in multiplicity, but this is death. Art also merges multiplicity in unity, but this is neither illusion nor death. The unity of art is a unity in the midst of life's multiplicity; it is the reality only of a moment's unity amidst ever-present chaos; it offers but moments of pleasure; it is the product of wholly human creative effort; and it offers a retreat for contemplation which is purely human. But what it offers is real, not illusory. The church and the literature of courtly love, the Virgin Mary and the theology of St. Thomas are all products of the human imagination. All are art and, as art, all are real (191).

These ideas receive final expression in the ultimate image of *Chartres*, human life conceived as a drama. "For us," the uncle tells the niece, "the world is not a schoolroom or a pulpit, but a stage, and the stage is the highest yet seen on earth." There are actually three stages in the book. The first is its frame structure: Henry Adams and the reader watch the uncle and the niece take their journey. The quotation here refers to the second and principal stage, where the medieval child performs while the uncle and niece watch and the uncle comments. The third is a stage within this stage, on which the great actors of the period perform while the uncle

[51] Acts 17:23.

and the niece identify with the common people as audience. The dramatic quality these stages give the book is enhanced by the physical presence of the uncle. As the embodiment of the twentieth-century point of view, he gives a dramatic quality to its main tension, that between the child and the old man. But the principal use of the drama in *Chartres* is as an image for a view of life. Both medieval man and the uncle, the child and the old man, view life as a drama. To the child, the play seems real: life is a conflict of human wills, overseen by the divine creator who gave man free will. The old man, however, sees the drama as an illusion, no more real than a play on a stage. Valid as art, it is only make-believe in life (106).

The uncle describes this use of the image most fully in discussing medieval French art, which, he says,

> starts not from facts, but from certain assumptions as conventional as a legendary window.... The fact, then as now, was Power, or its equivalent in exchange, but Frenchmen, while struggling for the Power, expressed it in terms of Art. They looked on life as a drama—and on drama as a phase of life —in which the bystanders were bound to assume and accept the regular stage-plot. That the plot might be altogether untrue to real life affected in no way its interest. To them Thibaut and Blanche were bound to act Tristan and Isolde. Whatever they were when off the stage, they were lovers on it. Their loves were as real and as reasonable as the worship of the Virgin. Courteous love was avowedly a form of drama, but not the less a force of society. Illusion for illusion, courteous love, in Thibaut's hands, or in the hands of Dante and Petrarch, was as substantial as any other convention;— the balance of trade, the rights of man, or the Athanasian Creed. In that sense the illusions alone were real; if the Middle Ages had reflected only what was practical, nothing would have survived for us.

Man is a force of nature, which, like all forces (according to the Dynamic Theory), seeks more force (power). But, because he perceives the multiplicity of nature as unity, man, when he is most distinctively human, seeks to increase his force indirectly. Out of his sense of unity he conceives ideas of what ultimate reality is and ideals of what society should be and seeks power by trying to realize these in his life and that of society.[52] As products of his distorted sense of reality, all such ideas and ideals are illusions. In struggling to realize them, he is trying to impose his own sense of order upon the anarchy of reality. He is trying to make his life a work of art (224).

Man makes this effort because he believes in his ideas and ideals. They prescribe how life should be lived; they also describe how it often is lived.

---

[52] See also *Chartres*, p. 252. Some aspects of the theory of fictions described in succeeding pages are summarized in Elizabeth Stevenson, *Henry Adams: A Biography* (New York: The Macmillan Co., 1955), p. 329.

Men in the twelfth century viewed life around them, especially life on the social levels above them, through the conventions of courteous love. It was thus that they viewed the relationship between Queen Blanche of France and Thibaut-le-Grand, her chief follower and supporter after her husband's death: "French convention [ideals] required that Thibaut should have poisoned Louis VIII for love of the Queen, and that this secret reciprocal love should control their lives." Therefore, when Blanche and Thibaut were on "the stage"—in the eyes and minds of their contemporaries—"they were lovers." The aristocrats who attempted to live by the code of courteous love knew that they were living according to ideals which human beings had deliberately chosen and then systematized into a scheme of behavior. They knew, that is, that they were play-acting, living life as if it were a drama. Nonetheless, courteous love was a definite force in society. It modified human behavior and conditioned the interpretation men placed upon the behavior of themselves and others. More important, in acting in accordance with it men were only doing consciously what they usually do unconsciously. Thus the uncle says that the supposedly courteous loves of Blanche and Thibaut "were as real and as reasonable as the worship of the Virgin." Both were human illusions, created by men out of their own unique sense of unity. The uncle emphasizes this point by asserting finally that courteous love is as real and reasonable a convention (or "fiction," as he calls it elsewhere) as "the balance of trade, the rights of man, or the Athanasian Creed." What the courteous lover did, all men do when they are most human—pursue power through ideals and thus make of life a drama (224, 252, 224).

It is significant that all the fictions the uncle lists affected large areas of human society. Later he says that all societies are based upon fictions. Commenting on the continued belief of the "ordinary man" in the Virgin after the failure of St. Louis' crusade, he says that "few of the usual fictions on which society rested had ever required such defiance of facts." Societies, that is, are unities whose coherence rests on man's sense of unity and its expression in fictions. What these fictions are depends, not upon human choice, but, with some flexibility, upon the position of society in the historical movement described in the Dynamic Theory of History. Without such fictions, and the dramas they lead to, man's life would be simply practical, a brutal struggle for power. It would also be always the same. The individuality of historical periods is due to the change in fictions produced by the forces of history. Fictions, therefore, give life and history their highest value, because they enable man, if only for a moment, to satisfy his desire for unity. The uncle says of the great ladies of the twelfth century that "they insisted on teaching and enforcing an ideal that contradicted the realities, and had no value for them or for us except in the contradiction." Because it contradicts reality, such an ideal can never be wholly realized nor even wholly pervade the minds of men in the mass. Commenting on the twelfth-century drama, the uncle speaks of "the illusion which men thought they thought their existence," implying what he calls elsewhere "the latent scepticism which lurks behind all faith." The social function of art is to increase faith by offering man a fuller embodiment of the ideal than he can ever realize in life. The business of the medieval glassworker, for example, was "to excite [the] illusions" of the "mediaeval pilgrim." The medieval cathedral constantly renewed and increased the faith which had originally motivated its builders (252, 211, 249–250, 96, 142).

Thus fictions contribute to the continuity as well as the unity of society. Moreover, once men have begun to live in terms of a fiction, the investment they make in time, money, and belief acts as a force of inertia to make them continue to believe in it. The uncle says of the Virgin that "society had staked its existence, in this world and the next, on the reality and the power of the Virgin; . . . her overthrow would have been the most appalling disaster the Western world had ever known." Therefore, "at least for a time, society held firm." The uncle considers this twelfth-century drama the greatest of all social dramas and its art, "on the whole, the highest expression of man's thought or emotion." Like all else in the multiverse, however, it too was transient and eventually gave way to new social dramas based on different fictions. Men lost faith, as they always do, disillusioned by experience and simply bored by the strain of belief. Disillusionment and boredom aggravated the destructive tendency which men have in common with other natural forces. Yet, according to the Dynamic Theory, it was finally not man but the nonhuman forces which rule history that destroyed the faith they had once created (252, 211).

The use of the drama as the ultimate image of *Chartres* suggests that Henry Adams' main concern is not with the facts of medieval life but with its fictions and the vision of life which they determined. The primary materials of such history are traditions, legends, art, philosophy, etc., the creative expressions of an age. The uncle admits that "tradition exaggerates everything it touches," but adds that it "shows, at the same time, what is passing in the minds of the society which *tradites*." The legends about Eleanor of Guienne, for example, reflect, "not perhaps the character of Eleanor, but what the society liked to see acted on its theatre of life. Eleanor's real nature," he says, "in no way concerns us. . . . For us, the poetry is history, and the facts are false." He might just as well have written, "For us, the *drama* is history, and the facts are false." The choice of "poetry" suggests his belief that such history has greater charm than a history of events. But he also believes that such history has greater significance than other history because of its concern with what is most important to man, the satisfaction of his desire for unity (198, 210, 224).

The highest expressions of human ideals are great religious images like the Virgin, and great personalities like St. Francis. But faith and life are brief; philosophy and especially art last longer. In them the limitations imposed by the flux of reality are at a minimum and thus in them the ideal can receive its most durable expression. When faith dies and the drama of the ideal is over, there remains "only the shell—the dead art—and silence." Yet such fossils survive as more than just monuments to the faith they originally expressed. For a small number of persons the dead art remains alive, capable of stimulating aesthetic if not religious feeling. "Honest tourists," the uncle says, "are seriously interested in putting the feeling back into the dead architecture where it belongs." *Chartres* is written by one of the supposedly small number of such people who respond to medieval art, for others with the same taste. It embodies the feelings and ideas Henry Adams had about the dead art and his understanding, in terms of this Dynamic Theory, of the drama of life out of which it emerged. His feelings take the form of nostalgia for a vanished perfection; his understanding, the form of irony because this perfection was never more than an illusion. In the work as a whole, feeling and understanding, illusion and reality, mingle and fuse into a complex and poignant image of the old man's vision of the world of childhood (40, 275).

CHAPTER VI

PESSIMISTIC NATURALISM AND "THE FALL" OF MAN

THE FALL AND THE ETERNAL QUESTION

Both *Mont-Saint-Michel and Chartres* (1904, 1913) and *The Education of Henry Adams* (1907, 1918)[1] are related to the Dynamic Theory of History as image to idea. *Chartres* portrays the thirteenth century as a period in which the child had faith, based upon illusion; *The Education* portrays the twentieth century as a period in which the old man has wisdom, based upon knowledge. Faith led the child to a never-ending effort to make reality conform to his illusion; the constant experience of disillusionment leads the old man to his wisdom. The child's motive produced a life of what he considered valid action; the "Henry Adams" of *The Education* spends most of his life trying to find a faith that will make such action possible.[2] He calls that effort the attempt to gain an education.

Late in the book the nature and persistence of the attempt is suggested, symbolically, when Adams responds to a political murder by asking: "Had one sat all one's life on the steps of Ara Coeli for this?" The church of Santa Maria di Ara Coeli (Saint Mary of the Altar of Heaven) in Rome is built upon the Capitol on the site of an important Roman temple. Mentioned as a Christian church as early as the eighth century, it was given in 1252 to the Franciscan Order to which it still belongs. Adams visited it on his first trip to Rome in 1860, primarily out of respect for Edward Gibbon, who conceived the idea of writing his *Decline and Fall of the Roman Empire* on its steps. Here Adams meditated on the same problem which, he believed, had puzzled and stimulated Gibbon a

---

[1] The page references to *The Education* in this chapter are to the Modern Library edition (New York: Random House, Inc., 1931) with an introduction by James Truslow Adams. Such references are between parentheses in the text.

[2] See critical note 49.

113

century earlier. Why had Roman fallen? Though he observes that "not an inch had been gained by Gibbon—or all the historians since—towards explaining the Fall,"[3] he found that he too "went on repeating . . . the eternal question:—Why! Why!! Why!!!" The "steps of Ara Coeli" meant the same thing for him that he believed they had for Gibbon: they stood for the fall of Rome and posed the "eternal question" why it had occurred.[4] But for Adams this question was more complex than it had been for Gibbon, to whom "the Fall" meant the collapse of the Western Roman Empire in the fifth century and the fall of the Eastern Roman Empire in the fifteenth century. Adams writes that "two great experiments of Western civilization had left [in Rome] the chief monuments of their failure, and nothing proved that the city might not still survive to express the failure of a third." The first failure was that of the Western Empire, but the second was that of the spiritual "empire" of the medieval church, which "fell" in the sixteenth century. The third is that of the economic empire which Adams felt ruled the contemporary world[5] (471, 91–92).

As Adams grew older, the fall came to have for him an even more inclusive significance. For one thing it came to stand for the failure of all political entities. Each of many journeys he made to the sites of other fallen empires in search of an answer to the eternal question ended with his return to Rome, where "the church of Ara Coeli seemed . . . to draw all the threads of thought to a centre." And yet the quest was equally relevant to the present. In reply to a hypothetical question why he was so interested in explaining the fall, Adams suggests, "Substitute the word America for the word Rome, and the [eternal] question [becomes] personal." For "Rome was actual; it was England; it was going to be America." The third great experiment in western civilization is primarily the economic experiment of American civilization. Why Rome fell might provide a key to the fall of America. The answer to the eternal question would not only explain the past, it might also make possible prediction of the future (367, 92, 91).

But the fall refers to more than empires. Adams says that on his first trip to Rome he often sat on the steps of the church of Ara Coeli at sunset, an appropriate time, according to traditional symbolism, for one to meditate on the fall. In the last pages of the book he returns to this symbolism, now in reference to his friend John Hay's last illnesses, which

[3] Mrs. Joan Jones, a graduate student at the University of Nebraska, has pointed out in an unpublished seminar paper numerous images of physical falling in *The Education* (e.g., pp. 433–434).

[4] See critical note 50.

[5] See Henry Adams, *Letters to a Niece and Prayer to the Virgin of Chartres*, with a niece's memories by Mabel La Farge (Boston: Houghton Mifflin Co., 1920), p. 98.

Adams compares to "the clouds that gather round the setting sun."[6] Somewhat earlier, he discusses his own old age in a chapter entitled "Twilight." The setting sun is associated with the ultimate fate of individuals as well as empires. In both cases the unity and the continuity of an individual entity give way to multiplicity: both undergo the fall. The eternal question is thus as relevant to men as it is to empires: it is the question of why both die (503).

In saying that he sat all his life on the steps of Ara Coeli, Adams means that he asked all his life why the fall occurs. Yet in *The Education* he presents each new area of experience as if he had entered it naïvely, expecting to find unity and coherence, only to find the fall in some form. Continuity fails in the history of coinage, architecture, law, art, thought, men, and women; the orderliness of formal education is a failure; every idea and generalization—mental unities—about diplomacy, political morality, or contemporary politics proves invalid. Religion's view of reality as unity has collapsed, and science's attempt to replace religion with Darwinism seems to Adams untenable. Everywhere he finds unity and continuity historically momentary, philosophically invalid. He depicts his life in *The Education* as a process of repeated disillusionment. The fall—the collapse of unity—comes to seem to him the basic experience of human life. The steps of Ara Coeli symbolize the ultimate fact in human life and pose the question why it is so.

Adams' movement toward disillusionment is paralleled by one kind of movement in the book, its linear progression from the relative unity of his childhood to his vision of the multiverse in his old age. The other kind of movement is also progressive, but circular rather than linear. Adams enters each new experience looking for some persistent unity or order. Finding none except the tendency for unity to become multiplicity and for sequence to break down, he wonders why. Finally, he asks what his own attitude should be to the kind of reality he discovers. This movement is from question to answer to attitude and back to question again. The form paralleling the movement is wavelike, question and answer being always the same. It is also cumulative, building toward two climaxes: the death of Adams' sister and the formulation of the Dynamic Theory of History.[7]

The Fall Exemplified

Of the many areas in the book in which the fall proves to be central, four are particularly significant: the life of the narrator; his

[6] This passage is a faint echo of Adams' use of Wordsworth's Immortality Ode in *Mont-Saint-Michel and Chartres.*

[7] See critical note 51.

experience with education; the history of the United States; and the history of woman.

According to the preface the "Henry Adams" who is the book's subject is not its author but a manikin created to serve author Adams' didactic purpose. He speaks of himself at times as a representative nineteenth-century man: in the preface he tells his audience that "the garment [of education] offered to them is meant to show the faults of the patchwork fitted on their fathers." Another role is best understood by examining his use of the Garden of Eden story. Late in the work he says that, in the course of his education, he was confronted with the fact "of growing complexity, and multiplicity, and even contradiction, in life, . . . as though he were still Adam in the Garden of Eden between God who was unity, and Satan who was complexity, with no means of deciding which was truth." Here, the Garden of Eden is an image of a supposed primal unity, in which the problem of Adam was the philosophical one of deciding whether unity or multiplicity was truth. In the first chapter of *The Education* Adams puns on the likeness between his name and that of the first man: in his childhood, he says, "no one suggested . . . a doubt whether a system of society which had lasted since Adam would outlast one Adams more." The likeness of names is used to suggest that Adams and his forebears share in the human nature all men have inherited from Adam. "Henry Adams" is Everyman (x, 397, 16).

He assumes yet another archetypal role when he calls himself a "weary pilgrim" and compares himself to a pioneer wandering along "his vague trail across the darkening prairie of education." Throughout *The Education* he refers to this metaphor of his life as a journey and himself as a wanderer. The only two figures with whom he briefly indentifies completely are two philosophical wanderers, Rasselas and Teufelsdröckh. He also compares himself to Odysseus, and to Dante and St. Augustine, both of whom he characterizes as wanderers. As in the works in which these figures appear (except for Odysseus), *The Education* unites two literary types, the spiritual or intellectual autobiography and the epic of journeying. Like his prototypes, Adams sees his spiritual journey as not only his own but that of Everyman. The journey itself he views as at least the profoundest metaphor for man's life, perhaps more than a metaphor. Late in life, returning to routine after a long trip, he writes that he

would rather, as choice, have gone back to the east, if it were only to sleep forever in the trade-winds under the southern stars, wandering over the dark purple ocean, with its purple sense of solitude and void. . . . He had not yet happened on Rudyard Kipling's "Mandalay," but he knew the poetry before he knew the poem, like millions of wanderers, who have perhaps alone felt the world exactly as it is.

The message is clear: to know the world Everyman must go a journeying (433, 396, 316).

Such a conception of man's relation to reality means that no valid answer to the eternal question can bring peace and rest nor can any symbol of such states be as valid as Ara Coeli. Nonetheless, symbols invariably occur in pairs in *The Education* and Ara Coeli has a counter symbol, Wenlock Abbey, a thirteenth-century English building restored by Adams' friend Charles Milnes Gaskell. At Wenlock the atmosphere is one of "profound peace," and the movement of time, so strongly emphasized in *The Education*, disappears: "One might mix up the terms of time as much as one liked or stuff the present anywhere into the past . . . without violent sense of wrong." Here Adams found something of what Henry Thoreau found at Walden Pond and T. S. Eliot at the "still center of the turning world." Appropriately, he found it in a humanly created monument of the Middle Ages. Yet no more than Chartres did this monument offer a permanent refuge. This is especially true of Wenlock, for *The Education* is a book about the discovery of reality, not the memory of a dream. Although Adams says that "he yearned for nothing so keenly as to feel at home in a thirteenth-century Abbey," he realizes that his feelings are finally "mere antiquarian emotion." Not only has the sense of reality which brought the abbey and Virgin into existence disappeared, but, according to the view Adams accepts, the medieval sense of reality was never anything but an illusion. Thus Ara Coeli, the dynamo, and the wanderer have a validity for all times which Wenlock Abbey, the Virgin, and the pilgrim never had [8] (290, 229, 228, 355).

This validity is the basis for Adams' own role as a wanderer. His personal journey began with his birth in 1838. Late in *The Education* he writes that "unity is vision; it must have been part of the process of learning to see. The older the mind, the older its complexities, and the further it looks, the more it sees, until even the stars resolve themselves into multiples; yet the child will always see but one." He presents his own childhood in these terms as a period of relative unity. Yet in the first six chapters of *The Education*—as, to some extent, throughout the book— the chapters go in pairs, one emphasizing unity, one, multiplicity.[9] For Adams' boyhood, the duality is between Boston and Quincy,[10] a duality emphasized by the old man but recognized even by the boy. Quincy, the symbol of multiplicity, comes first; then, Boston. Adams draws upon his use of Eden as a symbol to characterize Boston's manners: "The garden of Eden was hardly more primitive." The irony is obvious; nonetheless the allusion reinforces the unity symbol. In the world of Adams' childhood, Boston dominated Quincy, unity dominated multiplicity, as,

---

[8] See critical note 52.   [9] See critical note 53.   [10] See critical note 54.

according to Adams, it always does for the child. Here, for the only time in the first six key chapters, a unity chapter dominates the multiplicity chapter it is paired with. The New England of Adams' childhood is as close to being a unity as anything he ever experiences (398–399, 40).

Yet, like the original Eden, this one contains the seeds of its own destruction. From the beginning, the New England climate works to destroy Adams' sense of unity. Its harshness of contrasts tends to dichotomize rather than unify his experience. "The bearing of the two seasons on the education of Henry Adams . . . ," he writes, "was the most decisive force he ever knew; it ran through life, and made the division between its perplexing, warring, irreconcilable problems, irreducible opposites, with growing emphasis to the last year of study." Superimposed upon the basic dichotomy of winter and summer are the dichotomies of town and country, school and vacation. "Town was winter confinement, school, rule, discipline, ... restraint, law, unity," and the "effort to live"; the "country . . . was liberty, diversity, outlawry," "tropical license, ... the multiplicity of nature" (7–9).

Boston and Quincy are Adams' first unity and multiplicity symbols because in winter Adams went to school in Boston, in summer he spent his vacation in Quincy. As a child, though he felt Boston was superior he liked Quincy best. Even then he wanted to escape from Boston, a desire intensified by his feeling that he was "shut out of Boston as though he were an exile." Youth's liking for vacations partly explains this preference; Adams also notes that the Adams family had always been at odds with Boston and hence was never quite at home there. But the preference was further reinforced by the fact that Adams' paternal grandmother, the wife of John Quincy Adams, was from Maryland. Again using the Eden image to taunt New England, Adams characterizes his grandmother as the Eve who made him an exile in the New England garden. Even as a child, he says, "he might . . . have felt some vague instinctive suspicion that he was to inherit from her the seeds of the primal sin, the fall from grace, the curse of Abel, that he was not of pure New England stock, but half exotic." Climate and heredity explain to Adams why, even in the comparatively unified world of his boyhood, he was aware of the fundamental polarity of existence and also why he preferred what that world considered the wrong pole (51, 17, 19).

When he was twelve, Adams made his first escape from the unity of New England to the greater multiplicity of Washington, D.C. Although he hated the slavery he found there, his total reaction to the city was pleasurable:

> The impression was not simple, but the boy liked it: distinctly it remained on his mind as an attraction, almost obscuring Quincy itself. The want of

barriers, of pavements, of forms; . . . the freedom, openness, swagger, of nature and man, soothed his Johnson blood. Most boys would have felt it in the same way, but with him the feeling caught on to an inheritance. The softness of his gentle old grandmother . . . did not come from Boston. . . . He did not wholly come from Boston himself. Though Washington belonged to a different world, and the two worlds could not live together, he was not sure that he enjoyed the Boston world most.

Washington tends to replace Quincy as Adams' multiplicity symbol, and a new dichotomy is drawn. Boston dominates Quincy, but Washington tends to dominate Boston.[11] The symbol opposed to Washington is Harvard College. For Adams as a boy school had been the epitome of Boston and winter, of the discipline he hated, and Harvard was the climax of school. "From the first," he says, "he wanted to be done with it. . . . The first door of escape . . . led into Germany." But Harvard proved to be "instinct with life compared with all that [Adams] could see of the University of Berlin," and the German high school proved even worse. He escaped from Germany through a trip to Rome, another multiplicity symbol (and the counter symbol to Berlin). Just as his grandmother had been in part responsible for his liking Washington, so another woman, his sister, introduced him to Rome. Rome, he says, was "a gospel of anarchy and vice; the last place under the sun for educating the young; yet it was, by common consent, the only spot that the young—of either sex and every race—passionately, perversely, wickedly loved." Here is the same ironic identification of multiplicity (or anarchy) with Satan that appeared in Adams' interpretation of the Garden of Eden myth. Here is also the same love of multiplicity that appeared in his desire to escape to Quincy and summer. But important changes have occurred. Boston, a symbol of unity, had been central and dominant in Adams' New England. Washington, a multiplicity symbol, was stronger and the center of a larger world than either Boston or Harvard. But Rome, also a symbol of multiplicity, is the center of western civilization: "Without her, the Western world [is] pointless and fragmentary; she [gives] heart and unity to it all." Berlin's unity is more subordinate to Rome than Quincy's multiplicity had been to Boston. The movement from the beginning of *The Education* to Adams' visit to Rome is the movement of Adams' own growing experience from a dominant unity to a dominant multiplicity (44–45, 61, 75, 90, 93).

But, why, if Rome is multiplicity, does Adams say that it gives heart and unity to western civilization? Because, as the home of two great experiments of that civilization, Rome has given it what unity it has. Yet nowhere is the ruin of unity so evident. Hence it is not surprising that here

[11] See critical note 55.

Henry Adams loses his belief in a unity-dominated world. Rome, he finds, "could not be fitted into an orderly, middle-class, Bostonian, systematic scheme of evolution. No law of progress applied to it. Not even time sequences . . . had value for it." [12] Rome repudiates childhood's vision. From the steps of Ara Coeli Adams surveys the fall of his own youth as well as the fall(s) of Rome. The experience suggests a partial answer to the eternal question. The fall is not only something that occurs in the external world; it is also a matter of perspective. "The older the mind," Adams will say later,

> the older its complexities, and the further it looks, the more it sees, until even the stars resolve themselves into multiples; yet the child will always see but one. Adams asked whether geology since 1867 had drifted towards unity or multiplicity, and he felt that the drift would depend on the age of the man who drifted.

Increasing awareness of complexity—of multiplicity—is part of the process of human maturation (91, 398–399).

The belief that this change of awareness is a growth in one's knowledge of reality—that complexity, not unity, is real—is the basis for Adams' views on education. In his boyhood and youth he hated school; as an old man he explains why school was a waste of time and thus deserved hating. He says of the irreconcilable opposites which he believes permeate life that "the man who pretended they were not [irreconcilable] was in his eyes a schoolmaster—that is, a man employed to tell lies to little boys." His dislike for artificial unities appears in his hatred for the lecture system, which, he says, "could lead only to inertia." Mental development "required conflict, competition, contradiction." In Berlin he turned from school to what he called "accidental education," by which he meant simply following his own interests until they ceased to be interesting or were replaced by some greater interest. As opposed to the unity of formal education this was clearly an education of multiplicity. For Adams it was his primary means of education for the next forty years. Appropriately, it made of him a tourist and a wanderer, for wanderers alone, he says, feel "the world exactly as it is" (9, 303, 85, 316).

Despite this congruence of theory and practice, however, Adams is never satisfied with the haphazard character of accidental education. He wants a theory or system which can be used in schools. In the preface to *The Education* he says that the book was written to "fit young men, in universities or elsewhere, to be men of the world, equipped for any emergency." What he is trying to do is reconcile two irreconcilables,

---

[12] It is here, in connection with Rome, that Adams makes the eternal question apply to the collapse of temporal continuities as well as simply unities.

formal and accidental education, by combining the economy of the former with the reality of the latter. Recognizing that no system can conform to the multiplicity of reality, he sees that without any system the student wastes most of his energy. His object is to devise a system which will teach a maximum of reality with a minimum of waste. Eventually, when the student has passed beyond its limits, it can (and should) be discarded.

Adams also sees the movement from unity to multiplicity in American history. Here unity and order lay in the eighteenth-century America of the Founding Fathers, a period represented by moral principles, the Constitution, George Washington, and a republican form of government. By contrast, America from 1860 to 1900 is represented as a period of growing anarchy, of utilitarian morality, the collapse of the Constitution, Grant–McKinley–Roosevelt, and the growth of an American empire. The transition in morality is the same as that developed more fully in *Democracy*. Adams views the utilitarian morality of his own age as a morality of multiplicity; the a priori morality of the Founding Fathers he views as one of unity. His own attitude appears in his comment that "the Puritan thought his thought higher and his moral standards better than those of his successors. So they were. He could not be convinced that moral standards had nothing to do with it, and that utilitarian morality was good enough for him, as it was for the graceless." The morality Adams is concerned with is that involved in the seeking of political power. Observing that the newspapers of late nineteenth-century America "discussed little else than the alleged moral laxity of Grant, Garfield, and Blaine," he notes that, nevertheless, "the public nominated Grant, Garfield, and Blaine for the Presidency, and voted for them afterwards." His conclusion is that "the moral law had expired—like the Constitution." Of the expiration of the Constitution, he says that "the system of 1789 had broken down, and with it the eighteenth-century fabric of a priori, or moral, principles. Politicians had tacitly given it up. Grant's administration marked the avowal" (26, 280–281). Political leaders had changed in a similar way. "George Washington was a primary, or, if Virginians liked it better, an ultimate relation, like the Pole Star." But by 1870 such order had given way to anarchy. In that year, Adams says, he and many other Americans voted for Ulysses S. Grant, in part because of "the parallel they felt between Grant and Washington. . . . Grant represented order . . . . The soldier always represented order." But Grant proved to be lacking in the administrative force necessary to prevent corruption and establish order, and, in addition, incredibly simple and almost without intellect. "That, two thousand years after Alexander the Great and Julius Caesar," Adams concludes, "a man like Grant should be called—and should actually and truly be—the highest product of the most advanced evolution, made evolution ludicrous." Again, continuity breaks down and unity collapses (47, 260, 266).

The change from republic to empire is more complex. Throughout the period of Adams' manhood, the United States had grown in power and unity: "the National Government and the national unity had overcome every resistance." The Civil War enforced "unity and uniformity" on the American people; after the war Americans devoted a generation largely to uniting the country by a railroad system. Between 1898 and 1903, England, France, and Germany were brought into an American Atlantic system. To Adams it seemed possible that within sixty years the world would be an American empire that would bring "the just and fair allotment of the whole world among the regulated activities of the universe." He saw two great obstacles to the realization of this possibility. One was Russia, the last and "most unmanageable of all" the countries to be brought into an American system because it was animated by a force antithetical to that which characterized the United States. Adams calls this force "race-inertia." In defining "inertia" he says that

> he decided from personal experience that his mind was never at rest, but moved—when normal—about something it called a motive, and never moved without motives to move it. So long as these motives were habitual, and their attraction regular, the consequent result might, for convenience, be called movement of inertia, to distinguish it from movement caused by newer or higher attraction; but the greater the bulk to move, the greater must be the force to accelerate or deflect it.

Applied to the Russians, this definition seems to mean that their actions grow out of habitual rather than novel motives, that life in Russia is characterized by uniformity and continuity rather than variety and change, and that when once set in motion the Russian individual and nation tend to remain in motion simply out of habit and find it extremely difficult to alter their course. Adams calls Russia itself "a vast continental mass of inert motion, like a glacier." By associating it with cold and winter, he relates it to Boston, school, and unity: race-inertia is a force for the maintenance of unity (398, 226, 362, 439, 373, 423, 441, 440).

In contrast, America is a country of "acceleration." The American mind responds more readily to new rather than old attractions; it likes change and is more often motivated by the force of novelty than habit. The American "never had known a complete union either in Church or State or thought, and had never seen any need for it. The freedom gave him courage to meet any contradiction, and intelligence enough to ignore it. Exactly the opposite condition had marked Russian growth." Hence, whereas Russia is a "sink of energy like the Caspian Sea," a centripetal force absorbing and transforming other forces into its own torpid inertness, America is a "twenty-million-horse-power" dynamo, a centrifugal force pouring energy into other forces, making them explode or volatilize into their individual components. The problem is which type of force and which nation will dominate the future. Adams is uncertain. But by the end of *The Education* he has suggested the ultimate victor. Like the rest of the world, he is amazed at Japan's success against Russia in the Russo-Japanese War of 1904–1905. He says of Japan that its force could not "be mistaken for a moment as a force of inertia." A nation characterized by acceleration had defeated Russian inertia and thus it seemed to Adams that, though "inertia of race and bulk would require an immense force to overcome it, . . . in time it might perhaps be partially overcome" —either by the Russians themselves or by an outside force. As a result of the Russo-Japanese War, the task of creating an American world empire seemed on the way to completion as "even Russia seemed about to be dragged into a combine of intelligent equilibrium based on an intelligent allotment of activities" (411, 408, 409, 416, 464, 448, 503).

But there is a second and far greater obstacle to America's growth toward empire. As American unity has increased, so has American multiplicity. The question is which is increasing faster. "All one's life," says Adams,

> one had struggled for unity, and unity had always won. The National Government and the national unity had overcome every resistance: . . . yet the greater the unity and the momentum, the worse became the complexity and the friction. . . . The multiplicity of unity had steadily increased, was increasing, and threatened to increase beyond reason.

The danger is that multiplicity, increasing faster than unity, will destroy the latter. Adams develops this theme partly through the most pervasive analogy in the work, that between the development of the United States and the history of the Roman Empire.[13] On his first visit to Ara Coeli in

[13] William Jordy, *Henry Adams: Scientific Historian* (New Haven: Yale University Press, 1952), p. 66; Sister M. Aquinas Healy, "A Study of Non-Rational Elements in the Works of Henry Adams as Centralized in his Attitude toward Women" (Ph.D. dissertation, University of Wisconsin, 1956), p. 235; and John Brunner, "Henry Adams: His Decline and Fall" (Ph.D. dissertation, UCLA, 1956), pp. 409, 416, comment briefly on this analogy in *The Education*. Ernest Samuels, *Henry Adams: The Major Phase* (Cambridge, Mass.: Harvard University Press, 1964), p. 132, notes its appearance in the letters (e.g., HA to Charles Milnes Gaskell, April 25, 1895, and HA to Brooks Adams, Sept. [?], 1895, both in Henry Adams, *Letters of Henry Adams, 1892–1918*, ed. Worthington Chauncey Ford [Boston: Houghton Mifflin Co., 1938], pp. 67, 83) and two examples are cited in J. C. Levenson, *The Mind and Art of Henry Adams* (Boston: Houghton Mifflin Co., 1957), pp. 290, 301. Charles Andrew Vandersee, "The Political Attitudes of Henry Adams" (Ph.D. dissertation, UCLA, 1964), p. 267, cites an unpublished 1895 letter in which Henry Adams draws "analogies for his brother Brooks between conditions of America and the conditions of Rome that preceded its fall."

1860 he had noted that the eternal question of why Rome fell became personal when one "substitute [d] the word America for the word Rome": that is, the answer in Rome's case might well suggest the future of America. Almost forty years of further journeys found Adams returning after each one to Ara Coeli, still convinced that he had the right question, but still without an answer. All of these journeys, he says, carried

> camel-loads of moral [but] New York sent most of all, for, in forty years, America had made so vast a stride to empire that the world of 1860 stood already on a distant horizon somewhere on the same plane with the republic of Brutus and Cato, while schoolboys read of Abraham Lincoln as they did of Julius Caesar. . . . The climax of empire could be seen approaching, year after year, as though Sulla were a President or McKinley a Consul.

Earlier, he had said of United States senators, "They were Romans" (398, 92, 367, 45).

Yet disintegration, he believed, was approaching even more rapidly than empire. In Rome there had been only two kinds of force available (besides that of the military presumably), religion and the slave. Therefore, "when society developed itself . . . rapidly in political and social lines, it had no other means of keeping its economy on the same level than to extend its slave-system and its fetish-system to the utmost." (The admission of increasing numbers of Germanic barbarians is apparently the extension of the slave system which Adams has primarily in mind.) This extension continued "until the slave-system consumed itself and the empire too." Society then had "no resource but further enlargement of its religious system in order to compensate for the losses and horror of the failure." Religion was looked upon as a source of power as physically efficacious as an army: Constantine used "the Cross as a train of artillery, which, to his mind, it was. Society accepted it in the same character." It was also Constantine who attempted to turn the collective force of all religions extant in the empire into maintaining the unity of the Roman state system. The difficulty was that by the time Constantine gave official approval to Christianity, the Church, after three centuries of persecution, had become an independent and highly disciplined unity in itself. Rome was unable to consume and absorb this unity. Instead, it helped destroy the Empire. To Adams it seems that the fall of the Western Empire (the first fall of Rome for Gibbon, the first also for Adams) occurred because the Empire was forced by its own needs to extend its sources of power until they grew too powerful in themselves to be contained by the fabric of Roman unity and thus destroyed it. Reality forced the development of seeds within unity which eventually destroyed it, just as maturity had forced the knowledge upon Henry Adams which destroyed the sense of unity he had had as a child in Boston (480, 479).

Adams saw early twentieth-century America confronting much the same problem as Rome had faced in the years immediately before Constantine. The sources of energy were different, and the problem was one of many new sources of power rather than over-development of old forces, but the threat posed to unity was the same. Again using the Roman analogy, Adams writes that on his return from abroad in 1905 New York

> had the air and movement of hysteria, and the citizens were crying, in every accent of anger and alarm, that the new forces must at any cost be brought under control. . . . A traveller in the highways of history looked out of the club window on the turmoil of Fifth Avenue, and felt himself in Rome, under Diocletian, witnessing the anarchy, conscious of the compulsion, eager for the solution, but unable to conceive whence the next impulse was to come or how it was to act. The two-thousand-years failure of Christianity roared upward from Broadway, and no Constantine the Great was in sight.

These new forces were the mechanical ones brought into play between 1860 and 1905. The railways had united the country, but the new chemical, mechanical, electrical, and "ethereal" forces had unleashed energies which the country seemed wholly unable to control. Adams saw no help from Christianity in solving the problem but did see the need for a twentieth-century analogue of Constantine. Traveling on to Washington he found Theodore Roosevelt "training Constantines and battling Trusts. . . . The Trusts and Corporations stood for the larger part of the new power that had been created since 1840, and were obnoxious because of their vigorous and unscrupulous energy. . . . They tore society to pieces and trampled it under foot." Adams had little hope that a Constantine would be found: "the sole object of his interest and sympathy was the new man, and the longer one watched, the less could be seen of him" (499–500).

Although by 1905 the American world system seemed to Adams close to completion, requiring consolidation more than anything else, its total disintegration seemed even closer because of the anarchy which the new forces had brought. "For the first time in fifteen hundred years a true Roman *pax* was in sight," Adams says, but the irony is obvious. The *pax* at best will be but momentary; the movement toward multiplicity is greater than that toward unity. Just as Rome was forced to develop the forces which led to her fall, so America has developed the forces which must soon lead to the collapse of her unity (503).

Adams also sees profound differences between the United States and Rome. One is the extent to which women are involved in the national movement from unity to multiplicity. Woman's importance lies in her nature as a force: she is reproduction. Reproduction is a force of inertia

—and unity—comparable to the race-inertia of Russia. The human motives which decide it are relatively unchanging, the results of a constant attraction. Yet sex-inertia is vastly more powerful and important than race-inertia: "Sex is a vital condition, and race only a local one." For sex creates and maintains the continuity of the human race: "Of all movements of inertia, maternity and reproduction are the most typical, and women's property of moving in a constant line forever is ultimate, uniting history in its only unbroken and unbreakable sequence. Whatever else stops, the woman must go on reproducing." Woman is the greatest unifying force in existence. As the primary source and focus of the human sense of unity, she is primarily responsible for humanity's traditional sense of reality as unity: "She conceived herself and her family as the centre and flower of an ordered universe which she knew to be unity because she had made it after the image of her own fecundity." Yet even when this view was predominant woman's lot was not a happy one: "Tragedy [has] been woman's lot since Eve." The attraction she exerts upon the male has led to her own victimization. Hence, Adams says, "for thousands of years women [have] rebelled" against their maternal role, primarily through religion. Since modern man took that from them, they have rebelled by trying to become like him. Insofar as they have been successful they have had to "marry machinery" (441, 459, 446, 447).

In modern America this marriage has been facilitated by the opposition to sex of the Puritan tradition. Whereas "in any previous age, sex was strength," for the Puritans "sex was sin." As a result, "American art, like the American language . . . , was as far as possible sexless. Society regarded this victory over sex as its greatest triumph." In Rome, by contrast, Venus was a great power. Adams does not say how the movement from unity to multiplicity in Rome affected the role of woman, but he views the medieval Virgin as a continuation of the Roman woman goddess: "the Venus of Epicurean philosophy survived in the Virgin of the Schools." In America this goddess has disappeared: "this energy was unknown to the American mind. An American Virgin would never dare command; an American Venus would never dare exist." [14] For the first time in history woman's rebellion against maternity has been so successful that it threatens the continuity of the race. What the Puritans began, the new mechanical forces seem about to finish. The "twenty or five-and-twenty million steam horse-power created in America since 1840, and as much more economized, . . . had been socially turned over to the American woman," Adams says, with the result that "woman [has] been set free." As the culmination of that freedom she has become sexless. Adams' conclusion is a warning: "Inertia of sex could not be overcome without

[14] See critical note 56.

extinguishing the race, yet an immense force, doubling every few years, was working irresistibly to overcome it" (384, 385, 384, 385, 444, 447, 448).

THE QUESTION ANSWERED

It should be clear by now that Adams' answer to the eternal question occurs throughout *The Education*. But there are two culminating points, one near the middle of the book, one at the end. The former is the death of Adams' sister, the latter, his Dynamic Theory of History. The first presents Adams' sense of the nature of reality, the final answer to the eternal question. The second expresses his own understanding of the significance of that reality for human life, his limited personal answer to the question. Both answers—either specifically or by implication—tie together most of the threads of *The Education*, as ideas in the Dynamic Theory, as aspects of a concrete image in the death of Adams' sister.

The first climax is the image. Here Adams presents his own most intense experience as an image of reality. It is appropriate that that experience should be the death of his sister. The ultimate antagonists in man's experience are, he believes, woman and the rest of nature; the birth of a child represents the greatest assertion of order, the death of a woman, the final triumph of nature. Adams' sister is not represented as typical of his conception of woman: she travels alone in Europe and thus shares in the freedom enjoyed by American women; she is not characterized as a mother either. Yet she is said to exert the power of "the eternal woman," who "had her way" because she was "young, pretty, and engaging." Adams came to her death uninitiated into reality. "He had never seen Nature—only her surface—the sugar-coating that she shows to youth." The sugar-coating was also present here: "Never had one seen her so winning," Adams says of Nature. But now her beauty simply added to the horror of the death by its revelation of her malignancy: "Nature enjoyed [the death], played with it, the horror added to her charm." Even this traditional personification of nature as a woman disappears when Adams expresses his full sense of the reality that lies beneath the sugar-coating. "For the first time," he says, "the stage-scenery of the senses collapsed; the human mind felt itself stripped naked, vibrating in a void of shapeless energies, with resistless mass, colliding, crushing, wasting, and destroying what these same energies had created and labored from eternity to perfect" (87, 287, 288).

This experience was a part of accidental, not formal education. As a boy Adams had hated the unity and order of school and turned instinctively to Quincy and nature's multiplicity. Here he learned that the senses are as deceptive as the mind, and multiplicity a far greater horror than the most rigid unity. The experience initiated him into reality. But it was more than an initiation: it was also "the last lesson—the sum and term of education." For a few moments he penetrated the veil of the senses and touched ultimate reality. His experience was a naturalistic equivalent of the mystic's immediate knowledge of God. But unlike the mystic he found behind the veil not unity and harmony but anarchy and conflict. Thus for Adams the experience was one to be avoided, and, when forced upon him by circumstances, to be painfully endured (287).[15]

The experience also suggests the tragic irony of woman's life. As has been noted, in Adams' use of the Garden of Eden myth, God is unity; Satan, multiplicity; and the garden itself, a state of primal human unity. Multiplicity enters the garden through Eve. Here is the paradox of woman: she is the greatest force of unity and continuity in human life; yet through her, multiplicity enters Eden and the life of Henry Adams. His Maryland grandmother brings the South's multiplicity into the relative unity of the New England "Eden"; his sister takes him from Berlin's unity to Rome's multiplicity and thereby helps to make him a tourist and a wanderer. The solution to the paradox seems to be that woman's intuitive sense of reality, superior to man's reasoning powers, shows her where reality is, yet her nature leads her to view as unity the multiplicity she finds. Adams' sister is kin to Goethe's *Ewigweibliche* and Dante's Beatrice. All lead man to reality, but all fail to realize that this reality is not the perfection of their own unity but its fatal antagonist. It is their own destroyer whom they take as God and lead their best beloveds to. Thus woman is not only the victim of a man or a church or a machine; she is also the supreme victim of the multiverse, of that ultimate chaos to which, all unknowingly, she is so confident a guide!

As Adams considers the relationship between man and nature, he finds its ultimate expression in death, the collapse of human unity into the chaos of nature. Sitting all his life upon the steps of Ara Coeli he comes finally to see that the fall is the essence of life and the form of human history, whether of the individual, the group, or the race. In every case the human aspiration toward unity is frustrated, whether by personal failure, or death, or by the disintegration of human societies, large or small. The destiny of man and all his creations is to fail, and the death of a woman, the primary source of the human sense of order and of the aspiration for greater order, is the most basic expression of that failure.[16]

Adams' attitude toward this idea of reality has two distinguishable, if not wholly different, aspects, one represented by the Augustus Saint-Gaudens' sculpture at Rock Creek Park, the other, by the Dynamic

[15] See critical note 57.
[16] See critical note 58.

Theory of History. According to Adams, the Saint-Gaudens' figure represents "the Peace of God,"[17] which arises from "the acceptance, intellectually, of the inevitable."[18] In the letters (especially of his later life), as well as in *The Education*, Adams stresses his own practice of submission in the face of superior force: "My rule is to conform," he says; "it is the only path of freedom."[19] He considers this the attitude of the Stoic, calls Stoicism "perhaps the best" of all social anodynes for grief, and eventually names Marcus Aurelius as his "type of highest human attainment."[20] But there is another, less passive attitude which appears when Adams says that

> every fabulist has told how the human mind has always struggled like a frightened bird to escape the chaos which caged it; how . . . after sixty or seventy years of growing astonishment, the mind wakes to find itself looking blankly into the void of death. That it should profess itself pleased by this performance was all that the highest rules of good breeding could ask; but that it should actually be satisfied would prove that it existed only as idiocy.

This attitude is but a faint remnant of the resistance to nature which Adams says is part of the New England inheritance.[21] Yet it is strong enough to produce Adams' theory of reality, his Dynamic Theory of History. Midway in *The Education* he states that "in essence" history— like nature—is "incoherent and immoral." Again, however, he cannot simply accept the fact, and when at Troyes, France, the outbreak of chaos represented by a political assassination makes him realize how woman's—specifically the Virgin's—effort to give unity to human life has failed he still refuses to give up his search for an answer to the eternal question.[22] "Every man," he says, "with self-respect enough to become effective, if only as a machine, has had to account to himself for himself somehow, and to invent a formula of his own for his universe, if the standard formulas failed. There, whether finished or not, education stopped" (289, 460, 301, 472).

[17] HA to R. W. Gilder, Oct. 14, 1895, cited in Marian Adams (Mrs. Henry Adams), *Letters of Mrs. Henry Adams*, ed., Ward Thoron (Boston: Little, Brown and Co., 1936), p. 458.
[18] See Henry Adams, *Henry Adams and His Friends: A Collection of His Unpublished Letters*, compiled with a biographical introduction by Harold Dean Cater (Boston: Houghton Mifflin Co., 1947), p. cxviii n. 212; hereafter cited as Cater. (Quoted by Cater in his introduction, p. liii, from the "*Evening Star* [sic] for Monday, January 17, 1910, p. 13."
[19] E.g., HA to Mabel La Farge, October 12, 1905, in *Letters to a Niece*, p. 113.
[20] HA to Henry Osborn Taylor, February 15, 1915, in Cater, p. 769.
[21] Henry Adams, *The Life of George Cabot Lodge* (Boston: Houghton Mifflin Co., 1911), p. 16.
[22] See critical note 59.

Here, Adams does not simply accept the inevitable. He tries to make a formula to describe it. F. L. Lucas calls this effort the essence of tragedy and philosophy.[23] But Adams does not wholly believe in his formula. In his youth he had sought "some great generalization which would finish one's clamor to be educated"; now he seeks not "absolute truth" but, "among indefinite possible" formulas, the one which will "best satisfy the observed movement of the runaway star . . . called Henry Adams"—that is, the one that will best translate and generalize his own personal motion from unity to multiplicity into experimentally verifiable historical terms. The result is his Dynamic Theory of History and its attendant Law of Acceleration. The theory involves four absolutes: space, time, force, and motion. Space seems to be infinite; time, a linear movement; force, "anything that does, or helps to do work"; motion, "change of place and interconversion of forms." History results from the interaction of one moving force, man, and all other (moving) forces—nature—in space and through time. Nature forces man to grow, to appropriate more of its force for his purposes, and gradually diminishes man's own personal force in the process. Man has expressed this encounter with nature in two ways. During most of his history, his instinctive sense of reality as unity has led him to express the encounter as religion. During the past three hundred years, that instinct has been increasingly controlled by an empirical and rational method which is leading him to the realization that reality is multiplicity. This new view is expressed chiefly in science (224, 472, 473, 474, 453).

The primary expression of man's sense of unity in the religious period was the anthropomorphized deities he created. He also created images of a period in history when he and the rest of nature were in harmony—the Garden of Eden, for example. Science, in order to create its own view of reality, has had to destroy belief in such deities and images. In the nineteenth century the most pervasive scientific world-view was the evolutionary theory of Darwin and Alfred Russel Wallace, buttressed by the geological theories of Charles Lyell. Adams says that Lyell published his *Antiquity of Man* "in order to support Darwin by wrecking the Garden of Eden." Yet although evolution, like earlier scientific theories, did weaken religion, it did not wreck it. Noting that the St. Louis Exposition closed on Sunday, whereas the Virgin's Exposition at Coutances did not close at all, Adams says that "apparently the Virgin . . . had no longer the force to build expositions that one cared to visit [i.e., those held near the

[23] F. L. Lucas, *Tragedy in Relation to Aristotle's Poetics* (New York: Harcourt, Brace and Co., 1928), p. 60: "Tragedy . . . is man's answer to this universe that crushes him so piteously. Destiny scowls upon him, his answer is to sit down and paint her where she stands."

churches], but had the force to close them." Religion has persisted partly because it expresses man's profoundest instinct, partly because, once human beings have deeply invested in a belief, they do not easily give it up. But it has also persisted because the scientific world-views which have thus far challenged it have not been truly scientific. Instead of rejecting unity, they have only expressed it in scientific rather than religious terms. Adams says of Darwinism that "unity and uniformity were the whole motive of philosophy, and if Darwin, like a true Englishman, preferred to back into it—to reach God *a posteriori*—rather than start from it, like Spinoza, the difference of method taught only the moral that the best way of reaching unity was to unite" (225, 468, 226).

But though evolution "pleased everyone—except curates and bishops" and "was the very best substitute for religion," by the end of the nineteenth century continued application of the scientific method seems to Adams to have made the unity of Darwinism as untenable as religion: "Evolution was becoming change of form broken by freaks of force, and warped at times by attractions affecting intelligence, twisted and tortured at other times by sheer violence, cosmic, chemical, solar, supersensual, electrolytic—who knew what?—defying science, if not denying known law." Not evolution but catastrophism, or what Adams sometimes calls "the break," seems to him the law of change. This law finds its ultimate nineteenth-century expression in what Adams paradoxically decides is the scientific synthesis most in accord with the true nature and direction of science: James Clerk-Maxwell's kinetic theory of gases. "So far as he understood it," Adams says,

> the theory asserted that any portion of space is occupied by molecules of gas, flying in right lines at velocities varying up to a mile in a second, and colliding with each other at intervals varying up to 17,750,000 times in a second. To this analysis—if one understood it right—all matter whatever was reducible.

Nature is not a gradual evolution of lower to higher forms, but a chaos of particles in constant motion. "The only difference of opinion in science regarded the doubt whether a still deeper analysis would reduce the atom of gas to pure motion" (in that case Adams' list of absolutes would be only three—space, time, and motion) (225, 401, 431).

Such a conception of reality has no place for unity: "The scientific synthesis commonly called Unity was the scientific analysis commonly called Multiplicity. The two things were the same, all forms being shifting phases of motion." Here is the ultimate rationale for Adams' view that perhaps only the wanderer, of all men, has experienced the world exactly as it is. The constant anarchic motion of the wanderer is the human expression of the constant anarchic motion of all forces in reality.

The kinetic theory also explains why science must inevitably wreck the religious world-view. If reality is multiplicity, a continued increase in man's knowledge of reality must eventually destroy the unified world of man's childhood, that "Eden of [man's] own invention." Here the Garden of Eden, in its final use as an image of unity, is an image of the entire religious period destroyed by man's awareness of multiplicity. A far greater image of the religious view fares no better. Whereas the medieval child had retained his faith in the face of St. Louis' disastrous crusade, the old man, confronted at Troyes by a single murder, feels a scandalous failure of the Virgin's grace. This failure is to the life of Everyman what the death of his sister was to the life of Henry Adams, at once the greatest of all catastrophes and "the sum and term of education." The old man's vision in *Chartres* of the Virgin looking down "from a deserted heaven, into an empty church, on a dead faith" is the historical counterpart of Adams' own personal experience. For the race, as for the individual, the supreme expression of nature's hostility to man and his sense of unity is the death of a woman (431, 459).

In *The Education* the truth embodied in such experience first came to Adams as an emotion of overwhelming horror. At the end of his life, experience combined with a study of contemporary science (especially physical science) gives him a rational view of reality which corresponds to the felt experience:

> He found himself in a land where no one had ever penetrated before; where order was an accidental relation obnoxious to nature; artificial compulsion imposed on motion; against which every free energy of the universe revolted; and which, being merely occasional, resolved itself back into anarchy at last.

This scientific multiverse has its own symbol for infinite force. The religious universe centered upon a succession of woman goddesses, culminating in the Virgin. For Adams the dynamo becomes the symbol for the modern world: "Among the thousand symbols of ultimate energy, the dynamo was not so human as some, but it was the most expressive." The crucial difference between this symbol and the Virgin is that the latter is the greatest symbol man has ever created of his own humanity and the sense of unity which is his essence. It represents man at the zenith of his selfhood. The dynamo represents man at the nadir of that selfhood, his sense of unity almost gone, the reality of chaos on the point of breaking through his humanity. The absolute antithesis of the human Virgin is the nonhuman multiverse. The dynamo expresses the vestiges of unity that cling to twentieth-century science and twentieth-century man (457–458, 380).

To the world symbolized by the dynamo Adams' reaction is not the utter horror he felt after his sister's death. Instead, he reacts as he reacted to Boston, to school, and to everything else he didn't like: "All that a historian won was a vehement wish to escape. He saw his education complete, and was sorry he ever began it. . . . He repudiated all share in the world as it was to be." At the end of *The Education* he is on the verge of gaining his wish. Now, however, the only escape is death. His two best friends dead before him, he feels "the quiet summons to follow—the assent to dismissal." Putting aside the tragic attitude, he returns to a stoic acceptance of the inevitable. *The Education*, therefore, ends as a complete autobiography naturally does, with the author's anticipation of death. The fall in its most basic form, the death of a human being, is once again about to occur. For sixty-seven years, the unity called Henry Adams has been moving toward multiplicity. The end of that process will be the dissolution of the human individual into the chaos of nature. For Henry Adams as Everyman the eternal question will remain, but for Henry Adams, "Groombridge, 1838," the answers will no longer matter. His quest will have reached an end (458, 505).[24]

The Ultimate Symbolism

Like the journey in *Chartres*, this quest has an ultimate image which expresses its central emphasis. In *Chartres* the drama expresses man's illusion of order; here the ocean expresses the reality of multiplicity.[25] But whereas *Chartres* has only one key image, the ocean in *The Education* is part of a complex of water symbols: ice, snow, and glaciers; the ocean; and steam.[26] Of these only the ocean (and it only at the end of the book) is used to symbolize reality. Generally, the three symbols suggest three states of society or of the individual. Water is the normal condition. Ice and snow suggest an exaggerated retardation of human energy; steam, an exaggerated acceleration of energy. As usual in Adams' work, one extreme eventually proves to be real and at last absorbs both the other extreme and the norm.

The extremes are introduced in the first chapter, primarily in the contrast between Boston and Quincy, symbolizing, respectively, a rigid

---

[24] See critical note 60.

[25] See critical note 61.

[26] The ocean imagery in *The Education* is discussed more briefly in Tony Tanner, "The Lost America—The Despair of Henry Adams and Mark Twain," *Modern Age*, V (Summer, 1961), 304–306. Tanner compares it to similar images in Twain's later work and contrasts both with the ocean imagery in Emerson. A much fuller treatment, emphasizing the ocean, but also mentioning the glacier, appears in Brunner, "Henry Adams: His Decline and Fall," pp. 7–8, 51–52, 270–272, 275, 278, 368–369, 372–375, 376–379, 380–381, 385–386, 395–400. Individual footnotes here and in chapter 8 indicate specific likenesses and differences in our interpretations.

human unity and the multiplicity of nature. Adams emphasizes his hatred for rigid unities, especially for school. By associating Boston and school with winter, he also creates the first link between his unity-multiplicity dichotomy and the book's pervasive water symbolism. For winter is a rigid unity, a frozen time of ice and snow. This symbolic use leads directly into the snow, ice, and glacier imagery which appears later in the book. Adams also makes it clear in this chapter that unity is the false half of his pervasive dichotomy: "Winter and summer [27] . . . were hostile, and the man who pretended they were not, was . . . a schoolmaster— . . . a man employed to tell lies to little boys." This attitude remains constant throughout *The Education*. But Adams' early hatred for rigid unities soon becomes a more complex attitude (e.g., 31). A crucial instance appears in his account of his visit to Mont Blanc after his sister's death. After seeing the mountain as "it was—a chaos of anarchic and purposeless forces," he says that "he needed days of repose to see it clothe itself again with the illusions of his senses, the white purity of its snows, the splendor of its light, and the infinity of its heavenly peace." Here snow parallels light (and peace) as "illusions of [the] senses." Yet Adams has no feeling of hatred for it or for illusion; on the contrary, he is pleased by both. His boy's love for Quincy, summer, and the "multiplicity of nature" has been radically altered by his sister's death and its revelation that nature's multiplicity is an "insanity of force." Now snow and ice became beneficent illusions, protecting him from the reality of the multiplicity he has learned to abhor. (In addition, he looks here at the snows of Mont Blanc from a distance; since he is not forced to live in a frozen world, his response can be more purely aesthetic than it was when he was a boy.) (9, 289, 9, 288)

Also, because he is reacting against one extreme—that of multiplicity— he finds at least momentary satisfaction in the other. Later in the book— in his characterization of Russia—winter, ice, snow, and glaciers again appear as images of rigid inflexibility and again arouse his dislike as well as disbelief. He says that Russia's surface keeps "the uniformity of ice and snow" and finds its "image" to be "that of the retreating ice-cap—a wall of archaic glacier, as fixed, as ancient, as eternal, as the wall of archaic ice that blocked the ocean a few miles to the northward, and more likely to advance." As usual, he believes that unity is destined to be volatilized and thus prove transient, a temporary rather than a permanent reality. But here he takes no pleasure in his winter imagery. "The glacial ice-cap" is a "nightmare" he explicitly associates with Russian inertia, and he speaks

[27] Working from experience to image here at the beginning of the book, rather than from idea to image, Adams associates the "multiplicity of nature" with the summer life of heat rather than with a water image. Yet it is heat that melts ice and volatilizes water; the image, therefore, is related to the later use of steam as an image of multiplicity.

of the terror it arouses in "Germans, Scandinavians, Poles and Hungarians" (409, 411, 414, 412).

This usage is the climax of the unfavorable connotations of snow and glacier images. The climax of their favorable connotations comes in the final chapter. The connection between image and meaning is not made explicit there, but in context seems clear. Adams has described his failure to see any clear signs of the new man needed to bring the twentieth-century forces of multiplicity under control. After discussing what value his own Dynamic Theory might have in producing such a man, he says that "there, the duty stopped."

> There, too, life stopped. Nature has educated herself to a singular sympathy for death. On the antarctic glacier, nearly five thousand feet above sea-level, Captain Scott found carcasses of seals, where the animals had laboriously flopped up, to die in peace, . . . "probably from . . . instinctive dread of . . . [their] marine enemies."

Later in the same paragraph he equates the peace sought by the seal with his "own passive obscurity" (and contrasts it with the "exposure" of his friend John Hay). Like the seal, Adams has crawled up out of the ocean of life and reality onto a glacier, where he is momentarily safe from the disintegrative forces of reality. *His* glacier is his Dynamic Theory. As a theory it is a rigid unity and therefore a lie (told, indeed, by an avowed schoolmaster seeking to educate young men). But in this case the lie is a conscious artifice, created by Adams, after a lifetime of study, out of refusal to admit defeat and as a means of finding rest from the apparently infinite chaos to which his search for education has led. Like all such unities it is a transient thing, but also, like them, it is capable of making life easier for the old, whether they be seals or "tired student [s]" (501–502, 472).[28]

While Adams has been varying and developing this ice and snow imagery, his ocean imagery has undergone an even more thoroughgoing transformation. In the second chapter of *The Education*, he writes that "if he were to worry successfully through life's quicksands, he must depend chiefly on his father's pilotage; but, for his father, the channel lay clear, while for himself an unknown ocean lay beyond." This ocean is an image for the concrete world of things and events in which men live their daily lives. By the end of the book, however, the ocean has become an image for the context of ultimate reality in which everything exists. The kinetic theory of gases and its assertion that reality is chaos provide the basis for

[28] Brunner notes the glacier image, its use to symbolize Russian inertia, and its connection with the water symbolism in the book ("Henry Adams: His Decline and Fall," p. 51).

this transformation: reality, Adams says, is an "ocean of colliding atoms." This is no longer an ocean of water, palpable to the senses, but a supersensual ocean of gas molecules. The transformation has destroyed water as a normative image between extremes and made it the image of the extreme that is true: chaos or multiplicity. In the course of the book both ice and water have proved to be images of appearance, while impalpable gas molecules are shown to be the valid image of reality (26, 431).[29]

Man's relationship to this new ocean of reality is expressed in another image[30] reworked from an earlier usage. It appears in Adams' discussion of Karl Pearson's *The Grammar of Science*. Adams says that the scientists of his youth, "including Newton, Darwin and Clerk Maxwell, had sailed gaily into the supersensual, calling it:—'One God, one Law, one Element, / And one far-off, divine event,/ To which the whole creation moves.'" They refused to consider evidence or argument which denied this unity. "At last their universe had been wrecked by rays, and Karl Pearson undertook to cut the wreck loose with an axe, leaving science adrift on a sensual raft in the midst of a supersensual chaos."[31] The shift from Newton and Darwin's proud ship, sailing gaily into supersensual unity, to Pearson's raft adrift "in the midst of a supersensual chaos," vividly suggests the diminution both of science and of man which the new science had brought about. Henry Adams' own consternation is suggested when he remarks, soon afterwards, that "he found himself on the raft,

[29] Brunner observes that this "sea of supersensual chaos" (*ibid.*, p. 270) represents "the formless void of scientific phenomenalism" (*ibid.*, p. 51), of Ernest Mach and Karl Pearson. Characterizing the book as a whole as an account of Henry Adams' intellectual "odyssey" through this sea of chaos, Brunner notes that

Adams even had a ship. It was the recurring image of the Cunard liner, which always finally appeared from over the horizon of the narrator's thought to bear this voyager to some new land of contemplation. . . . The Cunarder became eventually a kind of spectral ship in Henry Adams' imagination, whereby he would seek to reckon, by triangulating from its future growth the moment when the modern world and the modern steamship must have their . . . stop. (*ibid.*, pp. 376–379)

For Brunner's view that in *The Education* this "sea of phenomenalistic chaos drifted into the dead ocean of entropy" (*ibid.*, p. 275), see critical note 67.

[30] A second image of this relationship is that of man as a deep-sea fish, who sees only the little area illuminated by the light he himself creates. See *The Education*, pp. 239 and 450, for the original and reworked versions of the image.

[31] Jordy, *Henry Adams: Scientific Historian*, pp. 234, 236, comments on what he calls this "oft-quoted metaphor." Brunner also notes the image ("Henry Adams: His Decline and Fall," p. 7), which he characterizes as Adams' "famous metaphor of scientific phenomenalism," and adds (*ibid.*, pp. 7–8) that "as he drifted saturninely through a sea of chaos, Adams could at length declare that his sensual raft was illusory too." He does not observe, however, that this raft is his Cunard liner viewed not from a human but from an absolute perspective.

personally and economically concerned in its drift": here the personal ship of Henry Adams of the beginning of the book has shrunk to a frail raft, on which he and all humanity are adrift in a shoreless chaos (452, 453).

Adams' role as a wanderer culminates in this image. His belief that perhaps the wanderer alone knows "the world exactly as it is" finds its supreme rationale in the kinetic theory's view of reality as composed of atoms in constant, erratic motion. Here the statement and its rationale both appear in an image of man as an infinitesimal atom, helplessly tossed about in the sea of reality. If Adams leaves man any comfort, it resides only in the suggestion that at least all humanity is together on the same raft (316).

The same image appears one final time in *The Education* as part of a full-scale, figurative account of human history, viewed in the light of the new conception of reality. "As history unveiled itself in the new order," Adams says,

man's mind had behaved like a young pearl oyster, secreting its universe to suit its conditions until it had built up a shell of *nacre* that embodied all its notions of the perfect. Man knew it was true because he made it, and he loved it for the same reason. He sacrificed millions of lives to aquire his unity, but he achieved it, and justly thought it a work of art. The woman especially did great things, creating her deities on a higher level than the male, and, in the end, compelling the man to accept the Virgin as guardian of the man's God. The man's part in his Universe was secondary, but the woman was at home there, and sacrificed herself without limit to make it habitable, when man permitted it, as sometimes happened for brief intervals of war and famine; but she could not provide protection against forces of nature. She did not think of her universe as a raft to which the limpets stuck for life in the surge of a supersensual chaos; she conceived herself and her family as the centre and flower of an ordered universe which she knew to be unity because she had made it after the image of her own fecundity; and this creation of hers was surrounded by beauties and perfections which she knew to be real because she herself had imagined them.

. . . Neither man nor woman ever wanted to quit this Eden of their own invention, and could no more have done it of their own accord than the pearl oyster could quit its shell; but although the oyster might perhaps assimilate or embalm a grain of sand forced into its aperture, it could only perish in the face of the cyclonic hurricane or the volcanic upheaval of its bed. Her supersensual chaos killed her.[32]

---

[32] The oyster is not the only—or even the most important—inhabitant of the ocean to be used symbolically in *The Education*. Brunner examines (*ibid.*, pp. 395–400) in detail the three ocean creatures—Pteraspis, Terebratula, and Limulus—Adams uses as recurrent images in *The Education* to suggest the flaws in Darwin's evolutionary theory and in all intellectual disciplines.

As the reference to Eden suggests, this passage presents Adams' version of the fall of man. At the same time it is a condensed and figurative account of the Dynamic Theory, more emotionally effective, and no less valid, for being expressed in images rather than concepts. This emotional intensity also owes something to Adams' use of the ocean instead of the dynamo as the antithetical symbol to the Virgin. The dynamo lacks the symbolic potency to compete with the Virgin and thereby lends itself admirably to Adams' belief that the movement of history is one of decline.[33] Yet when the primary focus of the Dynamic Theory is upon it and the Virgin, the perspective becomes too human to convey fully Adams' view of history and reality seen from the perspective of reality. By focusing upon the opposition between humanity (especially woman) and the ocean as a symbol of reality, he gives a stronger sense of reality's perspective and, therefore, much fuller expression to the whole of his vision (458–459).[34]

Water imagery is also used to characterize the movement of society toward anarchy. This movement is particularly advanced in the United States, the antithesis of Russia. Adams uses no water imagery for America but he does use a water image to characterize that aspect of American acceleration which seems to him most significant, its tendency to emancipate women from their natural role as mothers: "The woman . . . had been set free—volatilized like Clerk Maxwell's perfect gas [in the kinetic theory]; almost brought to the point of explosion, like steam." This is one of the two explicitly figurative uses of steam in *The Education*. Its appearance in conjunction with the kinetic theory of gases suggests that steam is the sensual analogue of the supersensual gas molecules that comprise reality. In his account of reality Adams invariably wants to stress the fact that it is supersensual; the use of steam as an image would thwart this intention. But here he is speaking of society and therefore of the physical world. The sensuous image of exploding steam becomes effective because it is easier to imagine individuals as droplets of steam than as supersensual molecules or atoms. Such an image is also closer to the kinetic theory than the image of man on a raft in chaos, for there man has the company of his fellows. Here, although exploding steam is a less vivid image, man is robbed of all comfort and becomes merely one of the isolated atoms of reality (444).

[33] See critical note 62.

[34] On p. 459, of *The Education*, Adams says of this figurative version of the Theory that "such seemed the theory of history to be imposed by science on the generation born after 1900." Subjected, that is, to the unity-creating mind of man, the scientific facts available in 1900 would take (unified) form as the Dynamic Theory. The coincidence of this form and that which Adams' mind gives to his own life (*The Education*, p. 472) provides a basis and a justification for his treating himself as Everyman.

The other use of steam is explicitly as an image of "supersensual chaos." It appears in the expressionistic picture of New York City which begins the final chapter of *The Education*. Looking out over the city, Adams says that "power seemed to have outgrown its servitude and to have asserted its freedom. The cylinder had exploded, and thrown great masses of stone and steam against the sky." The cylinder is the container in which water is turned to steam and used as a source of power, as in a locomotive. Here it is man's mind conceived as a containing and controlling force. New York's stone skyscrapers are viewed as the consequences of the explosion of that mind, unable to control the tremendous influx of new forces. This passage crystallizes the apocalyptic implications of the Dynamic Theory and *The Education* as a whole into a climactic image of humanity on the verge of destruction. In the religious period, men remembered—or thought they did—behind the discord of their personal experience the harmony and peace of Eden, the earthly counterpart of heaven. Here Adams sees within the stability of New York City and the routine of its people's lives an accelerating movement toward anarchy, a human counterpart of the chaos of the multiverse (499).

The Education ends with the juxtaposition of its major water images in two pictures. Within four pages steam, the sea, and the glacier all appear, the first in the description of New York, the others in the account of the seals crawling up on the glacier to die. Together, the images suggest the knowledge Adams has gained in sixty-eight years of searching for an education, and his reaction to that knowledge. He finds humanity on the verge of disintegrating into the chaos of reality, and, after failing to find the new man who might avert the disaster, he retreats from the horror of that reality onto the glacial *Civitas Intellecti* of the Dynamic Theory to await his death.

These conclusions also suggest a final answer to author Adams' lifelong struggle with the problem of illusion and reality. Reality is so great a horror, he seems to say, that only illusion makes life bearable.

CHAPTER VII

THE ULTIMATE SYMBOLS: I

FROM DRAMA TO MACHINE

Along with the symbols and myths in individual books by Adams, there are also certain symbols which recur throughout his work. Occasionally these become dominant in a particular work, but generally they are subordinate to some less common symbol. Of such symbols the three most pervasive and significant are the drama, the machine, and various water symbols. All three are concerned with what the relationship between man and nature (reality) is, or ought to be, and thus with the problem of distinguishing between illusion and reality. Because they pervade Adams' work, all reflect the movement of his thought from a qualified belief that man's will is both free and efficacious to a less qualified belief that man is simply a part of nature.

As symbols, drama and the machine are involved with the question whether man's life is more like a drama or a machine. Adams was always interested in drama. Elizabeth Stevenson says that "acting, rather than writing or reforming, seems to have been Adams's most conspicuous school role" as a Harvard undergraduate. After graduating he seems to have done no more acting, but he did continue to attend plays. In his writings, literature, and especially the drama, is mentioned the most frequently of all the arts. He calls "the dramatic art . . . the highest and most exacting in all literature," primarily because it performs what in his view is the highest accomplishment of literature, the creation of real and living characters. But to have a drama, characters have to be put into action; such action requires an idea or a motive. This idea is Adams' main concern. Even characters interest him primarily as the expression of a thought or "moral meaning."[1] Yet he looks for this meaning less in the

---

[1] Elizabeth Stevenson, *Henry Adams: A Biography* (New York: The Macmillan Co., 1955), p. 17; Henry Adams, *The Life of George Cabot Lodge* (Boston: Houghton Mifflin Co., 1911), p. 62; Henry Adams, Review of Tennyson's *Queen Mary*, in *North*

theater than in life. His concern with the drama is principally figurative and is based upon the fact that human life and history often seem to have some of the characteristics of a play. He means by "drama" a conflict between individuals or groups over some idea or motive, the whole having a unity like that of a drama, and leading to a final catastrophe or consummation. Such situations pose the question whether the "drama" of life is real, whether the course of life and history is actually decided by struggles among men over ideas (or simply for power), or whether this drama, like that on the stage, is only make-believe and forces other than men are the decisive factors in history.

In contrast to his early interest in the drama, Adams' interest in machines, in the usual sense of mechanical contrivances, was very slight until the end of the century. Yet the term "machine" frequently appears in his work throughout his life. He refers to the Constitution, the American government, and the U.S. Bank as "machines"; he speaks of "social machinery," of the United States and England as "money-making machine[s]," and of the American "economic machine."[2] In this figurative usage, a machine is a contrivance of man's reason and will, intended to help him do more work with less effort. The measure of its value lies in the kind and amount of work it does and its efficiency in doing it. All such machines and especially those that concern the whole of a society, such as political machines, have a constant tendency to become stronger than the human beings who create them and hence to transform men into machines. Such mechanization stifles individuality and emotion. This tendency is the great danger of machinery and is a principal concern of Adams in his figurative use of "machine." The danger is enhanced because, in Adams' work up to *The History* and according to the dynamic theory of history after that, nature itself functions mechanically. Its

---

American Review, CXXI (Oct., 1875), 424–425. (Cf., Introduction to present text in regard to intellectualism.)

[2] Henry Adams and Henry Cabot Lodge, Review of H. Von Holst's *The Constitutional and Political History of the United States*, in *North American Review*, CXXIII (Oct., 1876), 355; Henry Adams, "The Session," in *North American Review*, CXI (July, 1870), 59. Henry Adams, "The Session," in *North American Review*, CVIII (April, 1869), 611. HA to Brooks Adams, Mar. 8, 1903, in Henry Adams, *Henry Adams and His Friends: A Collection of His Unpublished Letters*, compiled with a biographical introduction by Harold Dean Cater (Boston: Houghton Mifflin Co., 1947), p. 537 (hereafter cited as Cater); Henry Adams, *The History of the United States During the Administrations of Thomas Jefferson and James Madison* (New York: Charles Scribner's Sons, 1889–1891), V, 207; VI, 400; HA to Sir Robert Cunliffe, Jan. 8, 1895; and HA to Charles Milnes Gaskell, Nov. 22, 1899, in Henry Adams, *The Letters of Henry Adams, 1892–1918*, ed. Worthington Chauncey Ford (Boston: Houghton Mifflin Co., 1938), pp. 63, 249; hereafter cited as Ford (1892–1918).

influence thus reinforces that of man-made machines and makes man's difficulties in controlling them all the greater.[3]

The simplest form of the drama symbol appears earliest in Adams' work. In "The New York Gold Conspiracy," which appeared in 1870, the drama is treated as a valid image of life. Adams hopes to show the public "how dramatic and how artistically admirable a conspiracy in real life may be, when slowly elaborated from the subtle mind of a clever intriguer, and carried into execution by a band of unshrinking scoundrels." The plot is the attempt by Jay Gould and Jim Fisk to corner gold in the late 1860's. The motives of the actors were not ideas or principles but greed and perhaps, in the case of Gould, the "hazard and splendour" of the operation. A theory was constructed for the occasion, according to which western farmers would benefit from the operation. Adams concedes some validity to it but notes that when the operation seemed to be in danger "nothing more was heard in regard to philanthropic theories of benefit to the Western farmer."[4] This is the only extended use of the dramatic analogy in Adams' work in which sheer greed is so important, ideas and principles so unimportant. Success of ideas and principles always means power for those who hold them, but in Adams' other works the heroes and heroines care more for the ideas and principles than for the power. In *Mont-Saint-Michel and Chartres* Adams *defines* a drama as a human struggle over an idea and distinguishes such a dramatic struggle from one which is purely practical or concerned with power for its own sake.[5] Yet if this aspect of the fully developed analogy is only partially present here, the other, even more essential aspect is completely present. Human life described as a drama has literal validity only if human actions are a decisive factor in human history—only if man's will is free and efficacious. In this essay the freedom and the efficacy of the wills of Gould and Fisk are emphasized; their conspiracy is checked only when a stronger will comes into action. It is this emphasis which makes "The New York Gold Conspiracy" the best extended example of the simple, or naïve, use of the dramatic analogy in Adams' work. In it, at least, the "drama" of life is treated as real, not make-believe.

The initial use of the machine as an image of human life also follows the dictionary definition: "Any person or organization that acts like a machine, as automatically and without intelligence or feeling." The figure appears infrequently in Adams' work up to 1880. In 1869 he speaks of "the

---

[3] Review of Von Holst's *Constitutional and Political History*, p. 361.

[4] Henry Adams, "The New York Gold Conspiracy," in *Westminster Review*, XCIV (N.S. XXXVIII) (Oct. 1, 1870), 422, 421, 431.

[5] Henry Adams, *Mont-Saint-Michel and Chartres*, with an introduction by Ralph Adams Cram (Boston: Houghton Mifflin Co., 1933), p. 224.

blind, unreasoning vote which follows mechanically a party standard."
In *Democracy*, J. C. Levenson observes that from Mrs. Lee's "initial
resolve to 'touch with her own hand the massive machinery of society' to
her final sense of a narrow escape from 'being dragged under the wheels
of the machine,' a persistent line of imagery implies that mechanization
has taken command and human reality has departed from politics." In
Esther, when Hazard feels that to be successful in New York he must
bring people with opinions of their own into the church, Adams notes
that it would be "small triumph to draw a procession of followers from
a class who took their opinions, like their jewelry, machine-made."[6]
Clearly, Adams does not believe in these cases that a man has to act like
a machine. Doing so is a matter of choice—and contemptible.

The dramatic analogy appears most frequently in Adams' work before
The History (1891) in the naïve form it takes in "The New York Gold
Conspiracy." Usually it is used in connection with American political life
or history and appears in short phrases: "this great historical drama" or
"each actor on the scene" or "a new generation . . . came on the stage."
When developed to any extent, it tends to be used in a more sophisticated
way. Adams implies the direction such usage will take in commenting on
the larger significance of the Gould-Fisk episode: "For the first time
since the creation of these enormous corporate bodies, one of them has
shown its power for mischief, and has proved itself able to override and
trample on law, custom, decency, and every restraint known to society,
without scruple and as yet without check."[7] This comment suggests that
Gould's and Fisk's attempt to corner gold is only the first of a series of
similar dramas, and these, in turn, but episodes in the larger drama of
society's attempt to control the corporations.

In another form taken by the dramatic analogy these tendencies
toward seeing the immediate drama as an example of a recurrent drama
and as part of a larger drama are developed further. The year before
"The New York Gold Conspiracy" appeared, Adams published an

[6] *New English Dictionary*, definition 3. Adams, "The Session" (1869), 618. J. C.
Levenson, *The Mind and Art of Henry Adams* (Boston: Houghton Mifflin Co., 1957),
pp. 87–88. (Henry Burt Rule, "Irony in the Works of Henry Adams" [Ph.D. dissertation, University of Colorado, 1960], p. 105; and Dennis S. R. Welland, "Henry Adams
as Novelist," in *Renaissance and Modern Studies*, III [1959], 35; also note the mechanical imagery in *Democracy*.) Henry Adams, *Esther : A Novel*, by Francis Snow Compton
[pseud.], with an introduction by Robert E. Spiller (New York: Scholars' Facsimiles
and Reprints, 1938), pp. 62–63.

[7] Henry Adams, Review of Henry Cabot Lodge's *Life and Letters of George Cabot*, in
Nation, XXV (July 5, 1877), 13. Henry Adams, Review of John Gorham Palfrey's
History of New England, in *North American Review*, CXXI (Oct., 1875), 473. Review of
Von Holst's *Constitutional and Political History*, 356. "New York Gold Conspiracy,"
436.

article, "Men and Things in Washington" (1869), in which he noted that the one universal prejudice among diplomats in Washington was their absolute disbelief "in theories of society and government." The basis for this prejudice was European experience—most immediately, a century of French political failure. Yet in Washington these same diplomats dealt with a government whose structure they were "expected to accept as perfect." This was a good deal to expect, Adams says, but notes that

> it affords a certain amusement to a clever foreigner to feel sure that he has the word to this prodigious charade which is performed under his eyes on a stage where he sits among the actors like a fine gentleman of Shakespeare's day. It is not surprising that he is a sharp critic when one reflects how profoundly ignorant he must believe the performers to be. To him the drama and its development appear almost as certain as a mathematical formula; the characters seem as familiar as the heroes of Corneille; the nation that, during an indefinite series of generations, throws itself alternately from the corrupt arms of a single man to the still more corrupt embrace of a number of men, is a sight as well known as a Greek chorus to a school boy. . . . With a drama so put on the stage, neither diplomats nor any other persons have a right to think Washington dull. It is true the play is somewhat long and the number of acts is unconscionable, but a similar tragedy when performed in Rome was longer still, yet not without interest to the bystander.[8]

Although Adams is making no effort to present a drama to the reader, his diplomat sees official life in the capitol as a "prodigious charade" and Adams comments on it as a drama. The use of "charade" suggests Adams' primary interest in the idea or motive of the drama. To his diplomat, who knows that the idea of this American political drama has recurred throughout history, the movement of the play seems predictable—even machine-like. Here the possibility of recurrence suggested for the drama of Gould and Fisk becomes actuality. Indeed, it is the chief source of interest for the supposed spectator. Yet the predictability it makes possible is not the same as necessity. Scientifically they may be the same, but in Adams' work necessity always has an element of "must" or "have to" about it, not simply of "will" or "does." In "Men and Things in Washington" the actors still make choices, still struggle, and still bring about events, even though a diplomat and a historian may be able to predict what those events will be. With some exceptions this is the view which prevails in Adams' work up to 1876. Thus Adams does not seem to identify completely with the diplomat here.

The next important use of the dramatic analogy is in *Democracy* (1880) and *Esther* (1884), where Adams presents his material in semidramatic

[8] Henry Adams, "Men and Things in Washington," in *Nation*, IX (Nov. 25, 1869), 455.

form. Both novels are a series of dramatic scenes, emphasizing dialogue; both contain a primary conflict between individuals over a central idea or motive; and both make the dénouement the result of a choice by an individual. Yet though in form both resemble "The New York Gold Conspiracy," they differ in other respects both from it and from one another. For one thing, elements of the recurrent drama described in "Men and Things in Washington" appear in both novels. Adams' chief concern in *Democracy* is the belief of Americans that their democratic government is unique in history for its moral purity. Baron Jacobi's assertion that, actually, American democracy has stronger tendencies toward corruption than other governments and Mrs. Lee's decision that it is no different from other governments suggest that the drama of democracy is part of the recurrent political drama of history and therefore partially predictable. In *Esther* the note of recurrence is struck even more strongly. In the second section of the book the painting of St. Cecilia on the walls of the church suggests the recurrence in history of transitional periods when individuals are forced to choose between the old world and the new and suffer because of their choice. Thus Esther's particular drama is only the latest form of a recurrent human drama. Although her own choice is not predictable, that of the world is, because such dramas in the past have always had the same outcome. This problem of the importance of individual choice to historical change is another and more essential difference between the conceptions of the drama of history in the two novels. In *Democracy* America's political decline from purity to corruption, although predictable, seems to have been the result of choices by individuals not of the action of forces stronger than individuals.[9] In *Esther* the movement from one phase of thought to another is intrinsic in history itself. Individual choice still exists, but man in the mass is obliged to enter the new phase of thought. Both Strong and Wharton simply assume that the new world is coming into being.[10] Here, for the first time in Adams' work, predictable drama becomes determined drama.

The dramatic analogy appears in *Esther* in still another way. All the characters (except the minister) agree that the new church is like a stage or an opera house. They seem to imply that religion is essentially a state of mind (or feeling).[11] When the members of a congregation are in this state of mind the church service is a public and communal means of expressing it, but when this state of mind does not exist, the services

[9] Henry Adams, *Democracy: An American Novel* (New York: Henry Holt and Co., 1908), pp. 71–75.

[10] *Esther*, pp. 28–29, 192, 255.

[11] See HA to Mabel La Farge, Oct. 6, 1894, in Henry Adams, *Letters to a Niece and Prayer to the Virgin of Chartres*, with a niece's memories by Mabel La Farge (Boston: Houghton Mifflin Co., 1920), pp. 75–76.

become a mere spectacle, a show, and the church, a theater, as they are here. The terms suggest that the disappearance of genuine religious emotion has made the church and its services not simply human, but a cheap and tawdry form of the human because they pretend to be still religious. The terms also suggest, for the first time in Adams' use of the dramatic analogy, that the drama is a form of art and, therefore, of illusion. Here illusion is associated with the meretricious. Adams emphasizes this connotation by using the adjective "theatrical" throughout the book rather than "dramatic." By "theatrical" he means what he will mean eight years later in calling Gothic art " a little theatrical and false."[12]

Esther also introduces a new motive for drama and therefore a new type of drama. "Men and Things in Washington" concerned a political drama. "The New York Gold Conspiracy" was a drama in which economics collided with politics and lost, but Adams suggested that it might prove prophetic of a future drama that would be wholly economic. *Democracy* introduced a third type, the love drama, combined with the political drama. *Esther* contains the love drama but also introduces a fourth type, the religious drama. In addition, *Esther* also implies a third way of living life, or at least of looking at life, besides those suggested by the drama and the machine. When Hazard says in his sermon that "you are NOT . . . . You were and are and ever will be only a part of the supreme I AM,"[13] he is suggesting that what is real is not the human but the divine, which is both supernatural and superhuman. This suggests the possibility that history is essentially the result neither of human effort nor of the interaction of natural forces but of the will of a deity. In this view history would be neither a drama nor a mechanical process but a sacrament, a continuous expression of the divine.

Adams was at work on his *The History of the United States During the Administrations of Jefferson and Madison* while he was writing *Esther*. Nine months after the novel was published,[14] he wrote the historian Francis Parkman that two volumes had already been written. He goes on to tell what he himself had learned from his work. "The more I write," he says,

> the more confident I feel that before long a new school of history will rise which will leave us antiquated. Democracy is the only subject for history. I am satisfied that the purely mechanical development of the human mind in society must appear in a great democracy so clearly, for want of disturbing elements, that in another generation psychology, physiology, and history will join in proving man to have as fixed and necessary development as that of a tree; and almost as unconscious.[15]

[12] HA to Brooks Adams, Sept. 8, 1895, in Ford (1892–1918), p. 80.
[13] *Esther*, p. 8.   [14] Cater, p. 128 n. 2.
[15] HA to Francis Parkman, Dec. 21, 1884, in *ibid.*, p. 134.

In *Esther* the movement of history is the movement of thought, a succession of new worlds based upon new conceptions of reality. The semidramatic form of the novel seems to overlie a deterministic view of history. In this letter to Parkman the determinism is explicit and emphatic. Individuals still choose, but the minds of men in the mass have a fixed and necessary pattern of development which they follow, not by choice, but mechanically and largely unconsciously. The mechanical analogy triumphs therefore. The key to human existence is neither God and His Providence, nor man and his will, but nature and her laws; history is to be understood neither as a sacrament nor a drama, but a machine. The dramatic analogy is only a form of expression, a kind of historical rhetoric—finally, an illusion.

Yet Adams' letter also makes it clear that Parkman is not to expect Adams' own history to be written from this new perspective. That is to be the task of the future, of the "new school . . . which will leave us antiquated." Adams identifies himself with an older school, apparently those who deal with history in terms of the dramatic analogy. In the main, his *History* (which appeared in completed form in 1891, seven years after *Esther* and this letter) bears out this contention. There is much in it that suggests even the simple drama of "The New York Gold Conspiracy." He writes that "all the actors in the drama" of Jefferson's commercial struggle with England and France "assembled, to play another act in a tragi-comedy of increasing interest." Later, he says that "the time had come when each actor" in Aaron Burr's plot "must take his place, and must receive orders as to the *rôle* he was to play."[16] Often such allusions introduce or conclude full-scale dramatic narrations of particular historical events. A striking example of this is the account of the Burr-Hamilton duel. Adams' method naturally lends itself to such treatment. As earlier in *Gallatin*, so here he presents documents interspersed by narration. The documents, of course, emerged from a living human context, and extensive use of them naturally tends to emphasize that context. It also leads to discussing them and history in terms of the conflicts between men, whether as individuals or groups. While such discussion often moves out of narration and into analysis, just as often it moves in the other direction and becomes drama.[17]

Another use of drama, involving content rather than method, is introduced in chapter 6 of the first volume ("American Ideals"). There

[16] *Ibid. The History*, III, 123, 252.

[17] For the dramatic qualities of *The History*, see especially William Jordy, *Henry Adams: Scientific Historian* (New Haven: Yale University Press, 1952), pp. 51–53, 64. Also, Stevenson, *Henry Adams: A Biography*, pp. 239, 245, 248, and Ernest Samuels, *Henry Adams: The Middle Years* (Cambridge, Mass.: Harvard University Press, 1958), pp. 399–405.

Adams comments on the paradox "—that the hard, practical, money-getting American democrat . . . was in truth living in a world of dream, and acting a drama more instinct with poetry than all the avatars of the East." This dream was the motive which incited men to come to America and to continue struggling when they got here. It was, Adams says, the American's "whole existence"; [18] he lived life as if it were a drama. The use of "dream" for the idea that motivates this drama revives the suggestion of make-believe associated with the drama in *Esther*. But here there is no connotation of the false or meretricious about the suggestion. The church services in *Esther* were false because they perpetuated a form from the past that had lost its vitality. American life in 1800 was make-believe for the opposite reason: it was lived in terms of a future form that was not yet an actuality. Whereas in *Esther* the ideal is dead, in *The History* it is the source of life. Adams' comparison of the American drama to that which an Eastern avatar lives suggests his own evaluation of how high the American aspired. An avatar believes himself the incarnation of a god and lives as if he were one. The American also lived remote from every-day realities and with great intensity, but he did so not as a contemplative but as a man trying to make earthly existence assume the shape of the ideal. In the case of the avatar the ideal is superhuman and supernatural. In the case of the American it was natural and human, and the result aspired to was a kind of earthly Paradise. Yet Adams sees nothing inferior in this secularity. He says that the American drama was "more instinct with poetry"—that is, more ideal, more beautiful, more imaginative—than that of the avatar.

In electing Thomas Jefferson, chief spokesman of the dream, as President in 1800 Americans signified that they wished the national dream to guide their political destiny. By the end of Madison's second administration this wish seems to Adams to have been on the way to being realized. As a dramatic historian he frequently suggests that particular events in this realization were the result of individual actions. His account of the Louisiana Purchase, for example, suggests that Jefferson, motivated by the practical aspect of the dream, effectively influenced the course of history. His criticism of Jefferson for betraying his principles in the negotiations leading to the purchase is also part of the dramatic view. Individuals can be so criticized if human actions influence history and if such actions are the expression of free and responsible men. If individuals do not influence history, such criticism is largely irrelevant except for personal relationships; if individuals are not free, it is unfair as well as irrelevant. But if they are both free and effectual, morality is not only relevant, it is of crucial importance for history, and moral criticism is a primary responsibility of the historian.

[18] *The History*, I, 172, 174.

In the letter to Parkman, Adams expresses his belief that history is not a drama but a mechanical process. In *The History* that belief also appears. Individuals in society may make choices, but society is "obliged" to seek new levels. History forces man to move in a certain direction and ultimately even dissenters from the movement help it along. Adams' problem is how to reconcile the largely dramatic form of his work with this deterministic philosophy. In *Mont-Saint-Michel and Chartres* he will do so by keeping the reader constantly aware that the drama he is presenting is as much an illusion as a play on a stage. In *The History* he does not do this. Often he can ignore the problem, partly because determinism is specifically mentioned only occasionally, partly because he believes that individual choices at odds with the movement of history can, for a time, affect that movement. When, for example, Napoleon's coup d'état "forced both France and England back on their steps," [19] the drama of history momentarily became actual drama.

Dramatic method and deterministic theory are, however, brought together at times. Sometimes a dramatic narration of events is followed by philosophic comment. At other times, there is a philosophic confrontation of the two views of history. The first way leads eventually to the technique used in *Chartres*. The most ambitious example of the second appears in the final chapter of *The History*. Adams begins by drawing a distinction. The dramatic view of history, he says, is concerned with the human side of history, that which appeals to dramatists and poets; it emphasizes the highest achievements and the most dramatic moments of the most brilliant civilizations. Such achievements are produced by individuals, and the concern of the dramatic historian, both in art and history, is with the individual, not the society. He is especially concerned with the hero, whom he considers a source of power, not simply an expression of the force of society. In this view, the hero is far more important than his society, which exists only to produce him and lives or dies in his success or failure. War is the condition which defines the hero; it is also his natural field of action. The scientific view of history, in contrast, is concerned with those aspects of history which interest the scientist. His principal interest is in finding general laws; in history he is concerned with the laws of human development. His object of study is that in history which lends itself best to this aim and to the scientific method: society as a whole. To him, the individual is important only as a social type. Moreover, his concern with society is not with its rare and exceptional moments, but with the commonplace, everyday lives of the mass of the people. [20]

Here the lines are clearly drawn. Dramatic history culminates in the hero in action; scientific history, in the operation of general laws. Which

[19] *Ibid.*, IV, 302, 300. See also III, 80; IV, 339.
[20] *Ibid.*, IX, 222–225.

view has the most validity is suggested when Adams says, "Should history ever become a true science, it must expect to establish its laws, not from the complicated story of rival European nationalities, but from the methodical evolution of a great democracy."[21] It is the scientific view which is the most valid. Yet scientific history was impossible until American democracy came into existence, for only through study of a society large enough to be representative of mankind, peaceful and stable enough to permit uninterrupted development, and uniform enough for the individual to be important primarily as a social type can general laws be discovered. For societies like those of Europe, composed of small nations constantly at war, where the systems are impermanent and conditions exaggerate the prominence of individuals, scientific history is not only inappropriate but impossible. In America the conditions of life make it possible and therefore both more appropriate and more valid than dramatic history.

Adams' own history is predominantly dramatic because, as he explains, the stress of European pressures forced the United States before 1815 into behaving like a part of European society.[22] In 1815, however, "a new episode in American history began. . . . New subjects demanded new treatment, no longer dramatic but steadily tending to become scientific."[23] The History is, therefore, appropriate to the time with which it is concerned, even though it lacks the validity that will be possible when history can be studied as a mechanical evolution rather than a drama.

In 1891, the same year in which the last volumes of The History were published, Adams wrote the poem "Buddha and Brahma." In it the narrator, an Indian rajah, contrasts the merits of two kinds of religious life, his own way and that of his friend Buddha. "Gautama's way is best," he says—to give up ordinary life and devote all one's energies to attaining union with the divine. But the Rajah could not find a way out of the world as Buddha did, and so has taken up the duties of his station and remained a Brahmin. Behind this life in the world, however, he, too, lives a life devoted to the divine. To his son he explains that

> . . . we, who cannot fly the world, must seek
> To live two separate lives; one, in the world
> Which we must ever seem to treat as real;
> The other in ourselves, behind a veil
> Not to be raised without disturbing both.[24]

In such a world the dramatic analogy is as invalid as it is in a world where only natural forces exist. Human action is "drama" but merely in the sense that it is make-believe, mere play-acting. In reality, history is a sacrament, the continuous expression of the will of Brahma. Here, as in

[21] Ibid., IX, 222.   [22] Ibid., IX, 220.   [23] Ibid., IX, 241.
[24] Henry Adams, "Buddha and Brahma," Yale Review, V (N.S.) (October, 1915), 82–89.

The History, Adams, who seems to speak through the Rajah, turns away from the dramatic view toward one which sees history as the product of superhuman forces. But now he presents this reality as divine rather than natural; for the only time in his work, life and history are presented as a sacrament. (This is one of the few places in all his work where religion is treated as having any validity whatsoever.) Nevertheless, the poem is like *The History* in its effort to find a system of thought which will adequately embody Adams' steadily growing sense that, ultimately, reality is non-human and nondramatic.

A Machine to Counter Chaos

Between "The New York Gold Conspiracy" and "Buddha and Brahma" there has been a steady erosion of Adams' always limited belief that history is a drama of human wills struggling over ideas and a correspondingly steady increase in his belief that history is a mechanical evolution of forces greater than man which his thoughts and actions express rather than initiate or control. Adams' effort to find a system of thought which will adequately embody this sense of history eventually leads him to formulate his dynamic theory of history. Yet by the time he does so he has ceased to believe that history is a mechanical process and come to view it as a meaningless chaos of those forces greater than man which control his movement. His theory, instead of expressing that chaos, represents a human rebellion against reality, intended to help man both to understand it and to exert as much control as he can over it. The theory is a "machine" in Adams' figurative use of the term, a human contrivance intended to do work. The first mention of Adams' belief that modern man needed such a theory appears in "The Tendency of History," his 1894 presidential letter to the American Historical Association.[25] Written to prepare the way for his brother Brooks' philosophy of history in *The Law of Civilization and Decay*, it proved also to be a harbinger of his own theory,[26] which is present by implication in *Mont-Saint-Michel and Chartres* and systematically formulated at the end of *The Education of Henry Adams*.

Assuming that nature is reality and man a part of nature, the theory gives an account of the deterministic relationship between them. In this

[25] Henry Adams, "The Tendency of History," in *The Degradation of the Democratic Dogma*, with an introduction by Brooks Adams (New York: The Macmillan Co., 1919), pp. 125–133.

[26] Ernest Samuels, *Henry Adams: The Major Phase* (Cambridge, Mass.: Harvard University Press, 1964), pp. 144, 344. Brooks Adams, "The Heritage of Henry Adams," in *The Degradation of the Democratic Dogma* (New York: The Macmillan Co., 1919), pp. 96–97.

view, the drama of history is illusion. This does not mean that history cannot be written as drama, but it does mean that the drama cannot validly be presented as history itself. In *Mont-Saint-Michel and Chartres* Adams preserves this balance. He never lets the reader forget that the drama of medieval life is, like all dramas, finally make-believe, that the reality is "Power, or its equivalent in exchange." [27] But medieval man at his best, like the American of 1800, struggled for power not directly but by attempting to realize an ideal, and thereby made of his life a drama. So men at their best always do, Adams believes. Indeed, what makes a multitude of individuals a society rather than a crowd, he believes, is a commonly held ideal. While such an ideal is always a fiction and the life it determines always make-believe, to the extent that it deviates from the direct pursuit of power, it is men's ability to believe in such fictions that enables them to act together as part of a group having a collective identity and pursuing collective goals. When belief in such an ideal declines, a society loses identity and direction as it disintegrates into a heterogeneous mass of individuals pursuing their own private interests and hence acting at cross purposes. Ultimately, since the power of any fiction is limited in space and time, such disintegration is inevitable. [28]

This theory of fictions first appears in *Mont-Saint-Michel and Chartres*. But a concern with the relationship between ideas and reality has been central to Adams' work from the beginning. More specifically, from his first book—*The Life of Albert Gallatin*—on, some aspects of this theory appear in every one of his major works. In each a specific, widely held fiction (or set of fictions) is shown to be an illusion. [29] What *Chartres* does is to present the theme as it appears in its final formulation in the dynamic theory and to make the drama the definitive image for that state of illusion in which the best and most human of human beings live.

[27] *Chartres*, p. 224.

[28] Adams' theory of the nature and importance of fictions appears in summary form in two brief quotations from other writers. The first appears in Edward Allan Chalfant, "Henry Adams and History" (Ph.D. dissertation, University of Pennsylvania, 1954), p. 209. Chalfant notes that in Adams' copy of Henry Maudsley's *Body and Will* (New York: D. Appleton and Co., 1894), he "scored the margin opposite the lines: '. . . it is plainly necessary for mankind to have its ideal, if it is to make progress; when it has lost the imagination of a state of perfection which never is but always is to be, it will have lost the impulse of evolution and have entered the path of its decline'" [p. 186, of 1884 ed.]. The second quotation describes that decline. It is from Gustave Le Bon and appears in Henry Adams, "A Letter to American Teachers of History," in *The Degradation of the Democratic Dogma*, with an introduction by Brooks Adams (New York: The Macmillan Co., 1919), p. 252.

[29] George Hochfield, *Henry Adams: An Introduction and Interpretation* (New York: Holt, Rinehart and Winston, Inc., 1962), focuses upon the importance of ideals in Adams' life and work in his excellent book. See especially p. 10.

Sometimes this image is associated with another, that of the child. According to the dynamic theory, it is the child who believes in ideals and in unity. As early as *Gallatin*, however, Adams says that in later life Gallatin had "outgrown the Jeffersonian dogmas." In *Democracy*, after listening to Ratcliffe argue that George Washington would have had to be less moral to win a modern election, Mrs. Lee asks herself, "In spite of Mr. Ratcliffe, is it not better to be a child and to cry for the moon and stars?"[30] In both cases belief in ideas or principles and therefore in life as a drama is associated with youth, whereas age and experience bring disillusionment and disbelief. In *Chartres* this contrast becomes the principal device through which Adams maintains that balance which must be kept between the dramatic analogy and reality if dramatic history is to be valid.

In the final chapter of *Chartres*, the old man shows the child beginning to grow up. Discussing St. Thomas Aquinas' theology, Adams shows medieval man turning to a mechanical view of life and history while still asserting a belief in free will and still defining the new view in terms of the medieval religious dream. Adams begins by changing Thomas' (and Aristotle's) "prime mover" to a "prime motor." This motor or machine is a simple and primitive form of the dynamo, Adams' symbol for the old man's twentieth-century world. According to *The Education*, Adams first discovered the dynamo in 1893 at the Chicago World's Fair and first felt it as a symbol of infinite energy (what Thomas called God) in 1900 at the Paris Exposition.[31] In his correspondence, he had already occasionally found it a useful image for tremendous force.[32] In *Chartres*, he uses it as a symbol of infinite energy, or God. He also says of Thomas' view of free will, crucial for the dramatic analogy, that it "seems to differ little, and unwillingly, from a system of dynamics as modern as the dynamo." The significance of these comparisons is made explicit when Adams explains that in Thomas' thought "by the term God, is meant a prime motor which supplies all energy to the universe, and acts directly on man as well as on all other creatures, moving him as a *mechanical motor* might do."[33] Nature is a mechanical system whose motive power is provided by God. Man is a part of this system, and thus his movement too is completely a mechanical process. Thus religious pantheism, as Adams calls Thomas'

[30] Henry Adams, *The Life of Albert Gallatin* (Philadelphia: J. P. Lippincott and Co., 1879), p. 560. *Democracy*, p. 144.

[31] Henry Adams, *The Education of Henry Adams*, with an introduction by James Truslow Adams, The Modern Library (New York: Random House, Inc., 1931), pp. 342, 380. But cf., Louise Fant Fuller, "Henry Adams: Pilgrim to World's Fairs," in *Tennessee Studies in Literature*, IX (1964), esp. 8.

[32] E.g., HA to Elizabeth Cameron, Feb. 18, 1901, in Ford (1892–1918), p. 317.

[33] *Chartres*, p. 368. The italics are added.

doctrines, denies man's free will—and the dramatic analogy—as much as scientific determinism does.

In this respect Thomas' system was a medieval precursor both of the unformulated scientific system implied in *The History* and of the dynamic theory of history. In another respect, however, Thomas' system and the theory—as it appears in *Chartres* and *The Education*—are antithetical. Both must treat unity as real in order to exist. But for Thomas that treatment is based upon a conviction—and an attempt to prove—that reality *is* unity; for Adams unity is only a necessary fiction. Before the twentieth century, Adams believes, belief in unity characterized both theology and science. But when, in the twentieth century, "unity turned itself into complexity, multiplicity, variety, and even contradiction,"[34] a scientific universe of harmonious laws began to seem as much an illusion, a reflection of man's desire to believe in unity, as a religious universe expressing the unity of God. The mechanical analogy, too (whether religious or scientific), with its assumption of sequence in history, began to seem as fictitious as the dramatic analogy. This discovery of the chaos underlying the unity asserted by both the mechanical and dramatic analogies constitutes the ultimate education of Henry Adams in *The Education*.

Both the machine and the drama figure prominently in the book. Adams sees twentieth-century man as increasingly dominated by his machines: "The new American . . . [is] the child of steam and the brother of the dynamo . . . ; a product of so much mechanical power, and bearing no distinctive marks but that of its pressure." Similarly, America's choice in 1893 of a single gold standard represents the acceptance of an economic system which will be "centralizing, and mechanical"—and lead finally to chaos. But if modern men as victims of their machines are moving toward chaos, men as actors in the drama of life have always moved upon a thin crust over chaos. In the climactic passage of the book, Adams describes the "sum and term of education" as it came to him during his sister's death.

> For the first time, the stage-scenery of the senses collapsed; the human mind felt itself stripped naked, vibrating in a void of shapeless energies. . . . Society became fantastic, a vision of pantomime with a mechanical motion; and its so-called thought merged in the mere sense of life, and pleasure in the sense.[35]

Here, the dramatic analogy is shown to be an illusion created by the senses and hence is completely stripped of all validity as a means of understanding reality. What Adams seems to mean by "a vision of pantomime with a mechanical motion" is that, when reality did not completely dissolve into

---

[34] *Ibid.*, p. 375.
[35] *The Education*, pp. 466, 344, 287, 288.

chaos, it seemed mechanical. The suggestion is that the mechanical analogy is a halfway house between the drama and chaos, more valid than the former, less so than the latter.

This suggestion is the key to Adams' eventual rebellion against the chaos which his sister's death revealed to him. After 1890, when he resumes the story of his life in *The Education*, he presents himself as struggling to formulate rationally "the sum and term of education" which her death had taught him. Eventually he decides that "Chaos [is] the law of nature; Order [is] the dream of man."[36] The word "dream" ties this formulation to the dramatic analogy, for "dream," as used in the chapter on "American Ideals" in *The History*, is synonymous with "idea," "principle," "convention," and "fiction" in being a general term for the motive of a human drama. In *The Education* the variety of human motives and fictions mentioned in *Chartres* is reduced to one basic and essential motive, of which all others are but expressions: the ultimate dream of man is that reality is unity; the ultimate drama is man's attempt to make the multiplicity of reality conform to that dream. But since the dream is an illusion, the drama must be always a tragedy. This total rejection of the validity of the dramatic analogy should logically have been accompanied by total submission to chaos. But while Adams accepts the reality of chaos intellectually, emotionally he rebels and then formulates this rebellion in intellectual terms as his dynamic theory of history.[37] In doing so he does not completely return to illusion by inventing a dramatic theory but compromises by viewing history as a mechanical process.

The assumption of sequence is the foundation of this theory. Its pattern of movement is derived from his observation that "the older the mind, the older its complexities, and the further it looks, the more it sees, until even the stars resolve themselves into multiples; yet the child will always see but one." The movement between the child's perception of unity and the old man's perception of multiplicity which Adams could observe in his own life became, when transferred to Everyman, the basis for a philosophy of history. Next he found a mode of perceiving reality which enabled him to express the movement from unity to multiplicity as a mechanical process. He says that in 1902, though he "never knew why . . . , he began to mimic Faraday's trick of seeing lines of force all about him, where he had always seen lines of will." Seeing lines of will leads naturally to viewing life in terms of the dramatic analogy. Seeing lines of force leads naturally to the mechanical analogy: "By this path, the mind stepped into the mechanical theory of the universe before knowing it." Again, as in the case of his sister's death, experience leads to a view of reality. But there, what was an unsought

[36] *Ibid.*, p. 451.   [37] See critical note 63.

experience actually plunged him into reality: "For the first time in his life, Mont Blanc for a moment looked to him what it was—a chaos of anarchic and purposeless forces." Here, perceiving lines of force is not perceiving reality but only a "trick" of perspective, while the lines of force themselves are "phantoms." [38] Thus the mechanical theory is a falsification of reality. Yet it serves a useful and valid purpose: it takes Adams out of the dramatic world of conflicting human wills into the abstract, nonhuman world of scientific force. In that world man and nature are two magnets determining lines of force, the relationship between them being one of greater and lesser strength. Nature, the stronger, gives direction; man, the weaker, automatically follows that direction. Here Adams had the mechanical explanation he needed for the change from unity to multiplicity. Now he was able to construct his dynamic theory of history, which views history not as chaos but as a mechanical process.

This mechanical movement explains the dramas of history. As man moves along the lines of attractive force provided by nature, he expresses his sense of reality at any given moment in terms of some mental unity, a "fiction" or "ideal." The dramas of history are man's efforts to shape reality to conform to those ideals. The great periods of dramas were the great periods of unity, those of instinct and religion. [39] Since they ended, both fictions and their symbolic expressions have lent themselves increasingly less to dramatic conception or treatment, especially when they followed the main movement of history toward an increasing emphasis on science. Because science has generally retained the human belief in unity, this emphasis has led to mechanical views of reality and nonhuman symbols. Adams' own theory is a mechanical one; its symbolic expression for the twentieth century is the dynamo. This modern symbol evokes in him the same desire to pray that symbols of infinite energy have always evoked in men, but it offers little for the dramatic imagination to feed on.

The importance and meaning of the dynamo changes radically between the two historical essays. Its most important use in Adams' work is in "The Rule of Phase Applied to History." The climactic image of that

---

[38] *The Education*, pp. 398–399, 426, 427, 289, 427.

[39] There is a difference in the three major versions of the theory in the periods into which Adams divides history. In *The Education* he is much less specific about their number and dating. The early period is religious; the modern period is scientific and extended from 1400 or 1500 to (apparently) 1900 (or perhaps even later, since Adams compares what happened in 1900 with what happened in 300 and does not consider the latter the beginning of a new period. See pp. 493–494, 482). In "The Rule" and "A Letter" the division between instinct and reason which had appeared in *Chartres* (and as religion and science in *The Education*) becomes a division into the period of instinct and the period of thought. Now religion is viewed as a part of the period of thought, though there is a very strong survival in it of instinct ("A Letter," p. 229).

essay is "the figure of nature's power as an infinitely powerful dynamo, attracting or inducing a current of human thought according to the usual electric law of squares." Here the last chapter of *Chartres* is brought up to date as St. Thomas' "prime motor" becomes a twentieth-century dynamo. In both cases the symbol stands for ultimate reality and suggests that the movement of man's thought is completely involuntary and mechanical. In "A Letter to American Teachers of History" its role is much diminished. "Very unwillingly," Adams writes, "can [the modern physicist] admit Reason to be an energy at all; at the utmost, he can hardly allow it to be more than a passive instrument of a physico-chemical energy called Will . . . ; a dynamo, mysteriously converting one form of energy into a lower." Here the dynamo has become a symbol for human reason considered to be a passive mechanism wholly moved by some other, greater force. What has happened to the symbol is that Adams, remembering that it takes force to make a dynamo move, has now asked what that force is. To Thomas Aquinas, as Adams interprets him in *Chartres*, the question would have been meaningless, for Thomas' God was a self-generating machine. By implication, therefore, Adams rejects Thomas' image. But he retains Thomas' belief in the unity of energy. Thomas believed this unity derived from a spiritual cause he called God; Adams describes it in "A Letter" as deriving from "a physico-chemical energy" he calls "Will," by which he means "nature's energy." This Will is not a fixed cause; but it is a single and continuous force. Adams infers its existence from the single direction in which not only human history but all nature is moving according to the second law of thermodynamics: to him, unity of direction, however great the multiplicity of force, means unity of energy. The law's assertion that "all nature's energies were slowly converting themselves into [unusable] heat"[40] means that the movement of nature's forces is not chaotic but a mechanical process of which man is a part.

In "The Rule" Adams had said that ultimate reality was unknowable, that the mind can never "reach anything but a different reflection of its own features." In "A Letter" he returns to the assertion of *Chartres* and *The Education* that it can be known. But now the twentieth century no longer seems to him to be approaching an awareness that reality is chaos. Instead it is becoming increasingly committed to the second law of thermodynamics—and therefore to the mechanical analogy—as the key to reality and to history. Adams himself seems to find this convenient law, which he says "is very rapidly becoming a dogma of absolute Truth,"

[40] Henry Adams, "The Rule of Phase Applied to History," *The Degradation of the Democratic Dogma*, with an introduction by Brooks Adams (New York: The Macmillan Co., 1919), p. 305.

the most believable unifying abstraction since he lost belief in "the great principle of democracy"[41] to which he had committed himself in 1863. The appeal of the second law lies not only in its widespread acceptance by scientists and its harmony with his own pessimistic interpretation of the movement of history, but especially in its incorporation of his belief in chaos into a mechanical theory of reality. The chaos of reality, simply by being in motion, is losing energy and eventually will be a motionless chaos, incapable of change. This law came closer than any principle Adams ever found to justifying that deliberate retreat from chaos to a mechanical theory which had initially been his own autobiography writ large.

Yet finally he asserted only the "convenience" of the second law as well as of the dynamic theory for himself and his age. He seems to have reserved final belief for his own formula in *The Education* that "Chaos [is] the law of nature; Order [is] the dream of man." In "The Rule," while denying that man can know reality, he notes that "one has learned to distrust logic, and to expect contradiction from nature, but we cannot easily prevent thought from behaving as though sequence were probable until the contrary becomes still more probable." Here the attraction of human thought toward unity (or sequence) is noted and, by implication, held to be suspect; nature is also said to be characterized by contradiction. But there is no direct assertion that nature is chaos or that man is on the verge of discovering it to be so. In "A Letter to American Teachers of History," a fuller statement appears. Adams notes that Lord Kelvin would not have insisted on the monism which his own law implied: "Almost in his last words he pathetically proclaimed that his life was a failure in its long effort to reduce his physical energies to a single term. Dying he left the unity, duality, or multiplicity of energies as much disputed as ever."[42]

A page and a half later Adams gives his own views the fullest and most explicit expression they receive after *The Education*:

> If the safety of society should seem now to depend on assuming a multiple cause, as of old on establishing the unity of creation, nothing obliges society to persist in its monist scheme . . . .
> So little essential is monism, that M. H. Poincaré lately startled the world by avowing that physicists used that formula only because all science would become impossible if they were not allowed to assume simple hypotheses . . . ;

[41] "A Letter," pp. 208, 230, 145. "The Rule," p. 295. "A Letter," pp. 260–261. HA to Charles Francis Adams, Jr., May 1, 1863, in Charles Francis Adams, Charles Francis Adams, Jr., and Henry Adams, *A Cycle of Adams Letters, 1861–1865*, ed. Worthington Chauncey Ford (2 vols.; Boston: Houghton Mifflin Co., 1920), I, 282.

[42] "The Rule," p. 271. "A Letter," pp. 238–239.

but this mental need of unity is also a weakness, which gives the degradationist an artificial and altogether unfair advantage. The convenience of unity is beyond question, and convenience overrides morals as well as money, when a vast majority of minds, educated or not, are invited to live in a complex of anarchical energies, with only the privilege of acting as chief anarchists. Bewildered and outraged they reject the image; but they find that of diffusion or degradation so simple and so natural as to satisfy every want. . . . Simplicity may not be evidence of truth, and unity is perhaps the most deceptive of all the innumerable illusions of mind; but both are primary instincts in man, and have an attraction on the mind akin to that of gravitation on matter. The idea of unity survives the idea of God or of Universe; it is innate and intuitive.[43]

Once again, as in *The Education*, belief in unity is said to be instinctive. Up to the present it has also been more convenient than anarchy. But just as degradation is triumphing over evolution, despite the latter's appeal to man's desire to believe in progress as well as unity,[44] so anarchy will triumph if it ever becomes more convenient. More significantly, Adams calls this "mental need of unity" a weakness and unity itself "perhaps the most deceptive of all the innumerable illusions of the mind." His own personal belief still seems to be that reality is "a complex of anarchical energies."[45] The monism of the dynamic theory is therefore not reality but only his own personal assertion of the "privilege of acting as chief anarchist" in such a world.

In his correspondence after "A Letter," some further relevant comments appear. In 1913 he wrote that "there is no such thing—I am confident,—as real consequence in history. The generations are actually separate and unconnected." A year later he said, "I suggest only that Kelvin's Second Law applies to all forms of energy alike. My quarrel with the physicists is that they are afraid to apply their own law."[46] Together, these statements seem contradictory. But in the light of all Adams has said previously, they seem to mean that after "A Letter" he continued to believe both that all change is chaotic and that for his own era the most tenable fiction of change as unity was that mechanical sequence described by the second law of thermodynamics.

A SPECTRUM OF DRAMATIC ROLES

In *The Life of George Cabot Lodge*, the one work Adams wrote (under his own name) after "A Letter," he does not develop the dynamic theory

[43] "A Letter," pp. 240–242.
[44] *Ibid.*, pp. 158–159, 160, 153.
[45] Henry Wasser, *The Scientific Thought of Henry Adams* (Thessaloniki: [n.p.], 1956), pp. 90–91, also analyzes this passage.
[46] HA to Charles Milnes Gaskell, Mar. 5, 1913, June 1, 1914, in Ford (1892–1918), pp. 610, 625–626.

further but instead returns to *The Education*'s sense of reality as chaos. Again he dislikes it, but now, instead of rebelling against it by formulating a theory of reality, he concerns himself more directly with how best to live in such a world. He examines the kinds of lives men may lead, particularly the two ultimate and antithetical human lives, those of the Savior and the King and Judge. Thus in *Lodge* Adams has come full circle in his use of the drama and the machine as opposing symbols. Moving from faith in the dramatic analogy to faith in the mechanical analogy to faith in chaos, he moved back to willed assertion of the mechanical analogy (the dynamic theory). Here he returns to a similar position in regard to the dramatic analogy. Now, however, instead of creating a dramatic theory of history he asks what, in the make-believe world of the human drama, is the best role for man to play. Consideration of the antithetical roles in *Lodge* leads to a consideration of these roles as they appear in other works by Adams and to discussion of a few other roles he emphasizes, particularly that of the "eternal woman" and her lover.

That *Lodge* returns to *The Education* rather than continuing the dynamic theory does not mean that there is no connection between it and the late essays. Appropriately, since these essays are assertions of the mechanical analogy, there is no specific mention in either of them of the dramatic analogy. Nonetheless, in "A Letter" Adams makes an important restatement of his final formulation of the dramatic view of life and history. He says of the physicists who follow the second law of thermodynamics that "their terms commonly require that they should treat man as a creature habitually striving to attain imaginary ideals always contrary to law." [47] Whether the "law" here be the chaos of Adams' ultimate formula or the second law of thermodynamics makes no difference to the rest of the definition. The dramas which men try to live are always illusions, always at odds with the reality of nature.

The Life of George Cabot Lodge illustrates this definition. Structured, like most of Adams' works, in terms of antitheses, it rests finally upon a contrast between two character types, defined in terms of their ideas, the simple nature and the complex nature. [48] The contrast is closely related to that in *Chartres* between the child (especially St. Francis) and the old man. Lodge himself, the poet son of Senator Henry Cabot Lodge, is presented as a "simple . . . nature". His basic characteristic is that he never loses a boy's "instinct of unity with nature," but "from first to last . . . identifie[s] himself with the energies of nature." In *Chartres* the uncle does not describe the usual medieval sense of nature, but he characterizes St. Francis, the epitome of the child, as seeing nature in God and feeling so completely at one with it that he preached to birds and addressed wolves

[47] "A Letter," pp. 249-250.   [48] *Lodge*, p. 12.

and fire as brothers. Lodge and other simple natures also believe that
nature is wholly good; Francis agreed. The simple nature concluded that
perversity, unintelligibility, immorality, and futility are found only in
man, and that civilization is at once a stimulus to the development of such
qualities in man and an expression of them. In this view man is "an
outrage;—society an artificial device for the distortion of truth;—civilization a wrong." [49] By contrast, the medieval child, though he believed in
man's sinfulness, also believed in the sacredness of the Church. St.
Francis, too, was somewhat less antagonistic to society and civilization
than the simple nature. He hated books and reason, but his attitude
toward the Church was not one of hostility but a combination of avowed
submission and actual willfulness. Yet the uncle's paraphrase of the
"Cantico del Sole" suggests that, in his view, both Francis' sense of
nature's perfect oneness with God and his acting out of an immediate
intuitive rapport with what he called God made a Church (and reason)
unnecessary. Also, his sense of nature's goodness and unity with God led
him to require his followers to leave society and civilization and hide
themselves in "absorption in nature." [50]

Lodge was devoted to poetry, especially that of Walt Whitman; to
mysticism, that of Buddha and "Liao Tze" (though he also praised
Christ); to idealistic philosophy, especially that of Schopenhauer and
Plato; [51] and to logic. Again, there are many parallels with the child. The
child cared for poetry and, though not usually a mystic, in his epitome as
St. Francis was both poet and mystic. Especially in the thirteenth century,
the child also loved logic. But this love signified the end of childhood,
for the essence of the child was that he felt rather than reasoned. St.
Francis, the embodiment of that essence, hated both philosophy and logic.
Yet even as a philosopher the medieval child was a "realist"—that is, an
idealist, like Lodge and other simple natures. "Realism, when pressed,
always led to pantheism," Adams says, and here the maturing child of the
scholastics harked back to his emotional beginnings. For St. Francis'
mystical sense of the unity of nature and God was "the simplest and most
childlike form of pantheism." [52] According to the definition of pantheism
in *Chartres*, Lodge's favorite authors were all pantheists, while Lodge's
own sense of the unity of God and nature made him, and other simple
natures, also pantheists.

The medieval child would, of course, have rejected all of these authors
as heretics. But the child was not an exclusively medieval phenomenon.
According to *Chartres* he dominated human history until the Renaissance,
and Adams' emphasis is upon the fundamental unity rather than diversity

---

[49] *Ibid.*, pp. 64, 11, 14, 12.   [50] *Chartres*, p. 330.
[51] *Lodge*, pp. 47–48, 121–122.   [52] *Chartres*, pp. 297, 339.

of his many manifestations.[53] Similarly, in *Lodge* Adams says of the simple nature's pantheism that "the Greek, or Oriental, or German philosophy changed the idea" of the Church—that "'there is no will save one, which is the Lord's'"—"only in order to merge the universe in man instead of merging man in the universe."[54] The "only" suggests that Adams saw no fundamental difference between the two views. The simple nature of *Lodge* seems to be fundamentally the same figure as the child described in *Chartres*.

There are also close parallels between the view of the modern world presented in *Lodge* and that which appears (or is implied) in *Chartres* (and also in *The Education* and the correspondence). The nineteenth-century world in which Lodge lived was not favorable to simple natures or to artists. Adams says of Boston that "the twenty-five years between 1873 and 1898 . . . [were] years of astonishing scientific and mechanical activity," just as they were in the world at large according to *Chartres* (and *The Education*, "The Rule," and "A Letter"). There was in Boston also the same "steady decline of literary and artistic intensity, and especially of the feeling for poetry," which, according to *Chartres* and the other later works, characterized the modern world. Such circumstances forced Lodge and anyone else who wished to be a poet into an attitude of revolt against society. This attitude proved ineffectual because society believed in itself so little that its only reaction was indifference. Adams says of Boston in *Lodge* that "society was not disposed to defend itself from criticism or attack. . . . [It] no longer seemed sincerely to believe in itself or anything else." In his correspondence he writes that all America is "a placid ocean of ignorance" or "a sort of flat fresh-water pond which absorbs silently, without reaction, anything which is thrown into it." Indeed, the world as a whole is "a sort of ocean which drowns poor artists."[55] This is not the twentieth-century chaos described in *The Education* but that torpid intellectual state described in the historical essays.

In the summer Lodge escaped from Boston to the family's vacation home at Nahant. There, next to the ocean, which he felt as "an echo or double of himself," he renewed his sense of identity with nature's energies and regained that sense of reality's simplicity and unity which Boston—characterized as a "complex" place—tended to destroy. Adams' account of this retreat suggests that he did not react to it as Lodge did and thus that he did not identify with the simple nature. Nahant, he says,

[53] Cf., *Ibid.*, e.g., pp. 340–341.

[54] *Lodge*, p. 179.

[55] *Ibid.*, pp. 6, 17. HA to Charles Milnes Gaskell, Dec. 17, 1908; HA to Royal Cortissoz, Sept. 20, 1911, in Ford (1892–1918), pp. 513, 572. HA to Edith Morton Eustis, Sept. 12, 1909, in Cater, p. 665.

seems to be actually the ocean itself. . . . There the winds and waves are alone really at home. . . . At the best of times . . . their restlessness carries a suggestion of change,—a warning of latent passion,—a threat of storm. One looks out forever to an infinite horizon of shoreless and shifting ocean.[56]

This description makes Nahant sound less like a place of simplicity and unity than a microcosm of that multiverse of anarchic force described by the kinetic theory of gases and imaged by the ocean in *The Education!*

Adams' attitude in *Lodge* seems to be that of what he calls a complex nature. Such a nature feels at home in complex Boston because his sense of reality, like that of Bostonians, is antithetical to the pantheism of Lodge and other simple natures. Adams explains that the Bostonian specifically had "for centuries . . . done little but wrestle with nature for a bare existence, and his foothold·was not so secure, nor had it been so easily acquired, nor was it so victoriously sufficient for his wants, as to make him care to invite the ice or the ocean once more to cover it or himself." The Bostonian and the complex nature agree with the old man in *Chartres* in viewing the relationship between man and nature as one of conflict rather than unity. To them the perversity, unintelligibility, immorality, and futility which the simple nature sees only in man and society seem equally characteristic of nature. Like the old man, too, they view civilization as the result of man's effort to diminish the influence of these characteristics of nature upon human life. Therefore, to them the attitude of revolt against civilization of Lodge and other poets "seemed unnatural and artificial." In nineteenth-century Europe, by contrast, the conditions of life were "less intimate" with nature than they were—or had been until recently—in Boston (or America in general) and therefore the simple nature's views "seem[ed] natural; indeed almost normal."[57] Adams' own opinion seems clear from the tone of his explanation of the Bostonian's view: he agrees with that view. Here not only *Chartres* but *The Education* and "A Letter" are at one with *Lodge*: all agree in viewing the relationship between man and nature as fundamentally hostile. In this respect the complex nature in *Lodge*, like the old man of *Chartres*, seems to speak for Henry Adams.

This inference gains support from the fact that in *The Education* Adams had already described Lodge's views as antithetical to his own. He says there that his party of Conservative Christian Anarchy "consisted rigorously of but two members, Adams and Bay Lodge. . . . While Adams . . . assumed to declare the principle, Bay Lodge necessarily denied both the assumption and the principle in order to assure its truth." The principle was Adams' ultimate view of reality, "that in the last synthesis, order and anarchy were one, but that the unity was chaos."[58] Lodge's

[56] *Lodge*, pp. 11, 12; 10–11.   [57] *Ibid.*, p. 16.
[58] *The Education*, p. 406.

denial apparently means that he asserted that in the last synthesis order and anarchy were one, and that the oneness was unity. This is the fundamental metaphysical principle of the simple nature; it is also the fundamental principle of the child.

Adams is less easily identified with the complex nature's belief that, since nature is hostile, men should co-operate in strengthening society and civilization. In later life he vacillated between a desire to accelerate the disintegration of society and a desire to retard it. His attitude here in *Lodge* will become clearer in the course of analysis.

As a simple nature, Lodge believed not only in the freedom of man's will but in its supremacy over all other forces in reality.[59] Thus he carried to its final expression the child's belief that life is actually a drama, a struggle between human wills over ideals. Appropriately, Lodge was not only a poet but a dramatist, whose "dramatic motive"—or imaginary ideal—"was always the same": the fundamental belief of the simple nature that ultimate reality is an "infinite Will which causes and maintains the universe" but exists only within its creation. This "Will is God; it is nature; it is all that is, but it is knowable only as ourself." "The Soul of Man [is thus] the Soul of God." Moreover, if reality is knowable only as an individual man, then its supreme expression is also man's supreme expression, the drama. The ultimate drama would be man's struggle to realize the highest ideal he is capable of conceiving. Since that ideal is God, the ultimate drama is a man's struggle to "raise the universe [i.e., the divine unity] in [himself] to its highest power" and thus become one with God. To realize this ideal an individual must sacrifice everything in his life, both within and without himself (including all human attachments) to the freedom and autonomy of the inner divinity until "man is slain, / And . . . God . . . / . . . lives!" At the end of *Herakles*, Lodge's last and most ambitious drama, his hero Herakles—a simple nature—has achieved this aim:

> I have prevailed by labors, and subdued
> All that man is below his utmost truth,
> His inmost virtue, his essential strength,
> His soul's transcendent, one pre-eminence!
> Yea, I have brought into the soul's dominion
> All that I am!—and in the Master's House
> There is no strength of all my mortal being
> That does not serve him now; there is no aim,
> There is no secret which He does not know;
> There is no will save one, which is the Lord's!

Herakles has wholly merged himself with the god within and thus become divine. His drama is called the drama of the "Savior" or "Sacrifice" or

[59] *Lodge*, p. 155.

"Pathfinder," for, though it is performed by an individual, it involves all mankind. All men carry the entire universe within themselves. Therefore, the Savior, whether Prometheus, Herakles, Buddha, or Christ, also "carries the whole of humanity in his person." In this he suggests Adams' account of the hero in the final chapter of *The History*. There Adams said that, "in the dramatic view of history, the hero deserved more to be studied than the community to which he belonged; in truth, he was the society, which existed only to produce him and to perish with him."[60] The Savior is the ultimate hero. He is all humanity, that "Greater Man" who, in becoming divine, raises "the whole of humanity within him" to "the divine level."

The motive for this drama is said to be the "oldest," "the most universal," and "the greatest in human experience." Yet motive and drama are valid only if there is, indeed, a creative principle which "is God . . . is nature . . . is all that is; but . . . is knowable only as ourself."[61] If any of these ideas are false, then motive and drama alike are invalid. Lodge, as a simple nature, believed in such unity and such a creative principle.[62] Adams, under the persona of the complex nature, did not. "The idea," he says of Lodge's motive, "is a part of the most primitive stock of religious and philosophical motives . . . but, in our modern conception of life, impossible to realize except as a form of insanity." This "modern conception of life" is the view of the complex nature—and of Henry Adams—that man's innate perception of reality as a divine unity—or even a universe— is a distortion of reality. Saviors are insane because they fail to realize that, like all men, they are anarchists in a multiverse where all forces are anarchic. "All Saviors were anarchists," Adams says, but adds that they were "Christian anarchists, tortured by the self-contradictions of their rôle." Like St. Francis in *Chartres*, they believed that the "inward voice"[63] was God and hence that they had no responsibility except to it and should accept no restraint except what it imposed. Adams and other complex natures, however, view Saviors (including St. Francis) as anarchists, acting in obedience not to a transcendental unity but to their own natures. In calling them "Christian anarchists" he seems to mean that the Savior's intention is to help mankind. The moral contradiction in his role arises in part from the cruelty involved in his necessary sacrifice of all human ties in order to make men divine.[64] An extreme example is Herakles' murder of his own children. But there is also a metaphysical contradiction in the

---

[60] *Ibid.*, pp. 109, 178, 109, 156, 110, 174, 179, 164, 165. *The History*, IX, 223.

[61] *Lodge*, pp. 165, 111, 164, 109.   [62] *Ibid.*, pp. 12, 47, etc.

[63] *Ibid.*, pp. 110, 110, 155.

[64] *Ibid.*, pp. 109–110, 169; HA to Elizabeth Cameron, Mar. 3, 1912, in Ford (1892–1918), p. 588.

role of the Savior. It arises from "the conception of a God sacrificing himself for a world of which he is himself a part," which Adams calls "a confusion of ideas,—a contradiction of terms."[65]

Finally, Saviors are said to be insane because, in order to "raise the universe [the divine Unity, the Soul or Will] in oneself to its highest power, its negative powers must be paralyzed or destroyed." The Savior must transcend all that is not unity, all multiplicity (including all human beings as individuals). The complex nature views this as a sacrifice not only of the Savior's humanity, but, since reality is multiplicity, of his sense of reality as well. "In reality," Adams says, "nothing was destroyed; only the Will—or what we now call Energy—was freed and perfected." The consequence of the Savior's attainment of divinity is a will developed to its maximum strength, freed from all social and rational control, and guided by a delusion of divinity which is actually the impulses of a nature completely divorced from reality. In a letter written in 1912 Adams cites a contemporary example of the Savior and describes the probable personal and social results of his aberration:

> I can not rid my mind of the idea that Theodore [Roosevelt] has read my *Life* of Bay [Lodge] and is doing *Herakles*. I can imagine no other explanation. He has risen above these safe human mediocrities. He looks on the insanity-process as part of the rôle. His first sacrifice is his own family. His friends come next. His followers come last. The asylum is the end.[66]

Herakles also contains a counter figure to the Savior: Creon, the "King and . . . Judge." His nature is implied in Adams' description of Herakles as "the Savior, not the Servant,—the creator, not the economist,—the source itself, not the conduit for 'these safe human mediocrities.'" Herakles severs himself from society and humanity in order to rise above men and merge with their source and creator. In so doing he himself becomes the creator and source and thereby raises all men to the divine level. Creon, "the man-of-the-world, the administrator, the humorist and sage," unites himself with his own society in order to become a conduit for the best that is in it. He tries, primarily through existing laws and institutions, to achieve and maintain justice and order. He would serve men as men, within the larger humanity of society. His life, too, is based upon ideals and, therefore, is also a drama and doomed to failure. Yet these ideals do not require an assertion of self but an acceptance of the traditional ideals of a human society. His drama is thus not one of increasing insanity but one of acting within the limits of the degree and kind of alienation from reality characteristic of his own society in order to keep it operating effectively. This is also true of his relationship to life in general.

[65] *Lodge*, p. 165.
[66] *Ibid.*, p. 110. HA to Elizabeth Cameron, Mar. 3, 1912, in Ford (1892–1918), p. 588.

Adams says of Creon that, at the end of his life, he "has accepted all the phases of life, and has reached the end, which he also accepts, whether as a fact or a phantasm,—whatever the world will,—but which has no more value to him than as being the end, neither comprehended nor comprehensible, but human." He accepts the processes of nature with the same completeness as the traditions of his society, and again tries to be as effective as possible within the externally imposed limitations. Such a character is a "complex" nature, and appealed so much to Adams that he wrote Lodge, "Of course Creon is my personal joy."[67]

The instinctive reaction of Creon to Herakles suggests Adams' own attitude toward the Savior: "Creon sees the hero, and admires him, but doubts what good will come of him to man. He lays down the law, as a King and a Judge must . . . . [His] reply to this 'estranged, rare man,' is that 'all men living are not ever free,' and that, if not pliant, they are broken." The Savior gains freedom by asserting the divine Will within him; the King and Judge finds it by submitting himself to the time and place in which he lives. Creon's view is one which pervades Adams' own work. Particularly relevant is his statement in a letter that "my rule is to conform. It is the only path of freedom."[68] Adams' choice between the two figures seems clear. But he never makes it explicit. At the end of the work he says that

> not only philosophers, but also, and particularly, society itself, for many thousands of years, have waged bloody wars over these two solutions of the problem . . . : but while neither solution has ever been universally accepted as convincing, that of Herakles has at least the advantage of being as old as the oldest, and as new as the newest philosophy,—as familiar as the drama of the Savior in all his innumerable forms. . . . Paradox for paradox, the only alternative—Creon's human solution—is on the whole rather more paradoxical, and certainly less logical, than the superhuman solution of Herakles.[69]

Perhaps Adams refuses to make a choice here because he wrote Lodge as a memorial biography at the request of his subject's parents.[70] In any case,

[67] Lodge, pp. 171, 168, 166–167. HA to George Cabot Lodge, Dec. 2, 1908, in Cater, p. 629.

[68] Lodge, p. 171. HA to Mabel La Farge [Oct. 12, 1905] in Letters to a Niece, p. 113.

[69] Lodge, p. 181. The contrast between paradox and logic here is a contrast between Adams and Lodge. Adams comments on Lodge's taste for logic; his own taste for paradox is exemplified throughout his work but especially in The Education. Adams' increasing interest in the King and Judge figure, the reasonable man, does not seem to have changed the low opinion of logic expressed in Chartres, where he contrasts it with the intellectual method of Francis Bacon (p. 331), and in The Education, where he calls it "the mirror of the mind" (p. 429) and also contrasts it, by implication, with the empirical method of Bacon (p. 484).

[70] HA to Elizabeth Cameron, Jan. 24, 1910, and May 29, 1910, in Ford (1892–1918), pp. 531, 543.

it seems clear, both from his comment to Lodge about Creon and from the letter in which he describes Theodore Roosevelt as a Savior figure, that his own hero is Creon.[71]

The contrast between these two figures is the more significant because the Savior and the King and Judge are the final and most extreme expression in Adams' books of a contrast in character types which recurs in his work from at least *Gallatin* on. Again and again Adams presents two individuals dedicated to the same ideal. One is so personally absorbed in the ideal that he is either unconcerned with making it socially viable, except perhaps by direct personal appeal to other individuals, or else is impractical in attempting to do so. The other is also dedicated to the ideal but thinks of its realization as a social—and often an institutional— enterprise in which he is only one of many participants. His sense of the ideal is often not so intense nor so intimate but he is usually more effective at making it socially viable.[72]

In the life of *Gallatin* and in *The History*, the dichotomy appears as the contrast between Jefferson and Gallatin. Jefferson is the absolute idealist who is at his best dealing with the ideal in its pure form but fails as a statesman (and even as an idealist) when he is put in the position of having to give the ideal practical embodiment through the machinery of society. He is particularly ineffectual against Napoleon, the incarnation of absolute opportunism, who though a hero to his people is portrayed by Adams as dedicated less to them or his country than to his own personal power. Gallatin is the practical idealist, dedicated to the same ideal as Jefferson, but primarily concerned with giving it social embodiment. It is he for whom Adams has the most respect and affection. In *Democracy* and *John Randolph* Adams' attitude is the same. In the former the principal conflict is between an aspirant to absolute idealism and another practitioner of absolute opportunism. Mrs. Lee wants to find in democracy an ideal to

[71] For other evidence, compare Adams' implied description of Creon (and the King and Judge) as an "economist" in *Lodge*, p. 168, with *The Education*, pp. x, 501, and HA to Barrett Wendell, May 18, 1910, in Cater, p. 683. But see also critical note 64.

[72] Charles Andrew Vandersee, "The Political Attitudes of Henry Adams" (Ph.D. dissertation, UCLA, 1964), portrays Adams as politically a consistent "conservative" (pp. 185, 226) and a "Federalist" (pp. 187, 189, 196)—emphasizing "commonsense" (pp. 131, 187, 196) and "practicality" (pp. 131, 175). His picture of Adams ideal, the "*practical* statesman" (p. 131), also appears in the description of "practical statesmanship" in Rule, "Irony in the Works of Henry Adams," pp. 168–171, and Jordy, *Henry Adams: Scientific Historian*, pp. 68–69. Robert M. Bunker, "The Idea of Failure in Henry Adams, Charles Sanders Pierce, and Mark Twain" (Ph.D. dissertation, University of New Mexico, 1955), esp. pp. 17–19, 35–36, 67, discerns an antithesis similar to my own in Adams' work but interprets it in the opposite way. He believes Adams is primarily sympathetic to what I call the impractical idealist and considers George Cabot Lodge, the "pure type of all Adams' heroes" (p. 17).

worship; Ratcliffe manipulates the ideal to gain personal power. The closest to a spokesman for democracy as the kind of ideal Mrs. Lee desires is Gore. But Gore's idealism, though articulate, is fraudulent, a mask for private ambition. When he fails to get what he wants from Ratcliffe, he maligns him, though he had earlier praised him, and leaves the scene. Mrs. Lee proves as ineffectual against Ratcliffe as Jefferson did against Napoleon. Only outside interference prevents her marrying him. Then she too flees, as Jefferson fled from responsibility when the embargo failed. But Adams does not condemn her, as he did Jefferson, because she has no official responsibility. She flees, as ultimately Jefferson did when his presidency was over, to the ideal in its pure form (in her case, to an image of the ideal, the fixity of the pole star), but her flight is a measure of the degree to which working democracy outrages the ideal upon which it is supposedly based. Adams has affection for Mrs. Lee—as he did not for a Jefferson he once characterized as "almost feminine" in some of his qualities—agrees with her decision about democracy as an ideal, and sympathizes with her flight—or with its symbolic significance at least. But primarily he identifies with Carrington, who in turn is identified with George Washington, an expression (here *and* in *The Education*) of the practical statesman or King and Judge figure at its best. Although Carrington knows far more than Mrs. Lee about the corruption in America and has no hope of being politically effective, unlike her, he does not abandon democracy but remains in its capital, practicing law and encouraging reform. In *Randolph* the narrator attacks a man who alternates between an impractical idealism pushed to the point of insanity and an indulgence of his emotions which also approaches insanity. In him the lack of self-knowledge in a Mrs. Lee—and possibly Gore—is pushed to an extreme. Such self-deceiving ambivalence looks forward to its ultimate expression in the Savior figure who murders his children in order to become God. In *Randolph* there is no pervasively important counter-figure to Randolph. Practical idealism is represented by the Adams family, however, and especially by John Quincy Adams.

In *Esther* and "Buddha and Brahma" the same dichotomy appears, but now Adams is concerned with religion and metaphysics rather than politics, and his attitude toward the two types of idealists has changed. In *Esther*, the minister Hazard, primarily a society and institutionally oriented idealist, is rejected because he serves an outmoded ideal. But there is another practical idealist, who serves the viable ideal in the book, George Strong, a scientist who wants to help make science—a co-operative enterprise—truer. Adams seems to identify more with him than with any one else in the book, though the identification in this case seems less specific than in any other of Adams' major works. Yet it is not Strong but

Esther, who is represented as knowing most by Adams and who claims his most respect and affection. And her relationship to the ideal is individual rather than social and through personal feeling rather than the intellect. In "Buddha and Brahma" the dichotomy is more central than in any other work by Adams until *Lodge*. Here he clearly identifies with the society-oriented figure, the Brahmin—literally a King and a Judge—has the most affection for him, and lets him make an eloquent plea for his way of realizing the ideal. Yet Adams seems to agree with his spokesman's assertion that Buddha's way of serving the ideal is best. Again, as in *Esther*, it is the individual who strives for the ideal outside of society and its institutions that realizes it most completely.

The discrepancy between Adams' attitude in these two sets of works is less great if one observes that when he is talking about politics he prefers the social idealist whereas when he is talking about religion, even though he continues to identify with the social idealist, he believes the individualistic idealist best realizes the ideal. In *Lodge* his attitude will become even simpler (though not so simple as it is in *Gallatin*). There, by having his two idealists define in radically different ways that *best* in human nature which both desire to stimulate and serve, he can have his social, practical idealist—far more than in *Gallatin*—know reality best, act in the best way, and be the character with whom he most identifies.

In *Chartres* the problem is once again more complex. In the third from the last chapter the individual idealist Abélard is pitted against the church-oriented William of Champeaux and St. Bernard. More than with any other figure in *Chartres* (or in *Esther* or "Buddha and Brahma") Adams identifies with Abélard, whose combination of philosophical nominalism and adoration of a woman is closest to his own position. He also likes Abélard better than the other two figures in this chapter, but his liking is limited by the knowledge that nominalism helped destroy medieval unity (and by his dislike of logic). But this contrast only prepares the way for the principal expression of the dichotomy in the book, the contrast in the last two chapters between St. Francis of Assisi and St. Thomas Aquinas. These two figures have previously been described as the final expressions in *Chartres* of its pervasive contrast between the child and the old man. George Cabot Lodge and the simple nature in *Lodge* have also been shown to have many similarities to the child and St. Francis, while the view of the narrator in *Lodge* (presumably Adams' view) is that of the complex nature and therefore much the same as the old man's. St. Francis in *Chartres* is also a Savior figure: "the nearest approach the Western world ever made to an oriental incarnation of the divine essence," the uncle says. In *Lodge* Adams dislikes the Savior but in *Chartres* he loves Francis more than any other figure except the Virgin. He also cares more for him than he does for Buddha in "Buddha and Brahma," even though Buddha appears in a poem which seemingly accepts the ideal to which both he and the Brahmin are committed, whereas the uncle in *Chartres* believes that Francis' ideal is an illusion. The key to this dilemma seems to be the fact that in *Chartres* the characters express the religious ideal of the Middle Ages as a whole in terms of the particular ideal of the twelfth century. St. Francis expressed the twelfth-century dedication to love as well as the medieval devotion to God, and therefore, unlike the Savior figures in *Lodge*, instead of losing his humanity in becoming "divine" he became "charity incarnate,"[73] the human epitome of man's highest attribute. The uncle calls him a reincarnation of Christ. In *Lodge*, Christ is described as having become an "estranged rare man," like all Saviors, through masculine self-assertion. In *Chartres*, however, the Christ of the twelfth century—and the other members of the Trinity—was the Virgin's child and wholly at one with her spirit of love and grace. Hence Adams loves the Christ reincarnated in St. Francis while he rejects the Christ of *Lodge*.

But, for all his love of Francis, the uncle cannot—because of his belief in anarchism—say of Francis what the Brahmin said of Buddha, that his "way is best." He does say that Francis "may . . . prove to have been [humanity's] ultimate expression," but this statement is not quite the same. Even an anarchist might see Francis as the supreme expression of man's Quixote-like role in the multiverse without seeing his way as best. Moreover, Adams makes a final decision dependent upon mankind's doubtful settling of the problem of what its collective goal is, or whether it even has one. He also acknowledges that, unlike Francis, who because he acted only for himself could "throw caution aside and trust implicitly in God"—even at the risk of suffering the fate of the children on crusade —"the Church, embracing all mankind, had no choice but to march with caution, seeking God by every possible means of intellect and study." He recognizes, too, that Francis' ability to absorb himself in the absolute was possible only for a few exceptional people, and that the rest of mankind "lived for the day, and needed [the] shelter and safety"[74] of a social institution. (Here, in muted form, the uncle shows the same awareness of society's needs and claims which the Brahmin had expressed.) Hence, while the uncle shows no sympathy for the Trinity or the Church when they come into opposition to the Virgin, and only a little more for William, Bernard, and the Church in their struggle with Abélard, he is more sympathic toward St. Thomas Aquinas.

[73] *Chartres*, p. 331. For St. Francis as a savior figure, see *Chartres*, p. 12. See also HA to Henry Osborn Taylor, May 7, 1901, in Cater, pp. 509–510.

[74] *Chartres*, pp. 340, 339, 342.

Thomas, like Francis, was an anarchist, but all men, according to *Chartres*, are anarchists in the sense that all are autonomous forces in an anarchic multiverse of force. The difference between the two men is a difference in the human faculty they believe should guide men's lives and the social consequences of that choice. The uncle notes that "the two poles of social and political philosophy seem necessarily to be organization or anarchy; man's intellect or the forces of nature."[75] If nature is chaos, following the forces of nature leads to anarchy. Organization requires intellect to create and preserve it. St. Francis, believing that he was obeying God's will, followed nature; the social consequences were anarchy. St. Thomas, also believing that he was obeying God's will—and also an anarchist[76]—used his intellect to create a rational image of the Church which became a powerful weapon in that institution's struggle to preserve its existence and integrity. Thus, like Gallatin, Thomas defined his dedication to his ideal in terms of a particular human society and its formal organization. He, too, sought to be the Servant, not the Savior. This fact is emphasized when the uncle says that he has chosen to talk about Thomas rather than some other theologian not out of personal choice but because the Church itself has chosen Thomas' thought as its greatest intellectual expression.[77] Adams does not identify with Thomas as much as he does with Abélard, nor feel for him the affection he does for Francis. He views the whole need for an intellectual expression of religion—which should be a matter of feeling, as it is in St. Francis—as a part of man's movement from youth to age and hence a sign of weakened strength. Yet man was not responsible for that change and Thomas filled society's need and demand for unity in the most vital way possible in the thirteenth century. In that role Adams treats him with admiration and respect as a "genius" and "a great artist."[78]

Neither Thomas nor Francis, however, is the principal figure in *Chartres*.[79] The book is about feeling and therefore its principal figure is a woman, the Virgin. Thomas excels in the masculine quality of reason, which at its highest creates not a community ruled by love but an institution ruled by justice. In *The Education of Henry Adams*, a masculine book focused upon the education of its male protagonist, Adams traces his protagonist's slow recognition and implementation of the value of rational organization in the midst of twentieth-century multiplicity. In the first part of the book Adams shows himself as a child rejecting the human and rational order of Boston and school and allying himself with the multiplicity of nature and "accidental education." Like St. Francis,

---

[75] *Ibid.*, p. 339.
[76] HA to Charles Milnes Gaskell, Dec. 20, 1904, in Ford (1892–1918), p. 444.
[77] *Chartres*, p. 344.   [78] *Ibid.*, pp. 345, 374.   [79] See critical note 65.

he follows the forces of nature. But this course, instead of resulting in an experience of universal order, leads him to the death of his sister and the realization that nature is chaos and man a part of that chaos. This realization affects both his theory of history and his code of action. He says of St. Francis in *The Education* that his "solution of historical riddles seemed the most satisfactory—or sufficient—ever offered." "Historical riddles" seem to be problems of tracing rational continuity—chains of cause and effect—in history. St. Francis did not believe in such continuities; he believed that the continuity of history, as of nature, was the continuous immediate presence of God in His creation. Therefore Francis "solved the whole problem by rejecting it altogether." Adams' knowledge of reality leads him to agree with Francis that history is rationally incoherent, but, unlike Francis, he knows that it is also "immoral" and "meaningless." [80] Francis' rejection of the problem left him with his faith in God; Adams' leaves him with chaos.

Nonetheless, Adams at first continues to follow nature, because it is reality, and eventually formulates his ideas as conservative Christian anarchy. As a conservative Christian anarchist, he has "no associate, no object, no faith, except the nature of nature itself" and "no motive or duty but to attain the end" [81]—the multiplicity of nature. Thus his sanity leads him initially to do deliberately what insane religious Saviors like St. Francis do unconsciously, encourage society's disintegrative movement toward anarchy—in Adams' case because he wants to destroy a society that is neither conservative nor Christian. In encouraging chaos Adams' role is as tortured as that of the Savior's in *Lodge*; both try to eliminate illusion from their lives (and those of all men) and make them wholly an expression of reality. But the Saviors sacrifice their sense of multiplicity to the innate human tendency to believe order more real, in the faith that doing so is both in accordance with truth and in the ultimate best interests of themselves and mankind. Adams sacrifices his desire for order to his discovery that multiplicity is real in the belief that he is acting in accordance with truth and perhaps with his own best interests. But he makes no claim to be acting in the best interests of mankind except insofar as he believes that no human state can be worse than the present.

Eventually, he rebels against multiplicity—though still acknowledging it to be reality—and against further progress into chaos—though still continuing to consider such progress inevitable. Still acting as a conservative Christian anarchist, he deliberately asserts his humanity and the human ideal of order, and undertakes to create a rational account of the whole of human experience, his dynamic theory of history. He does this basically

[80] *The Education*, pp. 85 (cf., p. 80), 367, 368, 301, 472.
[81] *Ibid.*, pp. 407, 406.

to satisfy "his own needs" but he also hopes to give young men of the twentieth century the understanding which will enable them to integrate the new forces discovered by science into the social order and thereby retard the movement of society toward chaos. As the Servant rather than the Savior, he is trying to serve the human ideal of order by helping to create the new man society is seeking in the final chapter of *The Education*. In "The Rule of Phase Applied to History" and "A Letter to American Teachers of History" this attempt to function in the role of intellectual King and Judge becomes even clearer as the dynamic theory ceases to be autobiography and avowedly becomes a means of creating order through serving a specific human institution, the university, and especially the department of history.[82]

This change—from destructive anarchy to constructive organization—in *The Education* parallels the shift from St. Francis to St. Thomas in *Chartres*. The difference is, first, that Adams understands, as medieval man did not, that the two means represented by the two men lead to antithetical goals (and that the medieval versions of both goals are impossible for men to achieve). A more important difference grows out of the fact that the destructiveness of Francis' anarchism was counterbalanced by the unifying power of the ideal of love he shared with his age. (Thus the twelfth-century Church accepted him, whereas even a hundred years later he "would have been burned."[83]) In the twentieth century, reason is all man has left to serve as a unifying force. In *The Education* and the historical essays, therefore, Adams is trying, by deliberately imposing a rational order upon his anarchism, to make it serve the one human institution which might attempt—albeit with little chance of success—to avert the impending disaster.

Thus Adams' ultimate role in *The Education* and the historical essays leads directly to his rejection of Herakles and acceptance of Creon in *Lodge*. The final appearance of the antithesis, however, is later, in a letter and an article. In 1915 Adams wrote to Henry Osborn Taylor about the latter's book, *Deliverance: the Freeing of the Spirit in the Ancient World* (1915). The book concerns "the various ways in which some of the wisest men of the Ancient World" reached "an adjustment between the instincts and faculties of human nature and the powers conceivably controlling its accomplishment and destiny."[84] Adams begins,

---

[82] HA to John Franklin Jameson, Mar. 20, 1909, in Cater, pp. 649–650. Cater, pp. 783–784. "A Letter," pp. 261–263, etc.

[83] *Chartres*, p. 336.

[84] From p. 1 of a new preface by Taylor to the 1933 edition of *Deliverance*, republished under the title, *Prophets, Poets, and Philosophers of the Ancient World* (New York: The Macmillan Co.).

Perhaps I ought to say first, that once, at the most trying crisis of my life, and of his—our old teacher in wisdom, Gurney, said to me that of all moral supports in trial only one was nearly sufficient. That was the Stoic. I cannot say that I have found it so, except in theory, but I am talking theory. Putting myself in that position I read your book.

You see at once what must follow—what did in fact follow. Of course all that goes before is futile except as failure; all that follows after is escape—flying the ring—by assuming an improbable other world. Logically the religious solution is inadmissible—pure hypothesis. It discards reason. I do not object to it on that account: as a working energy I prefer instinct to reason; but as you put it, the Augustinian adjustment seems to be only the Stoic, with a supernatural or hypothetical supplement nailed to it by violence. The religionists preached it, and called it Faith.

Therefore to me the effect is of ending there. The moral adjustment, as a story, ended with Marcus Aurelius. There you lead us with kind and sympathetic hands; but there, over the door to the religious labyrinth, you, like Lord Kelvin, write the word Failure. Faith, not Reason, goes beyond.

. . . . At the present moment, perhaps, the moral is somewhat pointed—to me decidedly peaked. If you are writing Failure over one door and Lord Kelvin over another [i.e., reason[85]], and the Germans over the third and last—that of energy without direction—I think I had better quit. I said so ten years ago, but I put it down to my personal equation then, and I cannot believe that you mean it now. Are we, then, to go back to Faith? If so, is it to be early Christian or Stoic?

The early Christian I take to have been abandoned long ago by the failure of Christ to reappear and judge the world. Whatever faith is to save us, it cannot be that. Is it, then, the Stoic?

. . . had I been the author [of the book], I . . . should very likely have labored damnably over the Buddhists and the Stoics. Marcus Aurelius would have been my type of highest human attainment. Even as it is, I would give a new cent to have a really good book on the Stoics . . . . I need badly to find one man in history to admire. I am in near peril of turning Christian, and rolling in the mud in an agony of human mortification. All these other fellows did it—why not I?[86]

Three adjustments are mentioned in this letter: the Stoic, the "early Christian," and "energy without direction." Stoicism is the control and direction of energy by reason. Specifically, Taylor describes it as a belief that men should live virtuously by rationally identifying their interests with those of the natural universe, which consists of matter permeated and ruled by a rational, material force.[87] The ethical essence of this position is that virtue consists in submission to reality and intelligent action in terms of that submission. In *Lodge* Adams notes that "step by step, like

[85] Cf., "A Letter," pp. 238–239.
[86] HA to Henry Osborn Taylor, Feb. 15, 1915, in Cater, pp. 768–769.
[87] Taylor, *Prophets*, pp. 174–177, 193–196.

a demonstration in geometry, the primitive man is forced into the attitude of submission to destiny or assertion of self." Adams views these two "contradictory conceptions of duty" [88] as the ultimate ethical alternatives. The King and Judge submits to destiny: Creon, for example, submitted both to nature and the society he lived in and sought to act as effectively as possible within those limitations. To Adams he was a "joy." Four years later he chose another King and Judge figure, the Stoic Roman Emperor Marcus Aurelius, as his type of highest human attainment.

Yet, though Stoicism is conducive to the King and Judge role, neither Creon nor the King and Judge figure in general is necessarily a Stoic. When Adams writes at the end of the letter that he is "in near peril of turning Christian," he is probably not saying that he is in peril either of choosing the role of Savior or of abandoning his preference for the King and Judge role. The "early Christian" mode of adjustment, he says in the letter, is the Stoic rational adjustment to a rational reality with an irrational supplement called faith "nailed to it by force." Its ethical attitude is still that of submission to a reality which is natural and rational, but now that reality is viewed as also having a supernatural and super-rational dimension. Insofar as submission is to both aspects of reality, this adjustment too can produce King and Judge figures. Creon could have been a Christian bishop or pope as well as a Stoic emperor.

Adams' sense of the possibility of becoming Christian as a "peril" and his desire for a book on the Stoics to offset the temptation parallels his assertion that the early Christian adjustment was "abandoned long ago by the failure of Christ to reappear and judge the world." [89] In his view the moral adjustment "ended with Marcus Aurelius" as the highest ex-pression not only of Stoicism but of humanity. He does not say, therefore, that Stoicism was a success; indeed, he specifically denies that it was or is, "except in theory." [90] But it was closer to success and, apparently, to reality than any other adjustment.

[88] *Lodge*, pp. 112, 115.

[89] See also HA to Elizabeth Cameron, Jan. 22, 1915, in Ford (1892–1918), p. 630: "Father Fay is no bore—far from it, but I think he has an idea that I want conversion, for he directs his talk much to me, and instructs me. Bless the genial sinner! He had best look out that I don't convert him, for his old church is really too childish for a hell like this year of grace." Note that the word "childish" is consonant with Adams' symbolism of the child and the old man.

[90] See also HA to Margaret Chanler, Sept. 9, 1909, in Ford (1892–1918), p. 523. After speaking of the possibly disastrous effect upon his relationship with the Lodge family of the death of George Cabot Lodge, Adams says, "Well! being a poor bit of materialised *Energetik*, I have no resource but the old one, taught by one's brothers in childhood—to grin and bear it; nor is this refuge much ennobled by calling it stoicism. The defect in this old remedy is that it helps others not at all, and oneself only by a sort of moral suicide."

Both the Stoic and early Christian adjustments involve a controlled direction of personal energy in accord with the supposed dictates of ultimate reality. Opposed to both of these adjustments is "energy without direction," which seems to be the other "conception . . . of duty" mentioned in *Lodge*: "assertion of self." The supreme expression of such assertion is the King and Judge's antithesis, the Savior, who instead of submitting to reality, which he conceives of as divine, tries to become that reality. As a result, Adams says, his "Will—or what we now call Energy —[is] freed and perfected." Energy perfected—apparently at its maximum intensity—and freed from all social or individual control is "energy without direction"; in *Lodge*, Adams' view is that its possessor is insane. In the above letter, "the Germans" are said to be pronouncing this mode of adjustment a failure. If by "the Germans" Adams means thinkers— paralleling Taylor and Kelvin—he would seem to be referring to the belief of Schopenhauer and his followers that the unimpeded operation of the irrational Will whose dynamism is the essence of reality results in the evils of conflict and suffering.[91] But if he means Schopenhauer, why does he say "the Germans" when Friedrich Nietzsche, who sees the uninhibited results of the Will as good rather than evil, is also German? It seems more likely that "energy without direction" refers to war,[92] which Adams seems to be saying "the Germans"[93] in World War I are demonstrating is a failure as a primary mode of human adjustment. He says "the Germans" rather than Europeans in general because at this time he believed both that Germany had begun the war and that it was losing it. By February, 1915, the Battle of the Marne, which had stopped the initial

[91] Adams' referring to Schopenhauer's followers, at least, as if they were contemporaries of Taylor is no more anachronistic than his referring to Lord Kelvin in the same way. Kelvin died in 1907, Eduard von Hartman, Schopenhauer's chief follower, in 1906. Moreover, as late as 1910 Adams says (in reference to another subject), "Edward von Hartman's introductory paragraph, I conceive to be the last word of life." (HA to Barrett Wendell, May 18, 1910, in Cater, p. 682.)

[92] It is interpreted in this way in R. P. Blackmur, "Henry Adams: Three Late Moments," in *Kenyon Review*, II (Winter, 1940), 20. Adams' attitude toward war shifted after *Chartres*. In *The History* he considered the ability and willingness to fight a necessity for national success and even survival. In *Chartres* war, along with women and poetry, was liked by the child (p. 29) and Adams is sympathetic to this taste as to the others. But horror for war appears in *The Education*, where he speaks of it as a "wild ocean" (p. 111) and as "chaos" (p. 289), both equivalent to calling it "energy without direction."

[93] In the four pages of Adams' published correspondence written between the beginning of the war and Feb. 15, 1915 (Ford [1892–1918], pp. 626–630), the date of the letter to Taylor, he refers to "the Germans" three times and to "the German" or "German" or "Germany" three other times, in every case meaning the country or its people.

German attack, was several months past, and the western front was settling down to the trench warfare and sporadic, indecisive battles that would characterize the war for the next three years. In a letter written on November 26, 1914, Adams expresses his attitude toward the apparent German failure: "The Germans are half mad with solitude and desperation," he says; "I pity them, but it would be worse for them if they won." [94] This sense of German failure seems to be the basis for what he says in the letter to Taylor. (If he meant the passage to have any specific philosophical significance, it might suggest that the German defeat at the Marne was proving Nietzsche, the exponent of aggressive war and thus of "energy without direction," wrong and Schopenhauer and his followers right.)

Three years after writing this letter, Adams describes not only the Germans but the entire Teutonic race as having exemplified, throughout its history, the mode of adjustment he calls "energy without direction." This, in effect, is the thesis of an article entitled "The Genesis of the Super-German" which appeared in April, 1918.[95] Its author, Father Sigourney Fay, a frequent visitor to Adams since 1915, said that Adams "wrote all of [it] except the very last part." [96] Apparently making extensive use of George Santayana's *Egotism in German Philosophy* (which Adams had recently read[97]), it argues that "three times since Christianity came into the world" the Teutons have "violently attacked" and tried to destroy "Celtic-Latin . . . religion and civilization": in the fourth and fifth centuries, Arian Teutons invaded the Empire; in the sixteenth century Protestant Teutons sacked Rome; in the twentieth century non-Christian Teutons attacked Belgium and France. Father Fay ascribes this history of aggression to the consistently "subjective" character of the Teutonic race and its consequent recurrent espousal of "the heresy of the superman." He traces the original conjunction of these two characteristics to the conversion of the Teutons in the early Middle Ages to Arianism—

at that time the form of Christianity most congenial to [themselves] . . . . Arianism in their minds took on a thoroughly Teutonic character . . . . What was everything to them was the teaching that a superangel had taken the body and the appearance of a man; for they supposed, like all the Arians, that the Logos took the place of the human soul in Christ, and that He, although all

[94] HA to Elizabeth Cameron, Nov. 26, 1914, in Ford (1892–1918), p. 628.

[95] Sigourney W. Fay, "The Genesis of the Super-German," in *Dublin Review*, CLII (April, 1918), 224–233.

[96] Cater, pp. cv, cxix (n. 216). (This is the same Father Fay that Adams refers to in n. 89 above.)

[97] HA to Elizabeth Cameron, Sept. 5, 1917, in Ford (1892–1918), p. 646: "I think I wrote to you of having read to me . . . Santayana's very clever essay on German Metaphysics."

the world was against Him, had beaten down all opposition and had finally triumphed over His enemies in this world, having first harried Hell. In other words, though Nietzsche was not to come for centuries, the Arian-Teutonic Christ was the superman. They denied, as all Arians did, original sin.

The effect of this doctrine "upon a race so intensely subjective" was that from the time the Teutons embraced Arianism, they "produced one great military leader after another," each an "irresponsible superman amenable to no one so long as he was justified by his emotions." "His will was the only law."

This tendency was seemingly eradicated by the conversions of the Arians to Roman Catholic orthodoxy, but it sprang to life again with Martin Luther. For the Catholic, Fay says,

> Faith . . . rests upon reason and is an extension, really, of human reason by the aid of a supernatural light. Luther, in direct contradiction, . . . set his face against any rational element at all in the act of faith. Faith for him depended entirely upon feeling. . . . The whole of religion was now inside of the soul; external authority counted for nothing, tradition counted for nothing, reason counted for nothing.

The subjectivism of Leibniz was a bridge from this definition of Christianity to the philosophy of Luther's "real disciple," Immanuel Kant:

> Martin Luther had cut the bridges between religion and reason; but, because he was not a philosopher, he could not cut all the bridges between the perceiving mind and the world perceived. This Kant did for him; and from Kant's day to ours the Teutonic mind has been imprisoned within itself. Everything had from henceforth to be stated in terms of . . . the experience . . . of the individual. If religion were to depend solely upon feeling, and one had not the feeling of religion, then religion naturally disappeared. . . . If morality depends merely upon a categorical imperative within us, there is no moral law without us which can be imposed upon us by the authority of the race. . . . Neitzsche follows Kant as logically as Kant follows Luther. . . . Neitzsche saw clearly that the categorical imperative . . . was but an inheritance from an age which had submitted itself to external standards in ethics if not in religion; but if there were no external standards in either the one or the other, there could be no guide left but the Ego, no ruling Deity but the Will. Here the Teuton breaks with Christianity.

In this essay (which Father Fay wrote to help prevent Ireland from allying itself with Germany in World War I[98]) Stoicism is not mentioned. The conflict is between Celtic-Latin religion and civilization, and Teutonic subjectivist heresies and their social consequences. But the definition

---

[98] Samuels, *The Major Phase*, p. 580.

of Catholic faith as "an extension . . . of human reason by the aid of a supernatural light" is a favorable restatement of Adams' hostile definition of "early Christian" faith in the 1915 letter to Taylor as the Stoic belief in reason supplemented by supernaturalism. The alliance of orthodox Catholicism with external authority, tradition, and reason is also akin to Creon's respect for the first two at least in *Lodge*. The most striking connection between the essay and *Lodge*, however, is the similarity in words as well as ideas between Fay's statement that Nietzsche's analysis left man "no guide . . . but the Ego, no ruling Deity but the Will" and Adams' statement in *Lodge* that in a successful Savior "Will—or what we now call Energy—is freed and perfected." The priest speaks of "Deity," the student of science, of "Energy," but they have in common the capitalized use of "Will" as well as the same idea. The latter similarity suggests that the Nietzschean superman is equivalent to the Savior. Fay himself brings the two together earlier in the article when he says that "though Nietzsche was not to come for centuries, the Arian Teutonic Christ was the superman." This Christ is not the Christ of Fay's Christian orthodoxy nor of the "early Christian" adjustment in the Taylor letter: he is not a Savior who has been transformed into an institution ruled by a King and Judge figure through a rational system of law. Nor is he the Christ humanized by the ideal of love whom St. Francis in *Chartres* is said to have reincarnated. He is, rather, Christ as the archetypal Savior described in *Lodge*, whose nature is now fully explained.

The contradiction in the Savior is that in the service of the greatest ideal he can commit the greatest of evils, even the murder of those he loves best. Equating him with the superman illuminates this contradiction by suggesting that the archetypal Savior and the superman differ primarily in their conscious motivation. The Savior believes that his actions express the spiritual essence of reality and are making him and, through him, other men more at one with its unity. The superman believes that his actions express that will-to-power which is the essence of reality (Adams calls it the tendency for all forces to grow) and that these actions are moving him toward the utmost individual development he is capable of and thereby differentiating him to the greatest possible extent from other men. The motivation of the two figures seems antithetical, but Adams, who agrees with Nietzsche's analysis of the ultimate nature of reality, believes the results are the same: an irrational, antisocial assertion of self, amoral and insane in its unrestrained pursuit of power, chaotic in its effects. The superman is simply a Savior without illusions acting directly out of the anarchic will-to-power which moves all forces in the multiverse.[99]

[99] The superman seems to be the ultimate expression of "what a brute the emancipated man [can] be," as Adams said in *Chartres* (p. 211).

According to Fay, from the time of its conversion to Arian Christianity to its conversion to Catholic Christianity, the Teutonic race was led by a succession of military Saviors or supermen, each of whom thought of himself as a "follower and imitator of the superangel who had dwelt in the body of a man" as Jesus Christ. The social chaos normally caused by the Savior was prevented by the absolute submission of everyone in the community to the irrational impulses of the leader. Such submission made the Savior-leader almost literally the embodiment of the community and the community a Savior-community whose total energy (or collective will) was without direction or control except by the uncontrolled will (or energy) of the leader. The nature of the society defined its principal activity: "energy without direction," here as in the 1915 letter, is war. Human relationships—legal or personal—and human beings themselves were primary obstacles to the insane drive of the Savior-race toward apotheosis—just as Herakles' children were to his insane aspirations toward divinity —and hence were also its inevitable victims.

The conversion of the principal Teutonic tribes to Catholic orthodoxy was a conversion to a rational Christian social order led by a King and Judge figure. Beginning with Luther, however, the Teutons steadily moved back toward their innate subjectivism and glorification of the superman. But one change had occurred. In throwing off Catholic Christianity the Teuton threw off all Christianity and when he finally found his essential nature once again in Nietzsche he had lost his Christian ideal or illusion. In the twentieth century the military Savior-race has become the race of the superman, fully conscious of its dedication to "energy without direction" as a mode of adjustment.[100] The object of its aggression, however, has not changed. As in the fourth and sixteenth centuries, so in the twentieth century, it is again the Celtic-Latin civilization of the Roman state and the Catholic church, which Fay views as constituting a continuous supraracial and supranational tradition based not upon following the forces of nature but upon the control and direction of nature by the human intellect, aided by supernatural light, and hence an expression of order rather than chaos. Celtic-Latin civilization is energy *with* direction; it is a Creon-civilization, a collective embodiment of the King and Judge figure.

It was in *The Education* that, while accepting "energy without direction" as a description of reality, Adams first (in his later work) emphatically rejected it as a moral prescription for personal and social "salvation." Instead he created an avowedly false materialistic monism as a means both of achieving personal order and of helping twentieth-century man retard

[100] In *The Education*, Adams characterized America as the country of the dynamo; but here Germany is the country of pure chaos.

the disintegration of society. Yet neither in *The Education* nor in the 1915 letter did he express much hope for the re-establishment of social unity. At the end of *The Education* he found Theodore Roosevelt trying to train the new King and Judge figures society needed but doubted his success. He did not point out the irony that a figure whom he characterizes in *The Education* as "pure act,"[101] privately called insane,[102] and compared to Lodge's Herakles should be trying to train King and Judge figures. Yet the irony in the case of Roosevelt was hardly greater than that Henry Adams—who characterizes himself as a "runaway star"[103]—should be trying to do the same thing by means of a philosophy of order he himself does not believe in. In the 1915 letter he reasserts his belief that no system succeeds on a personal level in a moral crisis and sees little hope for any on a social level. If there is a residue of hope, however, he seems to believe that it lies in the materialistic monism of Stoicism—or, more likely, in something akin to his dynamic theory as it appears in "A Letter to American Teachers of History."[104]

There is one other place in Adams' work in which nations or races or civilizations are viewed as playing the roles of Savior or King and Judge. On March 25 and May 2, 1897, eighteen years before the Taylor letter, twenty-one before the Fay article, Adams briefly mentions the idea in two letters about Rome. In the first he says that "the soul of Rome" is a "sense of finite failure" (an anticipation of his making Rome in *The Education* the center of the fall in western civilization). In the other he says that "the world contains only one or two great tragic motives in the historical drama, and Rome concentrates them." He explains what these motives are when he says in the first letter that "Rome . . . tells of the two first failures of western civilization: one political, the other spiritual," which he specifies more precisely as "the imperial and the papal failures."[105] He is considering the history of each of the two parts of what Fay calls Celtic-Latin religion and civilization a tragic drama. In terms of Adams' use of the dramatic analogy up to 1897, this is all that can be legitimately said of these brief passages. Yet Adams' continued use of the

[101] *The Education*, p. 417. "Pure act" implies "without reflection." Its implications for a God who is perfect and a human being who is not are quite different.

[102] HA to Elizabeth Cameron, Feb. 25 and Mar. 3, 1912; HA to Sir Ronald Lindsay, Sept. 28, 1912, in Ford (1892–1918), pp. 587, 588, 605.

[103] *The Education*, p. 472.

[104] Full discussion of the Taylor letter and the Fay article obviously requires some attempt to understand the seemingly contradictory attitudes in them toward instinct (or feeling) and reason. In order not to digress too violently from the subject of the present chapter, this discussion has been placed in Appendix II. For other critical commentary on the Fay article, see critical note 66.

[105] HA to Mabel La Farge, Mar. 25 and May 2, 1897, in *Letters to a Niece*, pp. 98–100.

dramatic analogy and his continued concern with Rome and the Catholic Church suggests that these passages might well have appeared in a letter written in 1917. If they had, *Chartres*, *The Education*, *Lodge*, the 1915 letter, and the Fay article would make it possible to infer a great deal from the little Adams says. The passages would then suggest that to consider the history of Rome and that of the Church as dramas is to consider each an attempt to create unity out of multiplicity in terms of an ideal on the level of an entire civilization, one a political unity through the state, the other a spiritual unity through the Church. Like all effective social dramas both codified their motive in a system of law and embodied it in an administrator (a King and Judge figure) responsible for securing and preserving social unity. In the case of Rome military conquest was rationalized as an ideal of political universality which was embodied in a system of increasingly supralocal law created first by the senate, or by the senate and the emperor, and administered by the emperor or others. In the case of the Church the anarchical individual drama of the Savior was transformed into a unifying social drama by the assertion of the Church that Jesus was the one true Savior, that his drama was the one true Savior-drama in history, and that the Church was his mystical body through which men could literally participate in a recurrent re-enactment of that drama. This transfer of the Savior's authority and even identity to what functioned as a human institution gave a supernatural sanction to the efficient rational organization led by the pope. This, in turn, enabled the Church to create a high degree of the spiritual unity which was its primary aim and a degree of temporal unity, which, however small, was surprisingly large in view of the prevalent social and political chaos and its own lack of military force.

In the first letter, Adams also says that at Rome "the third and last [failure of western civilization]—the material or economical—is there only in the vulgar ruin of a contractor's building speculation." In the second letter he clarifies the relationship of this drama to the others when he says that "Florence . . . never counts for a tragic motive. It is not quite as fat and gross as the Touraine . . . . but Florence was always mercantile; —never imperial or spiritual." The modern drama is economic, an attempt to unite the world through economic interest. Its chief actor is the businessman or financier, whom Adams usually refers to contemptuously as a "jew" or "gold-bug"[106] because his motivation is profit, a motive hardly ideal enough to create a drama, much less a tragedy. Yet Adams

---

[106] E.g., HA to John Hay, July 28, 1896; HA to Brooks Adams, Oct. 23, 1897; HA to Brooks Adams, Oct. 12, 1899; HA to John Hay, Oct. 18, 1893, in Cater, pp. 376–377, 422, 482, 292. HA to Elizabeth Cameron, June 10, 1888, in *Letters of Henry Adams, 1858–1891*, ed. Worthington Chauncey Ford (Boston: Houghton Mifflin Co., 1930), p. 388; hereafter cited as Ford (1858–1891).

always recognizes his power and influence and occasionally expresses
something like respect at his cunning and courage. There is respect as
well as irony in his statement that "Jay Gould . . . is certainly a great man,
worth writing about,"[107] although the greatness is more akin to that of a
Napoleon than a Marcus Aurelius or a St. Francis. The failure of this
drama, Adams suggests, will have neither pathos nor dignity but, like the
remains of the contractor's building speculation in Rome, will be merely
a "vulgar ruin."

This drama is the drama of man when he has lost most of his innate
perception of reality as unity and most of his ability to live as if life were
a drama. He has become more like other forces in the multiverse, pursuing
power directly rather than in terms of an ideal or a fiction. Thus, the
economic drama is close to the opposite end of the historical continuum
from the drama of the Savior. At the opposite end is the drama Adams
implies that the Germans are playing in 1918, a drama whose motive is
"energy without direction." But here the word "drama" has become a
misnomer, for the essence of drama is energy given direction by an ideal.
A drama based upon the "ideal" of "energy without direction" is a
contradiction in terms. In 1918, therefore, the drama has begun to
cease altogether to be a viable image for human life.

Opposed to both of these dramas is that of human love. Unlike them
it is a wholly human drama, indeed, the most human of all dramas. Contrasting it with a version of the religious drama, Adams wrote in 1889 of
a Buddhist friend that

> thousands and millions of men have taken his road before, with more or less
> satisfaction, but the mass of mankind have settled to the conviction that the
> only Paradise possible in this world is concentrated in the three little words
> which the ewig man says to the ewige woman. Sturgis [Bigelow] calls this the
> Fireside, and thinks he knows better. He looks for his Paradise in absorption
> in the Infinite.

Adams comments that any kind of a paradise in human life "is a dream":
personal dramas based on either motive are doomed to failure. But his
sympathies are with the love drama. This drama appears in *Gallatin* and
becomes of major importance in the two novels. It receives final and
autonomous expression in *Chartres*, where the twelfth century is depicted
as a period when love became the chief ideal of society on all levels.
The central role in this drama belongs to the woman, whose primary
characteristic is her power to give and evoke love, the most powerful
transforming and unifying force in human experience. Her lover, like the
Savior and the King and Judge, seeks to be one with the object of his love,

[107] HA to Elizabeth Cameron, Jan. 2, 1891, in Ford (1858–1891), p. 457.

but in this case that object is a woman. When men in the mass are moved by this ideal, society realizes a spontaneous and organic unity capable of building Chartres cathedral. The mechanical unity obtained by law supported by force, which the King and Judge represents as the embodiment of justice, is a feeble thing by comparison. Usually, this drama is the basis for the family and therefore for society. The story of Tristan and Isolde, however—which, Adams says, "served as a sacred book to the women of the twelfth and thirteenth centuries"[108]—shows how the love drama, because it involves only two individuals concerned solely with one another, may be radically opposed to society and religion. Yet the same Henry Adams who rejects the antisocial dramas of Napoleon and Herakles accepts and even glorifies the equivalent love drama. On its highest level this drama becomes a religion, the worship of a woman goddess who embodies the emotion of love and the force of reproduction. Such worship gives society the fullest voluntary unity human beings are capable of. The "last and greatest" of these woman goddesses was the Virgin Mary, whose cult was the final and highest expression not only of the medieval love-drama but of all such dramas.

A measure of the intensity of Adams' regard for this drama is his attitude toward Don Quixote. Cervantes' hero occasionally appears in Adams' writings throughout his adult life, but his two chief appearances are in *John Randolph* (1882) and *Chartres*. In the former, he is made the literary counterpart of the American statesman John Randolph,[109] "as pure a Virginian Quixote as ever an American Cervantes could have conceived." Randolph's *idée fixe* is suggested when Adams writes that he "figured as a political Quixote in his championship of states' rights, which became at the end his hobby, his mania." Here Cervantes' hero is a symbol for human idealism carried to the verge of insanity. A very different estimate appears in *Chartres*. Adams says that "every one is more or less familiar" with the "theories of courteous love, . . . if only from the ridicule of Cervantes and the follies of Quixote, who, though four hundred years younger, was Lancelot's child." The ideals of courteous love, he says, "were a form of religion, and if you care to see its evangels, you had best go directly to Dante and Petrarch, or, if you like it better, to Don Quixote de la Mancha. The religion is dead as Demeter, and its art alone survives as, on the whole, the highest expression of man's thought or emotion."[110]

[108] HA to Anna Cabot Mills Lodge, June 18, 1889, in *ibid.*, pp. 399–400. *Chartres*, p. 219.

[109] This was first noted in print by Levenson, *The Mind and Art of Henry Adams*, p. 103. It is fully developed by Henry B. Rule, "Henry Adams' Attack on Two Heroes of the Old South," *American Quarterly*, XIV (Summer, 1962, Part I), 179–184.

[110] Henry Adams, *John Randolph* (Boston: Houghton Mifflin Co., 1899), pp, 13, 32. *Chartres*, pp. 213, 211.

Don Quixote is still a creature of folly whose excesses made him the butt of his creator's ridicule, but now Adams views these as having been committed in the service of the one ideal worthy of such excess. Indeed, they are now accounted sacred and the book which describes them is considered one of the gospels of the religion of love.

In *Chartres* the uncle says of the twelfth-century love-drama that this "stage is the highest yet seen on earth." Yet less than a decade later Adams writes in *Lodge* that the motive for the drama of the Savior is the "oldest," "the most universal," and "the greatest in human experience." [111] Has he changed his mind ? To decide, it is necessary to compare the two dramas. Both are based, like all dramas, on the human illusion of unity: man projects his own essential illusion onto reality, gives it the name and form of a goddess or a god, and calls it ultimate reality and ruler of the universe. The dramas differ in the nature of the divinity each is concerned with and the kind of response proper to each. In the drama created by worship of Mary, the proper human response is love, the highest emotion man can feel. Insofar as the "human" can be identified with the sense of unity, love is also the most human emotion because it can produce the most complete social unity. In this drama there is no attempt to become the goddess. In the drama of the Savior, however, man attempts to become the god. The response to the divinity here is normally self-assertion, the quality man has in common with all other forces in the multiverse and therefore his least distinctively human quality. Moreover, since self-assertion produces social chaos and anarchy rather than unity, it is also the lowest human quality. The drama performed on the twelfth-century stage was the highest of all dramas which work within human limitations. The drama of the Savior is the drama of man losing both his humanity and his sanity in attempting to exceed those limitations. It seems clear that whatever Adams' attitude toward the love drama at the time of writing *Lodge*, he does not consider the drama of the Savior the "highest" drama in the sense of the *best* drama, as he did the love drama in *Chartres*.

Neither of these dramas can for long become that of an entire society. The drama of the Savior tends to dissolve society into individuals struggling to become divine. For a whole society to act out this drama as individuals would be suicide. But neither can men be motivated for long entirely by their highest emotion. Invariably society falls away from love into other motives. The only continuously effective motive for the social drama is one capable of development into a system of law such as that which formed the core of the political and papal attempts to unite western civilization.

[111] *Chartres*, p. 106. *Lodge*, pp. 165, 111, 164.

Adams first juxtaposes the love drama and the social drama involving the King and Judge in *Gallatin* where, in a work focused upon its subject's public career, he treats Gallatin's home life briefly but with interest and sympathy. *Democracy*, as both a novel and (in part) a comedy of manners, makes the love drama the principal means of expressing its theme. In effect, it concerns a woman's rejection of a potential lover because he is a fraudulent King and Judge. Again, as in *Gallatin*, the two roles are harmonious. In *Esther*, the love drama is even more central. Here Hazard, a King and Judge figure (with occasional flashes of the megalomania characteristic of the Savior), is rejected by the eternal woman not for lack of integrity but because of it. Esther rejects him because she knows she must believe in the ideal he is committed to if their marriage is to succeed and yet she cannot believe in it. Here, for the first time, the two dramas are incompatible, but they are so because the woman and the King and Judge figure have different ideals. In *Chartres*, the possibility of conflict between the dramas reaches a climax. The conflict is never so direct nor so intense as it is in *Democracy* or *Esther* but it is more basic because here there is no problem of integrity *or* incompatible ideals apart from the nature of the dramas themselves. The Virgin and St. Thomas Aquinas have equal integrity and share a common religious ideal. But the love drama of the first and the institutional drama of the second express the fundamental conflict between the primitive emphasis on feeling and the modern emphasis on reason which is subordinate only to unity versus multiplicity as the principal antithesis of the book. In the twelfth century the Middle Ages is represented as flowering in a devotion to love so great that it became the primary basis for the unity of society. Among the upper classes it was embodied in a system of law called the code of courteous love, which was administered by Queen and Judge figures like Eleanor of Guienne and Blanche of Castile. In this rational form the social drama of love was a form of self-conscious play, though it operated as a genuine social force. The real unifying force in society was the emotion of love itself. In the thirteenth century the love drama did not disappear but it did become subordinate once again, this time to an intellectual drama institutional in its concerns and emphasis.

In *The Education* the relationship between the two dramas, including their characteristic relationship in the Middle Ages, is viewed once again as complementary rather than conflicting. (In this regard, as in so many others, the view of *The Education* is basic to Adams' subsequent thought.) In "The Abyss of Ignorance" Adams shows himself searching for the attractive force which has determined the direction of change in history. He goes to the Virgin at Chartres and asks her to show him the force he seeks, which she calls God. She tells him that she and Christ together are love but that they "have little or nothing to do with God's other energies which are infinite, and concern [them] the less because [their] interest is only in man, and the infinite is not knowable to man." But she suggests that if he is "still troubled by [his] ignorance," he ask "the masters of the schools." So he goes to St. Thomas Aquinas, who tells him that

> To me . . . Christ and the Mother are one Force—Love—simple, single, and sufficient for all human wants; but Love is a human interest which acts even on man so partially that you and I, as philosophers, need expect no share in it. Therefore we turn to Christ and the Schools who represent all other Force. We deal with Multiplicity and call it God. After the Virgin has redeemed by her personal Force as Love all that is redeemable in man, the Schools embrace the rest, and give it Form, Unity, and Motive.[112]

Here there is no disagreement between the Virgin and St. Thomas. He says that love is one of the infinite multiplicity of forces he and the Virgin call God; it is sufficient for all human wants. Insofar as it affects human beings, it enables the woman to create the community of love her nature desires. But its effect is always partial. Human beings are also affected by other forces and these can be prevented from fostering social anarchy only by being organized by reason. Since Thomas is represented in *Chartres* as serving the Church rather than the salvation of individuals, it seems valid to infer further that for such rational organization to be practically meaningful it must be embodied in an institution administered by a King and Judge.

This account of the relationship between the Virgin and Thomas explains what occurs to Adams at Troyes two chapters later. The shock of the assassination and the immediate knowledge of chaos it renews in Adams does not make him desert the Virgin.[113] But he does realize anew the limitations of love's influence on man and therefore turns from making her his primary concern to giving his own rational organization to the other forces in the multiverse (in his dynamic theory of history). In the final chapter of *The Education* he expresses his concern at being unable to find the new men who will discover the means to integrate the new forces into a new social unity. This concern reflects his pessimism about the possibility of such an integration; but it also implies the hope that his book and his theory, which in the introduction he directed to young men, might be a means of training such men. His redefinition and restatement of the theory in "The Rule" and "A Letter" inevitably involved a con-

---

[112] *The Education*, pp. 427–428.

[113] See Frances Quinlivan, "Irregularities of the Mental Mirror," in *The Catholic World*, CCV (April, 1946), 65.

tinued interest in these new men and hence a continued renewal of his interest in the King and Judge figure. This found expression in his praise for Creon in the letter to Lodge and the later biography, in the 1915 letter to Taylor, and in the Fay essay.

In speaking of Marcus Aurelius in the 1915 letter Adams expresses a need for someone in history to "admire." It has been said that to admire is to love with the head while to love is to admire with the heart. The concern for organizing forces other than love that gave rise to Adams' renewed interest in the King and Judge figure was a rational concern; the process of organization itself was a rational pursuit; it is therefore appropriate that the emotion evoked by the practical administrator of such organization should be a rational emotion. Yet such admiration, although it seems to express a conviction that the King and Judge is a more effective agent of social unity than the woman can be except at rare moments, does not mean that Adams has ceased to love "the eternal woman." One wishes he had written in his last years a letter to Elizabeth Cameron (or some other woman friend) comparable to the Taylor letter. Lacking that, the best evidence for his later attitude toward the love drama appears in *Lodge*. There he comments briefly but with intense lyricism about the mutual love of Lodge and his mother and about his and his wife's love for one another. The most important material, however, appears in Adams' discussion of the character of Eve in *Cain*, a drama by Lodge which preceded *Herakles*. Adams says that,

> after the traditional development of the mediaeval drama, Eve is reproduced in the Virgin . . . . As, in the mediaeval conception, the rôle of the Virgin almost effaced the rôle of Christ, the drama of Cain ends by almost effacing Cain in the loftier self-sacrifice of the woman . . . . Perhaps some readers would find more meaning and higher taste in the drama had Lodge called it "Eve" instead of calling it "Cain"; but here the dramatist was developing his theme in philosophy rather than in poetry, and the two motives almost invariably stand in each other's light. The maternal theme is the more poetic and dramatic, but without the philosophy the poem and the drama have no reason to exist.[114]

The equation of Eve and the Virgin suggests that Eve's role in the drama is that of "the eternal woman." And though Adams explains and defends Lodge's emphasis upon Cain rather than Eve the phrase "some readers" seems a thinly veiled disguise for Adams' own opinion that Eve as the center of a love drama involving Cain and Abel would have been a more meaningful and tasteful drama than the one Lodge wrote. Clearly Adams has not lost his interest, affection, or respect for the love drama. Yet *Cain*

[114] *Lodge*, pp. 117–118.

contains no King and Judge figure and in his discussion of *Herakles* Adams makes no analysis of the hero's relationship with his wife Megara. Nor are the two dramas discussed together. Therefore, it cannot be said how Adams at this time would have defined the relationship between them and the relative value of each.

The evidence that *is* available, however, suggests that if Adams had made a final choice it might well have been the King and Judge. Here *The Education* seems to be an epitome of the movement of his thought. Quincy, at the beginning of the book, represents multiplicity; it also represents to the young Henry Adams the true, the good, and the beautiful. In "Chaos" Adams shows himself learning that truth is alien to the good and the beautiful. In the second part of the book he begins by pursuing truth. But in 1895 he rediscovers the beautiful, especially as it expresses the medieval love drama and its highest expression in the Virgin. The fullest expression of that rediscovery is *Chartres*, where the focus of interest is a world which believed this beauty was the controlling force in the universe. Adams' perspective, however, is a sense of truth which considers this beauty an expression of sexual force and hence, although a reality, one whose influence upon man is ultimately less than that of other forces. In this view twelfth-century belief was a supremely beautiful illusion. In *The Education* the renewed shock at Troyes both of this beauty's illusoriness and of truth's horror is portrayed as turning Adams away from the pursuit of truth *and* of beauty to the construction of a formula that is too much an expression of chaos to be beautiful and too much an ordering of chaos to be true. The value it ultimately seeks to realize is the good. And though Adams never rejected chaos (and therefore war) as supreme truth nor the love drama as supreme beauty, his emphasis at least seems finally to have rested where it had been in his early essays and *The Life of Albert Gallatin*, upon the goodness of him who is the servant of his society and of that justice which is its core.[115]

[115] Many other human types recur in Adams' work, chief among them the thinker and the artist.

CHAPTER VIII

THE ULTIMATE SYMBOLS: II

SOURCES AND EARLY USES OF WATER IMAGERY

Henry Adams' major symbol for the forces of nature is water. Water imagery is also the most pervasive symbolic element in his work.[1] Its meaning varies, like that of his other major symbols. It is always a symbol of reality and as such is a symbol of the forces, human and natural, which oppose the individual and his will, but it does not symbolize reality conceived in mechanical terms until this view comes to dominate Adams' thinking during the 1880's and after. In one of its main forms in this later period it is also a symbol of chaos, a concept of reality the machine cannot symbolize. The machine is organization; chaos is not. Also, "machine" always suggests some kind of machine-maker, whether human or divine, a notion almost always alien to Adams' thought about the nature of ultimate reality. In using the image, he seems, indeed, to be using the eighteenth-century image for reality without the belief in a divine creator which usually accompanied it. The absence of such an implication is another advantage of water symbolism as an image of his view of reality.

Yet the water imagery in Adams is frequently accompanied by machine imagery. A machine was defined in the previous chapter as a "contrivance of man's reason and will, intended to help him do more work with less effort." Water is not man's natural element and if he is going to be in it for more than a short time he needs something to help him, usually a mechanical contrivance—a raft, a boat, a ship. Hence although Adams sometimes figures man in relation to a watery reality as a fish or a swimmer, usually he *is* a ship or is on a ship. Of figurative ships which men are on, the most common is the ship-of-state, though Adams also speaks of a whole civilization as a ship. This usage is in accord with his frequent

[1] Besides his comments on water symbolism in *The Education* (noted in footnote 26 to chapter 6), John Brunner, "Henry Adams: His Decline and Fall" (Ph.D. dissertation, UCLA, 1956), also notes on pp. 50–53, 69, some of the water symbols in *Esther* and the works after it and relates them to one another.

references to governments as a whole or in their parts as "machines." The relationship between a ship and the water symbol expresses the relationship which Adams believes exists between man and reality. Particularly significant is the extent to which man can or cannot control the ship, for here Adams expresses the measure of his sense of human action as free or determined.

The source of Adams' water imagery and ship-water imagery is usually commonplace metaphors which constant use has deprived of much of their figurative quality—the "stream" of things, or events, for example, or "drifting with the current," or "a tide in the affairs of men." He also uses images that are still clearly metaphorical, but have become conventional —the ship-of-state, for example, or human life as being like a ship on the ocean of life. These commonplace images are given vitality (as was the dramatic analogy to a lesser extent) by being connected with his own personal interests and experience. In the first chapter of *The Education*, for example, he describes his boyhood pleasure in the color and sight of the ocean and his joy in the summer when he "waded in the brook, or swam in the salt ocean, or sailed in the bay." [2] In the same chapter he contrasts this pleasure with his hatred for the cold of winter. In a Harvard undergraduate essay [3] written ten years after the date given this chapter in *The Education*, he lists six favorite vacation memories, five of them connected with water: trips on the Hudson and St. Lawrence rivers; the sight of Niagara Falls; walking, sun-bathing and fishing on the southeastern coast and islands of Massachusetts; and an afternoon sail on the ocean. Later, a stream or a river, the ocean, snow and ice, Niagara Falls, sailing, and swimming would all become important images in his writings.

Such experiences are a part of most boyhoods, especially in New England. In Adams' case, however, neither the experiences nor his sensitivity to them ended with boyhood. He traveled all his life, and whether on the move or at home he was always especially sensitive to water. In a letter to an English friend, for example, he says of Washington, D.C., "I know of no other capital in the world which stands on so wide and splendid a river." In another letter, he writes that "our trip to Niagara was a real pleasure and a new experience." But most of his experience and awareness centered on the ocean. In 1863 he writes from England that some friends were "charmingly situated . . . with the ocean rolling under their windows; . . . the more I look at it, the more I feel how far the ocean is superior in grandeur to every other object in nature." Sometimes he feels this grandeur a challenge to more than contemplation:

[2] Henry Adams, *The Education of Henry Adams*, introduction by James Truslow Adams, The Modern Library (New York: Random House, Inc., 1931), p. 9.

[3] Henry Adams, "Retrospect," in *The Harvard Magazine*, III (March, 1857), 63–65.

The other day, arriving at San Francisco, I took my baronet out to the Cliff House, where the Pacific was rolling in its long surf in the light of a green and yellow sunset; and there I pointed to the Golden Gate and challenged the baronet to go on with me. Ignominiously he turned his back on all that glory, and set his face eastward for his dear fogs; and I, too, for the time, submitted; but the longing was as strong as ever.

Once actually at sea, however, Adams is rarely so happy. "Oceans are a bore" is one reaction, but a rare one. Generally he is miserable, for he invariably suffered from prolonged bouts of seasickness: "I have had to be much at sea, and every sea-voyage is to me worse than an ordinary fever; my misery is abject; I dread it more than any ordinary disaster."[4] Nonetheless, he continued to travel, and both calm and stormy oceans, boredom and seasickness, became part of his water imagery.

In 1863 he uses the ocean as a symbol of ultimate reality. "The truth is," he writes his brother Charles,

everything in this universe has its regular waves and tides. Electricity, sound, the wind, and I believe every part of organic nature will be brought some day within this law. But my philosophy teaches me, and I firmly believe it, that the laws which govern animated beings will be ultimately found to be at bottom the same with those which rule inanimate nature. ... Thus ... I look for regular tides in the affairs of man, and of course, in our own affairs. In every progression, somehow or other, the nations move by the same process which has never been explained but is evident in the ocean and the air.[5]

The universe is a great ocean, in which everything has its regular waves and tides. Organic nature, including human history, is as subject to this universal process as inorganic nature. One law rules all and the symbol for this "all" is the ocean. Man, therefore, has no free will; he is the helpless instrument of the universal process. This passage must stand at the beginning of any systematic analysis of Henry Adams' use of water symbolism because it is unique in his work. Its use of the ocean as an explicit symbol of ultimate reality does not reappear until *The Education* in 1907.

[4] HA to Charles Milnes Gaskell, Nov. 5, 1868, in Henry Adams, *Letters of Henry Adams, 1858–1891*, ed. Worthington Chauncey Ford (Boston: Houghton Mifflin Co., 1930), p. 148; hereafter cited as Ford (1858–1891). HA to Mary Eliot Dwight Parkman, Feb. 20, 1879, in Henry Adams, *Henry Adams and His Friends: A Collection of His Unpublished Letters*, compiled with a biographical introduction by Harold Dean Cater (Boston: Houghton Mifflin Co., 1947), p. 89; hereafter cited as Cater. HA to Charles Francis Adams, Jr., Oct. 16, 1863, in Charles Francis Adams, Charles Francis Adams, Jr., and Henry Adams, *A Cycle of Adams Letters, 1861–1865*, ed. Worthington Chauncey Ford (2 vols.; Boston: Houghton Mifflin Co., 1920), II, 93; hereafter cited as *Cycle*. HA to Elizabeth Cameron, Nov. 4, 1888, and Aug. 26, 1891, in Ford (1858–1891), pp. 395, 522; HA to Rebecca Gilman Rae, Nov. 8, 1890, in Cater, p. 210.

[5] HA to Charles Francis Adams, Jr., Oct. 2, 1863, in *Cycle*, II, 89–90.

The beliefs it expresses in progress and in a universe disappear from his thought by the 1890's. Its materialism is always basic to his thought, but the determinism and the assertion that there is one, basic natural process at work in all nature anticipate similar ideas in his work by twenty years or more. What makes the passage unique is the fusion in it of ideas which generally appear only in the later works with other ideas which are pervasive in the early works but later disappear.

Elsewhere, the ocean image has a normal form which exists unchanged to 1876: the ocean as the image of life, the world, reality, the whole disordered and changing mass of human and natural circumstance which human beings are a part of and in which they live. After 1876 various new forms of the image appear. But throughout all of these the normal image persists. It dominates all the water imagery to 1891 and the personal and political water imagery to the end of Adams' life; it is also the source of most of the new forms the imagery takes. It is the basic and most pervasive water symbol in Adams' work. In this normal image the ocean is a tremendous mass of boundless tidal movement, generally restless, though occasionally so calm as to seem stagnant, at other times extremely wild and turbulent, threatening the ships upon it with destruction. It is a beautiful, a magnificent, sometimes an awe-inspiring or even terrifying sight. In relationship to this ocean man is most often floating upon it, generally in a ship, though sometimes upon a raft. Yet he may swim in it, too, as a man or, more often, as a fish. Neither navigating nor swimming is ever easy. At best it is a challenging and exciting, though frightening experience, which requires patience, courage, skill, and perseverance to give one a chance of success. Even with these qualities, one may lose control of his movement and simply be swept along with the current. Without them, he hasn't a chance of directing his course. Up to 1876 Adams generally felt it was possible, though difficult, to swim or navigate successfully. After that, his belief decreased, until after 1891 he viewed man's movement as being, almost invariably, determined by the movement of the ocean (or a river).

WATER IMAGERY FOR THE SELF AND AMERICA

Adams often uses water images in connection with his own life. Most of these appear in the letters, although *The Education* also contains many. Generally, the image is that of a boat upon an ocean. As a young man Adams is interested first in getting his boat launched. Writing to his mother from Paris at the age of twenty-two, he tells her that his brother "Charles writes me a plan according to which I should study law in Washington. . . . I never knew before this how I liked Quincy and Boston, and how sorry I should be to cut loose of them altogether; but this course, which certainly is the one I should choose and follow, if it will go, finishes setting me afloat." Quincy and Boston are the shore and childhood; leaving them to go to Washington, D.C., is to launch Adams' own ship into the ocean and maturity. This is the normal ocean image: the ocean is "life" or "the world," especially as it is encountered outside the childhood environment. The image suggests perhaps a slight element of danger in venturing on the new element, but primarily the process is viewed as challenging and exciting. Thirteen years later, writing to his protégé Henry Cabot Lodge, who has been "wallowing in a boundless ocean of history," Adams, now thirty-five, has encouragement to offer: "One has a very helpless feeling the first time one plunges into a new existence, no matter what the medium is. . . . Patience is the salvation of men at all such emergencies. I have never found that fail to pull me triumphantly through." Here Adams characterizes his entering upon any new existence as an encounter with what seems at first to be an enormous, unstable mass, without order or coherence. Not skill but patience is the first requirement for survival. In figurative storms, however, other qualities are also needed. In 1862 he writes, "I have . . . found it necessary to take in every spare inch of canvas and run under double-close-reefed mizzen to gallant skysails before a tremendous gale."[6] Here Adams himself is explicitly a ship or on a ship. His position is dangerous, but his emphasis is not upon the power of the storm over him but, by implication, upon the skill, energy, intelligence, and courage needed to survive.

So far, survival has been Adams' main concern. But initiation occurs no more than once per ocean, and storms, though possibly frequent, are not constant. Under ordinary conditions, direction is the second concern of the voyager. Like other young men, Henry Adams had many plans; like them, he found these interrupted by the Civil War. Indeed, at times he felt that he had lost all direction. "Have we both wholly lost our reckonings," he asks his brother Charles in 1863, "and are we driven at random by fate, or have we still a course that we are steering though it is not quite the same as our old one?" In 1864, he has completely surrendered to this sense of having lost self-direction: "I am looking about with a sort of vague curiosity for the current which is to direct my course after I am blown aside by this one."[7] In both these passages he is again a ship and in both he is upon the ocean of circumstance. But now a new element in the

---

[6] HA to his mother, July 1, 1860; HA to Henry Cabot Lodge, June 11, 1873, in Ford (1858-1891), pp. 61, 253. HA to Charles Francis Adams, Jr., Jan. 22, 1862, in *Cycle*, I, 104.

[7] HA to Charles Francis Adams, Jr., May 1, 1863, and Oct. 28, 1864, in *Cycle*, I, 278; II, 210.

ocean has gained symbolic meaning: the ocean's tides and currents, which will direct a boat or a life if the individual does not.

This use of water moving in a direction reappears in a letter written in 1867, when Adams, back home once more, is feeling more sanguine about the future. Up to 1876 his attitude is generally more hopeful than pessimistic, and a sense of drifting or of being blown about by fate is the exception rather than the rule. Most of the time he simply assumes that he can direct his own course, and his primary interest is not in the problem of whether or not he has free will, but in specific goals and methods of achieving them. In 1867 he writes to Charles,

> I never will make a speech, never run for an office, never belong to a party. I am going to plunge under the stream. For years you will hear nothing of any publication of mine—perhaps never, who knows. I do not mean to tie myself to anything, but I do mean to make it impossible for myself to follow the family go-cart. . . . I shall probably remain under water a long time. If you see me come up, it will be with an oyster and a pearl inside. If not, why—so!

Here, "the stream" is the movement of contemporary life. Adams, instead of being on a ship, is swimming. To float atop or with the stream seems to mean to be fashionable, powerful, or famous. Diving beneath the stream seems to mean cutting oneself off from the contemporary world, its fashions and its celebrities, and getting into the deeper and more stable water underneath, perhaps to universal human nature. Such an excursion will destroy the possibility of success in politics, which depends upon identification with contemporary life. At the same time, it is the only way to get material for a literary or historical work. Adams hopes by the publication of such a work to rise to the top of the stream again and is willing to risk permanent obscurity on the chance of doing so. The danger of drowning would seem to be the danger of such obscurity. Certainly that is what Adams means when, two years later and still in the stream, he writes triumphantly, "Though I have no power whatever and am held up solely by social position and a sharp tongue, yet I float. . . . We fishes do swim!"[8]

Thirteen years later, in 1880, at forty-two, his retirement from Harvard and from the editorship of the *North American Review* now four years past, he no longer uses such energetic images. The ship of an active career has become a philosophical ship and Adams himself, a philosopher "in this ocean of life," forced to keep his "eyes fixed on the horizon-line or a star, if [he doesn't] mean to be sea-sick." After his wife's death in 1885, another change occurs: the philosopher becomes a wanderer. In 1878 he had

[8] HA to Charles Francis Adams, Jr., Nov. 16, 1867; HA to Charles Milnes Gaskell, Dec. 7, 1869, in Ford (1858–1891), pp. 136, 174.

written, "It is ludicrous to play Ulysses," but ten years later he is a "professional wanderer," not only "on what Mr. Longfellow was pleased to call life's solemn main," but on literal oceans as well. Describing his entertainment by islanders in the South Seas, he comments, "As usual I felt like Odysseus." The role no longer seems ludicrous, though it remains distasteful. Adams can say of the "purple ocean" that "I gaze over it by the hour, wondering what lies beyond," but he also says, "I . . . dread unnecessary oceans." Repulsion, indeed, is stronger than attraction, and it is only ennui that keeps him moving: "The object of such long expeditions . . . is to tire myself out till home becomes rest." [9]

In the decade from 1892 to 1902 the traveler did tire himself out and the long sea-voyages came to an end. Figuratively, however, they continued. But now the wanderer became a drifter, and though he can still call himself "Odysseus" it is a rare hero who will announce, even facetiously, that "I am but a waif on the waters of eternity." Humor has replaced energy and it, more than anything else, helps to make the general tone of hopelessness and helplessness bearable. From 1904 to 1918 the aged Adams becomes an "ancient mariner," and the change reflects a further increase in the tone of helplessness. In *The Education* he writes of this period of his life that, "after so many years of effort to find one's drift, the drift found the seeker, and slowly swept him forward and back, with a steady progress oceanwards. . . . The process is possible only for men who have exhausted auto-motion." The suggestions of age and helplessness are made more graphic when he compares himself in his letters to "a log" floating on the tide or a "stray straw on the ocean." Finally, no longer able to steer even his own ship, much less those of his friends, he is grateful for the affectionate attention given him by his "nieces." "As a wreck," he says, "I float on the waves . . . but they never float,—they paddle. They work terribly hard at paddling one. Never had I so much devotion. Why are not all wrecks brought here and paddled?" [10] The boat that in 1860 waited to be launched has become,

---

[9] HA to Henry Cabot Lodge, July 9, 1880; HA to Charles Milnes Gaskell, Aug. 21, 1878, Ford (1858–1891), pp. 326, 308. HA to Elizabeth Cameron, Feb. 10, 1894, in Henry Adams, *Letters of Henry Adams, 1892–1918*, ed. Worthington Chauncey Ford (Boston: Houghton Mifflin Co., 1938), p. 36; hereafter cited as Ford (1892–1918). HA to Elizabeth Cameron [May or June (?)] 1887, Nov. 27, 1890, May 17, 1891, in Ford (1858–1891), pp. 384, 447, 487. HA to John Hay, Jan. 4, 1891, in Cater, p. 233. HA to Charles Milnes Gaskell, Mar. 8, 1888, in Ford (1858–1891), p. 388.

[10] HA to Brooks Adams, Aug. 10, 1902, in Cater, p. 529. HA to John Hay, Dec. 4, 1900, in Ford (1892–1918), p. 302. HA to Isabella Stewart Gardner [Mar. 17, 1909?], in Cater, p. 647. *The Education*, p. 426. HA to Mabel Hooper La Farge, May 5, 1908; HA to Whitelaw Reid, Aug. 1, 1909, in Cater, pp. 616, 659. HA to Anna Cabot Mills Lodge, Aug. 10, 1913, in Ford (1892–1918), p. 615.

at the end of life, a wreck; the intrepid seaman of 1863 has become an ancient mariner, helplessly dependent upon others. But the basic image for the man and for the life has remained the same: Adams still sees himself primarily as a voyager upon the ocean of existence.

After 1876, Adams occasionally uses water images for other individuals besides himself, though never often enough to be important. The most significant extension of this form of water imagery is the relationship between it and national character suggested by certain images common to *Esther* and *The History*.[11] In *Esther* the relevant images appear in the artist Wharton's description of the novel's heroine. She is "one of the most marked American types" he has ever seen. She is imperfect in figure and in features, he says; nonetheless she interests him:

> She gives one the idea of a lightly-sparred yacht in mid-ocean; unexpected; you ask yourself what the devil she is doing there. She sails gayly along, though there is no land in sight and plenty of rough weather coming. . . . She picks up all she knows without an effort and knows nothing well, yet she seems to understand whatever is said. Her mind is as irregular as her face, and both have the same peculiarity. I notice that the lines of her eyebrows, nose and mouth all end with a slight upward curve like a yacht's sails, which gives a kind of hopefulness and self-confidence to her expression. Mind and face have the same curves.

He adds that he has "passed weeks trying to catch" the type. But "the thing is too subtle, and it is not a grand type, like what we are used to in the academies." Many of these characteristics reappear in Adams' description in *The History* of the schooner used as a privateer in the War of 1812, a vessel Adams characterizes as uniquely American and makes the symbol of the national character. The American is said to be intelligent, rapid, and mild; the schooner is described as being built not to attack and fight, but to encounter the enemy quickly and, if necessary, to fly and escape.

> To obtain these results the builders and sailors ran excessive risks. Too lightly built and too heavily sparred, the privateer was never a comfortable or a safe vessel. Beautiful beyond anything then known in naval construction, such vessels roused boundless admiration, but defied imitators. . . . She could not bear conventional restraints.[12]

[11] Elizabeth Stevenson, *Henry Adams: A Biography* (New York: The Macmillan Co., 1955), p. 244, also notes this likeness.

[12] Henry Adams, *Esther: A Novel* by Francis Snow Compton [pseud.], with an introduction by Robert E. Spiller (New York: Scholars' Facsimiles and Reprints, 1938), pp. 26–28. Henry Adams, *The History of the United States of America During the Administrations of Thomas Jefferson and James Madison* (9 vols.; New York: Charles Scribner's Sons, 1889–1891), IX, 236, 240; VII, 318–319, 320.

As Esther, "one of the most marked American types," is imaged by a yacht, so the American national character is imaged by the privateer; no other nation has an equivalent to either. The primary quality of both is lightness and grace; neither is in the grand style. Both, indeed, are so slight or so lightly built as to be, or seem to be, in constant danger of capsizing and seem out of place on the ocean (whether literal or figurative); yet both have, or reflect, a certain gay confidence and hopefulness in the face of such danger. Neither is belligerent, yet both seem courageous. Esther finds that she cannot bear the "conventional restraints" Hazard hopes to impose upon her; if she were to submit she would be as pathetic as the captured privateers after the British shipbuilders had imposed "conventional restraints" upon them. The ships were no longer the same; Esther would not be the same woman.

This is Adams' view in the 1880's of the American national character in terms of his ship and ocean imagery. It is not his view of the nation as a political unity. The schooner is not the ship of state, but of American individualism, which is depicted in *The History* as detracting from the effectiveness of the political expression of society as a whole. The symbol Adams uses for the social whole, as a political entity, is the ship-of-state. In the novel *Democracy* he explains his heroine's restless desire to understand democracy by saying that it was "the feeling of a passenger on an ocean steamer whose mind will not give him rest until he has been in the engine-room and talked with the engineer." The ocean steamer here is the American ship-of-state; Mrs. Lee is a citizen of the state and a passenger on the ship, who feels she must visit the engine room, the center of social power, because it is there that the ship's movement is controlled. She goes to Washington, D.C., because it is the engine room of the American ship-of-state. Years earlier, Adams used the same image in reference to his own life in Washington, and also anticipated Mrs. Lee's reaction to her visit: "One appreciates least the success of the steamer, when one lives in the engine-room. I swear I feel as though I ought to give my soul a thorough washing."[13]

The ship-of-state differs in appearance from the schooner. The latter is characterized as lightly built and graceful. The ship-of-state is the great ocean steamer which appears in *Democracy*. In his first mature essay, "The Great Secession Winter, 1860–61," Adams says that, after the Virginia election of 1860, "the country began to wake from its despair. Slowly the great ship seemed to right itself, broken and water-logged it is true, but not wrecked." In *John Randolph*, two decades later, the

---

[13] Henry Adams, *Democracy: An American Novel* (New York: Henry Holt and Co., 1908), p. 10. HA to Charles Francis Adams, Jr., Feb. 23, 1869, in Ford (1858–1891), p. 152.

"uncomfortable boat" of the doctrine of states' rights is contrasted with "the broader and stancher deck of the national ship of state." [14] In *The History*, it is not the graceful and beautiful schooner but the sturdier and more practical steamboat which will help realize the social dream of a united and developed America and thus aid in the creation of a greater and more powerful ship-of-state. The steamboat itself is not the ship-of-state, but it is a ship of society, not of the individual.

As with personal ships, the chief problem of the ship-of-state is to stay afloat. The second problem is to make progress toward a goal. In the passage just quoted from "The Great Secession Winter" heavy seas threaten to sink the great ship. Even on peaceful seas there is the constant danger of rocks. Sometimes sheer good luck will, for a time, keep the ship from foundering, but eventually such luck will run out. So Adams writes of American financial problems after the Civil War that "the time had now come when the tide which had thus far floated the country over all its perils had reached its highest point and had begun to ebb." When the lucky tide ceases to flow, intelligence and effort must take its place. "A quiet and easy resumption," Adams writes, still of postwar financial problems, "is a port into which this country is destined neither to drift nor to drive; it has got patiently to beat there, in the face of wind and tide." In these early uses of the image, it is clear that Adams assumes that the ship can be guided and directed by man. This faith corresponds to the faith in free will found in the earlier personal images. In both cases the faith steadily declines with the passing of time. In 1900, he writes, "I laugh to see our Senate hitting and kicking at England whenever it can, scratching and biting, and all the same, dragged along, just like France and Germany, because we are all in the stream together." In the case of the political ship, however, such absolute determinism is never so completely pervasive as it becomes for Adams' personal ship. When he writes of the United States in 1899, for example, that "we are plunging about in pretty heavy seas, without headway," [15] there is implied the need for forward motion or progress and therefore its possibility.

The main responsibility for giving the ship direction and seeing that it makes progress rests with the President. In 1870 Adams says that the President "resembles the commander of a ship at sea. He must have a helm to grasp, a course to steer, a port to seek; he must sooner or later

[14] Henry Adams, "The Great Secession Winter, 1860–1861," in *Proceedings*, Massachusetts Historical Society, XLIII (1909–1910), 680. Henry Adams, *John Randolph* (Boston: Houghton Mifflin Co., 1899), p. 252.

[15] Henry Adams, "American Finance, 1865–1869," in *The Edinburgh Review*, CXXIX (April, 1869), 522. Henry Adams, "The Independents in the Canvass," in *North American Review*, CXXIII (Oct., 1876), 444. HA to Elizabeth Cameron, Mar. 26, 1900 and Feb. 5, 1899, in Ford (1892–1918), pp. 276, 213.

be convinced that a perpetual calm is as little to his purpose as a perpetual hurricane, and that without headway the ship can arrive nowhere." The critical administration for Adams' own life and for his generation was that of General Ulysses S. Grant. He says that, at the time of the election, "almost the entire public . . . expected to see [President Grant] at once grasp with a firm hand the helm of government, and give the vessel of state a steady and determined course." But "the President . . . assumed at the outset that it was not his duty to steer; that his were only duties of discipline." Because Grant failed to assume the responsibility Adams thought belonged to the executive, the ship-of-state drifted far off her rightful course. A quarter of a century later he says of McKinley that "his constitutional incapacity to act, or to move at all except when floated by a stream, begins to reach imbecility." [16] In the course of the twenty-five years between Grant and McKinley, Adams himself had given up the role of an active member of society and even that of a philosophical wanderer, and saw himself as simply abandoned to the "drift" or the "stream." His thought paralleled this change, and *The History*, published in 1891, expressed a belief in complete historical determinism. Nonetheless, he is as severe on McKinley for lacking strength and decisiveness in the presidential role as he was on Grant in 1870!

After 1903 Adams stops using the ship-of-state image, partly at least because his interest now lies less in political problems and more in the problems of society as a whole. During the period from 1861 to 1903, however, when he is using the image extensively, the ocean in which the ship-of-state floats is almost always the same normal ocean upon which the personal ship of Henry Adams floats. Both float upon an ocean of human and natural circumstance viewed as an antagonistic and constantly threatening force.

INNOVATIONS IN WATER IMAGERY, 1878–1891

In the period from 1878 to 1891 two important variations appear in the ocean image and one in the ship-of-state image. The first occurs in *The Life of Albert Gallatin* when Adams calls the nineteenth-century court of Louis XVIII of France "an accident and an anomaly, a curious fragment of the eighteenth century, floating, a mere wreck, on the turbulent ocean of French democracy." [17] Here is one of the occasional instances when Adams uses the ship-of-state image for a country other than the

---

[16] Henry Adams, "The Session," in *North American Review*, CXI (July, 1870), 34. *Ibid.*, pp. 32, 34. HA to Elizabeth Cameron, Feb. 19, 1899, in Ford (1892–1918), p. 218.

[17] Henry Adams, *The Life of Albert Gallatin* (Philadelphia: J. B. Lippincott and Co., 1879), p. 563.

United States. It is also one of the rare occasions when the political ship-of-state becomes a wreck. But neither of these variations basically alters the image of the ship. The important innovation is that for the first time the ship-of-state is simply the government of a country, rather than the country as a whole. The division this makes between government and people is, of course, partly what Adams wishes the image to suggest. Yet in making it do so, he has also modified the rest of the image. When the ship is the whole country, the ocean it floats in is one of human and natural circumstance. The citizens of the country are at once passengers on the ship and a part of the ocean, for the ocean is composed partly of natural forces and partly of human desires and actions, both inside and outside the country. In this new image the domestic human element is separated from the natural elements and the foreign human elements and considered an ocean in itself. Thus the ocean of democracy is an ocean of wholly human circumstance, made up entirely of human beings, and specifically of the citizens of a particular country.

An even more important innovation in the ship-of-state image and an equally important variation in the ocean image appear in the novel *Democracy*. The novel dramatizes Adams' rejection of the "private religion" of democracy he had avowed in 1863. He still calls democracy the best form of government, but there is a great difference between this opinion and his earlier reverence. This difference can be measured by comparing the ship-of-state imaged by the great ocean steamer of the first chapter with the last form the image takes in the book. There Adams sees "humanity floating in a shoreless ocean, on [a] plank, which experience and religion long since condemned as rotten." [18] This plank is the basic principle of democratic government, majority rule. However, since American democratic society is only that principle writ large, the plank is also the ship-of-state. Instead of being a passenger on a great ocean liner, Mrs. Lee, along with the rest of democratic humanity, has only a rotten plank between her and the ocean. No wonder she feels that her nerves are shaken to pieces and longs for the fixity of the polar star. In *The Education* this image of humanity helplessly adrift on a plank or a raft in a boundless ocean will become Adams' final image of the general human situation. In both books it expresses a sense of man's loneliness and helplessness amidst vast nonhuman forces. Indeed, even in *Democracy* the image expands beyond its specifically political denotation to suggest the general human situation. For this rotten plank is the *best* political and social principle man has ever found. What he floats on without it, or whether he floats at all, it is hard to imagine. It is partly the desperation of

[18] HA to Charles Francis Adams, Jr., May 1, 1863, in *Cycle*, I, 282. *Democracy*, pp. 181–182.

this "best" human situation, partly the sense that an even worse situation is more common, that makes the image so effective.

The particular nature of the ocean contributes much to this effect. By placing all humanity on the plank Adams has eliminated the human element from the normal ocean image. What remains is an ocean of wholly natural circumstance. Moreover, the adjective "shoreless" tends to destroy the sense of natural circumstance as being that which man regularly confronts in his daily life. It tends to raise this ocean of natural circumstance to a higher power, as it were, to make it an image of ultimate reality, of that ocean of nature in which all things exist. As a purely natural ocean, of course, it is the antithesis of the purely human ocean of democracy which floats the wreck of Louis XVIII's court. As a purely natural ocean, it also goes much further in the direction of its own final form than the purely human ocean does at this point. Only in *Esther*, published two years later, is there an image of reality in this earlier period so much like the image that will dominate *The Education of Henry Adams* twenty-seven years later.

In this primary period of innovation in Adams' water imagery (1878 to 1891), still another variation appears, far more important for the period itself than the new oceans. This image depends upon the fact that water moves in a direction, whether momentarily, as in the ocean tides, more permanently, as in the ocean currents, or always, as in a river. For Adams this movement symbolizes the movement of man in time. After 1883 this movement and its images become increasingly important in his work and finally find expression in a new image. Up to 1883, the few images of such movement, such as the "stream," make it a part of the ocean. In 1883, however, it assumes an independent form by becoming a river.[19]

The first significant appearance of the river as a symbol is in a letter written in 1883. Adams contrasts Albert Gallatin, "the most fully and perfectly equipped statesman we can show," with Jefferson, Madison, and Monroe, who appear to him

> like mere grasshoppers kicking and gesticulating on the middle of the Mississippi River. There is no possibility of reconciling their theories with their acts, or their extraordinary foreign policy with dignity. They were carried along on a stream which floated them, after a fashion, without much regard to themselves.

At the end of the letter he adds that

> the element of individuality is the free-will dogma of the science [of history], if it is a science. My own conclusion is that history is simply social development

---

[19] Though cf., Ernest Samuels, *Henry Adams: The Middle Years* (Cambridge, Mass.: Harvard University Press, 1958), pp. 79, 440 n. 12.

along the lines of weakest resistance, and that in most cases the line of weakest resistance is found as unconsciously by society as by water.[20]

The first and last sections of this letter seem inconsistent. In his biography of Gallatin, Adams shows how Gallatin, with the same basic ideas as Jefferson, Madison, and Monroe, is far more rigorous in applying them and much more honest in modifying or abandoning them when they prove impractical. Gallatin does not, therefore, simply float with the stream, refusing to see the contradictions between his theories and the acts which circumstances force upon him. In this characteristic lies the contrast Adams draws between him and his fellows. Yet the lesson which Gallatin's integrity teaches is that circumstances are stronger than either principles or men. This is what Adams suggests in the second passage here; indeed, he goes further and denies that individuals have any important effect on history. The river moves at the same rate and in the same direction whatever men do and whether or not they are aware of what is going on. Usually, they are not so aware.

In terms of the movement of history, this determinism would seem to make Adams' claim that Gallatin is superior to his fellows meaningless. All are equally victims of circumstance. Men do, of course, live as individuals as well as elements of humanity and history, and, as an individual, Gallatin, as Adams presents him, has more of honesty and integrity than do his fellows. But Adams gives no reason why such qualities should be considered admirable. In later, similarly deterministic utterances, he will make it clear that the individual can live at odds with the stream and, in extraordinary circumstances, even slow down its movement. Such a possibility gives some room for individuality to affect history and some pragmatic basis for making moral judgments of individuals. In this letter, however, little such leeway is admitted. Adams' praise of Gallatin seems based upon little more than a cherished prejudice remaining from the wreck of a metaphysic admitting the existence and efficacy of free will.

Adams uses the river here as a symbol of history, specifically, of social development. By using the Mississippi River, the greatest of American rivers, he underscores his belief in the dominance of circumstances and the helplessness of individuals in that development. This sense of the omnipotence of circumstances, along with a belief that society is moving in a direction, seems to be the basis for the use of the river image in general. The ocean, despite its tides and currents, cannot so effectively image both of these ideas at once.

[20] HA to Samuel Jones Tilden, Jan. 24, 1883, in Cater, pp. 125–126. Brunner (68–69) relates the water symbolism in this letter to that in *The History* and *The Education*.

In 1884, the year following this letter, that accelerated portion of the Niagara River which comprises Niagara Falls appears as an important symbol in the novel *Esther*. As a symbol, the falls has at least two meanings.[21] It is primarily the symbol for the new world mankind is entering: that is, like the river, it is a historical symbol suggesting movement toward the future. But now this movement is seen as intellectual rather than social development; the river of history is a river of thought. The identity of a historical era is determined by the idea it adheres to. All such ideas are particular versions of absolute truth. In western civilization the movement from the classical to the medieval to the modern world has been evolutionary. Along with the ideas and symbols of this process, Adams presents a symbol for ultimate reality and absolute truth. This symbol is the ocean, which, unlike the falls, with its steady, directional movement, is a mass of confusion and contradiction, simultaneously caressing and cruel. Set against this symbol, the new world of the falls seems to be only a happy interlude amidst a much harsher reality. The falls' other meaning has a more immediate relevance to Esther's own life. Dynamically rather than statically conceived, the falls suggests the abrupt and terrific change in human thought as it moves from one world into another. Such a change often seems to be accompanied by suffering for individuals, as it is for Esther.

The primary emphasis of the book is upon Esther's personal tragedy, but this is set, not against the ocean, but against the promise of the new and better world symbolized by the falls. The falls is the most important symbol in the book. For the first and only time in Adams' work a water symbol is a major structural device. Only in *The Education* are water symbols more important, and there if they were eliminated from the book its argument and structure would remain the same whereas in *Esther* both would be radically incomplete.

The larger framework suggested for the novel by the contrast between the falls and the ocean has a striking similarity to the pattern of symbols in *The Education* and *Chartres*. Poetry and the ocean form the absolute human and natural antithesis in *Esther*; the drama and the ocean are the corresponding antithesis in the latter works. The Church and the falls are the opposing symbols of religion and nature here; the Virgin and the dynamo are the opposing symbols of religion and science there. The similarity suggests that Adams' later period begins with *Esther*. (In

[21] Sister M. Aquinas Healy, "A Study of Non-Rational Elements in the Works of Henry Adams as Centralized in his Attitude toward Women" (Ph.D. dissertation, University of Wisconsin, 1956), pp. 278–279, notes that the falls resembles the democratic ocean in *The History* in that both "represent natural forces which determine the destiny of society and of individual man—whether he will or no."

Democracy the American spirit rejects democracy as an ideal worthy of religious veneration; in *Esther* it also rejects the ideal embodied by the Church and accepts a new religious ideal, embodied in a natural object rather than a human being or a human creation.) Yet there are also profound differences between the pattern here and that in the later work. The difference is suggested by the contrast between the benign influence of the falls and the predominantly malign influence of the ocean of chaos in the later works. Man's proper response to the falls would seem to be that of submitting to its influence, whereas his proper response to the ocean is to minimize its influence as much as possible. Thus in the later works the spiritual naturism of *Esther* becomes pessimistic naturalism, modified by a humanism which looks to man rather than nature for desirable patterns and standards of human behavior. Paradoxically, the primary expression of this humanism is Adams' naturalistic dynamic theory of history. Its basic principle appears in *Esther*, though only by implication. Niagara Falls makes obvious, for the first time in Adams' use of water imagery, the fact that water follows the law of gravity and falls downwards. In *Esther* no symbolic significance is attached to this fact, but in the later works "the fall" becomes the fundamental process of nature. (In "A Letter to American Teachers of History," the falls itself reappears when Adams notes that the Niagara River gains power "by degrading its own energies." [22] Here the downward movement of the falls and the symbolic significance of that fact has become the reason for its use.) Thus in *Esther*, despite basic differences between it and the later work, Adams seems to be feeling his way toward the images and the relationships between them which he will later use.

Though *Esther* is more deterministic in its ideas than *Democracy*, it too is presented in a semidramatic form in which the deterministic element in history is subordinated to individual human choice. In *The History* (which appeared in 1891, seven years after *Esther*, though Adams had been working on it even before he wrote *Democracy*), Adams has a more rigorous obligation to history. Hence, as has already been suggested, his partial dramatization of his material gains an ironic quality by being contrasted with the impersonal and deterministic forces which really control history. At climactic moments involving the latter, he occasionally uses water imagery. Here, for the first time, the two most pervasive images in Adams' work, the drama and water, come into direct conflict. In discussing the ultimate consequences of the Napoleonic era, Adams writes that

[22] Henry Adams, "A Letter to American Teachers of History," in *The Degradation of the Democratic Dogma*, with an introduction by Brooks Adams (New York: The Macmillan Co., 1919), p. 241.

The workings of human development were never more strikingly shown than in the helplessness with which the strongest political and social forces in the world followed or resisted at haphazard the necessities of a movement which they could not control or comprehend. Spain, France, Germany, England, were swept into a vast and bloody torrent which dragged America, from Montreal to Valparaiso, slowly into its movement; while the familiar figures of famous men . . . were borne away by the stream . . . ; each blind to everything but a selfish interest, and all helping more or less unconsciously to reach the new level which society was obliged to seek.[23]

Here is a supplement to the 1883 letter which clears up its ambiguities. The image is a torrent or a stream rather than a river, but again it refers to the movement of history as social development. Again this development is largely unconscious. And again—and even more emphatically—it is unaffected by individuals. Even a Gallatin is "borne away by the stream," and those who oppose it ultimately only contribute to its movement. This is the final expression of the river image's original emphasis upon the forces which move the individual. Now the individual not only has no power to effectively resist the stream, he actually contributes to its movement even in resisting.

The next development in the river image is its reassociation with the ocean image, not as an ocean current but as a movement toward the ocean as its ultimate goal. This combined image is Adams' most complex and comprehensive water image up to this time. It appears for the first time in his work in the final chapter of *The History*, at the end of his contrast between dramatic and scientific history, in which he says that the United States is the first country whose history can best be studied scientifically— that is, as reflecting the laws of social development rather than the lives and actions of heroes. "Travellers in Switzerland," he says,

who stepped across the Rhine where it flowed from its glacier could follow its course among mediaeval towns and feudal ruins, until it became a highway for modern industry, and at last arrived at a permanent equilibrium in the ocean. American history followed the same course. With prehistoric glaciers and mediaeval feudalism the story had little to do; but from the moment it came within sight of the ocean it acquired interest almost painful. A child could find his way in a river-valley, and a hoy could float on the waters of Holland; but science alone could sound the depths of the ocean, measure its currents, foretell its storms, or fix its relations to the system of Nature. In a democratic ocean science could see something ultimate. Man could go no further. The atom might move, but the general equilibrium could not change.[24]

[23] *The History*, IV, 301–302.
[24] *Ibid.*, IX, 225. Edward Allen Chalfant, "Henry Adams and History" (Ph.D. dissertation, University of Pennsylvania, 1954), pp. 210–211, after noting Adams' comparison of the United States to the flow of the Rhine, points out in footnote 23 the

There seem to be two rivers of history here, the Rhine and an unnamed American river. Both seem to be rivers of social development, for both find a common goal in the "democratic ocean." This ocean is another expression of the purely human ocean already examined in connection with the court of Louis XVIII in *Gallatin*. A third and new image is that of the glacier. As the beginning of history, it suggests a primitive condition characterized by an equilibrium having an irresistible tendency to become disequilibrium, just as the ocean at the end of history is the final equilibrium which cannot change. Here, because it is used for the European beginnings of the transplanted culture of America, it is not a very relevant image. Later in Adams' work it will become more so.

The crucial question is whether the movement from glacier to river to ocean is a movement of progress. In the first chapters of *The History* Adams is certain it is; this view continues throughout most of the work. In the final chapter, however, he grows doubtful. Viewed in the light of his later works, the extended water figure just cited implies the same uncertainty— or even the later pessimism. For in this passage, as in *Esther*, the fact that rivers move by falling is essential to the image, though again no symbolic meaning is attached to the fact. But the history of the river image in Adams' work is the history of the gradual attribution of symbolic meaning to each of its major physical characteristics. It was the directional movement of tides or currents in the ocean which first made the river, in the letters, an image of contemporary life; in the 1883 letter the irresistibility and irreversibility of this movement in a river made it an effective image of history and its deterministic movement. In *Esther*, other characteristics were given meaning. At the end of *The History* it is the

---

likenesses of this image to that of the stream which is carrying society to a new level (*The History*, IV, 301-302): "Here again [Adams] uses a water metaphor, speaking of a 'stream,' 'a vast and bloody torrent,' suggesting an irresistible river into which all were drawn, but which none could 'control or comprehend.'" Chalfant then denies that Adams' statement is deterministic by adding that "the stream *is* the sum of [men's] several actions." Healy, "A Study of Non-Rational Elements in the Works of Adams," p. 631, says, "The ocean is the major symbol of democracy itself, and many are the symbols of the vast currents of that ocean, to say nothing of the rivers and streams which perpetually flow into it." Samuels, *The Middle Years*, pp. 358-359, views Adams' use of the stream imagery as one of the keys for discerning the influence of Herbert Spencer upon *The History*. He relates the Rhine image to the river image in the letter to Samuel Jones Tilden (Jan. 24, 1883, in Cater, 125-126) and cites comparable usages in Spencer's *First Principles*. Henry Burt Rule, "Irony in the Works of Henry Adams" (Ph.D. dissertation, University of Colorado, 1960), after noting (p. 148) that Adams' frequent telescope-like perspective in *The History* led him to note and record "the irony of man's helplessness as he was swept away by forces he could neither control nor comprehend," says that "to express this irony, Adams often used the stream metaphor." (In two footnotes, p. 149, Rule cites the Tilden letter and *The History*, IV, 300-302.)

physical fact that rivers often begin with glaciers, or ice and snow, and end in oceans which is made symbolically significant. It was perhaps to be expected, therefore, that eventually the falling movement of the river would also acquire a symbolic meaning. That such a meaning would associate the fall with progress, connected in conventional symbolism with an upward movement, was unlikely. The most likely possibility was that it would make some use of the pessimistic implications conventionally associated with falling.

The ocean image in Adams' work does not show such systematic development. The normal ocean of human and natural circumstance which appears most often up to this time can, as has already been pointed out, be either stormy or calm. Separated from this ocean, the ocean of natural circumstance or of reality perhaps suggests more of storm than of calm, but at most this is only a suggestion. The one occurrence of a purely human ocean thus far has been the "turbulent ocean of French democracy." In *The History*, however, Adams views the democratic ocean as a calm ocean which may cease to move at all. The social condition it images is a maximum of equality among individuals, which tends to decrease individual differentiation and produce a monotonous uniformity in national character. Such uniformity can lead to the stifling of all individuality and thus to social stagnation. This tendency of the human ocean to become a "dead ocean" is the direction the image will generally take in the later works, while the ocean of nature will tend to become the ocean of chaos it is in *Esther*. Hence, Adams tends either to be bored by the extreme calm of the human ocean or made seasick by the constant storminess of the ocean of nature.[25]

Water Imagery from *Chartres* to *Lodge*

In *Mont-Saint-Michel and Chartres* and again in Adams' last work, *The Life of George Cabot Lodge*, the ocean of natural chaos reappears. The closest Adams comes to making the meaning of the image explicit in *Chartres* is his remark, late in the book, that "an economic civilization troubles itself about the universe much as a hive of honey-bees troubles about the ocean, only as a region to be avoided." The nature of this ocean appears in the first paragraph of the book, where Adams writes that St. Michael stands "on his Mount in Peril of the Sea, watching across the tremor of the immense ocean." As in *Esther*, a divine personage looks out across the ocean of chaos and contradiction. But this is no pagan divinity of nature. St. Michael is the representative of the Church, a supreme expression of the human belief in unity. His antagonist is the multiplicity of the sea, constantly surging against the rock upon which the Church stands. In *Lodge* the human world is Boston. A few miles away at Nahant, however, one "looks out forever to an infinite horizon of shoreless and shifting ocean." The two are antagonistic once again. The sea tends "to revive some primitive instinct in boys, as though in a far-off past they had been fishes, and had never quite forgotten their home." [26] Obedience to this instinct leads to rebellion against civilization and a search for greater harmony with nature. The human mission of St. Michael is to kill this instinct; unity, the Church, and civilization can survive only if it is destroyed. But St. Michaels always fail: both literal and figurative rocks eventually always succumb to the sea's destructive power. In Michael's case the physical rock which supports the mount still stands, but the rock of faith which upheld his Church has disappeared. Only the lifeless art, silence, and the eternal sea remain. Lodge's fate is different. He never loses his sense of unity with nature, and thus dies still a child, believing that civilization is evil and nature, good.

A substantial percentage of all the water imagery in Adams' published work appears in *The Education of Henry Adams*.[27] The ocean is the principal image. During most of the book it takes the form of the normal ocean image, but in the later chapters it becomes the natural ocean of chaos. The ocean imagery is closely related to the book's most important structural element. This element grows out of the wavelike form assumed by the recurrent experience which Adams views as the basic experience of his life. Throughout his youth, and to some extent always, he depicts himself as believing in unity as he enters each new area of life; realizing at some point in his accumulation of experience that unity is false and multiplicity true; collapsing into disillusionment; and then regaining a measure of what he eventually decides is man's instinctive sense of unity. The form of this experience appears structurally as a tendency for chapters in *The Education* to occur in pairs, one emphasizing unity, the other multiplicity. The analogy between this alternation and the ebb and flow of the ocean means that the most important structural element in the book

[26] Henry Adams, *Mont-Saint-Michel and Chartres*, with an introduction by Ralph Adams Cram (Boston: Houghton Mifflin Co., 1933), pp. 345, 1. Henry Adams, *The Life of George Cabot Lodge* (Boston: Houghton Mifflin Co., 1911), p. 11.

[27] I counted approximately 345 passages in all of Adams' work which significantly mention water, whether literally or figuratively. I found 74 such passages in *The Education*, or 21 percent. Other commentators have cited several instances which I missed, both in Adams' work in general and in *The Education*. These do not seem to me to affect my interpretation of the use and meaning of water symbolism in *The Education* and in the work as a whole. Nor do they seem to me to affect my conclusion that *The Education* contains a sizable percentage of the total number of such symbols in Adams' work. But they do show that my statistics are only approximate.

and its chief symbol express one another and that both organically embody the theme: that history has alternated between periods when man creatively asserted his sense of unity and those when that sense grew weak and he was moved by the chaos of reality to assist it in destroying his own creations; that in the twentieth century he is in the period of most intense social and individual chaos in history; and that the little chance he has of surviving or delaying his doom—or even the better chance he has of meeting that doom with dignity—rests, as always, upon his effective assertion of his dream of order.[28]

The cyclical rhythm of Adams' experience is also progressive and moves toward two climaxes: first, his full realization that reality is chaos and, second, an assertion of order as his own final human response to that knowledge. The first climax makes little use of water symbolism;[29] indeed, the first twenty chapters do not make nearly so much use of it as the second part of the book does.[30] Three pages after the latter begins, Adams' crucial statement that perhaps only the wanderer has "felt the world exactly as it is" concludes one of the most vivid water images in *The Education*: that in which Adams wishes he could "sleep forever . . . , wandering over the dark purple ocean, with its purple sense of solitude and void." Later, in "The Abyss of Ignorance," Adams depicts himself as deciding that the kinetic theory of gases is the key to the nature of reality and changing the normal ocean image to "an ocean of colliding atoms" to fit the new conception of reality. In "The Grammar of Science" the

[28] Brunner, "Henry Adams: His Decline and Fall," pp. 368–369, observes that for purposes of his *Education*, Adams accepted the modern multiverse at Pearson's evaluation—as a supersensual chaos. It was his phenomenalistic chaos ["in which absolutes dissolved into relationships . . . . in which time and space became modes of human perception merely" (p. 270)], aqueous, vague, indeterminate, that Adams was striving to create through the symbolistic technique of the *Education* . . . a tentative effort . . . to make his writing . . . as amorphous as the dimensions of supersensual chaos itself.

In other passages (*ibid.*, pp. 366, 381–383) Brunner further correlates the water symbolism with Adams' use of symbolist and stream-of-consciousness techniques.

[29] The word "void," which appears in the phrase, "vibrating in a void of shapeless energies" (*The Education*, p. 288) appears again in Adams' characterization of the bird which appears "suddenly and inexplicably out of some unknown and unimaginable void" and in the succeeding description of the human mind waking, "after sixty or seventy years . . . to find itself looking blankly into the void of death" (*ibid.*, p. 460). Between these passages Adams expresses his desire at one point "to sleep forever . . . , wandering over the dark purple ocean, with its purple sense of solitude and void" (*ibid.*, p. 316). Thus a key word in Adams' description of his sister's death, which refers to the meaninglessness of ultimate reality (and, later, of death), is eventually used to characterize his chief symbol of that reality. (See also *ibid.*, p. 504.)

[30] Brunner also observes this fact, "Henry Adams: His Decline and Fall," p. 375.

significance of that decision for man's relationship to nature is expressed in Adams' ultimate formula—"Chaos [is] the law of nature; Order [is] the dream of man"—and in his ultimate (explicit) water image—man as "adrift on a sensual raft in the midst of a supersensual chaos." [31] Twenty-five years earlier, in the novel *Democracy*, Adams had seen humanity floating on a rotten plank in a shoreless ocean. There, as here, it was the destruction of a cherished ideal which evoked the ultimate image. But there the idea had been a political ideal, and the image, whatever its general implications, an image of man's political situation. Here, the shattered ideal is the ultimate human ideal, man's belief in unity, and the image is explicitly of the total human situation. Yet in both cases the image is basically the same ship and ocean image Adams had been using during the almost fifty years which had passed since he wrote his mother about the plans which would finish setting him afloat.

In the final chapter of *The Education* Adams uses the glacier as an image of the dynamic theory and describes himself as a seal crawling up on the glacier to die in peace. This ice image appeared once before in Adams' work, in the ice-river-ocean image at the end of *The History*. In *The Education* it has the same fundamental meaning: it is a primitive condition of energy, an inert potential, which ultimately will dissolve and become part of an ocean. But the process by which it does so is different in *The Education* from what it was in *The History*. There the melting glacier became a river which fell to an ocean of water where it lost all motion and energy in a final equilibrium. Here, the river hardly appears at all— though it could easily have done so. The *basic* structural element in *The Education* is the linear movement of the protagonist in time, a movement emphasized by the insertion of parenthesized dates at the beginning of each chapter. The river is a natural image for such movement and Adams' use of it, as in *The History*, often contains a temporal element. But to have used it here, in *The Education*, would have been to emphasize the work's linear structure at the expense of the more important alternating structure and thereby suggest that history is a single, massive movement toward a goal. This symbolism would have violated the primary contention of *The Education* that "Chaos [is] the law of nature" and hence that history is "incoherent." [32] Therefore, instead of using the ice-river-ocean figure, Adams uses the ice-water-steam figure. In this figure ice (the inertia of Russia or woman or the dynamic theory) becomes water but then continues to absorb energy until the water explodes into isolated molecules

---

[31] *The Education*, pp. 316, 431, 451, 452.

[32] *Ibid.*, pp. 451, 301. It is at this point that Brunner and I differ crucially in our interpretation of the water symbolism in *The Education*. See critical note 67.

of vapor moving with maximum speed and energy in a supersensual ocean. Here too man has a goal, but his movement toward it is disconnected and catastrophic. Instead of flowing toward a quiescent equilibrium he disintegrates in a violent explosion.

This imagery is clearly more appropriate to Adams' ultimate point of view. For the dynamic theory, however, the ice-river-ocean image is more appropriate, for the theory rests upon the admittedly false assumption that history does have a single, massive, linear movement. The omission of the river image from *The Education* suggests Adams' subordination there of the theory to his ultimate view. In the later historical essays, and the letters written at the same time as they, both images are used.[33] The idea of distinct phases in history is described in terms of the ice-water-steam imagery, while the river-ocean image is used to describe the unity of movement which the theory emphasizes. When the goal of history is described, however, it is generally, though not always,[34] the quiescent equilibrium of *The History*. This fact suggests that the essays are less concerned than *The Education* with the increase in man's supply of non-human force and more with his own loss of energy as a force. In the letters Adams wrote at the time the essays were current, he says that this loss has reached its final period in the twentieth century. In 1909, for example, he writes,

> Society no longer shows the intellectual life necessary to enable it to react against a stimulus. My brother Brooks insists on the figure of paralysis. I prefer the figure of diffusion, like that of a river falling into an ocean. Either way, it drowned Bay [Lodge, the poet], and has left me still floating, with vast curiosity to see what vaster absence of curiosity can bring about in my Sargasso Sea.[35]

This is the usual river of history, given a meaning similar to that assigned in *Esther* to Niagara Falls as the movement of thought. The image itself, however, is that of the last chapter of *The History* (without the glacier). There the river was history as social development, and the ocean was the diffusion of society in the ocean of democracy. Here the river of man's developing social thought also moves into an ocean where that thought becomes diffused. But there the movement was ostensibly one of progress, and the fact that the river falls to reach the ocean was not even mentioned. Here, its falling, and the symbolic significance attached to that fact,

[33] E.g., "A Letter," p. 213.

[34] "A Letter," pp. 145, 249; Henry Adams, "The Rule of Phase Applied to History," in *The Degradation of the Democratic Dogma*, with an introduction by Brooks Adams (New York: The Macmillan Co., 1919), pp. 281, 309.

[35] HA to Henry James, Sept. 3, 1909, in Ford (1892–1918), p. 522.

becomes one of the two principal elements in the image's meaning. That the river falls means that man's thought has steadily lost energy: its movement is one of decline rather than progress.

The ocean here is not the ocean of nature of *The Education* but the human ocean of *The History*. It is also a "democratic ocean." In 1910 Adams writes that "the *Letter* [*to American Teachers of History*] is intended as a historical study of the scientific grounds of Socialism, Collectivism, and Humanitarianism and Democracy and all the rest. . . . I maintain that . . . we are already in principles at the bottom,—that is, at the great ocean equi-potential,—and can get no further." The ocean that man has degenerated to is the ocean of democracy, "equi-potential" here being equivalent to "equilibrium" in the passage from *The History*. But in this ocean all the worst fears Adams had expressed in the final chapter of *The History* have been realized. His prediction there was that, "if at any time American character should change, it might as probably become sluggish as revert to the violence and extravagances of Old-World development." [36] At this point he is speaking specifically about America. But in *The History* image the Rhine too flows into the ocean: Europe, too, has been moving toward democracy. Hence, what is said of America tends to be true for Europe. The letters also suggest that the river and ocean are European as well as American. In both cases the movement has been steadily toward the ocean of democracy and in both cases that ocean has proved to be an inert sea of stagnation.

In "The Rule" and "A Letter" the images change somewhat. River and ocean become specifically images of "Thought" or of "psychical energy." In the passage just cited, in which Adams images society's lack of intellectual life by comparing it to a river falling into an ocean, he is equating the river with man's intellectual development, and the ocean with his state when that development ends. Yet society is also emphasized; there is not the complete abstractness which appears in a "current of Thought" or an "ocean of . . . thought." [37] This greater abstractness enables Adams to give his ideas both broader applicability and more precise expression than he could get using the less abstract terms. In "A Letter," for example, he treats man's thought as a degraded form of the force called Will, which exists in the most primitive forms of life. In this case, greater abstractness gives his ideas and his images a far more general applicability than they would have if he had written strictly in terms of human society and history. But the greater abstractness is also more appropriate to his view of history, which is that history *is* something more

---

[36] *The History*, IX, 225. HA to Raphael Pumpelly, May 19, 1910, in Ford (1892–1918), p. 541. *The History*, IX, 241.

[37] "The Rule," p. 281. "A Letter," p. 235. "The Rule," pp. 281, 309.

abstract than social development. In *The Education* Adams investigates every aspect of human life and activity, seeking continuity. His investigation proves a failure in every case but two, the biological continuity given the race by woman's inertia of sex and the intellectual continuity created by the mind's pervasive tendency to view reality as unity.[38] Thus the most valid way of studying history (except as a biological succession of human beings), is to study it as a movement of thought.

Adams uses the river image to mirror this kind of history too. In terms of thought, the river and ocean image of *The History* and of the letters just discussed becomes in "The Rule" an "ethereal current of Thought," which "is conceived as existing, like ice on a mountain range, and trickling from every pore of rock, in innumerable rills, uniting always into larger channels, and always dissolving whatever it meets, until at last it reaches equilibrium in the ocean of ultimate solution." The image of the initial ice, which was used in *The History*, reappears. The actual process of the river diffusing in the ocean is also described later in the same essay as "the subsidence of the current [of thought] into an ocean of potential thought, or mere consciousness . . . like static electricity." In "A Letter" Adams translates this highly abstract "scientific" expression back into somewhat more concrete historical terms. The river of history will end in an "ocean of statistics," that is, in a mass of separate facts unrelated by a coherent body of meaning. Another passage from the letters shows how this translation can be further translated into specifically social terms. In 1909 Adams writes a woman friend that "I am glad that you mean to resume your duties in New York society. Except for women, society is now an infinite solution; a mere ocean of separate particles; and you can help it to one little centre. I own that the centre will do nothing; but it may play itself to be real."[39]

The final expression of this ocean image appears in "A Letter to American Teachers of History." The essay itself is Adams' longest, fullest, and most objective version of the dynamic theory of history, as well as its final form. In *The Education* the theory is the view of history "imposed by science on the generation born after 1900." It makes use of the law of gravitation and the formula of squares. But it is also avowedly an attempt to chart the movement of history according to the course of Adams' life and thus is his own autobiography *writ large*. In "The Rule" the theory is emancipated from *The Education* and from the explicit autobiographical analogy. Here Adams tries to chart the course of history according to the law of solutions, Willard Gibbs' "Rule of Phases," and

---

[38] *The Education*, pp. 441, 456.

[39] "The Rule," pp. 281, 308–309. "A Letter," p. 249. HA to Margaret Chanler, Sept. 9, 1909, in Ford (1892–1918), p. 524.

the law of squares. In "A Letter," however, he found a single scientific principle, supposed to be true of all nature, which harmonized with the theme of his theory: the second law of thermodynamics. According to this law, Nature is steadily losing energy "until, at the last, nothing [will] be left except a dead ocean of energy at its lowest possible level . . . and incapable of doing any work whatever, since work [can] be done only by a fall of tension, as water does work in falling to sea-level."[40] In *The Education* no mention was made of nature's energies undergoing any change; by implication therefore they were static; thus man's dissipation of his own energy simply restored him at last to the ocean of chaos. Now, nature itself undergoes the same dissipation as man; like him, it moves or changes in time and has a history. Thus, in "A Letter" the dynamic theory has escaped not only from being a form of autobiography but even from being a philosophy simply of human history. It has become the historical aspect of a theory of reality. It is a special theory implying a general theory, a dynamic theory of nature, as it were.

Adams says in "A Letter" that, among the "number of figures" which the "degradationist can produce from his stores of energies" to illustrate his argument, one is "water, which expands or contracts, according to the temperature, or falls according to its position."[41] Thus, in his final version of the theory, both volatilization and falling are images, not only of the degeneration of man (as they were in *The Education* and "The Rule"), but of nature as well. Yet falling seems a better image here. Volatilization (or expansion) was appropriate for man's development toward absorption by a reality that did not itself develop. For "A Letter's" view that the fall is the basic process of all nature, the image of man and nature falling toward a common goal seems better. It is also more appropriate for the "dead ocean of energy" which "A Letter" says is the common goal of man and nature. Such an ocean is the natural equivalent of the human "democratic ocean" of *The History*, or the "ocean of potential thought" of "The Rule," or the ocean of socialism, collectivism, and democracy in the letters of 1909 and 1910. It is that dead human ocean raised to the higher power of a dead natural ocean, of which the human ocean is only a part. This "dead ocean" of nature appears only in "A Letter," but it is the culminating expression of this particular ocean image in Adams' work.

In terms of imagery he has used earlier, this ocean image implies the ice-river-ocean series. Adams says in "A Letter" both that falling water is an apt figure for the process of degradation[42] and that the second law of thermodynamics likened energy "to a falling substance tending to an

---

[40] *The Education*, p. 459. "A Letter," p. 145.
[41] "A Letter," p. 213.   [42] *Ibid.*, pp. 211, 213.

ultimate ocean of Entropy." The next step would be to use ice as an image for the initial state of nature. Such a state would be one of total inertness and maximum usable energy. But the image is not used. Adams does say (supposedly paraphrasing Lord Kelvin) that "creations always grow . . . higher in tension as you go backward," but he adds that "all [creations] are still subordinate and even trivial when compared with the primary creation of energy itself, about which no one knows anything except its name,—Nature." His own speculations about this primal state of energy do not suggest that it was a state aptly imaged by ice. His physicist-persona says that "nature is full of rival energies, and,—for anything we know,—may once have been full of hostile energies; but, hostile or friendly, its infinite variety of Forms . . . and Complexities, had taken order . . . before man . . . or any other . . . life, or vital energy, ever stirred!" In other passages, it becomes clear that this state of order *was* preceded by a state of "hostile energies." Adams' physicist says that "geology suggests . . . that, after at least fifty million years of conditions which made life impossible except under water, these anarchic forces [which prevailed at the beginning] dissipated themselves so far as to settle into an equilibrium." Adams also quotes a contemporary de-gradationist's assertion that "the Disorder towards which a collection of molecules moves, is in no respect the initial chaos rich in differences and inequalities that generate useful energies; on the contrary it is the average mean of equality and homogeneity in absolute want of co-ordination."[43] These passages suggest that the degradationist (and, therefore, "A Letter") views nature as having been, at its creation, in a state not of inertness, but of violent anarchy (except for the operation of the second law), with a maximum amount of energy available to do work. Constant dissipation of this energy led eventually to an unstable equilib-rium—or, rather, to a multitude of equilibriums—also subject to dis-sipation, and tending to become anarchy once again, now, however, without any usable energy.

Adams never created an image for this whole process. Clearly, the ice-river-ocean imagery would not have been appropriate. He does, however, use a specific image for what he says in "A Letter" will be the final state of nature. Nature's history will end in a "dead ocean" of absolute quiescence.

But what of man? What is his fate to be? In *The Education* Adams says that, like all other forces, man "must continue" to absorb new force, until "the reservoirs of sensuous or supersensuous energies are exhausted, or cease to affect him, or until he succumbs to their excess." The first alternative is unlikely; the second suggests the dead ocean of energy, but

[43] *Ibid.*, pp. 242, 202, 223, 225, 257.

in *The Education* no reason is given for believing in its possibility. The third alternative suggests volatilization or explosion into the multiverse. In regard to this possibility Adams says that, "thus far, since five or ten thousand years, the mind had successfully reacted, and nothing yet proved that it would fail to react—but it would need to jump." In the final chapter, however, the new man with the new mind is not to be seen, though everywhere men are crying for him. "The cylinder had exploded," Adams says, and this seems to be the threat and the danger in *The Education*: that man will not react or will not react quickly enough, and the new forces will explode him into the ultimate "ocean of colliding atoms." [44]

At the end of "The Rule of Phase Applied to History" Adams poses two possibilities for man as he enters the final phase of his thought. All evidence points to the

> subsidence of the current [of thought] into an ocean of potential thought, or mere consciousness, which is also possible, like static electricity. The only consequence might be an indefinitely long stationary period. . . . In that case, the current would merely cease to flow.
>
> But if, in the prodigiously rapid vibration of its last phases, Thought should continue to act as the universal solvent which it is, and should reduce the forces of the molecule, the atom, and the electron to that costless servitude to which it has reduced the old elements of earth and air, fire and water; if man should continue to set free the infinite forces of nature, and attain the control of cosmic forces on a cosmic scale, the consequences may be as surprising as the change of water to vapor, of the worm to the butterfly, of radium to electrons. At a given volume and velocity, the forces that are concentrated on his head must act.

Adams is ambiguous, but he seems to mean that man may either explode or mutate. The last, of course, is an unpredictable possibility. Stagnation or explosion thus remain the chief possibilities. In "A Letter" he is much less explicit about the future. He comes closest to an opinion, however, when he says that the degradationist views history as "a record of successive phases of contraction, divided by periods of explosion, tending always towards an ultimate equilibrium in the form of a volume of human molecules of equal intensity, without coordination." The tendency of history is toward equilibrium, but there is a possibility that one of the periods of explosion may be so violent as to destroy man before he reaches equilibrium. Of equilibrium itself Adams says that it is "death." Thus, in the degradationist's view, society is "condemned to a lingering death, which is sure to tend towards suicide." [45] (This last possibility would apparently come in the periods of explosion.)

[44] *The Education*, pp. 487, 498, 499, 431.
[45] "The Rule," pp. 308–309. "A Letter," pp. 213, 248, 190.

As expressed in terms of these oceans of chaos and stagnation, Adams is not altogether certain what man's ultimate fate will be, but he does reduce, to his own satisfaction, the probabilities to two, neither of which offers man any hope for a better life. It is also clear that Adams believes the present age to be an age of crisis. Generally, though not explicitly in "A Letter," he views it as the age of transition into the final phase of human history.

WATER IMAGERY FOR WESTERN CIVILIZATION

This situation and Adams' final notion of what man's fate will be are forcefully suggested in another water image which appears in his letters, first in 1901, then from 1912 to 1914. As early as 1891 he had written that "the deluge is coming, and the Church and State are sinking beneath the waves." In 1901 the image becomes more specific: "For years past I have watched the big ship lurch over, and at every roll she has gone more near the point of danger, but this time I think the equilibrium lost for good." In the same year he writes again that "Europe is done! . . . Positively I sit here, and look at Europe sink, first one deck disappearing, then another, and the whole ship slowly plunging bow-down into the abyss; until the nightmare gets to be howling. The Roman Empire was a trifle to it." [46] Here the ship-of-state, the "great ship," has become the ship of Europe and the ship of western civilization. The ship is sinking. In the image from "The Great Secession Winter, 1860-61" the American ship-of-state had come close to sinking and in the image from *Gallatin* the French ship-of-state was a wreck floating on the ocean. But now, in 1901, the great danger implicit in the image of ship and ocean has become an immediate actuality for Europe and an immediate probability for the whole of civilization. Only in the exploding cylinder of steam in the final chapter of *The Education* is there such another image of impending doom, and there it is only the suggestion of a frightening possibility, not the assertion of an immediate actuality.

After 1901 this apocalyptic image disappears from Adams' published work for over a decade, only to make an abrupt and culminating reappearance in connection with the sinking of the "Titanic" in 1912. Adams had reserved quarters on the ship with the intention of going to Europe on the return part of its maiden voyage. [47] The universal horror at its sinking was thus intensified for him by a sense of his own narrow

[46] HA to John Hay, Nov. 14, 1891, in Cater, p. 254. HA to John Hay, Jan. 10, 1901; HA to Elizabeth Cameron, April 8, 1901, in Ford (1892–1918), pp. 309, 328.

[47] HA to Elizabeth Cameron, Feb. 18, 1912, in Ford (1892–1918), p. 585.

escape from personal disaster. On April 16, 1912, two days after the event, he wrote to Elizabeth Cameron that

Saturday evening will be a date in history. In half an hour, just in a summer sea, were wrecked the *Titanic* ; President Taft; the republican Party; . . . and I. We all foundered and disappeared. Old and sinful as I am, I turn green and sick when I think of it.

I do not know whether Taft or the *Titanic* is likely to be the furthest-reaching disaster. The foundering of the *Titanic* is serious, and strikes at confidence in our mechanical success; but the foundering of the Republican Party destroys confidence in our political system. We've nothing to fall back upon.

In a work . . . called the *Education of Henry Adams*, I figured on the values of society, and brought out my date of stoppage,—did I not,—at 1917. I feel today as though I were shaving it close. The confusion and consternation here are startling. If it were a question only of a Democratic administration, they were resigned to that, but no one knows whether the people want representative government at all. They seem to want an Athenian democracy without representation. Last night the Lodges came to dinner. . . . I listened to the talk. . . . Through the chaos I seemed to be watching the *Titanic* foundering in a shoreless ocean.

By my blessed Virgin, it is awful! This *Titanic* blow shatters one's nerves. We can't grapple it. Taft, *Titanic* ! *Titanic*, Taft! and . . . I! Where does this thing end!

He still planned to go to Europe, however, saying "I've shifted my passage to the *Olympic* on May 4. Of course, the *Olympic* has a bad record; but nerves are now so shaken that no ship seems safe, and if I am wrecked, I might as well go under." [48]

Five days later, he wrote again to Mrs. Cameron. "No doubt," he says,

you have been imagining how grim and ghastly this last week has been among us here. . . . The strain gets on my nervous system. . . . Only in history as a fairy tale, does one like to see civilisations founder, and to hear the cries of the drowning. . . . The sum and triumph of civilisation, guaranteed to be safe and perfect, our greatest achievement, sinks at a touch and drowns us, while nature jeers at us for our folly. I said it all, seven years ago, in my *Education*, and nature has beaten me by fifteen years on my mathematics.

Most curious is the supplementary foundering of the Republican Party, which everyone has forgotten. Politically we are drifting at sea, in the ice, and can't get ashore. [49]

48 HA to Elizabeth Cameron, April 16, 1912, in Ford (1892–1918), pp. 594–595. Thirty-two years earlier Adams used the phrase, "shoreless ocean," in *Democracy* to describe the medium in which the rotten plank of democracy floated. Here, as there, it suggests the chaotic ocean of nature. (It also appears in *Lodge*, p. 11, where it seems to mean the same thing.)

49 HA to Elizabeth Cameron, April 21, 1912, Ford (1892–1918), p. 595.

Thus it was not the sinking of the "Titanic" alone which made so profound an impression on Adams, but that coupled with Theodore Roosevelt's break with President William Howard Taft. The two catastrophes fused in his mind to evoke an image of the simultaneous sinking of the "Titanic," of his own personal ship, and of the ship of the Republican party. Five days later the image had become even more comprehensive. The foundering of the Republican party had become the foundering of the whole American ship-of-state, while that of the "Titanic" had come to represent the foundering of the ship of western civilization. The result was an image of universal disaster that had an overwhelming emotional effect.

Indeed, the agony expressed in these letters is the most intense in all Adams' published work except in the scene of his sister's death in *The Education*.[50] The situations are related. There a woman dies and Adams is plunged into the chaos of reality. Here a ship sinks and a political party is destroyed, and Adams has a comparable vision of chaos. In both instances Adams is not the anarchist who even enjoys chaos but a man horrified and terrified by the sudden rent in everyday's illusion of stability and order. Here, too, the apocalyptic vision of Europe which appeared in the 1901 letter reaches its climax as Europe becomes all western civilization. The most fundamental expressions of western man's impulse to order, the great machines created by science and political thought, have collapsed, leaving humanity drowning in the resulting chaos. This is the climax of Adams' use of water imagery. In *The Education* he presented a philosopher's view of man precariously adrift on a sensual raft in a supersensual chaos, though he added that he was himself a passenger upon the raft and personally concerned in its fate. Here there is no need for him to state that he is part of the situation. His cries of suffering are sufficient evidence. Significant too is the diminution of his own size implied by the restoration of the raft to a great ship once again. Now he is not the philosopher gazing at his own and other man's fate *sub specie aeternitas*, but a little man in imminent danger of drowning. The size of the ship(s) only makes the more terrifying his realization that it offers no security.

The emotional effect of this experience upon Adams was so intense partly because of the nature and magnitude of the events and of his own

[50] Cf., Chalfant, "Henry Adams and History," p. 374: "The ['Titanic's'] disaster on her way to New York affected him as perhaps nothing had since 1870, when his sister died of tetanus." Chalfant appears to be thinking of the description in *The Education*. The death of Adams' wife probably affected him more than either of these events, but he never described it. See Charles R. Anderson, Introduction [to Henry Adams], in his *American Literary Masters* (New York: Holt, Rinehart and Winston, Inc., 1965), II, pp. 324–325, for a discussion of the relationship between Adams' feelings about his wife's death and his description of his sister's death in *The Education*.

personal involvement in them. But equally important was the intimate relationship they had with his inner life. From the time of his earliest letters he had imaged, first his own fear and insecurity in the world, then the precarious situation of man in general (as this fear and insecurity partly led him to see it) in a ship, great or small, floating on an ocean. By thus imaging or symbolizing an emotion, one partly escapes from it. At the same time the image or symbol becomes a means by which external persons or events can gain access to the inner self. If the self be sensitive or weakened or both and the external person or event powerful, the resulting influence can be a profound one. Adams demonstrated his own understanding of this phenomenon in describing Esther's reaction, when she was under great strain, to Niagara Falls. There, the influence was a beneficent one. Here, Adams was not so fortunate. After a lifetime of expressing his worst fears in a particular image, that image suddenly came to life. The nightmare of fifty years became reality.[51]

The extent of his suffering can be gauged by his plea to Mrs. Cameron at the end of the first letter to "telegraph at my expense if you see light." But apparently no light came, for in the second letter he wrote that "I find it impossible to shake off this nightmare." Inevitably, perhaps, for a person at once so sensitive and so old as Adams was, his own personal ship became part of the nightmare. Five days after the second letter, ten after the "Titanic" sank, the psychological crisis resulted in a stroke, which prostrated Adams for a month and from which he never entirely recovered. Three months later, on July 29, he told a friend, in a dictated letter, that "somehow or other something happened to me, and I haven't yet found out what it was. My lady friends all say it was the 'Titanic' disaster, and the Doctor says that possibly they are right. I know nothing else that it could have been."[52]

Two years later, on June 1, 1914, similar imagery appears in a letter Adams wrote from Paris to an English friend. "I will send you St. Augustine," he says,

[51] A figurative anticipation of the "Titanic" disaster appears in a letter to Charles Francis Adams, Jr., Nov. 8, 1910, in Ford (1892-1918), p. 553:

What seems to me really curious and new is that the whole people seems almost as much puzzled as I, and get no further than to want to vote against everybody and everything, but don't do it. They buck up against the top-heavy fabric of protection, and daren't even speak loud, for fear of its tipping over like an iceberg on their crowded ship. The risk of a general disappearance of all civilised society has become a nightmare in Europe. Even the newspapers discuss it constantly.

Brunner, "Henry Adams: His Decline and Fall," p. 52, notes the relationship between Adams' response to the "Titanic" disaster and his use of water symbolism in general, especially in *The Education*.

[52] HA to Elizabeth Cameron, April 16 and 21, 1912, in Ford (1892-1918), p. 595. HA to Margaret Chanler, July 29, 1912, in Cater, p. 738.

—that is, Bertrand's Life of him. It will illuminate our path. I've said so long that the world has gone to the devil, that I now enjoy seeing the process. In those days people—some people—thought they could escape into the next world, but now they know they are going to be drowned, so they dance and play ball. No one cares. I do not exaggerate. No one anywhere, socialist, capitalist, or religionist, takes it seriously or expects a future. The life is that of the fourth century, without St. Augustine. We each hope for ourselves to escape in time, but no one looks for more than one generation. . . . I calculate only on a year or so. . . .

Calculated in terms of energy, the whole problem becomes simpler, but I am puzzled to convert our vital energy and thought into terms of physical energy. As I measure it, our reserves of mental energy are already exhausted, but the exhaustion may be only apparent. Our mathematicians think well of themselves still. I see that their thought is better trained, but I doubt its energy. Nowhere else can I see thought at all. . . .

. . . I suggest only that Kelvin's Second Law applies to all forms of energy alike. My quarrel with the physicists is that they are afraid to apply their own law.[53]

Again, as in the "Titanic" letters, mankind is in imminent danger of drowning. Again, drowning suggests a catastrophic dissolution of western civilization into anarchy. The allusion to the fourth century compares this chaos to that of the Western Roman Empire finally overwhelmed by barbarian invaders. It would seem that, while man may not be totally annihilated by this situation, he will at least live in social chaos, without the ability to respond creatively to nature's forces and hence without hope for another rebirth of civilization. Man as an effectual force is thus about to be extinguished and his history, to come to an end.

The ocean here seems to be the natural ocean of chaos, as it does in the "Titanic" letters, but now the image is not connected with *The Education* but with the second law of thermodynamics and therefore with the final version of the dynamic theory in "A Letter to American Teachers of History." That Adams, under extreme emotional strain, should refer in the "Titanic" letters, not to "A Letter," written just two years earlier, but to *The Education* implies that in his own sense of his later writings *The Education* was the key work. It may suggest, too, how strongly he came to think of his work after *Chartres* as part of a single project. The likeness in imagery between the "Titanic" letters and this 1914 letter also indicates a strong belief in the dynamic theory despite his conviction that ultimately reality was anarchy and hence unpredictable. More important, the likeness shows how narrow the gap between the two views could become. The imminence of man's fate in both letters makes the factor of predictability relatively unimportant. Of the two possibilities

[53] HA to Charles Milnes Gaskell, June 1, 1914, in Ford (1892–1918), pp. 625–626.

for that fate suggested by the dynamic theory in "A Letter," the actuality is closer to explosion than stagnation. Man is about to be extinguished as an effective force not as the result of a gradual loss of energy but by being overwhelmed by chaos. This was the kind of fate predicted by Adams' ultimate view (and the Dynamic Theory) in *The Education*. For all practical purposes, therefore, at this point the two views have become one.[54]

[54] See critical note 68.

CHAPTER IX

THE PATTERN OF IDEAS

After struggling for a lifetime with the problems connected with illusion and reality, Henry Adams came to two conclusions: first, that man is "a creature habitually striving to attain imaginary ideals always contrary to law,"[1] and, second, that "Chaos [is] the law of nature; Order [is] the dream of man." He states the implication of these views for human life in a late letter: "I always expect the worst, and always find it worse than I expected."[2] The best way to live such a life, he says in another late source, is to "accept . . . , intellectually, . . . the inevitable." "My rule is to conform," he says in a third source. "It is the only path of freedom."[3]

Up to 1892 he was principally concerned with determining the validity and value of democracy. This concern was based upon an initial commitment described in a letter written in 1863: "I have learned to think De Tocqueville my model, and I study his life and works as the Gospel of my private religion. The great principle of democracy is still capable of rewarding a conscientious servant."[4] The principal literary service he rendered this principle was his massive investigation of the relative practicability of Jeffersonian and Federalist ideas in American political and social history in the early nineteenth century. Jefferson was the principal spokesman for the democratic dream, which Adams believed

[1] Henry Adams, "A Letter to American Teachers of History," in *The Degradation of the Democratic Dogma*, with an introduction by Brooks Adams (New York: The Macmillan Co., 1919), p. 250.

[2] HA to Henry Cabot Lodge, Sept. 5, 1909, in Henry Adams, *Henry Adams and His Friends: A Collection of His Unpublished Letters*, compiled with a biographical introduction by Harold Dean Cater (Boston: Houghton Mifflin Co., 1947), p. 663. The quotation which follows is found on p. cxviii n. 212.

[3] HA to Mabel La Farge, Oct. 12, 1905, in Henry Adams, *Letters to a Niece and Prayer to the Virgin of Chartres*, with a niece's memories by Mabel La Farge (Boston: Houghton Mifflin Co., 1920), p. 113.

[4] HA to Charles Francis Adams, Jr., May 1, 1863, in Charles Francis Adams, Charles Francis Adams, Jr., and Henry Adams, *A Cycle of Adams Letters, 1861–1865*, ed. Worthington Chauncey Ford (2 vols.; Boston: Houghton Mifflin Co., 1920), I, 282.

most Americans accepted. Its basic ideas were that man is naturally in harmony with nature, that both are intrinsically good, that man's will is free, that man and his ideas are stronger than circumstances, and that the best and most virtuous society is one which gives the individual the most freedom for self-development in a predominantly rural and agricultural setting. Adams' investigation led him to conclude that man is not in harmony with nature, that nature is not good, that man is prone to corruption, that his freedom is very limited, that circumstances are always stronger than men and ideas, and that the highest human development requires discipline in terms of an ideal and is usually found in urban areas rather than in the country. Thus American experience seemed to demonstrate that the ideas, not of the Jeffersonians but of the Federalists, were more in accord with reality. Adams believed in this period that man lives best when he lives in terms of reality. He admired most the man who, like Gallatin, tests his beliefs by acting upon them and then modifies them insofar as experience proves them false, but who does this slowly and carefully, avoiding the extreme of the opportunist as well as that of the doctrinaire.

Despite his own disillusionment with Jeffersonianism, he did not, at this time, accept the extreme Federalist view that democracy itself is an unworkable form of government which must inevitably lead to anarchy. In 1880 he compared majority rule to a rotten plank "floating in a shoreless ocean" but thought men had "thus far floated better by its aid" than by that of any other political principle. In 1912, however, he expressed his loss of all belief in democracy. "A Letter to American Teachers of History," he said, was "intended as a historical study of the scientific grounds of ... Democracy.... I maintain that ... we are already in principles at the bottom,—that is, at the great ocean equi-potential,—and can get no further."[5] The world had arrived at democracy, but in doing so had achieved, not man's highest political goal but his final descent into chaos.

By this time Adams' concern with democracy and politics was subordinate to a broader interest. From 1892 on, the context of his work was human intellectual history, and he was testing the validity and value of the fundamental human belief that reality is unity. More generally, he was testing the full component of what he believed to be the innate and instinctive beliefs of man: that his will is free and efficacious; that man, nature, and God are fundamentally in harmony and comprise a unity whose source is God; and that religion offers a higher truth than science.

[5] HA to Raphael Pumpelly, May 19, 1910, in Henry Adams, *Letters of Henry Adams* (*1892–1918*) ed. Worthington Chauncey Ford (Boston: Houghton Mifflin Co., 1938), p. 541.

After examining these beliefs in the context of history and his own experience, he concluded that God is an illusion, that man's will is controlled by motives induced in him by external forces, that his efficacy as a force is negligible, that nature is ultimate reality, that it is multiplicity, and that man and nature are irreconcilably opposed in a war in which man is invariably defeated and eventually destroyed. The instinctive beliefs of mankind proved to be as invalid as their particular expression in optimistic naturalism. Yet Adams' emphasis in this later, more ambitious testing was more on the ideas he found to be valid than on those he found invalid. In the early period he was primarily critical of the American political expression of eighteenth- and nineteenth-century optimistic naturalism. In the later period he asserted his own version of late nineteenth-century pessimistic naturalism.

This assertion took the form not of a miscellany of truths, which would have accorded best with his notion of reality as chaos, but of a unified system, the dynamic theory of history. Adams himself declared that, as a unity, this system could only be a falsification of reality and hence an illusion. He justified it as an expression of his own human rebellion against chaos and for its usefulness to himself and possibly others. Both the theory and its justification marked a change in his attitude toward the relative value of illusion and reality. In his early period he believed men should live primarily in terms of reality or in terms of ideas that are harmonious with reality. In the late period he believed that men cannot help but live partly in terms of illusion and that they live best when they do so. Such illusions vary in value. His own dynamic theory, he believed, was based on reality but also offered refuge from reality through its unified account of history. His experience with this personal illusion was just the opposite of his experience with the American dream. Instead of his faith decreasing, it increased, until, in his final formulation of it in "A Letter to American Teachers of History," he made its central principle one that he believed was "rapidly becoming a dogma of absolute Truth,"[6] the second law of thermodynamics. At the end of his intellectual development he found a working principle (though not an absolute belief) to which he could commit himself once more with at least some of the completeness (if not the enthusiasm) with which in 1863 he had committed himself to the principle of democracy. Appropriately, he made this commitment in the same work in which he expressed the total loss of his belief in his earlier faith.

The realities Adams finally arrived at leave man with only two ways to be effectual. He can abandon his uniquely human sense of unity and become a passive or active agent of destruction and chaos. Or, he can

[6] "A Letter," pp. 260–261.

assert his human sense of unity and be a creator. Yet as a creator he can create only as the artist does: he can create illusion but not reality. The fullest assertion of his creativity leads to total withdrawal from reality into illusion and hence to what modern man calls insanity. Don Quixote is the literary type of such human beings; St. Francis is Adams' favorite human example. Both made their lives complete works of art, masterpieces of illusion. Usually, however, men neither lose their humanity nor become insane, but assert their creativity within the bounds of society, the basic product of human art.[7] A society is the product of the collective sense of unity of its members. It is their means of warding off nature's assaults both from without and from within upon their sense of unity and upon their desire to live in circumstances which satisfy that sense. This sense is strongest in the woman, at once the source of its most basic and its highest expression. As the embodiment of the force of reproduction, she is the source both of the biological continuity of the race and of love. Love is the most powerful as well as the highest expression of the human sense of unity and is the strongest unifying force in human existence. The more a society is ruled by love, the closer it comes to perfection. Normally, however, love's influence operates primarily in the little society of the family, rather than in society as a whole. One of Adams' two favorite masculine types is the Lover, who makes the "eternal woman" and her child the center of his life.

The weakness of love as a unifying force is that, for all its strength, its influence is never continuous. Even in personal relationships, human beings are not capable of always acting in terms of their highest emotion. Thus, though love can and should be the basis for the family, it needs to be supplemented even there by another unifying force: justice. The state must be founded upon justice. This force operates in individuals as a flexible system of moral standards commanding wide social acceptance and in the state as a system of law administered by a sovereign government. Adams' other favorite masculine type is the King and Judge, who embodies justice rather than love and is concerned with the state and the good of society as a whole rather than with the family and the good of the woman and her child.

The two types are not necessarily at odds, of course, and may indeed be simply the private and public aspects of the life of a single man. Both, moreover, thrive best in the most human environment, the city. For, since man and nature are always at war, man gains the maximum of social unity only by creating a fortress to protect him against the disintegrating influence of nature's multiplicity. The city is that human fortress and

---

[7] See Elizabeth Stevenson, *Henry Adams: A Biography* (New York: The Macmillan Co., 1955), pp. 321–322.

within it man finds, at best, a momentary freedom to develop fully his humanity.

The highest human creations are religions and works of fine art. Religion is the worship of ultimate reality conceived as unity and given the form of an anthropomorphized deity. It is at once the profoundest expression of man's sense of unity and his profoundest illusion. Art, at its highest the concrete expression of religious faith, is less an illusion because it pretends to less truth. By emphasizing beauty instead of truth it becomes the highest expression of the only validity possessed by any human creation—the validity of art. Yet though religion and art are purer (more ideal) expressions of man's essence than society, both are at their best when they express their society and thus exert a unifying influence upon it. The highest religion and the source of the greatest works of art is a religion of love, centering in a woman goddess, because such a religion both expresses the highest possible kind of society and exercises the most intensely unifying influence upon that society. Twelfth-century France, in some of its aspects, was such a society; its greatest work of art, Chartres cathedral, both expressed and helped unify that society.

At best, man lives in a society in which all he does serves and is served by the human sense of unity which makes society possible. Unfortunately, man is not just human; his desires are not wholly motivated by his sense of unity nor wholly directed toward its furtherance. He is also a part of the rest of nature and has the same characteristics as other forces. Motion, for example, is characteristic of all forces and thus Adams says that, of all men, perhaps the wanderer alone has "felt the world exactly as it is." Unless a whole society moves, wandering is not conducive to social unity, yet societies have always found a way to make a place for the wanderer, whether as pilgrim or tourist, in order to exert some control over him and thus keep him within the social unity. Far more dangerous to society is the destructive tendency men have in common with other forces. This too can be controlled in some measure, but, given time enough, every society will eventually become its victim. Adams says of the decline of courteous love, for example, that "man, with his usual monkey-like malice, took pleasure in pulling down what he had built up." [8] Thus, if external nature does not destroy man's social unity, nature within him will eventually do so.

In his later life, Henry Adams himself was strongly moved by both creative and destructive impulses. Individual participation in a harmonious social whole was his ideal, but it was an ideal he himself never

[8] Henry Adams, *Mont-Saint-Michel and Chartres*, with an introduction by Ralph Adams Cram (Boston: Houghton Mifflin Co., 1933), p. 248.

realized. In *The Education of Henry Adams* he assigned the responsibility for this partly to his own temperament, partly to the environment in which he was reared and educated, partly to what he felt was the disintegration of modern society. Confronted with the impossibility, as it seemed to him, of achieving the ideal society he thought he desired and with the degradation of the actual society he was living in, he tended increasingly to vacillate between a concern for the preservation of society and a deliberate fostering of the forces which were bringing about social chaos. He never completely solved this dilemma, but his choice in 1915 of Marcus Aurelius as "my type of highest human attainment" perhaps suggests his final attitude. Marcus Aurelius exemplifies the King and Judge figure and is the antithesis of the socially destructive anarchist.

Adams' own primary role was, finally, that neither of a preserver nor a destroyer, but of a profound and witty man of the world, mediating between the two realms of thought and action. It is in this role that his principal value seems to lie. Disinclined to action by temperament, provoked to action by background, led to thought by temperament and background, dissuaded from too much reliance upon thought by both temperament and background, Adams ultimately combined these tendencies into works which provide a bridge between action and thought, between experience and its meaning, a bridge difficult to achieve in any age, but particularly so in our own complex and chaotic era. This bridge is largely provided by the "imaginative symbolism"[9] which this study has attempted to show pervades Adams' work. Such symbolism is a fusion of experience and significance which stimulates the emotions as well as the intellect and thereby becomes capable of influencing conduct. In Adams' work it is not mere rhetorical ornament but a primary means whereby he realizes his dual purpose of explicating experience and of making that explication an active influence upon the lives of others.

[9] Sir Leslie Stephen, *History of English Thought in the Eighteenth Century* (3rd ed.; 2 vols.; London: John Murray, 1902), II, 329.

APPENDIX I

THE UNITY OF THE DYNAMIC
THEORY OF HISTORY

The three major statements of the dynamic theory of history appear in chapters 33 and 34 of *The Education of Henry Adams* (1907),[1] "The Rule of Phase Applied to History" (written, 1909; revised, 1910–1912), and "A Letter to American Teachers of History" (written, 1910).[2] A fourth statement, explaining the theory as it appears in *Mont-Saint-Michel and Chartres* (1904), appears in a letter written in 1905,[3] a few months after the book's publication. A fifth incomplete and largely figurative statement appears on pages 458 and 459 of *The Education*. (These last two statements describe more fully than the major account in *The Education*—though not so systematically—what seem to be the full implications of *Chartres* and *The Education* as a whole.) Other relevant comments appear in *Chartres* and the correspondence.

Adams always asserts the essential unity of the theory.[4] Analysis of the statements just cited reveals some differences among them but suggests that basically Adams was right. An abstracted version of the theory, composed of only those elements common to the three major versions (those in

---

[1] Henry Adams, *The Education of Henry Adams*, introduction by James Truslow Adams, The Modern Library (New York: Random House, Inc., 1931), pp. 474–498.

[2] Both "The Rule" and "A Letter" are in Henry Adams, *The Degradation of the Democratic Dogma*, with an introduction by Brooks Adams (New York: The Macmillan Co., 1919), pp. 137–311.

[3] HA to Henry Osborn Taylor, Jan. 17, 1905, in Henry Adams, *Henry Adams and His Friends: A Collection of His Unpublished Letters*, compiled with a biographical introduction by Harold Dean Cater (Boston: Houghton Mifflin Co., 1947), pp. 558–559; hereafter cited as Cater.

[4] HA to Whitelaw Reid, Sept. 13, 1908; HA to Barrett Wendell, March 12, 1909; HA to John Franklin Jameson, March 20, 1909, in Cater, pp. 623, 646, 649–650. Also, Cater, pp. 781–782. HA to William James, Dec. 9, 1907; HA to Henry James, May 6, 1908; HA to Elizabeth Cameron, Feb. 28, 1910; HA to Raphael Pumpelly, May 19, 1910, in Henry Adams, *The Letters of Henry Adams, 1892–1918*, ed. Worthington

The Education and the two essays), contains all of the most essential ideas of each version, with one exception, in a coherent account faithful to the individual pattern of each particular version.[5] This abstracted version makes twelve points: (1) Man's innate perception of nature is a projection of his own mind into nature,[6] and therefore inhibits his knowledge of nature.[7] (2) Hence the dynamic theory of history, like all generalizations, is not absolute truth, but a device, analogous to a scientific hypothesis, which is more or less valuable as it fits the known facts, organizes them in a usable formula, and thereby makes prediction possible.[8] (3) According to the theory, reality is one in the sense that everything is force or energy.[9] The sum of all forces is called nature. Because nature is one, laws can be formulated which apply to all forces.[10] (4) Man is a force.[11] Hence, formulas useful in studying physical science also are useful in studying him—and his history.[12] (5) History is the interaction between man and the sum of other forces, or, as is often said, between man and nature, where "nature" means not the sum of all forces but the sum of all forces except

---

Chauncey Ford (Boston: Houghton Mifflin Co., 1938), pp. 485, 495, 536, 542. J. C. Leverson, *The Mind and Art of Henry Adams* (Boston: Houghton Mifflin Co., 1957), p. 366, argues that the different "scientific figure" in each of the three major versions of the theory necessarily determines three different theories. This appendix counters such attempts to separate the versions of the theory by emphasizing what they have in common.

[5] See critical note 69.

[6] *The Education*, p. 476; "The Rule," pp. 309–310, 295–296; "A Letter," pp. 240–242.

[7] *The Education*, pp. 475–476; "The Rule," pp. 294–295, 309–310; "A Letter," pp. 240–242.

[8] *The Education*, pp. 488, 492; "The Rule," pp. 270–271, 305–308, and Cater, p. 783; "A Letter," pp. 240–244, 190, 260–261, 166, 179–189, 234–235.

[9] *The Education*, p. 474; "The Rule," p. 299; "A Letter," pp. 140, 145, 208. Adams' ultimate view is monistic in the sense that he believes everything is force or energy. (A force is anything which does or helps to do work [*The Education*, p. 474]. Energy seems to be what a force uses—or uses up—in doing the work. The two terms are equivalent, two different ways of talking about the same thing. Ernest Samuels, *Henry Adams: The Major Phase* [Cambridge, Mass.: Harvard University Press, 1964], p. 449, notes Adams' tendency to identify "force" and "energy.") But Adams' ultimate view is pluralistic in the more important sense that he believes there are many kinds of force, without any relation to one another except conflict (cf., "A Letter," pp. 328–329). The dynamic theory assumes that this variety of force is ultimately one and hence that a law true of one kind of force (e.g., the rule of phase) is true of all forces.

[10] *The Education*, pp. 489, 492; "The Rule," pp. 269–271, 277; "A Letter," pp. 146, 149–150, 208, 260.

[11] *The Education*, p. 474; "The Rule," pp. 273, 281–284, 299, 301; "A Letter," pp. 208, 216.

[12] *The Education*, pp. 492, 496; "The Rule," pp. 283–284, etc.; "A Letter," pp. 150, etc.

man. Because nature is infinitely stronger than man,[13] history is the (irreversible) motion in time of man in response to the attractive power of nature,[14] without regard to man's conscious desires—and often contrary to them.[15] (6) This relationship has been continuous in the past and will be so in the future as long as man can respond to nature's attraction.[16] (7) The relationship has two aspects. On the one hand, in responding to nature's attraction man learns how to use an ever increasing quantity of its force for his own purposes.[17] But man pays for this gain by a compensating decrease in his ability to effectively control this increasing supply of force.[18] (8) The operation of these processes has been accelerated in the course of history and especially since the Middle Ages.[19] (9) The movement of history, though continuous, occurs not uniformly but by leaps from one "phase"[20] to another.[21] (10) One of the greatest such leaps was that from religion to science as man's primary means of comprehending and dealing with reality. This occurred between 1400 and 1700.[22] (11) Another phase began about 1900.[23] (12) In entering this new phase man is moving into an extremely dangerous period in his history, about which Adams makes a number of predictions.[24]

Because there is no systematic presentation of the dynamic theory in the *Mont-Saint-Michel and Chartres*—indeed, no mention of it by name —it has not been included in the foregoing synthesis. Both in *The Education* and the correspondence, however, Adams says that the former was written to exemplify the theory. The fullest implications of *Chartres* from this

[13] *The Education*, pp. 474, 484, 485; "The Rule," pp. 305, 310; "A Letter," pp. 234–235.

[14] *The Education*, pp. 474, 484, 485; "The Rule," pp. 305, 280, 299; "A Letter," pp. 181, 198, 234–235.

[15] *The Education*, pp. 483, 485, 486; "The Rule," p. 299; "A Letter," pp. 158, 183, 208.

[16] *The Education*, pp. 478, 487; "The Rule," pp. 281–282, 304–305; "A Letter," pp. 216, 168.

[17] *The Education*, p. 474; "The Rule," p. 304; "A Letter," pp. 233–235.

[18] *The Education*, pp. 496–497; "The Rule," pp. 308–309; "A Letter," pp. 234–236.

[19] *The Education*, p. 492; "The Rule," pp. 289–290; "A Letter," p. 229.

[20] *The Education*, pp. 479, 493; "The Rule," p. 268; "A Letter," p. 214.

[21] *The Education*, pp. 477, 482, 486–487; "The Rule," pp. 277, 296, 306–307; "A Letter," pp. 170, 148, 160–162.

[22] *The Education*, pp. 482–484; "The Rule," pp. 287–288, 290, 295–296; "A Letter," p. 140.

[23] *The Education*, pp. 486, 498; "The Rule," pp. 307–308; "A Letter," pp. 140, 258–261.

[24] *The Education*, pp. 496, 494–498; "The Rule," pp. 306–309; "A Letter," pp. 179–189.

point of view appear in a letter Adams wrote to Henry Osborn Taylor in 1905, a few months after the first printing of *Chartres*:

> I am trying to work out the formula of anarchism; the law of expansion from unity, simplicity, morality, to multiplicity, contradiction, police. I have done it scientifically, by formulating the ratio of development in energy, as in explosives, or chemical energies. . . . The ratio for thought is not so easy to fix. I can get a time-ratio only in philosophy. The assumption of unity which was the mark of human thought in the middle-ages has yielded very slowly to the proofs of complexity. . . . Yet it is quite sure . . . , that, at the accelerated rate of progression shown since 1600, it will not need another century or half century to tip thought upside down. Law, in that case, would disappear as theory or *a priori* principle, and give place to force. Morality would become police. Explosives would reach cosmic violence. Disintegration would overcome integration.[25]

For the most part this follows, with some omissions, the theory as it appears in chapters 33 and 34 of *The Education*. The comment about law giving way to force, morality to police, does not appear in the later formulation, however. Neither does the even more explicit pessimism of the final sentence, although it appears in other parts of *The Education*.[26]

A fuller assessment of *Chartres'* harmony with the theory may be gained by measuring it against the abstracted version presented earlier. (1) Man's tendency to perceive reality as unity in terms of some idea is commented upon and said to produce a life based on illusion, not truth.[27] (2) Adams' assertion that "the rights of man, or the Athanasian Creed" were "convention[s]" and "illusions" (p. 224) suggests his belief that all generalizations are true only as conveniences. Since the theory is not presented in abstract form, nothing is said of predictability. (3) There is no mention of force or energy as the ultimate reality nor of the all-inclusiveness of scientific laws. Nature is not defined as the sum of forces. (4) Man is said to be a part of nature (pp. 196–197), and the pursuit of "Power" is said to be the essence of his existence (p. 224), though he is not specifically defined as a force. Social energy is not said to be subject to the same laws as physical energy. (5) Nature is also shown to control man (pp. 374–375, 377). (6) The necessary continuity of their interaction is not specifically mentioned, although Adams' account of "the slow decline"—"inch by inch"—of medieval art suggests that the movement of history has been continuous at least since the Middle Ages (pp. 374–375). (7) Man's increas-

[25] HA to Henry Osborn Taylor, Jan. 17, 1905, in Cater, pp. 558–559.

[26] *The Education*, pp. 398, 444, 499–500, etc.

[27] Henry Adams, *Mont-Saint-Michel and Chartres*, with an introduction by Ralph Adams Cram (Boston: Houghton Mifflin Co., 1933), pp. 224, 376. Page numbers in the text are to this edition.

ing control over nonhuman force is not mentioned, but the decrease in his own energy and in his belief in unity in the course of history is (p. 127). (8) The idea that man has declined since the Middle Ages frequently appears (pp. 9, 61, 196, 240, 248, 345, etc.), though there is no mention of any acceleration in the change. (9) The sharp distinctions between the centuries suggests that history moves in leaps (pp. 1, etc.). (10) The shift from religion to science in the period between the thirteenth and twentieth centuries as man's primary means of knowing reality and the great change that shift signified is frequently suggested, especially, perhaps, by the juxtaposition of St. Francis and St. Thomas in the final chapters and the comparisons made between them (pp. 321, 33, 358). (11) There is no reference to 1900 as the beginning of a new period. (12) There is no mention of the twentieth century as a crucial period, aside from the references to it as the period of Everyman's old age, though there are some prophecies about it.

Thus analysis suggests that the main outlines of the theory do appear in *Chartres*. The opening pages of chapter 5 of the present text demonstrate that it is even closer to the theory as it appears in *The Education*. Missing are some specific points, abstract formulation, and the scientific terminology Adams uses in chapters 33 and 34 of the later work.

The most obvious difference between the various versions of the theory is the relative prominence in each of the dichotomy of unity and multiplicity (or order and chaos) and the attitude each takes toward that dichotomy. In *The Education*—and *Chartres*[28]—the dichotomy is the dominant idea of the theory and of the work. Indeed, Adams says in *The Education* that he thought of it as "A Study of Twentieth-Century Multiplicity" and of *Chartres* as "A Study of Thirteenth-Century Unity." The monism of the dynamic theory is an avowed artifice constructed to satisfy Adams' human need for order. The two later essays, however, contain no explicit acceptance of the earlier work's belief that reality is chaos. Indeed, they hardly mention the unity-multiplicity dichotomy at all. What they—and Adams' correspondence after they were written— do say of it, however, suggests that their "convenient" monism also rests upon a more fundamental acceptance by Adams of the chaos of reality. (This is discussed in detail in chapter 7 of the present text.)

This dichotomy is involved in a more important difference in the major versions of the theory. This is the enlarged scope of the theory in the essays and the continuity between nature and man which this enlargement involves. In chapter 8 of the present text it is noted that in "A Letter" the monistic theory of human history described in *The Education* becomes a monistic theory of nature as well. In *The Education* it is suggested that the

[28] *Ibid.*, pp. 319, 348, 366–367, 374–375.

life-cycle of man is like that of the other forces in the multiverse: he tends to grow by absorbing other forces until he is destroyed by being absorbed by some stronger force or by the sum of other forces. All other forces undergo the same cycle; nature, however, the sum total of forces, does not. In "A Letter," both individual forces *and* the sum of forces are subject to the second law of thermodynamics; the basic characteristic of both is their steady loss of energy able to do work. Both tend therefore toward a state of final quiescence, but, since man's end precedes that of nature, he has the alternative possibility of being destroyed in a violent explosion. Moreover, the fundamental antagonism between man and nature remains: "His Will and that of Nature," Adams says, "have been constantly at strife, and continue to be so." [29] Nevertheless, there is much more continuity between nature and man in this version of the theory than in the others. The difference is an essential one.

Chartres is involved in another important difference between the three major versions of the theory, the varying prominence of woman in each. In *Chartres* and in *The Education* as a whole she is the dominant symbol; in the essays she is not mentioned once. Her importance in the former works is explained in *The Education* when Adams says that woman, as the embodiment of the force of reproduction, is the source of the only unbroken sequence in human history and the physiological source and center of the innate human sense of reality as unity. Thus it is the emphasis upon the unity-multiplicity dichotomy in *Chartres* and *The Education* that makes the Virgin's role so important in them. The absence of that dichotomy explains why she does not appear in the later essays. Yet Adams says in "A Letter" that man's greatest achievements (since he learned to speak an inflected language [30]) were the religion and art of the Middle Ages.[31] So he could have mentioned the Virgin. The reason why he did not is suggested by the fact that even in *The Education* she is not mentioned in either of the two chapters (33 and 34) which systematically explain the theory. For her importance to be clear, those chapters must be supplemented at least by chapter 25, "The Dynamo and the Virgin," and pages 458 and 459 of chapter 31, "The Grammar of Science." In these passages, the basic aspects of the theory are presented in partly figurative terms. When Adams turns from such figurative expression to abstract exposition, the Virgin disappears. She does so apparently because in the two abstract chapters Adams is appealing to a different state or part of the mind than he is in his figurative statements of the theory. In the latter he is appealing to feeling as well as thought so he uses symbols as

[29] "A Letter," p. 250.
[30] *Ibid.*, p. 195.
[31] *Ibid.*, p. 229.

well as abstractions; in the former, his appeal is wholly to thought.[32] In the historical essays he also appeals wholly to thought; moreover, the audience he addresses is not nieces, nor even young men, but his fellow historians. In *Chartres*, he writes, "The scientific mind is atrophied . . . when it comes in contact with the eternal woman"; in "The Rule" and "A Letter" he is trying to persuade his colleagues to be more scientific. Yet his position is not that science (or reason) is better than feeling, but rather that, having lost the ability to feel, his colleagues should submit themselves to the discipline of what their own age does have to offer. He omits the Virgin, therefore, because the audience he is appealing to is unable to respond to her, while it might be capable of responding to his scientific analogies.

The major difference between "The Rule of Phase Applied to History" and "A Letter to American Teachers of History" is primarily a difference of emphasis. "The Rule" tones down the pessimistic implications of the theory more than any other version; "A Letter" emphasizes them more. In both essays, for example, the movement of history represents a decline, but this is mentioned explicitly only once in "The Rule," while in "A Letter" it is emphasized.[33] Again, "The Rule" is concerned with the possibility of all substances (except thought) being soluble in some other substance; in "A Letter," explosion, diffusion, and dissolving are said to be different forms of (or terms for) degradation.[34] "The Rule" suggests that the process it describes tends toward a final "equilibrium" in "an ocean of potential thought, or mere consciousness," which might involve for man only "an indefinitely long stationary period." In its last phases, however, if thought should release the power of the atom and electron, "the consequences may be as surprising as the change of water to vapor, of the worm to the butterfly, of radium to electrons." "A Letter" suggests the same basic tendency in history but adds that "stable equilibrium is death" and concludes, in regard to the possible sudden discovery of new forces, that the second law condemns mankind to "a lingering death, which is sure to tend towards suicide."[35] Here the mutation metaphor of the worm and the butterfly has disappeared and only the degeneration metaphor of radium and electrons and the explosion metaphor of water to steam remain.

There is the same shift in the attitude toward reason in the two essays. Like *The Education*, both view reason as induced in man by the forces of

[32] It is at this point that figures become completely detachable devices, useful only for explanation, as described in the Introduction to the present work.

[33] "The Rule," p. 297. "A Letter," pp. 195, etc.

[34] "The Rule," pp. 269, 281. "A Letter," pp. 211, 213.

[35] "The Rule," pp. 281, 309. "A Letter," pp. 248, 190.

nature.[36] Both view it as a late and inferior manifestation of the force which appears in older forms of life as instinct.[37] In "The Rule," however, reason is treated as an active agent. It is, indeed, said to be (1) the expression of "the attractive or inductive mass" of nature in man, through which (2) he reduces more solid energy states to the least solid state, that of thought, and thus (3) gains control of more of nature's force. Thus (4) thought "gives to human society its forward movement."[38] In "A Letter," however, reason is (1) little more "than a passive instrument" of nature for (2) "accelerating the operation of the second law of thermodynamics" and thereby (3) increasing the absorption of man's "psychical will" by nature's "physical energy." Thus (4) reason is a primary means for moving man and itself toward their final state of degraded energy—for reason too "must submit to the final and fundamental necessity of Degradation."[39] In "The Rule" reason is exalted; in "A Letter" it is depreciated. But what it is said to do is similar—if not the same.

There are, however, some real differences between the conceptions of reason in the two essays. Reason has less independence in "A Letter." Yet in one way it fares better. Although its tendency is said to be toward the illusion of unity, there seems to be at least a faint possibility that it can know reality. In "The Rule" it is said to be wholly incapable of doing so. Here "A Letter" is closer to *The Education* and *Chartres*, which suggest that reason can know reality and in the twentieth century is coming to do so.[40]

These and other differences in the theory can be attributed largely to Adams' belief that, if the theory is convenient, it can be expressed in the terms of any science. In a preface to the first version of "The Rule," he calls the theory "a scientific formula," which to him means that "the statement in one set of terms implies that it can be made equally well in all." But perhaps the variation in terms is a matter of strategy too. In *Chartres* Adams says that analogies "are figures intended to serve as fatal weapons if they succeed, and as innocent toys if they fail."[41] This comment (orig-

---

[36] *The Education*, p. 474; "The Rule," p. 305; "A Letter," pp. 198–199.

[37] "The Rule," p. 297; "A Letter," pp. 224–225.

[38] "The Rule," pp. 280, 281, 289, 280.

[39] "A Letter," pp. 208, 230, 234, 208.

[40] "A Letter," pp. 208, 240–242. "The Rule," pp. 294–295, 309–310. *Chartres*, p. 375: "The daily evidence of increasing and extending complexity" suggests both that man can know reality and that he is beginning to do so. *Education*: That twentieth-century scientific thought (pp. 400, 401, 431, 450–453) has come to the same belief that reality is chaos which Adams discovered through personal experience (pp. 288, 289, 398) implies that reason can know reality and in the twentieth century is coming to do so.

[41] Cater, p. 782. *Chartres*, p. 291.

inally made about the uncle's presentation of Abélard's and William of Champeaux' debate) describes, better than anything else Adams ever said, his strategy in presenting his theory. Each version is basically the same set of ideas and attitudes expressed in a new analogy or series of analogies. What Adams is most concerned with is the pattern which these have in common, not the differences they involve. However serious these may seem to some of his readers, they do not seem to be so for him. He sees his dynamic theory as one.

APPENDIX II

"FEELING" AND "REASON"
AFTER *CHARTRES*

In his 1915 letter to Henry Osborn Taylor, Adams takes specific exception to one fundamental aspect of Stoicism, its emphasis upon reason. "As a working energy," he says, "I prefer instinct to reason." [1] This preference appears in all his work after *The History* and also in *Esther*. It is surprising, therefore, to find him, in 1918, upholding reason against feeling in the article by Father Fay. [2] The seeming contradiction requires some explanation.

In Adams' expression of preference for instinct as a working energy, the qualifying adjective "working" is important. His preference for instinct (or feeling) is always as a means of *apprehending* reality and of creating unity. He does not prefer it as a means of *comprehending* reality, nor does he believe that man in the twentieth century can any longer rely upon it as the primary means of creating unity. Instinct is man's most sensitive index to reality. [3] But instinct also leads man to apprehend and comprehend reality as unity and thus motivates him to try to give more unity to the immediate multiplicity he perceives. [4] In every work after *The History*,

[1] HA to Henry Osborn Taylor, Feb. 15, 1915, Henry Adams, *Henry Adams and His Friends: A Collection of His Unpublished Letters*, compiled with a biographical introduction by Harold Dean Cater (Boston: Houghton Mifflin Co., 1947), p. 768; hereafter cited as Cater.

[2] Sigourney W. Fay, "The Genesis of the Super-German," in *Dublin Review*, CLXII (April, 1918), 228–229, 231–232.

[3] Henry Adams, *The Education of Henry Adams*, introduction by James Truslow Adams, The Modern Library (New York: Random House, 1931). On p. 288, Adams' own most intense experience of chaos comes through feeling (see paragraph four of this appendix). On p. 370, Adams' remarks about La Farge suggest that reason is not the best mode of apprehending reality. See also paragraph three of this Appendix.

[4] *The Education*, p. 456: "The direction of mind [which includes both feeling and reason], as a single force of nature, [has] been constant since history began. Its own unity [has] created a universe." On pp. 458–459, the fact that the woman, who lives by

and in *Esther*, whenever instinct dominates reason the result is some kind of monistic view of reality. Esther finds her way by feeling to the waterfall and the monism it symbolizes, a view truer than that of the Church, Adams suggests, but not so true as the chaos and contradiction symbolized by the ocean. In *Chartres* the dominance of feeling in the life of the child also found its ultimate expression in a religious sense of reality's unity and an effort to make human life conform to that unity. In both works reason is depicted as usually viewing reality as unity, but this commitment is neither so invariable nor so intense as that of feeling.

In a letter written in 1909 Adams says, "I like best Bergson's frank surrender to the superiority of Instinct over Intellect. You know how I have preached that principle, and how I have studied the facts of it. In fact I wrote once a whole volume—called my *Education* . . . —in order to recall how Education may be shown to consist in following the intuitions of instinct." [5] This statement is true in that *The Education* does show that (as Levenson says) Adams found those objects which were most meaningful in his education "not by seeking but by passive receptivity, not by plan but by accidental education." [6] Otherwise the statement is only partly true. For one thing it is not entirely true to Adams' idea in *The Education* of the relationship between instinct and reason. "Education" means two things: the ability to act effectively and the ability to understand truly. A perfectly educated human being would both act and think correctly by instinct. [7] His actions would be effective both because they were adapted to the end in view and because they were, whether he was

---

feeling, has an especially strong sense of reality's unity suggests that feeling is more strongly allied to the sense of unity than reason. On p. 385, the Virgin is said to have exercised "vastly more attraction over the human mind than all the steam-engines and dynamos ever dreamed of." The Virgin was a "symbol of power" (p. 388), more specifically, a symbol of infinite power as unity; her attractive power was exerted upon feeling (especially love, p. 428). This fact also suggests feeling's being more committed to unity than reason. In Henry Adams, *Mont-Saint-Michel and Chartres*, with an introduction by Ralph Adams Cram (Boston: Houghton Mifflin Co., 1933), p. 224, it is suggested that men tend to try to unify the multiplicity they perceive in terms of fictional ideals. Part of this attempt is the creation of works of art, aesthetic expressions of ideals (p. 104 and *The Education*, p. 385).

[5] HA to Margaret Chanler, Sept. 9, 1909, Henry Adams, *Letters of Henry Adams, 1892–1918*, ed. Worthington Chauncey Ford (Boston: Houghton Mifflin Co., 1938), p. 524.

[6] J. C. Levenson, *The Mind and Art of Henry Adams* (Boston: Houghton Mifflin Co., 1957), p. 325. Cf., Charles R. Anderson, Introduction [to Henry Adams], in *American Literary Masters*, ed. Charles R. Anderson (New York: Holt, Rinehart and Winston, Inc., 1965), pp. 331–332; and Sister M. Aquinas Healy, "A Study of Non-Rational Elements in the Works of Henry Adams as Centralized in his Attitude Toward Women" (Ph.D. dissertation, University of Wisconsin, 1956), pp. 31–32.

[7] *The Education*, p. 370.

entirely conscious of it or not, in accord with a formula for the universe harmonious with the major axioms and postulates of his age and therefore acceptable and meaningful to other men as well as himself. But in terms of *The Education*, neither such action nor such thought is wholly valid. In absolute terms effective action is that which increases the force (or power) of the actor, yet when one acts in terms of any formula one always diminishes to some extent the effectiveness of one's actions because such formulas are always false. Since they are created by instinct (or reason under the impetus of instinct) they cannot be otherwise, for instinct innately and almost inescapably views reality as unity, not as the chaos it really is.

The statement is even less true as an account of Adams' description of his education in *The Education*. His own cumulative knowledge that reality is chaos is gained not from instinct alone but from reason's analysis of the significance of the object or experience which instinct leads him to. There is one important exception. His initial and most complete knowledge of reality is gained wholly through feeling. In *The Education* he says of the experience of his sister's death that "impressions like these are not reasoned or catalogued in the mind; they are felt as part of violent emotion; and the mind that feels them is a different one from that which reasons; it is thought of a different power and a different person."[8] The agony of his experience is not only personal grief for his sister; it is also the result of an experience of chaos so intense that his emotions and even his senses, a perceptive apparatus designed to translate chaos into order, are forced to transmit chaos instead. In Adams' view this apprehension was crucial in his personal life: it was "the last lesson—the sum and term of education." Nonetheless, he portrays himself in *The Education* as requiring some thirty years of study and further experience, always accompanied by analysis, before he decided that his crucial apprehension of reality had also been a valid comprehension.[9] For him, certainty of comprehension requires reason as well as feeling.

Reason too tends to view reality as unity,[10] but it is by nature a more neutral faculty. When instinct becomes weak, reason eventually ceases to

---

[8] *The Education*, p. 288. The following quotation is on p. 287.

[9] There are at least three distinguishable ways in which Adams talks about chaos in *The Education*: (1) He shows himself learning from specific particular or cumulative personal experience (a) that reality in general is chaos (e.g., pp. 288, 289, 382, 398, 418, 472), (b) that history is chaos (e.g., pp. 301, 368), and (c) that twentieth-century society is rapidly moving toward chaos (e.g., pp. 398, 404–405, 444, 499–500). (2) He shows himself learning from study that twentieth-century thought tends to assert that reality is chaos (e.g., pp. 398–399, 400, 401, 431, 450–453, 457–461).(3) He makes generalizations, without referring to specific personal experience or study, about human beings or nature in general as chaotic (e.g., pp. 406–407, 433).

[10] *The Education*, pp. 456, 429–430, 432, 451.

interpret nature in terms of an a priori assumption of unity and begins simply to follow nature: it becomes objective rather than subjective, inductive instead of deductive. In *Chartres* and *The Education* this is what Adams sees as having happened in western civilization since the Renaissance.[11] In the twentieth century man has lost so much of his instinctive energy that he is in imminent danger both of realizing that reality is chaos and of having his society dissolve into that chaos. Whereas in earlier centuries "the illusions of his senses"[12] which gradually returned to Adams after his sister's death would have been accompanied by a return to some kind of faith in order, in the late nineteenth century Adams, as an individual and as Everyman, is so weak that he can never wholly return to such a faith.

The view that feeling (or instinct) creates unity and that its decline has enabled reason to discover chaos is the pervasive view in both *Chartres* and *The Education*. Adams makes a statement in the former, however, which seems to contradict this view: "The two poles of social and political philosophy," he says, "seem necessarily to be organization or anarchy; man's intellect or the forces of nature." In context this statement is part of a contrast between St. Francis and the scholastics. It seems to mean that organization is the product of intellect and that feeling leads to anarchy. When Adams adds that these two choices "seem to be the only roads that can exist, if man starts by taking for granted that there is an object to be reached at the end of his journey,"[13] he only makes the passage seem all the more incongruous in a work largely devoted to extolling the social unity created by feeling in the eleventh and twelfth centuries. Father Fay's article, however, takes the same attitude toward feeling and reason. In this respect, then, the passage in *Chartres* poses

[11] *Chartres:* This point must be inferred from a number of other ideas. On pp. 196 and 159, Adams suggests that reason and science have replaced feeling and religion. On pp. 311–312 and 331, he implies that Bacon's inductive method is the essence of science's use of reason. On p. 287, he makes it clear that the deductive or logical method was the essence of scholasticism. In the Jan. 17, 1905, letter to Henry Osborn Taylor (in Cater, 558–559: see Appendix I of this text, p. 234), he says that the inductive method is leading science to the "proofs of complexity" and thereby discrediting the medieval "assumption of unity" (Cf., *Chartres*, p. 375).

The Education, pp. 484–486. (This reference is to the abstract, systematic account of the Dynamic Theory. However, Adams accepted many of the individual ideas in the theory. It was primarily the pattern of the whole which was "only a spool on which to wind the thread of history without breaking it" [p. 472]. On p. 435, he says that the theory measures "motion down to his own time, *without assuming anything as* true or untrue, except relation [italics added]." That is, the theory *does* assume that "relation" —continuity in history—is true.)

[12] *The Education*, p. 289.

[13] *Chartres*, p. 339.

the same problem in regard to that book as a whole which the Fay article does to the whole of Adams' later work.

What Adams seems to mean in this *Chartres* passage is that when feeling is either extremely strong or extremely weak it leads to anarchy. Feeling always follows the forces of nature. In the case of St. Francis, it was so strong that he saw man, nature, and God as a perfect unity and believed that whatever he did when he acted according to his own intuition of God was in harmony with nature and the essential character of all men. From Adams' point of view such behavior actually disregards the realities of both society and nature and is therefore usually destructive both of the self and of other human beings. The children on the Children's Crusade were destroyed by their attempt to live this way; the Saviors in *Lodge* destroyed others in their attempt to do so. Yet the danger to society posed by Saviors has been minor compared to that posed since the Renaissance by the decrease in man's vital energy and therefore of his ability to react to reality in terms of feeling. When feeling is strong, but not strong enough to create Saviors, it tends to be focused not upon the divine within but upon some expression of divinity external to the individual (the Virgin or the Church, for example). It also leaves the individual still with a strong sense of the disunity in reality, with the realization that an increase in unity requires social co-operation, and with the desire and the power to effect such an increase. These were the characteristics of feeling, according to *Chartres*, when it produced the Crusades of the eleventh century and the churches of the twelfth century. But when man's vital energy and his ability to feel begin to decline, feeling becomes less outward in its focus and tends to lose both its drive and its power to effect social unity. (Thus, as reason is turning from the subjectivity of scholasticism to the increasing objectivity of science, feeling is turning from the objectivity of social action to the subjectivity of private impulse.) In *The Education* Adams' gaining an education basically by following "the intuitions of instinct" means that he follows the forces of nature and, therefore, chaos. But in his time there is no social vision of unity powerful enough to provide an external focus for this personal feeling. In an enervated world of multiplicity he follows an increasingly private path. Experience dictated by circumstances and feeling, and analyzed by reason, leads him to the increasing realization that reality is multiplicity. This results in an irreconcilable division in feeling and therefore in himself. No longer can he both follow nature and believe in unity. Henceforth he must sacrifice one or the other of these natural tendencies.

His initial decision is to sacrifice what he has discovered is his illusion of unity to his desire to follow nature. This is in accord with man's ancient belief that good consists in acting in harmony with ultimate reality. For Adams doing so means both accepting chaos as reality and acting in accordance with that chaos. The only social obligation involved is that of accelerating society's movement toward chaos. This reaction has a forced quality; the tone of the passages in which it appears is an odd mixture of affectation and desperation. These qualities are much less in evidence when eventually Adams rebels against the suppression of feeling's—and man's—belief in and desire for unity. In this rebellion he uses reason to assist feeling, as he does in the rest of *The Education*, but now, instead of using it as a means of analysis, he uses it as a means of synthesis, of creating the unity which feeling desires and hence of suppressing feeling's opposing tendency to follow the forces of nature.

It is in this context that Father Fay's article is to be understood. Fay's (or Adams') argument is that the subjectivism of the Teutonic race and its tendency to submit to a leader who also acts subjectively has led it to behave with the insane destructiveness characteristic of the Savior in *Lodge*. The second and third outbreak of this Teutonic Savior-complex came in modern times: Martin Luther's Reformation and the German aggression of 1914–1918. It is appropriate that Luther should coincide with the Renaissance, for both manifested the shift in western civilization from feeling as an objectively focused and social faculty to a subjective and private faculty. In the Fay article Adams traces this development in German thought after Luther from Leibniz to Kant to Nietzsche, but *Chartres* and *The Education* suggest the same development in western civilization in general as a result of the general weakening of man's vital energy and therefore of feeling. Thus Adams' preference in the Fay article for Roman Catholic reason over Protestant feeling is not necessarily a rejection of feeling in general but of feeling when it is subjective and anarchic. His acceptance of reason, similarly, is not necessarily a preference for reason in general but the same recognition which appears in *Chartres*, and most notably at the end of *The Education*, that, when feeling becomes subjective and private, only reason can create and maintain the lines of communication and connection which make human society possible.

CRITICAL NOTES

The following Critical Notes are examinations of some of the major problems in Adams' criticism in the context of that criticism. In order to break the flow of argument as little as possible, the works made use of have been cited in the briefest possible way, the intention being to refer the reader to the List of Works Cited, p. 309 for the full citation. In cases where only one work by an author is made use of, a parenthesis contains the author's name and the page number (e.g., Brunner, 21). Where more than one work by an author is considered, the name and page are separated by a letter, which also appears in the List of Works Cited (e.g., Levenson, a, 21). The only variation from this system is in the case of Ernest Samuels' three-volume biography, where the author's name and the page number are separated by a Roman numeral indicating the volume referred to (e.g., Samuels, II, 314). Adams' own works are cited by short title and page number, as elsewhere (e.g., *Gallatin*, 76). Citations to the several collections of Adams' letters follow the shortened citations used in the footnotes (e.g., Cater, 86).

1. One of the most vexing questions about Adams is the extent to which he turned from an emphasis on reason to an emphasis on intuition, feeling, and instinct in his later work. Spiller (a, 1096–1097) and Samuels (III, 262, 305) claim that he became a man of feeling and intuition. Healy's fine dissertation is a massive examination of nonrational elements in all of Adams' work. While granting that Adams "could never forego completely his allegiance to reason as a strong guiding force in life" (32), she argues (1) that "throughout the whole of [his] work, the direction of his thought develops with increasing intensity toward the conclusion that intuitive instinct . . . is superior to reason as a guide to existence" (600) and (2) that though he did not believe that intuitive instinct leads to absolute truth (which she doubts that he believed in) (601) it "taught more about existence . . . than reason ever could" (602). Wasser (12) and

Levenson (b, 136–137) believe that he was a man of reason in the late work. My position, which is between these extremes, is developed primarily in chapter 7 and Appendix II. Closest to my view is that of Brunner (See critical note 68).

2. Charles Francis Adams, Jr., in the second half of an anonymous review in *The Nation*, XXIX (August 28, 1879), is the only other commentator to note the connection I draw between Gallatin's acceptance of French theory, his wilderness experience, and his political career. (Proof of authorship is given in a letter from Charles Francis Adams, Jr., to E. L. Godkin, Oct. 30, 1880, quoted in part in Evelyn Page, "The Man Around the Corner," *New England Quarterly*, XXIII [Sept. 1950], 402–403, and cited in Samuels, II, 437 n. 31. Also discussed in Samuels, II, 64–66.) According to Charles Adams' paraphrase of his brother's account of Gallatin's school days, Gallatin

> became intimate with two young fellows ... who were thoroughly impregnated with the teachings of the French philosophy. The war of American independence was then absorbing the attention of Europe, and these young gentlemen conceived the idea that the unsophisticated wilderness was the field in which human nature, freed from social trammels, would achieve the best results. So two of them ran away to America; and the third, Badollet, presently followed. It was a foolish escapade. ... The wilderness ideal was, however, *as Mr. Adams well points out* [italics added], the key to Mr. Gallatin's subsequent political life; it was the echo of that French philosophy which was the bond of sympathy between himself and Jefferson (144).

Here Charles Adams gives to the wilderness a centrality and emphasis in the work which I try to show it has only implicitly. He makes a connection between Gallatin's schoolboy acceptance of French philosophy and a schoolboy interest in the American wilderness which Henry Adams does not. More important, he sees the emigration of Gallatin and his friends as motivated by their Rousseauistic ideals, a motivation Henry specifically denies. Only once, and then briefly, does Henry connect Gallatin's frontier life and his political career (*Gallatin*, 76). Hence Charles stresses what his brother tends to minimize; he sees as explicit and emphasized in the book the pattern of coherence which I see as de-emphasized and often absent from it though implicit in its material.

3. One pole of critical opinion about Carrington is represented by Speare (290), Wilson (203), and Hume (140–141), who consider him the hero and the best man in the novel. Closest to my own view is that of Stevenson: "The human philosophic center [of the novel] was ... for Adams ... the young Southerner who had lost everything in the war, who did nothing in the alien present but practice a little quiet law, but who

saw and understood—out of experience, out of tragedy" (173). Yet the focus of the novel is never on Carrington except in the second idyll with Sybil; he doesn't get the space that Mrs. Lee and Ratcliffe do; he is neither active nor effectual enough to be properly called the "hero"— even though he does save the heroine. Saveth (a, 232) considers him more principled than Ratcliffe and "just weak enough to interest Madeleine." Yet even at this time, over two decades before *Chartres*, Adams considers man's submission to woman not as weak but admirable, as Sister M. Aquinas Healy has shown. The Civil War background for Carrington's lack of energetic participation in the present is examined in some detail in the idyll with Sybil; Adams says that his "spirits were nearly exhausted after twenty years of strain" (257). Adams himself used a similar justification for a similar life after his wife's suicide. Aiken is more severe than Saveth. Carrington, he says, "lives in Washington in the anomalous position of a private citizen who, while practising his profession as a lawyer, is content merely to observe the chicanery of the politicians whose power he affects to despise" (vi). I find no evidence that he despises power; what he despises is corruption. His passivity is explained, if not justified, by the remarks made above in answer to Saveth. (Aiken quotes Henry Thoreau against such passivity; but Thoreau also said, "It is not a man's duty, as a matter of course, to devote himself to the eradication of any, even the most enormous wrong; he may still properly have other concerns to engage him.")

4. Most critics view Ratcliffe as an almost unmitigated villain. Rule and Howe feel that he is treated more sympathetically. While granting that he is "the personification of the degeneration of American democracy" (b, 108), Rule argues that Adams was trying to give him complexity enough to avoid caricature. Thus he notes that Ratcliffe has instincts of refinement and that he is the one character (other than Mrs. Lee presumably) who changes in the course of the book. Rule also believes that "throughout the novel Adams ironically presents his villain in such a way that he towers over his polished and conventionally moral foes and sycophants like Gulliver among the Lilliputians" (b, 111). Howe believes Ratcliffe is more powerful than Adams intended, that, although the villain, he has the most life of anyone in the novel (because of Adams' hatred for him) and that he is admirable insofar as he at least has taken the risks of deep involvement in life (179–180). I would agree with Rule's basic assertion that Adams tries to humanize Ratcliffe. Moreover, his assertion that Ratcliffe has improved is undeniable: the force Adams attributes to woman (and especially to a woman like Mrs. Lee) affects every male—supposedly for the good. But the improvement in Ratcliffe is in matters of taste, not of morals, and therefore not as significant as Rule suggests. Nowhere does

Adams imply that Mrs. Lee could ever have made him a moral man; on the contrary, he suggests that Ratcliffe might have corrupted her. As for Ratcliffe's stature, that is in the book—and intended by Adams. But its effect is not to make Ratcliffe more sympathetic but more appalling because more formidable. The same may be said of Howe's claim for his power as a character. In the same way, the respect Ratcliffe's involvement in experience arouses is, in the book, always secondary to the horror—and fear— it causes because it makes him a more formidable embodiment of evil.

5. Jacobi represents a type Adams presented sympathetically earlier in his career as an anonymous diplomat in the article "Men and Things in Washington" (1869) (to be discussed in chapter 7). There, as here, the type takes an attitude toward democratic government that Adams himself would assume in *The Education* and in his later life in general. In the article, however, Adams does not express approval of the diplomat's views; here he seems much closer to doing so, for Jacobi is describing the state of democratic society after human nature (as presented in the novel) has had another hundred years of free operation. Levenson's assertion (b, 91) that Jacobi is the epitome of Jamesian European villainy seems mistaken. Jacobi's corruption is never dramatized; it is only avowed and he is the person who avows it. What is portrayed is his personal relationships. In these Jacobi is the acme of affectionate kindness toward Mrs. Lee and Sybil and detests the stupidity, boorishness, arrogance, and hypocrisy of Ratcliffe. Adams seems to approve of all these attitudes. Aiken also seems to feel that Jacobi is presented unsympathetically. Trying to build a case for some sympathy by Adams for Ratcliffe, he says that in the final scene Ratcliffe is "caned . . . by that impotent old roué, Baron Jacobi" (x). The implications are quite different in the book. After describing Ratcliffe shoving the eighty-year-old diplomat aside, Adams says, "The Baron, among whose weaknesses the want of high temper and personal courage was not recorded, had no mind to tolerate such an insult from such a man" (368). Aiken's sympathies are with Ratcliffe; the book's are with Jacobi.

6. Gore is the most controversial figure in the novel. The problem is whether he speaks for Henry Adams in affirming the democratic faith. Critical opinion runs the gamut from those who, like Speare (305), view him as the spokesman for Adams' supposed personal idealism to Milne (61), who says that he "represents cynicism." Healy (160–161) feels strongly that Gore is not Adams' spokesman. She presents two arguments for Gore's credo also being Adams'—(1) that Gore is a literary man and historian from Massachusetts and (2) that Gore's points parallel Adams' expression of American ideals in the sixth chapter of *The History*. But she also presents three arguments against Gore's view representing Adams': (1) Gore has serious personal deficiencies (noted earlier by Hume [134]);

(2) other statements by Gore contradict his supposed "credo" (those given in my text: Healy was my source for this inconsistency in Gore); (3) the optimism of Gore's speech is out of character for Adams; and (4) there is evidence that the passage is ironic. For example, its conclusion, "Have I repeated my catechism," suggests to Healy that Adams leaves the reader "with the impression that Gore has been ironically parroting a political litany once learned by rote" (161). (Here Healy is close to Hume's earlier notice of Gore's flippancy [134]. I am indebted to Healy—and to Hume—for my notice of this flippancy, although I disagree with their interpretation of its significance.) My account of Gore in the text takes into account all of these points except whether or not Gore's "optimism" is inconsistent with Adams' view. This point—at least as regards Adams' attitude in *Democracy*—will be considered later in this chapter.

7. This characterization does not mean that Mrs. Lee does not have faults. The narrator points out three at least. Sybil points out others to Carrington during their ride in Arlington (256–257) and Mrs. Lee herself thinks of still others when Carrington calls her perfect (262–263). Nonetheless, Carrington does call her so and here, as elsewhere, it seems to me that Carrington speaks for Henry Adams. (I agree with Healy [174], who quotes Speare [303] to the effect that Mrs. Lee is the "most high-minded person" in the book.) Of commentators who tend to be primarily critical of Mrs. Lee, the most important are Vandersee, Aiken, and Rule. Vandersee considers her going to Washington an "aimless little game," her motives "selfish, or at least dubious" (143). It seems to me that Adams' critical characterization admits the first criticism, but only as one subordinate aspect of a quest profoundly serious and meaningful. Since the quest is a personal one, it is selfish in a sense, and since Mrs. Lee's motives are mixed and confused, and not altogether known to her, they can be said to be dubious, but neither selfishness, in a bad sense, nor dubiousness is Adams' emphasis. Aiken makes a more telling criticism when he says that Mrs. Lee "has plainly abandoned American democracy to the Ratcliffes" (xii). For all good men and women in America to do this would certainly be a bad thing, as Aiken implies; yet Mrs. Lee's case reminds me of Thoreau's argument that high-minded individuals who withdraw from their society in protest against its immorality serve a useful function for that society (as well as themselves). The most trenchant criticism is that by Rule who points out that Adams avoids the flat characterizations of melodrama by using irony to give human complexity to both his villain and heroine. The irony he stresses in Mrs. Lee's character is "the variance between her lofty idealism and her selfish, hard attitude toward the people with whom she comes in contact" (b, 114). He then considers her manipulation of men, her enjoyment of her power over

them, her amusement at their quarrels, and concludes that there is some truth in the opinion of Mrs. Clinton, Mrs. Lee's most envious and vindictive rival, that Mrs. Lee is a "heartless coquette" (116–117). The weakness of this perceptive analysis is that it is conducted in a completely serious and perhaps hostile manner, whereas Adams' tone is one of amused delight. Under these different kinds of scrutiny Mrs. Lee's character does not change but it looks different. The same qualities are often noted by those who like and those who dislike cats (compare 95, 96, and 100 of *Democracy*), but the resulting pictures of cats are quite different. Rule is particularly hard on the flirtation Mrs. Lee carries on with Senator Clinton because of Mrs. Clinton's backbiting hostility (97–98). Clearly Mrs. Lee cannot be accused of behaving in this instance according to the Sermon on the Mount. But just as obvious is Adams' relish for this example of femininity—and the implication that the reader will enjoy it equally as much. There is indeed "some truth" in Mrs. Clinton's opinion, but Rule's emphasis is on the "truth" whereas it ought to be on the "some" if he is concerned to present the book's attitude. More valid is his noting of Sybil's description of Mrs. Lee's refusal to feel since her husband's death and her advice to Carrington not to marry Mrs. Lee. But Rule fails to note that Mrs. Lee feels a good deal at the end of the book and that it is Sybil who there urges him to propose again when she and Mrs. Lee return.

That Mrs. Lee is not free from flaws does not mean that she cannot represent the ideal to Adams any more than similar feminine traits in the Virgin of *Chartres* deterred him from making her his ultimate ideal. Indeed this is Adams' triumph in both cases (though more so in the case of the Virgin, who is treated less satirically): that in creating a woman whose sensibility is a touchstone for the ideal, he creates a real and feminine woman rather than the wooden prig Nathaniel Hawthorne contrived for a similar purpose in *The Marble Faun*.

8. Aiken is very critical of Carrington for giving this information to Mrs. Lee. "Carrington considers it entirely right and proper," he says,

> to violate the rules of his "profession" because of an overriding duty to an individual person whom he also loves; he barely considers the possibility that there may be . . . obligations to a party or to a country that claim precedence over both his professional duties and the demands of personal honor. . . . The implication, clearly, is that in refusing to destroy Ratcliffe's public career Carrington himself must accept some responsibility for the fact that Ratcliffe, although defeated in love, is still as powerful as ever in politics, and may well become the next President. (xi–xii)

In answer to Aiken it should be noted first that it is Carrington's awareness that he is breaking his professional code which leads him to use the information he has only as a final resort. His moral problem is not one of right and wrong but which of two wrongs is worse—to allow Mrs. Lee to marry Ratcliffe without knowing a crucial fact or to break his professional code. He makes the decision only when he has to, and I see no evidence that Adams thought he made the wrong choice. Aiken's other, more serious, charge is anticipated by Carrington in the letter, when the latter says that he cannot tell his story to the public because the evidence was burned at the time he went through the papers with Mrs. Baker, so that Ratcliffe would simply laugh at his now unprovable assertion. Indeed, making his information public might even redound to Ratcliffe's favor. Whether at the time Carrington saw the evidence he should (or even could) have stolen it is something not mentioned in the book, but his handling of the moral problem with Mrs. Lee suggests that he could have brought himself to do such a thing only if there was a clear and present danger of Ratcliffe's becoming President. Yet Baker had died two years before and Ratcliffe's chance at the presidential nomination had come just the previous spring. To have betrayed a professional trust on the chance that two years later a man would become powerful enough to warrant such betrayal seems a much more dubious moral venture than that involving Mrs. Lee.

9. Colacurcio (a, 60) contends that Adams makes the basic point at issue between Mrs. Lee and Ratcliffe not his immorality but his pragmatism. He supports this assertion by an analysis of their final interview, in which he says that Ratcliffe argues so cogently his assertion that the complexity of life makes inevitable some violation of moral obligations that Mrs. Lee retreats from her original position that she will not marry him because he is immoral to the "weaker ground that she is not 'fitted for politics.'" Actually, her original decision to reject him because he is immoral by her intuited standards remains unchanged. What changes is her decision about *how* to refuse him. Remembering his apparent honesty, believing he has acted by a moral code of his own (335), aware of her own culpability in earlier accepting his immorality (358–359), and believing it is not her business to judge him (342), she decides to refuse him without either breaking with him or criticizing him. In the course of their interview she makes seven different attempts to refuse him. In the first (344–345), fifth (362–363), and sixth rejections (365) she simply refuses him; in the second (346–347) and third (354) she declares that she and Ratcliffe are unfit for one another and in particular that she is unfitted for politics; in the fourth (361) she makes this argument more specific by stating that she will not lead a life where good and evil are mixed together and she is "put in a position where I am perpetually obliged to maintain that immorality is a virtue"; finally, she says that she will not marry a man who ought to be in prison for what he has done. Of the reasons she gives, those

in the second and third refusals are simply stratagems, sugar-coated half-truths. That in the fourth refusal is a rejection of Ratcliffe's pragmatism, but a rejection whose basis is moral: Mrs. Lee refuses the immorality of a life which requires her to maintain that vice is virtue. Her final reason (in the seventh refusal) is purely moral: Ratcliffe has done things which are not only immoral by her standards but deserving of prison. In light of this analysis, it is difficult to see how Colacurcio can maintain that "in a sense the novel goes out of its way to have Mrs. Lee reject Senator Ratcliffe not as the self-interested blackguard he is but as a fairly consistent exponent of the whatever-*must*-be-done theory of politics." Though her final reason shows that Mrs. Lee has failed in her effort to refuse Ratcliffe without stating her real reason, that reason is not his pragmatism but his immorality.

Colacurcio's argument that Mrs. Lee's shift to a weaker position results from a loss of self-assurance because Ratcliffe presents so cogently the argument Colacurcio considers crucial does not seem to fit the text either. Adams says that when Ratcliffe finished stating this argument he found Mrs. Lee "lost in meditation over the strange vagaries of the senatorial mind" and therefore that *he* turned to "another line of argument" because "he rightly judged that there must be some moral defect in his last remarks, although he could not see it, which made persistence in that direction useless" (357). If anyone lost composure here it would seem to be Ratcliffe rather than Mrs. Lee. Her loss of composure comes later, when Ratcliffe asks why she did not criticize him earlier for a political act even "less defensible," he says, than the one she is being so severe upon. She loses her self-possession at this point because of the guilt she now feels at having countenanced this and other such actions. But this shame does not lead her to take a weaker ground for refusing Ratcliffe than she had done earlier in their interview. Instead, in this third refusal she simply applies the reason given in her second refusal (that they are unfitted to one another) specifically to herself and her unfittedness for politics. By her fourth refusal she has completely recovered her composure. There she does grant Ratcliffe his sincerity, as Colacurcio says, but neither there nor anywhere else in the interview can I find any evidence of Colacurcio's assertion that she admits that "her ideas . . . were naïve" and that "her standards of purity would, no doubt, mean the end of democratic government." On the contrary, her acceptance of his sincerity is followed by her sharp refusal "to be put in a position where I am perpetually obliged to maintain that immorality is a vice."

To describe the position Mrs. Lee supposedly retreated from in refusing Ratcliffe, Colacurcio quotes a statement by her which he ascribes to a conversation with Sybil preceding the Ratcliffe interview. Actually, the passage is something Mrs. Lee thinks to herself during the interview. Colacurcio goes on to say again that this position was not Mrs. Lee's final word, that she now grants Ratcliffe his position and denies only its adequacy for her. The position she finds inadequate for herself (at this point in the interview) is to take the "profits of vice" and to "maintain that immorality is a virtue"—a position which will make her immoral by her own standards. The position she grants Ratcliffe is that of being thus immoral by her standards. But she does agree not to judge him for being so and acknowledges that she is not competent to reform a world which lives this way. Contrary to Colacurcio, however, this tolerance is not her final word. When Ratcliffe's obstinacy goads her into finally giving her real reason for refusing him, she also judges him, not only by her personal standards but also by the social standards embodied in the law.

In the final sentence of his analysis, Colacurcio says that Mrs. Lee breaks with Ratcliffe "only when he tries most blatantly to bribe her with the power of his eventual presidency." It is true that Mrs. Lee has kept to her initial resolve not to break with Ratcliffe through five rejections of her attempts to refuse him. But it is not his attempt to bribe her that finally provokes her to make the break. The attempted bribe is only one of several factors which lead to the sixth refusal. Mrs. Lee's impatience has steadily increased throughout the interview and at this point she loses control of herself because, Adams says, "she was exasperated by [his] obstinate disregard of her forbearance, [his] gross attempt to bribe her with office, [his] flagrant abandonment of even a pretense of public virtue," *and* his attempt to seize her hand. To her, "the mere thought of his touch on her person was more repulsive than a loathsome disease" (364–365). Yet it is only *after* the refusal provoked by these feelings, when Ratcliffe persists in arguing with her and finally calls her a "heartless coquette" (366), that she tells him the real reason for her refusal and breaks with him. Perhaps a feeling of guilt helped to break down her reserve at this point. Perhaps her vanity was piqued by Ratcliffe's citation of Mrs. Clinton as authority for his accusation. But whatever the immediate causes, they were only the final exacerbations of a patience strained to the breaking point.

The foregoing analysis seems to me to destroy the evidence for Colacurcio's concluding assertion that Adams' supposed refusal "to let the battle between Ratcliffe and Mrs. Lee ever be fairly joined on theoretical grounds" suggests "that in Adams' view they might be practiced without dishonor *by somebody*." The answer Mrs. Lee makes to Ratcliffe is that of her intuited absolute moral standards. What this implies—if anything —about Adams' own view would seem to be that he too believes in such intuited standards. In regard to politics, Mrs. Lee's answer would seem to imply not so much the possibility of honorable "pragmatism" as the conclusion Adams expresses in *The Education* : that to engage in politics is inevitably to accept a measure of dishonor. Colacurcio agrees; where we differ is in what seems to me his exaggerated assessment of Adams' sympathy with the aspects of the pragmatic view which he describes.

10. Curiously, only two other critics have noted this passage, although Healy calls it "very significant" (162). She claims it is ironic and paraphrases its content as follows: "Experience, says Adams, has long since contradicted the theory of natural goodness; reason contradicts trust in mere majority, which may be wicked as well as good; yet America has 'floated' better by majority rule than the popes did by principle. When society ceases to 'float,' it will repent of its trust in the majority" (162). The first two clauses here suggest that the democratic doctrine Adams means is majority rule *and* the belief in man's natural goodness which often lies behind it. It seems to me, first, that belief in natural goodness is not a very humble belief and therefore does not contrast well with the "proudest" of political principles. But more important, the passage seems to me to be concerned only with the doctrine or principle of majority rule (which *is* humble enough for such a contrast) and that what Adams says *both* experience and reason contradict is the viability of that principle. Healy's interpretation of "floated" derives from an image used later in the chapter: the narrator says that "underneath the scum floating on the surface of politics, Madeleine felt that there was a sort of healthy ocean current of honest purpose, which swept the scum before it, and kept the mass pure" (196). Healy applies the contrast between that which floats superficially and that profounder something which lies beneath the surface to the earlier image. To me it seems more likely that the second image reflects *Madeleine*'s limited understanding at this point, her hope, which proves false, that the corruption she sees is only appearance and that beneath it lies a healthier reality. In the earlier image the *narrator* sets up a standard by which her limitations (and those of the second image) can be measured. It suggests that what appears to be is the reality; that the healthy undercurrent does not exist; and that it is on the surface, amidst the scum, that the plank of majority rule (a synecdoche for democratic society) floats without ultimate direction. Even if eventually society is politically organized by a new principle or a more effective application of majority rule—Adams suggests the possibility of one or the other in the chapter's second paragraph—it too will be a means of enabling men to float on the shoreless ocean of reality. (Healy also makes a fallacious implication, at least, in her contrast between papal principle and democratic lack of principle. Adams is contrasting two principles, as he shows when he calls the papal principle the "prettier principle.")

Greifer, who identifies Adams' attitude with Mrs. Lee's, says that "the disillusionment [which Greifer finds in the passage] is not merely in the wickedness and corruption of democracy, but in its damned viability as well" (10). After quoting a few lines from the passage, he comments: "Henry's dismay is well grounded. What else remains when one discovers that man's hopes are staked on a democratic idea which, if better than the ideas of the Old World, already had gone wrong in 1817" (11). The first sentence here also seems to me to misinterpret Adams' meaning. I do not see how the viability of democracy in the passage could be characterized as "damned." Adams begins with what he calls the proudest of all political principles—that of the papacy; by implication the principle of majority rule is a humble principle. Then he admits the seemingly insurmountable weaknesses of the latter. But at the end he asserts its superior viability and suggests that therefore society will continue to live by it (whereas by using the word "did" rather than "have" he suggests not only that the prouder principle was never so viable but that the time when that principle had comparable importance has passed). Greifer's second sentence suggests that, in his case, even more than Healy's, misinterpretation grows out of a failure to understand what the democratic principle is that Adams is talking about in the passage. Earlier in his article Greifer makes it clear that "the democratic idea" is that ultimate hope for democracy which appears at the beginning of *The History*: "[To] lift the average man upon an intellectual and social level with the most favored" (I, 9). But in this passage in *Democracy* Adams is not talking about this idea. The "democratic idea" is treated in *The History* as an eminently proud principle and therefore also offers a poor contrast to the "proudest" political principle. Moreover, the context again seems to me to make it clear that Adams is talking about the humbler principle that human beings know their own interests well enough so that majority rule is the best form of government.

11. Welland (who lists some other associations of bird images with Esther in the novel [38]) views the principal tension of the book as being expressed in the "dual imagery of the natural force of the sea and the natural vulnerability of the bird" (40). The value of this insight lies in its recognition of the existence of the ocean symbol and of Esther's association with birds (one is reminded that birds are a traditional symbol for the soul). Its weakness lies in Welland's failure to recognize that his juxtaposition (like my own of art and the ocean) operates in the background of the book, not the foreground. The bird and the ocean are never explicitly juxtaposed; their opposition therefore is only implicit. (Adams will make brilliant use of the bird image in *The Education* in noting the traditional comparison of human life to a bird flying in and out of a hall into the darkness [460].)

12. Healy and Brunner (237) are the first critics to note Adams' use of
the falls as a symbol. Healy is also the first to note that Esther's response
to it is prepared for by her role in the rest of the book (192–193). Rule
(b, 132–133) is the first to note that the symbol is also prepared for by the
nature imagery Esther is associated with throughout the novel. Colacurcio
(a, 62–63) gives the fullest list of these images. Samuels (II, 256) and
Hochfield (a, 52) stress the obscurity of the falls' meaning, without noting
the dependence upon symbolic perception which this intellectual obscurity signifies. Healy (192), Welland (39), Rule (b, 132), Bell (159), and
Samuels (II, 256) seem to agree that the falls symbolizes natural force as
ultimate force. Only Samuels, however, notes the male humanity which
Esther ascribes to her symbol and he too fails to note that it is a humanity
without human failings (*Esther*, 258). In Bell's case, this failure leads him
to argue that the falls "anticipates Adams' image of the dynamo, the
faceless might of nature made manifest" (159). The fullest discussion of
the falls' meaning is in Hochfield (b, 52–53), who calls it a "natural
symbol" of "eternal truth," which is "an ultimate energy, . . . life itself."
His interpretation rests primarily on Esther's final remarks to Strong in
chapter 9 of the novel and hence will be discussed in a critical note (15) to
my analysis of that passage. It should be noted here, though, that Hochfield's identification of the falls with life leads him (b, 113) to associate it
with the Virgin rather than the dynamo (though he does not say the falls
anticipates the Virgin). Brunner, who speaks (237) of "the thundering
pantheistic symbolism of Niagara" says that there "Esther doubtlessly
heard the inner voice of nature which her creator was to realize eventually
as *élan vital*." Later, he says of the Virgin that "she was . . . *élan vital*"
(225). Thus he suggests that the falls anticipates the Virgin. It seems to
me that there is no one-to-one correspondence between the falls and either
the Virgin or the dynamo. The falls is the modern symbol of the infinite
as natural energy, which Esther sees as having masculine human life. It is
not a machine; it is also more to Esther than just a natural symbol. That
is why she can fall in love with it and enjoy her rapport with it. The later
Adams of *Chartres* and *The Education* also sees the modern symbol of the
infinite as a symbol of natural energy, but the symbol is a machine (the
dynamo) and the energy is not that of life. The dynamo lacks not only
maleness but humanity. Moreover, it suggests a pessimistic view of man's
immediate future rather than the optimistic view suggested by the falls.
The eternal woman finds nothing in it to love, though she may choose to
be victimized by it. The energy of life in Adams' later work is expressed
not in the modern symbol but in the outworn medieval symbol, in the
Virgin (and all her pagan predecessors), who is human but female rather
than male. All other energy is symbolized by the Trinity, which the Virgin,

at the height of her power, loves and rules as her child but which she scorns as the machine of divine justice. What has apparently happened to Adams' symbolism (to oversimplify) is that Esther has merged with the falls, which has split in two, the woman becoming the embodiment of the life and sexual (male-female) aspect of the falls while the remaining, non-living, purely mechanical energies are embodied in the dynamo. Moreover, the dynamo is stronger in the modern world than the falls is said to be and therefore the prognosis for the future is pessimistic rather than optimistic. The continuity between the falls and the Virgin can be traced with the help of Simonds, who notes (579) that Adams' first response to Saint Gaudens' memorial statue for Marian Adams was "the Petrarchan phrase he had quoted in *Esther*: '*Siccome eterna vita e veder Dio.*'" It is Hazard who repeats this phrase when he first sees Niagara, but his explanation of why he does so—because "the sight of it suggests eternity and infinite power"—allies his basic response with that of Esther. Simonds also cites Adams' friend Spring-Rice as having said (582) that *Chartres* is "'like the monument in Rock Creek, in memoriam . . . .' For in that book Henry Adams said for Clover Hooper . . . what the St. Gaudens figure, 'beyond pain and beyond joy' was therefore beyond saying." (Spring-Rice then quotes the final paragraph of *Chartres*.) But if Adams' response to Chartres could be paraphrased in the Petrarchan phrase of Wharton and Hazard, and if the climactic scene of the book in the Court of the Queen of Heaven evokes emotions from the uncle paraphrasable by the entire Petrarchan fragment from which the phrase is taken, Adams' first response to the dynamo (as described in *The Education*) was a comparable desire to kneel and pray. It was not a response of love, it is true, and to this extent the Virgin is closer to the falls. Yet in Adams' later view the nonvital forces symbolized by the dynamo are always stronger than the vital forces symbolized by the Virgin; in these terms, the dynamo is a more valid symbol of that ultimate reality for which Niagara, even in *Esther*, was considered only a partial symbol.

13. Blackmur (d, 300–301) characterizes her as "the spirit of the wide places, the earth goddess of the mountains and prairies from which she came, all problems to her are but artificial forms of the simple problem of assent." If she is an earth goddess, she is a very attenuated one compared with, say, the heroine of Willa Cather's *My Ántonia*. Her powers of assent also seem to be more limited than Blackmur suggests: she denies both Wharton and his view of life and is desperately rebellious against her own lack of self-consciousness.

14. Although Colacurcio's analysis of the pragmatic element in *Esther* (a, 64–67) is a major contribution to commentary on the novel, it makes its point partially by distorting important passages in the book. Colacurcio

describes three pragmatic temptations which Esther refuses. The second of these is in the first of the two arguments between Strong and Esther. Colacurcio accepts everything Strong says as expressing what he believes. But the narrator says of Esther (192), before the argument, that Strong had decided to help Hazard; it seems to me Strong's arguments reflect that decision more than his own beliefs. Colacurcio says that Strong's refusal to answer Esther's question whether religion is true (198) is based on Strong's belief that "he is not competent to answer directly." But Esther says to Strong, "You think the whole church a piece of superstition. I've heard you say so, and I want you to tell me why" (200). What Esther says seems to be true, while Strong's answer is an evasive one, though not dishonest (cf. 191). Colacurcio goes on to say that Strong here "gives the impression of saying what, at one level of his mind, he really believes. But struck by Esther's extreme earnestness, he goes on to answer her from another level." What Adams says is that "Strong was forced out of this line of defense and found himself in an awkward position . . . . Strong was staggered and hesitated." That is, Esther had torn through the nets of sophistry in which he had tried to catch her. Strong's own attitude toward what he has said is that "in his own eyes his conduct so far seemed a little cowardly and ridiculous" (201–202). He would hardly have felt this way if he had been arguing candidly. The key to what seem to be Colacurcio's distortions is that they fail to take into account the tactical nature of Strong's argument and therefore exaggerate the extent to which Strong is a pragmatist.

The same thing is true of Hazard in what Colacurcio calls Esther's third pragmatic temptation. Colacurcio prefaces Hazard's desperate, final resort to "a version of Pascal's wager" by calling it "the example of his own deepest faith." But Adams says that Hazard was "willing perhaps to stretch his own points of conscience in the effort to control hers" (290). Later Colacurcio reverses himself and asserts that "Hazard's shift from the language of Descartes to that of Pascal represents a complete about-face, at least tactically, and brings the argument for religion into plainly pragmatic terms." What began as Hazard's final belief has become a tactical maneuver. Similarly, when Hazard, convinced of the righteousness of his cause (254), goes even farther in his pragmatism in the hope of securing his prey, Colacurcio fails even to mention the possibility that he is desperately using any means to gain his ends and simply accepts the argument at face value. For the second time pragmatism as tactic is confused with pragmatism as belief and therefore given a greater importance in the book than it actually has.

Colacurcio also explains Esther's final rejection of Hazard as based on "a pragmatism of her own. . . . She insists on the right to a belief and a

style of life more congenial to her nature than what Hazard proposes."
But this is not what she herself insists on. She says of her belief that she
can't be a clergyman's wife that "I can't reason it out, but I feel it" (269).
She is after the truth and she believes that feeling leads her to truth.
Colacurcio may interpret her assertion as meaning that she insists on a
belief and life congenial to her nature, but that is not what *she* believes or
says. Furthermore, Colacurcio says that Esther rejects the "fleshliness"
of Christianity simply because it is "distasteful" to her. But in Esther's
view her feelings ("taste" Colacurcio calls it) are the means she has of
knowing truth, and her feelings reject Christianity. Adams seems to agree
here that the felt response to reality as symbol is the best way to truth.
Only if all intuitional epistemologies can be equated with pragmatism can
Esther's intuitionalism be so designated.

15. I owe my awareness of the crucial importance of this figure of
speech to Esther's interpretation of the meaning of the falls to Hochfield,
although I disagree with much of his interpretation. He says (a, 52–53)
that

> the cataract symbolizes to Esther the vast and steady flow of an ultimate energy,
> of life itself, that satisfies its transcendent purpose through the fullest pos-
> sible realization of itself within its individual particles. Life is its own end so
> far as the individual is concerned, but each life has its unique truth, or prin-
> ciple of integrity, which it contributes to the total and eternal meaning of life
> as a whole. There is no single abstract faith by which eternity is circumscribed;
> eternity is the mysterious wholeness of life comprising the innumerable partic-
> ularities of living truth . . . . This is Esther's view of reality, of transcendent
> good (or at least necessity), which is the source of her individual meaningful-
> ness. The obligation it lays upon her is fidelity to the truth of her own nature.

(1) Esther does sense the falls as ultimate living (indeed, masculine)
energy but I see no evidence that this energy satisfies its purpose through
individuation of its unity. On the contrary, since what the reader knows is
limited to what Esther believes, the primary purpose of ultimate energy
would appear to be to reabsorb its individuated particles into itself, just
as the water of Niagara, falling in individual particles, moves toward
reabsorption of those particles in the mass of water at the bottom of the
falls. Thus life is not "its own end" for the individual. Hazard, Wharton,
and Esther all share the same drive to move out of self into a reality
greater than self (though in Hazard this seems to be a desire to enlarge
the self, while in Wharton and Esther it is a desire to escape the self based
on a hatred for the self). Strong is not so passionately concerned because
he has achieved a kind of success at losing himself in science and is no
proselytizer. (2) It might be argued more plausibly that *in this world* the

ultimate energy achieves its purpose in individuation, yet this argument too is contradicted by the fact that the most mature characters in the novel seek to transcend self while still in this world. (3) I also see no evidence that each life has its unique truth. As a matter of fact, Wharton and especially Strong and Esther share in the same "truth," the "truth" of the modern and future world. Hochfield's statement would be more plausible if he took the ocean rather than the waterfall as Adams' final symbol, but he does not do so. Yet even if he had, the narrator's apparent suggestion, through his use of the ocean, that reality is a multiplicity of contradictory truths, is still not a claim that each individual has his own truth. The assertion that only thought is immortal does suggest that each individual ought to search out the truth and to stand by what he perceives (in the sense of Ralph Waldo Emerson's distinction in "Self-Reliance" between an opinion and a perception). I see nothing, however, which would prevent an individual who is incapable of strong belief in any thought from accepting that of another person, and thereby participating, to the extent that he can believe in it, in the immortality of that truth (if it is indeed a truth). (4) The obligation to one's individual integrity if one has faith in a truth arises not because reality realizes itself in the individual but because it is in the essence of the self (what Christianity calls the soul) that the truth which makes man not an isolated self but a part of reality exists. One is faithful to the self in order to gain immortality but it is an immortality not of the self but of immersion (or loss) of the self in the whole of that nonself which exists in the essence of an individual who has hold of a truth. Thus, paradoxically, Esther is faithful to herself not to keep that self but to lose it in something greater and truer; to give it up to Hazard would be only, at best, to stifle it. (5) I see no evidence either that the sum of truths Hochfield mentions would equal reality; there is more of an implication that no abstract truths are true, that only symbols grasped through feeling give one access to reality. (6) It also seems clear that though "wholeness" —implying unity—may be a good word for the modern truth implied by the falls, it is a poor word to use if the ocean—with its suggestion of chaos —is a truer symbol for reality.

Esther does not make it clear whether there are many kinds of truth or simply many aspects or versions of the same truth. Her response to the falls, however, suggests that Hazard's belief expresses only one aspect of the whole of truth. The ocean symbol seems to imply that there are not only versions and aspects of truth but different kinds of truth, and that these are often contradictory. Truth appears to be multiple, not one. Even less clearly answered is the question whether there is a future world. Strong deals with the idea only as a possibility, and with the motivation of persuading Esther to marry Hazard. He does say that "thought is eternal" (272), but he seems to doubt that the human mind can apprehend truth at all. This doubt is in harmony with his idea of science as progressing toward truth, though it adds the possibility that science will never attain its goal. The idea that thought is eternal is also in harmony with his stated belief that "as for forms of faith it seemed to him as easy to believe one thing as another" (220), since it is thought, not the form of thought, that he has asserted is immortal. In either case immortality need not be in a future world: thought could be immortally immanent under a variety of forms in this world.

16. The question of what the theme of *The History* is, is one of the most disputed problems in the scholarship and criticism concerned with the work. Most critics view the theme in terms of the work's historical content and see it as either (1) America's achievement of unity in political organization and/or national character (e.g., Jordy, 81) (2) the failure of Jeffersonian principles (e.g., Hochfield, a, 63); or (3) some combination of these (e.g., Levenson, b, 121, 135–136). The principal other view is that the theme is (4) that men are controlled by forces stronger than themselves (e.g., Samuels, II, 349–350). Some commentators view the work as having a number of major themes. Most, with the exception of those who deny that *The History* is deterministic (see critical note 18), emphasize all four suggested themes in their discussion.

The fundamental weakness of the fourth-mentioned theme is that it argues that Adams was writing the kind of history he was trying not to write: an exemplum for a theory. Moreover, in pursuit of his avowed aim of simply stating the facts in sequence, Adams eschews all mention of determinism in the introductory chapters. In the conclusion, determinism enters into his contrast between dramatic and scientific history, but he says there (as he does in a letter to Francis Parkman, Dec. 21, 1884, in Cater, 134) that *The History*, dealing as it does with events before 1815, is not scientific; more important, his account of future scientific history is not of history which will take determinism as its theme but of history which will be presented from that philosophical perspective. In *The History* the determinist's remarks appear in the narrative as authorial comments. Their position suggests that their function is to relate the narrative to the final frame of reference of the work. In the foreground are the historical events and their immediate thematic significance. Among critics who deal with theme in terms of this latter level of the work, George Hochfield makes the most elaborate and trenchant case for the theme's being the failure of democratic idealism. Hochfield sees chapter 6 of Volume I of *The History* as the key to the work (a, 56). The basic weakness of his argument is that this chapter is but one—albeit the climactic one—

of six introductory chapters which Adams considered so much a unit that initially he proposed they be separated from the rest of the work as an introduction. Analysis of the subject matter of these chapters reveals this unity and its importance for determining *The History*'s theme. Chapters 1 and 2 are concerned with the problem of national development—physical, economic, intellectual—in America and the physical and especially mental obstacles to it in 1800. Chapters 3, 4, and 5 are an account of the intellectual characteristics of the three major regions of the United States, with emphasis upon the elements in each which stimulated or inhibited national development. These three chapters thus continue and develop chapter 2. Chapter 6 is concerned with the ideals which for democratic Americans determined the goals of national development and assisted in that development. The opposition to this idealism is also presented. All six introductory chapters are therefore concerned with national development and the forces which favor or oppose it. The much disputed questions at the end of chapter 6 strike the highest note in the chapters: can the national development realize the highest hopes of Americans? But this is only the ultimate aspect of the basic problem of national development which appears in all the chapters. In the narrative portion of *The History*, Adams' concern is with the whole problem, including the ultimate problem, and only occasionally (especially at the end of the work) does he focus upon the latter. His most pervasive and primary concern in the work (though not his own principal personal concern— see p. 70 of this text) is with what development is achieved, not with measuring that development against the democrats' highest hopes.

The passage in the work which gives strongest support to Hochfield's view is the final paragraph of chapter 7 of Volume I, where Adams says of the points Jefferson made in his first Inaugural Address that "the history of his Administration will show how these principles were applied, and what success attended the experiment" (I, 217). Since in chapter 6 Adams calls Jefferson the primary spokesman for democratic ideals, this paragraph would seem to be a restatement in terms of the concrete political situation of the questions at the end of the previous chapter. I would agree that such a relationship exists. But note that Adams does not say that the *whole* of *The History* is concerned with the testing of the Jeffersonian or democratic ideals but only Jefferson's administration. If the first four volumes are taken by themselves, Hochfield's view is much more tenable. Hochfield himself says that "with the collapse of the Embargo policy the interest of *The History* for the student of Adams' mind is at an end. The important questions have been answered" (84). Of the thirty-two pages he gives to *The History*, he devotes only three to its last five volumes. He is correct, it seems to me, in asserting that the first four volumes have a dramatic movement and that in them Adams' principal concern is with the failure of Jeffersonian principles rather than with national development. I would agree that this emphasis dominates his account of the Louisiana Purchase and of the Embargo—the climax of this emphasis, of Jefferson's administration, and of the first four volumes of the work. But the climax of the work as a whole is the War of 1812, which takes up three-fourths as much space as the account of Jefferson's whole administration. Nor is Adams' account of the war primarily a dirge for the failure of Jefferson's principles. (It could have been, as Adams' treatment of the Louisiana Purchase shows.) Instead, Adams' position is that of the ardent but objective patriot, elated at American victory and American gallantry in defeat, humiliated by defeat and especially by any cowardly or stupid behavior. The importance given the war by its position in the work, the space devoted to it, and the tone in which it is described, suggests that it is the climax to the national development which took place between 1800 and 1812 and was the ultimate instrument both for forging a national identity (or unity) and giving it at least the beginning of a position in the world.

Of all the views of the work's theme which I do not accept, the most tenable seems to me that which views the theme as the national development's triumph over Jeffersonian states' rights principles. But this view seems to me to oversimplify Adams' account of what occurred. The basic thematic irony of the work is not that the national development occurred at the expense only of Jeffersonian ideals, but that it occurred at the expense of both Virginia Republicans and New England Federalists *and* all the other movements which opposed it. If this view of the theme were to be rephrased as the triumph of national development over all forces opposed to it, it would be more accurate—and also very close to the view that the theme is the attainment of a crucial stage in national development. "Attainment" (or a similar term) seems to me a better term than "triumph," however, because it connotes less of a voluntaristic philosophical frame of reference. My own term, "crystallizes," suggests voluntarism even less and also has positive metaphorical implications of determinism. (Closest to my view is that of Brunner, who, though concerned with Adams' work after *Chartres*, comments that in *The History* Adams "traced the determined path by which a crude, disorganized society—despite a vacillating leadership—yet managed to become a centralized democracy" [16]. Brunner's final phrase emphasizes Adams' belief that the democratic tendency in America is stronger and more basic than the national tendency. My counterpart to this phrase, "democratic nationality," is Adams' own phrase and stresses the emphasis in *The History* upon the national tendency.)

17. Hochfield argues (a, 55–56) that, since Jefferson's and Madison's policies express the ideals of the people, Adams' political history is also a social history. To an extent this seems to be true. But it should be recalled that Adams specifically warns against *identifying* the people with their leaders when he says that "readers will be troubled, at almost every chapter of the coming narrative, by the want of some formula to explain what share the popular imagination bore in the system pursued by government" (I, 176). Adams never presents such a formula.

18. As noted in critical note 16 above, the question of whether or not *The History* is deterministic is a much disputed problem. Some critics have asserted that the forces which Adams says move history are primarily or entirely the people (e.g., Jordy, 87) or the "activities of powerful men" (Vandersee, 170). To me it seems perverse to read the quotation in the text (IV, 301–302) as meaning that either of these was the creator of a movement which "obliged" society to seek a new level. It makes better sense to read the passage as meaning that all of society—the people and their leaders—was obliged by something outside itself to seek a new level. (This "something" is best described by Ernest Samuels: Adams, he says, is "not explicit about the nature of the great undercurrent forces in American life . . . . The very difficulty of scientific measurement continually threw him back upon a *mystique* of force, a hypostatized something that mysteriously united all phenomena, physical and psychic, into a cosmic machine" [II, 374]. Saveth comments that "force, as Adams used it, belongs to that category of 'fictitious entities' which John Stuart Mill said are 'imagined as accounting [for] the more mysterious phaenomena' but which are really 'substitute[s] for explanation of the phaenomena of organized beings'" [b, xx]). Of the critics who argue that Adams is not a determinist (e.g., Vandersee, 170), many do not feel it necessary even to mention the external evidence for determinism, which consists primarily of two letters Adams wrote in which he explicitly stated his deterministic beliefs and related them to *The History* (HA to Samuel J. Tilden, Jan. 24, 1883, in Cater, 125–126; HA to Francis Parkman, Dec. 21, 1884, in *ibid.*, p. 134). Jordy cites none of this external evidence, yet claims that Adams agreed with Comte that a nation has an "inevitable destiny" (113; also 118–119) and says that the control of circumstances over individuals is reflected in Adams' sprinkling of analogies from physics throughout the work (93, 94 n. 53). But to Jordy these circumstances are "the people," whom he views as being, in *The History*, "the embodiment and the culmination of all national power . . . a kind of mystical prime mover in history. As such, the people almost mechanically determined national destiny" (87). The people's choice determines history, Jordy says, but what determines what their choice will be? If it be something internal to

the people, as Jordy suggests, then man, if not men, creates history. This seems to be denied by the passage in the text (IV, 301–302). Jordy's determinism seems to me to founder upon this equation of the forces that determine history with the people. Chalfant argues against even Jordy's kind of determinism, urging that the scientific analogies which Jordy mentions are infrequent and untypical of *The History* and used only as an expository device (203 n. 2). It seems to me perverse to read such passages as page 298 of Volume I, pages 301–302 of Volume IV, and pages 69 and 123 of Volume VI as making use of scientific analogies in a way that is unimportant, purely expository (as probably they *are* in I, 333, 338, 445, and perhaps 276, for example), or nondeterministic. Moreover, there are enough such passages to make it clear that their presence in Adams' much-revised work is deliberate. Their brevity seems to be the result of Adams' focus in the work upon the kind of material Chalfant views as the *only* material in *The History*—human action. The documents are the centripetal center and source of this focus. Yet, just as they move out into narrative, so narrative has a constant centrifugal tendency to push out beyond human action toward philosophical significance, and specifically toward a deterministic frame of reference. Adams' tight rein upon this tendency is not intended to eliminate such significance but to compress it as much as possible so as to keep the focus on the history. As a result, the brief philosophical passages are like burning matches, which, though themselves a source of light, function primarily to ignite the prepared, fact-laden mind of the reader into violent—and convincing—illumination.

This determinism creates problems for Adams the moralist, but I do not believe Hochfield (a, 68–71) is successful in his effort to go to the verge of determinism (he says that "the idea of necessary movement in history according to some kind of law, whether it be mechanical, evolutionary, or atomic, *left its impress* [italics added] on the *History*" [70]) and then draw back in order to make the moralist and the determinist consistent is successful. Equally interesting is the contradiction between Adams' scientific, in the sense of deterministic or naturalistic, point of view and his scientific, in the sense of (Rankean) objective, method of writing history. Ultimately both of these conflicts will be resolved in terms of determinism in *The Education*.

19. Samuels (II, 359) describes the Spencerian equivalent (and source, he says) of Adams' conception of the equilibrium in the "democratic ocean." In the passage quoted by Samuels, Herbert Spencer calls this state one of "quiescence." Samuels comments that "this equilibrium did not imply the death of society or the 'degradation' of its societal energies; on the contrary society would have reached its highest state, a state of

'moving equilibrium' and not one of complete stasis." Samuels implies that Adams accepted Spencer's evaluation as well as his idea and image. (Brunner, 373, 50–51, 68–69, seems to agree.) But Adams' use of the image must be read in the context of his doubts earlier in chapter 9 about the danger of such a social state's stifling individual as well as national progress. It is clear that Adams is at least uncertain that the final social state is a desirable one. In the text I will try to show that analysis of the implications of the symbols suggests that Adams was much more than uncertain about its desirability.

20. The relationship between *Chartres* and *The Education* has been much disputed among Adams' scholars. Aside from the comments in *The Education*, Adams' assertion of the connection between the two books appears only in letters (Cater, 623, 646, 649–650; Ford [1892–1918], 485, 495, 536, 542). Levenson (b) and Samuels (III) both made use of unpublished Adams material and apparently found nothing to contradict what is suggested by the letters already published. In these the first statement that the two books are connected appears in a letter to Henry Osborn Taylor of Jan. 17, 1905 (Cater, 558–559, quoted in Appendix I, p. 234, in present text), the year after the first private printing of *Chartres*. Nothing written while that work was being composed suggests that Adams intended to write a sequel.

Doubt whether the two works were conceived together suggests a doubt about whether *Chartres* embodies the dynamic theory of history and especially whether it embodies the version of the theory which appears in *The Education*. At the beginning of chapter 5 of the present text, I try to demonstrate that the elements of the theory as it appears in *The Education* also appear, in detail, in the earlier book. (In Appendix I, I try to show that *Chartres* also embodies, for the most part, the many elements of the theory which are common to the three systematic accounts of it in *The Education*, "The Rule of Phase Applied to History," and "A Letter to American Teachers of History." Differences in idea and emphasis, however, between these essays and the two earlier works, along with Adams' much vaguer statements about the former's relationship to the latter suggest that the essays were conceived after the earlier works had both been completed [cf., Levenson, b, 358, 365–366].)

Yet even if *Chartres* embodies the theory, other problems remain. (1) Did Adams write *Chartres* primarily to express the theory? (2) Do *Chartres* and *The Education* in their final form comprise a single intellectual whole? An imaginative whole? Both? Because they are closely related, these two questions will be discussed together. As early as 1925, Creek argued (86) that Adams' purpose in writing *Chartres* was not to embody his theory but to escape from the present. Since then a few critics—J. T.

Adams (218), Blunt (48–49), McIntyre (160)—have accepted Adams' statement in *The Education*. Others—notably Levenson (b, 354–355), Hochfield (a, 101, 114), and Samuels (III, 307, 311–312) (all in major works on Adams)—have developed in various ways Creek's belief that a more personal motive was precedent, both in time and importance. The effect of this emphasis is to minimize the connection between the two books. Hochfield also argues (a, 114) that the avowed intellectual relationship between the books was not systematically carried through and finally fails. Spiller (a, 1097–1100) and Anderson (333, 341), by emphasizing the books as works of art, are able to assert that they represent a single work of the imagination without having to deal with Hochfield's problem. My own analysis of the two works reveals a remarkable similarity in their structures: in each the first half of the book (relative to the second half) emphasizes feeling, the second half, reason; in each this division gives rise to two climaxes, a climax of feeling at the end of the first half, of reason at the end of the second half; in each the first climax is the death of a woman, symbolizing the inevitable destruction of human unity by nature's chaos, the second, a rational system which functions—or it is hoped will function—to preserve order in a world where instinct is no longer able to do so. Adams' own statement that the last three chapters of each work "make one didactic work in a disguise" (in a letter to Barrett Wendell, Mar. 12, 1909, in Cater, 646) also seems to me to be valid: the last chapter of *Chartres* especially, in its ideas, in the scientific terminology used to express them, and in its use of the image of the dynamo looks forward to the abstract account of the theory of history in *The Education*. These parallels and correspondences suggest that, whatever the manner or order in which Adams initially conceived the two books and whatever gaps there may be in their intellectual coherence, they do comprise in their final form a single imaginative *and* intellectual work.

Perhaps the close similarity of structure, particularly, was adopted deliberately in order to stress the unity lying beneath the fundamental difference in method of the two works. Although Colacurcio has rightly noted (b, 697–698) how the impersonalizing of autobiography in *The Education* goes with the personalizing of history in *Chartres* to make the books more alike than two more representative specimens of their genres would be, Anderson (338) notes an even more fundamental opposition of method:

> the over-all strategy of shifting between objective and subjective modes. The predominance of one over the other is reversed in *Chartres* from what it was in the *Education*. There the style was mainly dry, hard, and sharp because the persona was exploring the unknown, pitting his intellect against the hopeless multiplicity of the modern world. Here [in *Chartres*] the style is mainly warm

and lyrical, giving a sense of re-exploring the familiar to recover a lost unity, the beauty of art if not religion in the Middle Ages.

In each case the method is dictated—even necessitated—by Adams' sense of his material. His sense of the Middle Ages as a period of feeling led him to appeal to feeling in *Chartres*; *The Education*, by contrast, appealed primarily to reason because it was concerned with a period when reason was the only unifying faculty man still had. Between two books aimed at such different aspects of the sensibility, the kind of intellectual coherence Adams describes in the thirty-third chapter of *The Education* could perhaps exist only in the very general way he describes in the 1905 letter to Henry Osborn Taylor (noted in the first paragraph above).

21. *The Education* (475, 495). *Chartres* (375): From the thirteenth century on "the universe has steadily become more complex and less reducible to a central control. . . . Unity turned itself into complexity, multiplicity, variety, and even contradiction."

22. *The Education* (474). *Chartres*: In conjunction with the quotation in critical note 21, the point is implied on pp. 366–367.

23. *The Education* (474). *Chartres* (375, 377): "The fault, then, was not in man if he no longer looked at science or art as an organic whole or as the expression of unity. . . . The trouble was . . . in the universe itself which presented different aspects as man moved."

24. *The Education* (474–475). *Chartres* (224): "The fact . . . was Power or its equivalent in exchange."

25. *The Education* (475, 458–459). *Chartres* (224): See the rest of the paragraph referred to in critical note 28 here. That all men tend to live as "Frenchmen" do is suggested by the list of illusions at the end of the paragraph, especially when this is conjoined with the reference to "the usual fictions on which society rested" (*Chartres*, 252).

26. *The Education* (475–476). *Chartres* (104): At his utmost man tries "to rival the energy, intelligence, and purpose of God," creator of the ultimate created unity, the universe.

27. *The Education* (458–459). *Chartres* (211): "Eleanor [of Guienne] and her daughter Mary and her granddaughter Blanche knew . . . what a brute the emancipated man could be; and as though they foresaw the society of the sixteenth and eighteenth centuries, they used every terror they could invent, as well as every tenderness they could invoke, to tame the beasts around them." More specifically, "Eleanor and her daughters were using the power of earthly love to discipline and refine the courts." On "courteous love" as a unifying force, see p. 224 of *Chartres*.

28. *The Education* (384–385, 388–389). *Chartres* (245): "The twelfth and thirteenth centuries were a period when men were at their strongest; . . . yet these marvels of history . . . ;—all, without apparent exception,

bowed down before the woman." For the equivalence of "faith" and "feeling," see critical note 31 below. The justification for my use—in this note and in critical notes 31 and 32—of chapter 25 of *The Education* in the present correlation of the dynamic theory in that work and in *Chartres* [whereas I do not use chapter 25 in Appendix I] is that it develops the role of woman suggested in the figurative version of the theory given on pp. 458–459 of *The Education*. In Appendix I, I discuss why the Virgin is not mentioned in the abstract version of the theory in chapters 33 and 34 of *The Education*.

29. *The Education* (475). *Chartres* (104): "Like all great churches . . . , Chartres expressed . . . an emotion, the deepest man ever felt—the struggle of his own littleness to grasp the infinite."

30. *The Education* (475). *Chartres:* This belief pervades the book, as the present text suggests. Adams' own position is a twentieth-century form of nominalism. See especially p. 224, and note p. 142, where Adams says that the function of the glass workers at Chartres "was to excite . . . illusions."

31. *The Education:* On pp. 383–385, Adams makes his supreme example of "faith" the Virgin, "the highest energy ever known to man, the creator of four-fifths of his noblest art." On p. 483, he calls the Middle Ages "the great epochs of emotion," characterizing them on p. 481 by their architecture, glass, mosaics, sculpture, poetry, war, and love—that is, by the dominance of art and emotion. *Chartres:* Adams equates "faith" with "emotion." See, for example, p. 321, "In essence religion was love; in no case was it logic. Reason can reach nothing except through the senses; God . . . must be known . . . by emotion." On p. 196, he says that "archaic instincts" give one the ability to "feel," but that most modern men can only "study"—i.e., use their reason. On p. 317, he speaks of "the love of God—which is faith—and the logic of God—which is reason." On p. 106, he says that the purpose of the journey is "to feel Gothic art," with the implication that this is the only way actually to know art.

32. *The Education* (384–385, 458–459). *Chartres:* On p. 330, Adams calls the twelfth century "the most perfect moment of art and feeling in the thousand years of pure and confident Christianity." On p. 196, he says that in this period man gave his affection and worship to "the last and greatest deity of all, the Virgin." He says the study of her "lays bare the whole subject of sex," and he asserts, on pp. 196–197, that "perhaps the best starting-point for study of the Virgin would be a practical acquaintance with bees, and especially with queen bees." He also identifies the Virgin with such sex and mother goddesses as Astarte, Isis, Demeter, and Aphrodite as an example of "the eternal woman" on p. 196.

33. *The Education* (483–484, 481). *Chartres:* "The essence" of thirteenth-century art and, by implication, of all medieval art—"the despotic

central idea—was that of organic unity" (374). On p. 330, Adams says that the late twelfth and early thirteenth centuries comprised "the most perfect moment of art and feeling in the thousand years of pure and confident Christianity." But the period also marked the end of perfect Christianity and the approaching end of the whole period of man's childhood and its faith in unity (374–375). St. Francis, in whom the age—and perhaps mankind (340)—found its utmost embodiment of the human sense of unity, was as close to the first beginnings of man as to the "artificial society" (217) of the twelfth century. The art of his "Cantico del Sole" "seems to go back to the cave-dwellers and the age of stone" (341). See also p. 358.

34. *The Education* (484): The entire chapter 33 suggests the basic change that occurred—science (and therefore reason) supplanted religion (and therefore faith, which is feeling according to *Chartres*). Chapter 25 suggests that the dynamo (and technology) replaced the Virgin (and therefore art). See especially pp. 383–385. *Chartres:* See p. 104, where Adams balances religion against science, a miracle against a dynamo, a cathedral against a world's fair. Note also pp. 371 and 374, where St. Thomas' method and work are said to be modern, scientific, and technical. On p. 196, Adams says that "the scientific mind is atrophied, and suffers under inherited cerebral weakness, when it comes in contact with the eternal woman." Most modern men "cannot feel"; they "can only study."

35. *The Education* (484). *Chartres* (311, 331. See also 287 for medieval method).

36. *The Education* (475–476, 495). *Chartres* (375): In conjunction with the passage there, consider the implications of the alternatives posed on p. 288 and p. 366.

37. *The Education* (484, 485 ["The mind resumed its illusions"]). *Chartres* (371): Missing from *Chartres*, however, is the idea in *The Education* (496–498) that the attraction of nature has constantly put new forces at man's command until he has reached the point of no longer being able to control them and thus faces, in the twentieth century, a great crisis which only a "new social mind" will be capable of dealing with. In *Chartres* (138) man has simply grown old; his turn to empirical reason is a part of that aging process and hence his discovery of reality's multiplicity seems to be—though Adams does not explicitly say so—a function of old age. *The Education* also makes far more explicit Adams' belief that the woman's force of reproduction is the most basic source of man's sense of unity (458–459, 384–385).

38. *The Education* (459, 496; cf., 499–500). *Chartres:* This seems to be the social implication of the change in man's sense of reality mentioned on p. 375.

39. *The Education:* This idea is not part of the Dynamic Theory in *The Education.* It is implied by the narrator's description of the theory as the autobiography of "Henry Adams" expressed in terms of history as the autobiography of Everyman on pp. 472–473. It is also made explicitly on pp. 398–399, where Adams says that the child sees unity; old age, multiplicity. On p. 481, he suggests the intensity of premodern man's response to the stimulus offered him by the possibility of immortality. *Chartres:* On p. 8, the uncle suggests the energy of the child; on p. 138, he suggests that twentieth-century man has reached the age when neither his senses nor his memory is very reliable. On p. 375, he says that modern man is learning that reality is not unity but multiplicity.

40. *Chartres:* For the Middle Ages as the world of man as a child, see especially pp. 2, 87–89 (also 286). For the idea that the Middle Ages was at one with all of premodern history in this respect, note the characterization of St. Francis as childlike (341), and of his point of view as akin to that of the "cave-dwellers" (341, 358) in contrast to the scientific modernity of St. Thomas (358). For the modern world as the world of man in his old age, see especially p. 138, but also pp. 29, 127, 196. The importance of the child to *Chartres* (and its Wordsworthian context) has been previously noted by Brunner (101), Samuels (III, 262–263), and especially McIntyre (164–165, 171) and Anderson (337). Anderson also briefly notes (338) its juxtaposition with the old man (and how here too there is a structural parallel with the two Henry Adamses of *The Education*—the innocent seeker for unity and the experienced narrator who knows that order is only the dream of man). But Samuels asserts that the child's point of view— "affirming the primary authority of intuition"—is also Adams', a point which this chapter and portions of chapter 7 emphatically deny. McIntyre's excellent discussion contains a number of references to the child not included here. Anderson's brilliant insight is discussed in critical note 45.

41. Critics have varied widely as to the historical validity and the genre of *Chartres.* Reviewers and early critics frequently considered it a work of history, though concerned with the meaning or spirit of history rather than with facts. Bassett, for example, wrote (199) that it was "probably the best expression of the spirit of the Middle Ages yet published in the English language." Later critics have tended increasingly to develop the view, most ably stated by Henry Osborn Taylor (c, 593), among the reviewers, that the book is primarily subjective and its value, primarily literary. Here, too, however, opinions have varied from that of Cargill, who sees it (328) as a "prose poem," to that of Levenson, who claims (b, 245–248) that its genre lies between Walter Pater's "appreciations" and Jacob Burckhardt's cultural history, with the balance inclined to the latter. It seems to me the most relevant documents for Adams' own view are his

letter to John Hay on Jan. 9, 1892 (Cater, 262–263; quoted in part by
Levenson, b, 235); his letter to Henry Osborn Taylor on Jan. 17, 1905
(Cater, 558–560); and his letter to Mabel La Farge on Sept. 15, 1908
(*Letters to a Niece*, 121). The letter to Hay describes what Adams meant
by the term "Travels," which he put into the opening pages both of
Tahiti and the first printed edition of *Chartres*. "A rag-bag of everything"
is the phrase he uses. In the second letter he says that he cares "very
little whether my details are exact, if only my *ensemble* is in scale," which
suggests more order and coherence than the rag-bag image, with no
necessary diminishing of inclusiveness. The new principle which determines this emphasis on order is that of relevance: "To me . . . ," he says,
"the middle ages present a picture that has somehow to be brought into
relation with ourselves" "I have no object but a superficial one, as far
as history is concerned," he adds, suggesting an inherent opposition
between history as essentially an antiquarian pursuit and his own purpose.
In the third letter he suggests the importance of subjectivity in the work:
"I was at Chartres yesterday," he says, "to see whether I myself had
changed. . . . I saw nothing to correct. After some ten years of reflection,
it seems to me I got it pretty right." Obviously, Chartres had not changed
in ten years; what Adams was doing was testing his emotional relationship
to Chartres to see if he had changed. This suggests that *Chartres* was his
personal response to the church. Yet there is also the implication that his
sense of not having changed attested to an objective validity in his response.
Together, these letters suggest that Adams thought of *Chartres* as a study
of medieval culture as a coherent whole, organized so as to be relevant to
the twentieth century and presented as a subjective view of the period
which (though based upon a study of facts) centered in an emotional apprehension that transcended the personal and achieved universal validity.

42. Rule asserts (b, 218) that, "on the whole, there is very little irony
in *Chartres* . . . . When he entered the poetic stage-world of *Chartres*,
Adams was able to let his emotions flow unchecked by irony" except in
the chapter on St. Thomas. However true of verbal irony, this comment
fails to note that the essence of the whole book is the thematic irony
created by the contrast between the appearance the medieval child saw
and the reality seen by the twentieth-century old man.

43. Levenson (b, 249–258) and Samuels (III, 207–213) explore in some
detail Adams' relationship to the nineteenth-century cult of the Middle
Ages. Neither, however, notes the uniqueness of Adams' treatment. Adams
accepts, with variations, the nineteenth-century image of the Middle Ages
as a period of unity, but he sets this image not in a context of Romantic
or Christian belief in unity but in a belief in chaos. He presents the romantic image of the Middle Ages as medieval man's illusion, an iridescent

bubble in which he mentally dwelled and through which he saw the reality of chaos transformed into the unity of his heart's desire. This context of irony rather than faith intensifies the poignancy of a past which not only no longer exists (because of its pastness) but never really existed at all except in men's minds and therefore is doubly irrecoverable.

44. The problem of Adams' ultimate belief has been a subject of much controversy, with a tendency to focus upon this book and "A Prayer to the Virgin of Chartres." Most Roman Catholic critics deny that Henry Adams was a Catholic, a Christian, a supernaturalist of any kind. Most other critics agree, though Cargill (328 n. 147) says that the "Prayer" shows him "abandoning science altogether for mysticism" and Commager (a, 262) says that "the wonder is that he did not follow Newman . . . . The Virgin and her church not only solaced the emotions they satisfied the intellect." Most critics see a combination of emotional attraction and intellectual disbelief as the essence of Adams' position in both works. Samuels (III, 305), however, argues (as does McIntyre) that "in the New Jerusalem, faintly envisaged within the pages of the *Chartres*, rational science would yield the final authority to the mystical intuitions of vital instinct. . . . In the *Chartres* [Adams] took his stand with Nietzsche and their fellow instinctualists for the claims of Dionysiac man." More specifically, Samuels says (III, 236) of the Virgin in *Chartres* that Adams' "double skepticism [of theology and science] paralleled that of both Samuel Butler and Shaw and brought him to the Mother as the embodiment of the life force, the instinct behind all instinct." This assertion is of a piece with Samuels' belief that the child represents Adams' point of view in *Chartres*. In both cases it seems to me that Samuels fails to see that Adams' praise of instinct and feeling is countered by his belief that instinct does not know reality—which is chaos—is opposed to that reality, and is eventually always doomed to defeat by it. The strongest evidence Samuels presents is not in his analyses of Adams' works but the quoted phrase inserted in the following passage (III, 262–263, 622 n. 7):

> Adams had difficulty making up his mind about the nature of intuition especially as his latent idealism continued to erode his positivist leanings. Perhaps he came closest to identifying the drift of his thought when, near the end of his life, he quizzically admitted that though he was "a Unitarian mystic" he included the Virgin in his "faith." (HA to Elizabeth Cameron, Feb. 16, 1917)

Without more context, the reader unacquainted with the letter cannot form his own judgment of what Adams meant by it. It seems, however, to be in agreement with Adams' claims to being a stoic and a Bergsonian, and with their manifestations in the doctrine of Will in "A Letter to American Teachers of History." But all of these seem to me a consciously contrived, admittedly artificial overlay upon a basic belief that reality is chaos and any form of unity, illusion. What seems to me a definitive presentation of this position appears in Harry M. Campbell's "Academic Criticism on Henry Adams: Confusion About Chaos," *Midcontinent American Studies Journal*, VII (Spring, 1966), 3–14. Campbell's article is the only criticism of Adams' criticism that has been printed, though there is some in unpublished dissertations, notably that of Healy. The rapid proliferation of Adams' criticism since 1948 and especially in the past dozen or so years, together with the fact that Campbell deals with the single most basic question in interpreting Adams' work, makes his excellent article a crucially important one. Also relevant here is Brunner's brilliant analysis of the relationship between Adams' vitalism, his theory of history, and his ultimate view (see critical note 68). My own similar views are developed at length in chapter 7 of the present work, especially in the analyses of *The Life of George Cabot Lodge* and Father Fay's article, and in Appendix II.

45. The nature and validity of Adams' version of the medieval Virgin has been the most emotion-charged problem in *Chartres* criticism. Catholic critics have disavowed her validity, although their attitudes have varied from the hostility of Blunt (e.g., 49) to Heeney's suggestion (185) that Mary herself would have forgiven Adams his heretical vagaries because of his love for her. Samuels argues (a, 1144, 1146) that Fulton Sheen accepts Adams' view. Sheen does quote Adams twice (see below) with evident approval, but he makes no comment as to the validity of Adams' view in general (though again, see below). Blunt argues (47, 49) that Adams' view of the Virgin of Majesty is the synthetic view of anti-Catholic prejudice, specifically of Edward B. Pusey's *Eirenicon*, which John Henry Newman answered. Samuels agrees (III, 277) that Adams probably knew of the controversy, but points out what Blunt does not mention, that Newman in his reply dissociated the church from "the superstitious abuses cited by Pusey, abuses [which Newman said,] 'do but scare and confuse me.'" It was these abuses, Samuels says, that Adams cited to sustain his thesis. Healy (419, 452–455) and Heeney (183–185), however, deny that Adams offers any valid evidence for such abuses in the Middle Ages, point out that Adams' evidence consists solely of the popular legends of Mary, and cite Sister Mary Vincentine Gripkey's analysis of these legends, an analysis avowedly incited by the assertions of Adams and others (Heeney, 183–184 n. 63). Healy cites similar analyses of two other bodies of Marian legend. All the studies deny that degree of autonomy and power which Adams assigns to Mary vis-à-vis the Trinity. Heeney concludes (165) that Adams "out-legends the legends" and compares his paraphrase of one legend with a translation by a French Abbé to

demonstrate her point (187–191). It seems to me, however, that while she shows that Adams exaggerates the Virgin's role, she fails to demonstrate the invalidity of his major point—that what the Virgin asks for she gets. The Trinity's problem in the translation Heeney uses is not whether to grant the Virgin's request, as Heeney suggests, but only *how* to grant it in a way that will preserve their consistency. The most thorough and convincing account of the omissions and distortions in Adams' view both of the Virgin (131–152) and of the Middle Ages in general (98–182) is in Brunner, who examines Adams' views in a context of comprehensive knowledge of all the medieval works Adams cites and many more besides. Most critics emphasize Adams' own claim that the Virgin is a sex goddess. Samuels notes (a, 1143) that in this role she is a creation of nineteenth-century anthropology. Yet Samuels also says (III, 229) that, "for Adams, as for Rosetti and Renan, Mary symbolized the disinterested quest for Beauty" and compares her to Henry James' "similar quasi-mystical religion of aesthetic excellences." In the second of these views Samuels seems to me basically mistaken (as he is in his general exaggeration of Adams' Pre-Raphaelitism and especially of his espousal of its mysticism). In *The Education*, Adams specifically (385, 387) dissociates his concept of the Virgin as a force from the conventional nineteenth-century sense of her as sentiment or taste. Yet there is a partial truth in what Samuels says. For in *Chartres*, although Adams describes Mary as like Isis, Demeter, and Venus, says that she "lays bare the whole subject of sex" (196), and thus makes her a goddess of sexual force, as he does in *The Education*, the feeling which the uncle creates about her is not directly sexual but that highly sublimated feeling about women familiar in Victorian literature and eminently in the Pre-Raphaelites and Henry James. (Awareness of this difference leads Healy to argue that Adams' presentation of the Virgin in *Chartres* and *The Education* is inconsistent, a charge I comment on in critical note 56.)

In chapter 16 of *The World's First Love* (179–181) Fulton Sheen asserts that gaining equality has made women unhappy and urges a return to

> the Christian concept, wherein stress is placed not on *equality* but on *equity*. Equality is law . . . Equity is love . . . . In particular it is the application of law to an individual person . . . . Equity goes beyond equality by claiming superiority in certain aspects of life. Equity is the perfection of equality, not its substitute.

Then, after telling the Old Testament story of Esther and King Ahasuerus, he explains that

> this story has been interpreted through the Christian ages as meaning that God will reserve to Himself the reign of justice and law, but to Mary, His

Mother, will be given the reign of mercy. During the Christian ages, Our Blessed Mother bore a title which has since been forgotten, namely, Our Lady of Equity. Henry Adams describes the Lady of Equity in the Cathedral of Chartres.

But if equality is law, and equity as love is not only the perfection of equality but its superior in certain aspects of life, then if God is law, Mary as equity would seem to be the perfection of God and superior to Him in certain aspects of life. Two pages later (183–184), directly after quoting Adams' statement in *Chartres* (245) that the great men of the twelfth and thirteenth centuries all "bowed down before the woman," Sheen uses two more later quotations from Adams (250, 252), but without quotation marks. Using Adams' words, he says in the first of these that "without Mary, man had no hope except in atheism, and for atheism the world was not ready. Hemmed back on that side, men rushed like sheep to escape the butcher, and were driven to Mary." The implied image of God (or the Trinity) as a butcher and the implication that Mary is superior to Him, even if only "in certain respects," indeed bring Sheen, as Samuels says, startlingly close to Adams.

46. Levenson (b, 238–239) and Anderson (335–336) also observe this two-part division in the book. Following the former, Anderson sees the architectural emphasis of the first half as laying a foundation for a dramatic presentation of the life of the period in the second half. Anderson views this foundation (as I do) as primarily one of gaining a feeling for the period, upon which the uncle can rest a more rational commentary in the second half. A more adequate statement of both insights might be to say that in the first half Adams builds a foundation for the second half by creating in the reader a felt sense of medieval man's universe, in which he can then show medieval man acting in the second half. Beginning in his account of Mont-Saint-Michel with the church building—the most tangible and therefore sensuously available medieval work of art in the book—Adams develops a feeling for medieval man's sense of the universe as, in effect, a great church. He continues to do so in his account of Chartres, but now the emphasis shifts to the deity who ruled this church universe as her home in the twelfth century. Having created a felt sense of this cosmic background in the first half of the book, the uncle, in the second half, can show the life of the people who both created and were created by this world. There is still much discussion of art, but now, instead of focusing upon the art first and then upon the life as the source of the art, he focuses upon the life first and then upon the art as the expression of the life.

47. Critics have frequently noted that the three parts of *Chartres* move from a masculine to a feminine and then back to a masculine emphasis.

In part this is true, but the rational masculinity of the thirteenth century has a distinctly mechanical quality which looks forward to the twentieth century and its pervasively asexual and mechanical character, as described in *The Education*.

48. In 1937, Blunt, after attacking Adams' conception of the Virgin in *Chartres*, says (52) that Adams "may have read Saint Thomas . . . , but he does not understand him. Some one should riddle his writing on Saint Thomas. He is as accurate about the Schoolmen as he is about the Virgin." Until 1965, however, the only analyses of the Aquinas chapter were, briefly, in Samuels (III, 299–303), somewhat more fully in Sandelin (417–422), and Wasser (31–36). Criticism has been equally sparse (Wasser, 36–39, and Rule, b, 218–222). Brunner (252–261), however, is excellent. In 1965 Colacurcio (b) moved in the direction of carrying out Blunt's proposal though he approaches Adams in a more indirect and sophisticated way than Blunt did. His strategy is, first, to accept what he says is the opinion agreed to by critics in general, that Adams was a man of letters rather than a "professionally committed academician," second, to argue that *Chartres* is a work of personal vision rather than of intellectual history, and, finally, to show how "distortions" in Adams' view of St. Thomas spring from "biases" in Adams' mind. By constantly taking into account the personal nature of *Chartres*, he prevents what amounts to a sustained attack on Adams' presentation from being outflanked by those critics who emphasize Adams the artist rather than Adams the thinker or historian. The biases which he lists are: (1) Adams' rejection of the philosophical validity of all metaphysics, and consequent interest in the system of Aquinas only as art; (2) his preference for science over metaphysics, and consequent presentation of his artistic Aquinas in scientific terms; and (3) his belief in the dynamic theory of history, which asserts that history since the twelfth century has declined from faith to rationalism, and consequent presentation of Thomas as the beginning of that rationalism. In terms of these biases Colacurcio emphasizes a number of specific distortions in Adams' presentation. First, under the first bias, he notes that the "architectural analogy . . . determined what parts of the system were to be considered" and that "one result of this approach is that Adams discusses less than one-fifth of the entire *Summa Theologiae*," including "what seems to many modern thinkers the most vital and relevant part of the system, the theory of natural law" (b, 700). Colacurcio does not mention those parts of Aquinas' system which the architectural analogy *does* enable Adams to discuss: the existence of God, the creation of the universe, and man's free will, among others. Adams would probably argue that these are the basic problems any religious metaphysic must deal with—and it would seem legitimate for him to question the viability of a system in which such problems were

less "vital and relevant" than "the theory of natural law." The second distortion appears under the second bias. Here Colacurcio says that Adams' attempt to translate Thomas' metaphysical terminology into its scientific equivalent causes "something very queer" to happen "to Thomas' first argument for the existence of God." Instead of translating the argument as, "I see motion; I infer a mover," Adams translates it as, "I see motion; I infer a motor." Colacurcio says that "mover" "describes a being as an agent rather than as a nature. Thus [it] signifies any being which acts in any way whatever to produce motion (change) of any sort whatever. 'Motor,' on the other hand, with its unmistakable materialist and mechanist suggestions, is clearly inappropriate to Thomas' notion of God as Pure Spiritual Act" (b, 701). He then argues that "the real reason for the substitution" is Adams' love for the dramatic and his desire to create a "dramatic confrontation" (b, 702) between the metaphysician and a modern mechanic. What Colacurcio fails to observe is that the term fits Adams' understanding of Thomas' God and His relationship to the universe. "By the term God," Adams says, "is meant a prime motor which supplies all energy to the universe, and acts directly on man as well as on all other creatures, moving him as a mechanical motor might do" (368). Denying that in Thomas' system either man or God—"after the single, unalterable act of will which created" (363)—has free will, and arguing therefore that God acts mechanically, Adams views Thomas' God as a being who is more accurately described as a "motor" than a "mover," with its implications of an agent with volition. Whatever the dramatic reason for the change (and Colacurcio could also have pointed out that Aquinas' "motor" looks forward—in Adams' view—to the immensely more complex dynamo and therefore fits the theory of history which Colacurcio views as another of the personal biases conditioning Adams' interpretation), it is justified by Adams' understanding of what Thomas says and hence can be controverted not by arguing that Adams mistranslates a word but only by demonstrating that Adams' notion of the mechanical nature and action of Thomas' divinity is inaccurate. The third distortion is related to this second one. Colacurcio points out that Adams chooses only one of Aquinas' five proofs for the existence of God, the first one, and argues that he did so because of his second bias, because it "seems, deceptively, the most scientific [proof] and therefore lends itself most readily to a 'scientific' discussion. It would be very difficult to do *this same sort of thing* [italics added] with the third way, from contingency, or with the fourth, from degrees of perfection" (b, 702–703). It may be true that Thomas' other arguments would be less translatable into scientific terminology, but in saying this Colacurcio is only saying that to Adams they would therefore seem less "vital and relevant" to the scientific world of the twentieth century. But to note this is to miss the major point: that Adams or his mechanic would probably hit at the same point in these arguments where they find the first argument most vulnerable, the supposed necessity for a stopping place in the chain of causation. (According to Rudolf Allers, "God," *The Dictionary of Philosophy*, ed. Dagobert Runes [New York: The Philosophical Library, 1942], p. 118, "A basic factor in [Aquinas'] demonstrations [of God's existence] is the impossibility of infinite regress.") The third argument, which Colacurcio says "has been consistently found to be the most cogent" (b, 703 n. 11), prevents an infinite regress in necessary things by referring to the second argument's demonstration that in efficient causes it is not possible to go on to infinity. But that demonstration depends upon acceptance of the scholastic notion of efficient cause. Confronted with this argument the mechanic would probably not have recourse to David Hume's redefinition of cause but would instead reply in much the same way as he did to the first argument:

> What you say may be good logic, but it is not proof. You say that efficient causes cannot "go on to infinity, because in all efficient causes following [each other] in order, the first [member] is the cause of the intermediate cause, and the intermediate is the cause of the ultimate cause [or last member], whether the intermediate cause be several or one only." [*Summa Theologica*, Question II, Third Article.] But I know only events, not the supposed true order of causes, and when I consider a number of events which seem to be connected by cause and effect, all I can see is that any event in that series has a cause (or many causes), that that cause was itself the effect of a preceding cause, and so on indefinitely. I see no empirical reason to believe that there must be the kind of pattern you describe and therefore no reason why there has to be a first efficient cause.

One can infer that Adams would have thus criticized the second and third proofs in terms of the inadequacy of their attempts to prevent an infinite regress from a passage in a letter he wrote to Margaret Chanler, Sept. 9, 1909 (Ford [1892-1918], 523-524). There he says that "what I like most in the schoolmen is their rule of cutting infinite sequences short. They insist on stopping at the prime motor at once. Bergson and all the speculators who follow Kant . . . become scared and stop, without explaining the reason for stopping. They give me no sort of help. Time and space are conditions of Thought, and so far good; but I can reckon an infinite hierarchy of them in mathematics, one just as good as the other,—concepts of concepts,—and why, in space, should I stop?" When Adams says that he "likes" the schoolmen's practice, he does not mean that he agrees with them. Otherwise, why make the mechanic's criticism of Aquinas' first proof in *Chartres* so apparently devastating? But he does indicate how crucial the problem was for him.

This analysis suggests that one reason Adams chose to use Thomas' first argument rather than the third may well have been that, unlike the second or third arguments, it was not dependent upon a traditional philosophical conception like "efficient cause" but more purely empirical. The same point applies even more strongly to the other argument Colacurcio mentions, that from degrees of perfection, whose major premise is that "among beings there is one more and one less good, one more and one less true, one more and one less noble; and such more and less occurs in other things of this kind." The assumption here that "good," "true," and "noble" are absolutes offers little to the empiricist.

(Colacurcio goes on to assert that "the earlier debate between Abélard and William of Champeaux displays the same freedom with texts for the sake of irony." Here again Colacurcio echoes the charge of Yvor Winters [to whom Colacurcio acknowledges himself indebted] that Adams' "procedure is to be witty rather than intelligent" (398). Campbell seems to me to have adequately answered this charge in the article referred to in critical note 44 above. Colacurcio offers no evidence for his assertion.)

Colacurcio lists three other "similar distortions" under this second bias without presenting arguments or evidence against them. In two of these he dismisses Adams' view primarily by rejecting the analogies Adams uses, without arguments or evidence as to how essential these were to Adams' over-all presentation of his point.

The crucial distortion which Colacurcio deals with under this third bias is what he calls Adams' assertion "that his Aquinas is really the father of modern scientific rationalism." "It would not be difficult to dispute Adams' view," Colacurcio says. "One could easily show . . . that Adams is far less scrupulous than Aquinas was in distinguishing faith, theology and philosophy; that once the proper distinctions . . . are made, Aquinas seems far less rationalistic than even many of his contemporaries. . . . It would not be difficult to prove, in short, that the 'Christian philosophy' of the *Summa Theologica* is far less a logical tour de force than Adams makes it seem" (b, 709). Adams never says that Thomas is more rationalistic than his contemporaries; the uncle says that he chooses to talk about Thomas rather than another scholastic because Thomas stands "at their head as type" (344), chosen so not by the uncle but by the Church. Aquinas' fatherhood of modern rationalism is therefore presumably as the type of scholasticism rather than as an individual thinker. In a footnote Colacurcio suggests the invalidity even of this view by mentioning an "account [by Etienne Gilson] of the 'meaning' of Thomism in the history of philosophy almost opposite to that which Adams suggests" (b, 709 n. 18). But that another commentator—even a famous one—has a different view from Adams is no conclusive demonstration that Adams has distorted the historical significance of Thomas and scholasticism. What Colacurcio (and Blunt) fail to note and to deal with is that Adams' interpretation and criticism is not based solely upon his own avowedly nonprofessional reading of the *Summa* but also upon the commentaries of authorities, both in and outside of the Church. When, for example, Adams makes his climactic point, that Thomas' doctrine of matter and form is "frank pantheism," he says that "so it appeared to Duns Scotus" (357). Adams uses this strategy of citing a famous critic of Thomas at a number of points, citing Descartes and Pascal (347, 348–349), "many theologians" (350), M. Jourdain (356), Father de Régnon (370), and "the Franciscans and the Jesuits" (371). He also refers to the church council which in 1276 condemned Aquinas' doctrines (360–361). Were all these critics subject to Adams' twentieth-century biases? Surely some of them speak with as much authority as even Gilson? And though Colacurcio may demonstrate to his own satisfaction that Adams is mistaken simply by arguing from Thomas and Adams and citing Gilson, others may rightfully wonder (1) if Adams cites his authorities correctly, (2) what their place is in the commentary and criticism of Aquinas, (3) what claim they have to be considered authorities on Thomas, and (4) how Colacurcio would answer their arguments. Only when this is done will the student of Adams' work have a clear idea of the *viability* of Adams' view of Thomas in Adams' time and in ours. (Perhaps that is at least as important as the *validity* of his view.) Such a discussion would also enhance the writer's claim to pronounce on the validity of Adams' view, because it would show the reliability of those theologians and philosophers Adams admittedly leaned on in formulating his own highly metaphorical account of Thomas' doctrines.

49. There has been much dispute as to Adams' purpose in *The Education*, occasioned (or at least facilitated) and partly justified by Adams' own various and often contradictory accounts of it as a "shield of protection in the grave" (Ford [1892–1918], 495), a tribute to John Hay (Cater, 592), an attempt to educate himself (Ford [1892–1918], 485, 526; Cater, 619), an attempt to teach others (Ford [1892–1918], 472, 546), an experiment in literary form (Ford [1892–1918], 490; Cater, 614), a study of history (Cater, 609), and a study of education (Ford [1892–1918], 524; Cater, 609, 621, 623, 649–650). In *The Education* itself, several purposes are suggested. In the Preface Adams says that he wishes to educate young men to be effective in the twentieth century by showing them the faults in the education of their fathers and in particular by discussing what elements in his own education had "turned out to be useful, and what

not." In the Editor's Preface he quotes the passage in the text in which he says that his purpose in *Chartres* and *The Education* together is to measure the motion of man from the Middle Ages to the present, *The Education* being "A Study of Twentieth-Century Multiplicity." In the third paragraph of the text, the speaker suggests that he is writing a "story of education." In the same paragraph he suggests another purpose when he says that though the practical value of his story of education is uncertain, "every one must bear his own universe, and most persons are moderately interested in learning how their neighbors have managed to carry theirs." This statement makes explicit the autobiographical purpose first suggested in the Editor's Preface by Adams' statement that he used to say "half in jest, that his great ambition was to complete St. Augustine's 'Confessions.'" This suggestion is extended as well as modified by his references in the Preface to two other famous autobiographies, those of Rousseau and Franklin—even though he treats them as concerned with education as well as self-portrayal and characterizes Rousseau's book as a "monument of warning against the Ego" in such a work. Clearly, Adams does not wish to be thought of as writing autobiography for his own sake, to display himself. Rather, like St. Augustine, his avowed model, he is writing an autobiography focused upon his personal search for the nature of reality and man's relationship to it (described in terms of history rather than theology) and the kind of behavior dictated by such knowledge. Like Augustine, he views himself as both a particular individual and a representative man and sees the results of his search as relevant to both aspects of himself. Hence he offers his autobiography as a didactic work useful to others. That he avowedly (in the Preface) manipulates the life of the particular individual to make it more representative and therefore more validly and effectively didactic pushes the autobiography in the direction of "poetry" and away from "history." Doing so, expands, as Sayre says (123), the work's autobiographical purpose and nature, but it does not obliterate it. The title of the work emphasizes this purpose. It is also made clear at the end of the Preface where Adams notes that for his didacticism to be effective the effaced ego of the work "must have the air of reality; must be taken for real; must be treated as though it had life. Who knows? Possibly it had!" Thus obliquely and facetiously he reminds his reader that the story of education he is about to read is that of an actual human being.

The argument that *The Education* is basically fictive, or poetic, rather than historical or scientific, was advanced by Spiller (a, 1097–1100) and others, substantiated by the massive research of Samuels (e.g., I, 8–52; see vii–x), and has been carried farthest by Anderson (321–322) and by Brunner (96–97). Adams does say in the letters that the work is basically an experiment in literary form, written for the sake of the form rather than the content. But his assertion is contradicted by other statements in his letters, and implicitly by the clearly subordinate role the problem of form is given in the Editor's Preface. Yet even if it were true, it is also true that, nowhere, so far as I know, inside or out of the work, does Adams ever suggest that the image of himself which appears in the work is not true both to his sense of the facts of his life and to the image he has of that life. Nor does it seem to me to be so. Indeed, the greatness of *The Education*—like that of the *Confessions* and other great autobiographies—lies in the fact that it is history as well as poetry, that it shows the imagination involved in life and hence has a different kind of value than a primarily fictive work.

50. Adams makes the symbolic meaning of the steps of Ara Coeli clearest on page 340 of *The Education*: "One sat down to ponder on the steps beneath Richard Hunt's dome [at the Chicago Exposition] almost as deeply as on the steps of Ara Coeli, and much to the same purpose. Here was *a breach of continuity—a rupture in historical sequence* [italics added]." Levenson (b, 313, 322, 341) seems to see the symbol as having the same meaning as I do, and as posing the same question, though he apparently believes that the fall Adams is concerned with is specifically that of Christianity. Samuels (III, 374) seems to view the symbol as meaning "the collapse of [Adams'] eighteenth century world" and, apparently, "the transformation of the Western world in his own lifetime." MacLean's (336) treatment will be included in my discussion of Wenlock Abbey as a symbol. Sayre (101) notes that "the steps of Ara Coeli become a constant symbol in *The Education*. Why man? Why his societies? What orders and destroys them?" These questions seem to be questions involved with "the eternal question" and implied by it but they are not the eternal question itself nor do they refer to the fall—the phenomenon symbolized by Ara Coeli which poses the question. Brunner notes the symbol, its recurrence and its importance (408–413), attributes to it the same meaning that I do, and views that meaning, as I do, as inspiring the eternal question (371, 408). He also sees the falls that Adams was concerned with as the two falls of Rome and the possible fall of America (371, 408). He believes that Adams found his own answer to the question in the second law of thermodynamics (413), which he believes is the basis for the dynamic theory of history throughout Adams' later work. I do not agree with this contention, but I do agree that the dynamic theory is Adams' answer to the eternal question. (See also critical note 52.)

51. Critical discussion of the structure of *The Education* centers upon whether it has two or three major parts. Levenson, Samuels (III, 350), and Chalfant (339) say three. All view "Chaos" and/or "Failure" as the

end of the first part; they disagree as to where the third part begins. Samuels believes that *The Education*'s structure follows that of Thomas Carlyle's *Sartor Resartus:* the Everlasting Nay, the Centre of Indifference, and the Everlasting Yea. Though the analogy is significant, Samuels seems to me to make it invalid by emphasizing it too much and thereby distorting *The Education*. The most obvious difference is that Adams' "Yea" is not "everlasting" but very tentative and limited. Moreover, there is no real "center of indifference" in *The Education;* though the "no" is less strong in the last part of the book than in "Chaos," it is as strong as in the chapters preceding "Chaos." Levenson says (b, 333) that "The Dynamo and the Virgin" is the "second climax" of the book, thereby suggesting that the succeeding chapters form a third part. Yet just a few pages earlier (b, 326) he gives wide circulation for the first time (cf., Samuels, III, 338 and 633 n. 41) to the crucial piece of external evidence for a two-part structure: a letter to James Ford Rhodes, Feb. 10, 1908, in which Adams compares *The Education* to a centipede that crawled twenty sections downhill and then fifteen up a little for the view (compare letter to Whitelaw Reid, Sept. 9, 1908, in Cater, p. 621). Sayre (121) seems to return to the three-part division but considers the second part to be the omitted twenty years when Adams applied his early education. Though Sayre does not say so, the crucial *internal* evidence for this division is Adams' own statement near the beginning of the chapter, "Twenty Years After (1892)," that "education had ended in 1871; life was complete in 1890; the rest mattered so little!" (316; see also 313–315). This statement suggests that the actual book is in two parts because the second, or middle, part of the life was not education at all, but application. Anderson (325–326), citing the letter to Rhodes as evidence, also emphasizes the two-part division. (See also critical note 58 below.)

52. Folsom (169–170) points out that "just as Adams had sat on the steps of Ara Coeli pondering the ruins of two civilizations and speculating on the possible end of a third, so he was to lie on Wenlock Edge and ponder the disruption of the Kingdom of Siluria, the Middle Ages, and the possible dissolution of the modern world." (He is apparently referring to pp. 228–229 of *The Education*.) Folsom seems to view this likeness as meaning that Ara Coeli and Wenlock Edge are to be equated. MacLean's implication (336) that the steps of Ara Coeli are symbolic of timelessness would harmonize with my interpretation of Wenlock as meaning timelessness and Folsom's equation of Ara Coeli and Wenlock. But to me the steps of Ara Coeli do not seem a symbol of timelessness. Adams does quietly meditate there, but he never says that they offer him the "profound peace" (290) he finds at Wenlock. Instead, from the beginning the steps offer him the irritant of the fall and the eternal question. (See

critical note 50 above.) Wenlock, however, *seems* to offer him peace, and that it proves to be an outlook on the same problem that Ara Coeli confronts him with is ironic. What has happened is that a seeming unity symbol has proved to be a multiplicity symbol: the peace and timelessness that Wenlock seem to offer are illusions. MacLean seems to me to misread the meaning of the steps of Ara Coeli; Folsom, to equate them and Wenlock without realizing the irony involved in the equation.

53. Blackmur (a, 607–612) and Chalfant (340) have argued that the chapters are arranged in triads rather than pairs. This division seems to me to founder as early as the third chapter. (See critical note 55 below.)

54. Koretz (201) says that Quincy symbolizes "the Newtonian universe of balance, harmony, and order," while Boston looks forward to "the coming age in which unity and order have been destroyed." This seems to me a very partial view of the meaning Adams assigns the two places. In his most explicit discussion of their meaning (7–11) Adams equates Quincy with "diversity" and "the multiplicity of nature" and Boston with "unity" and the rigid discipline of school. These meanings would seem to be antithetical to those ascribed to the symbols by Koretz. But the problem is more complex. Insofar as Quincy is multiplicity and Boston unity, Quincy looks forward to the ultimate expression of spring, summer, sensuousness, and nature's multiplicity: the description of the death of Adams' sister in "Chaos." Boston, by contrast, looks forward to the ultimate expression of autumn-winter (p. 473), analysis, and the human desire for order: the Dynamic Theory of History and the law of acceleration. But something has happened along the way: Adams has reversed his attitude toward his opposing symbols. The death of Adams' sister reveals the horror that lies behind nature's beauty; the Dynamic Theory shows the (relative) security that may lie even in the most rigid humanly constructed order. Yet Adams loved Quincy more than he hated Boston; he hated the multiverse more than he liked his theory. The Virgin and the dynamo also express this polarity and further reveal the complexity of Adams' attitude toward it. The Virgin seems to be closer to Quincy—to the spring and summer of Everyman's life, to the sensuousness associated with natural beauty. Yet the Virgin represents the unity of the twelfth century and the Middle Ages generally: she is the counterpart for Everyman of the sister who is destroyed by nature's multiplicity in "Chaos." She is Everyman's image of nature when he is so much younger and more ignorant than "Henry Adams" that he views his transfer of allegiance from the Trinity to her as an escape, not to multiplicity (which was Satan), but to a new kind of unity, one looser, more illogical, and freer than the mechanical, Boston-like unity of the Trinity. The dynamo, by contrast, is associated with autumn-winter (p. 379) and

especially with the autumn and winter of Everyman's life and the analysis associated with man's mind. Yet the dynamo represents the multiplicity of the twentieth century (see critical note 62 below); as the Dynamic Theory it is Henry Adams' twentieth-century counterpart for the mechanical theology developed by Thomas Aquinas. It is an image of nature and man when Everyman has such age and wisdom that he views what is actually a final great effort of man to give order to multiplicity (the dynamo) as a symbol of multiplicity. As the Virgin is a looser unity than the Trinity, so the dynamo is a "tighter" multiplicity than the ocean of colliding atoms. This version of the polarity illuminates its American political expression. Quincy is associated with the loose eighteenth-century kind of federalism, embodied for Adams in the Constitution and George Washington (335, 343–344), which permits much individual freedom—a political analogue of the Virgin. Boston, however, which Adams associates with State Street and capitalism, foreshadows America's embrace in 1893 of a rigid, mechanical ordering of American government (and society), which is opposed to the Constitution and hangs on the verge of chaos (398), just as the dynamo does. In the case both of the Virgin versus the dynamo and of eighteenth-century American government versus twentieth-century American government, Adams prefers a unity that permits a large degree of freedom. He likes freedom more than he fears anarchy. Only when forced to choose between chaos and a rigid order does he prefer the latter.

55. Blackmur (a, 607–610) argues that Washington represents a synthesis of Quincy and Boston: that it is multiplicity trying to be unity. Adams does present Washington as the scene of such an effort, but earlier he presented Quincy as the scene of a similar effort. The problem is stated abstractly in the passage in which Adams says that the effort to run order through chaos is the aim of education (12) and exemplified concretely in the description of John Quincy Adams' taking the boy Henry to school and thereby forcing him to participate in the family's commitment to the order of society. This incident suggests the limited, eighteenth-century federalism which Adams admired. The scale is larger in "Washington" but the motif or problem is the same. The likenesses between "Quincy" and "Washington" (and Rome) seem to me both more pervasive and more significant than the differences. Adams goes to both places on vacation in spring or summer (just as he does to Rome); both are described very sensuously (as is Rome); the beauty of nature is emphasized in both (though it appears only in one brief phrase about Rome); in both (as in Rome) the emphasis is upon diversity or freedom and "want of forms" (Rome is "a gospel of anarchy"). In contrast, Boston is associated with winter and school, and there is no sensuousness and no nature

except momentarily in the final (transitional) paragraph: Boston is associated with unity. Harvard has the same characteristics, except that in it (perhaps because it is followed by Berlin, another unity place), there is no sensuousness at all. Berlin is treated the same way except that again sensuousness and nature appear briefly in the final paragraph, apparently as a prelude to Rome. Sensuousness also appears at the beginning of the chapter in connection with the trip from London to Berlin. Finally Adams explicitly makes Washington (45) and Boston antithetical (he does the same thing with Rome and Boston [91]), as he had Boston and Quincy in the first chapter. He also says of Washington that "it remained on his mind as an attraction, almost obscuring Quincy itself" (45), while of Mount Vernon (in the same chapter) he says that it was "only Quincy in a Southern setting" (48). (The difference between Washington's and Mount Vernon's relationship to Quincy does suggest that there is a dialectical progression in the pairs of chapters as well as repetition, Rome and Berlin marking the first climax of the dichotomy and of the progression.) This reminiscence of Quincy in Washington has its counterpart in the anticipation of Washington (and of Adams' liking for it and association of it with Quincy) in the "Quincy" chapter in the person of Adams' paternal grandmother, who is presented as helping to alienate Henry Adams from Boston by heredity because she was from Maryland, thereby making him one-fourth Southern.

56. Healy (501) argues that there are inconsistencies in Adams' presentation of the Virgin in *Chartres* and in *The Education*, and within *Chartres* itself:

> In the *Chartres* he identifies the Virgin as a goddess of absolute and anarchic power, worshipped in her own right in a "church of her own," independent of the Christian Church. Throughout the *Education* he stresses her identity as sexual force. But in his final statement he lays at her feet the historical "failure of Christianity." What is one to make of such contradictory, irreconcilable ideas?

But Adams does not say that the Virgin is always such an autonomous power; only in the twelfth century was she so. Even then, he says, she was nominally part of the Christian Church and the principal source of its strength. Since then, though her power and that of Christianity have waned, she remains, he says, the strongest weapon the Church has to conjure with. The source of this strength, in the past *and* the present, is the fact that she is an image of sexual force. As Healy says, this fact is stressed in *The Education*, but it is also made emphatically explicit in the opening paragraphs of the second half of *Chartres* (196) and is present by implication throughout Adams' discussion of the great ladies of the twelfth century and the courteous love tradition in literature. Since, in Adams' view, sexual force is the principal source of the strength of the Christian Church, at least since the twelfth century, it is hardly surprising that what seems to him the failure of the Virgin's grace at Troyes should also seem the failure of Christianity or, to put it as Healy does, that he should view the failure of Christianity as essentially her failure.

The emphasis on her illogic in *Chartres* seems to me largely accounted for by differences in what Adams is concerned with in the two books. In *Chartres* he is concerned with woman in relation to man and the Virgin in relation to a rigidly logical, masculine Trinity; in *The Education* he is concerned with woman and the machine, and woman and the multiverse —the Virgin versus the dynamo and the ocean. The Trinity *is* called the "machine of divine justice" in *Chartres*, but it is primarily male and therefore alive, whereas the dynamo and the ocean are neither human nor alive and therefore it is the Virgin as the symbol of life which is emphasized.

57. The symbolic significance of the death of Adams' sister is discussed in Levenson (b, 319–320), Sayre (115), and, most notably, in Koretz (201–202) and Anderson (325). Adams' loss of faith in nature in this experience is expressed, in part, as a loss of faith in nature as an embodiment of the feminine principle (288, 282). In "The Virgin and the Dynamo" Adams, in effect, separates from Mother Nature what was, for the nineteenth century, her essential aspect of fecundity (see Nuhn, 189–190) and assigns it to a Virgin Mary who has been separated from the supernatural and made a purely human mother and woman image. In opposition both to Mother Nature's chaos and indifference and to the orthodox Virgin's passive submission to the (illusory) machine of divine justice represented by the Trinity, Adams' Virgin is the friend of humanity. It is to her that Adams gives that affection which as a child (according to *The Education*) he had given to nature (8–9). (The study of his Maryland grandmother, Louisa Adams, in "Quincy," is, therefore, a kind of early study of the feminine principle that will eventually become Adams' chief "deity.") But see critical note 59 below.

58. Among the most disputed questions concerning *The Education* are those involving Adams' portrayal of himself as a failure. Roelofs, Anderson, and Baym all argue, in various ways, that the portrayal is not a sincere self-portrait but a deliberate distortion. The best evidence that the portrayal is basically sincere is that Adams presents the same image of himself in his late letters on the rare occasions when he mentions or implies something about his own success or failure (e.g., Ford [1892–1918], 318, 414–415, 566 n. 3). He never calls himself a success and only

CRITICAL NOTES 291

once even comes close to doing so (Ford [1892–1918], 416–417). Such evidence suggests that Roelofs (231) and Anderson (323–324) are mistaken in arguing that Adams makes his subject a failure simply in order to emphasize his themes and assist his didacticism. Certainly his portrayal does perform those functions, and clearly, as has been shown (Anderson, 320–325; Samuels, III, 355, 359–361, 368–369), Adams distorts the literal facts of his life, in order for those functions to be more effectively performed. But I see no reason to deny Adams' account in *The Education* of these themes as emerging from his self-image—rather than vice versa. It seems to me that his self-image determined his Dynamic Theory, from which the themes are derived. He then modified his picture of his life to emphasize the validity of the theory and of the themes. But he did not *create* the image of himself as a failure for artistic or didactic purposes. The presence of the failure image in the late letters is not such strong evidence against Baym's argument (217) that Adams was consciously adopting a pose familiar in nineteenth-century literature. But Baym offers no evidence that this was Adams' intent. Hence, his important insight does not necessarily mean anything more than that autobiographers, like poets, dramatists, and historians, work within the climate of opinion of their own era and view their material in terms of images common to that climate. (Roelofs argues [221–222] that Baym's argument is answered in the Preface to *The Education*, where Adams specifically says he is not displaying his own ego.)

59. Levenson (b, 340–341) brilliantly comments about this passage:

> The *historical tramp*, as he now called himself, reached his limit of free kinetic vibration one day at Troyes . . . . The old vision [of chaos] recurred and this time forced him to devise his answer. Overwhelmed by the new sciences of multiplicity, he had consented to the proposition that "the historian must not try to know what is truth, if he values his honesty; for, if he cares for his truths, he is certain to falsify his facts." Yet even then he had added that "though his will be iron, he cannot help now and then resuming his humanity or his simianity in face of a fear." The fear had come and with the experience at Troyes, Adams committed himself to the humanity of the modern manikin. . . . By contriving a formula, reason could convert his multiverse into a universe—for himself at least.

Levenson notes here that the Troyes experience is a repetition of that recurrent experience of chaos which appears throughout *The Education*. What he does not note is the striking parallels between this experience of chaos and its results and the two chapters which climax and conclude the first half of the book. In "Chaos" the death of his sister caused Adams to lose his childhood faith in nature, personified as a woman, and to decide that God, if he existed, could not be a person. In "Vis Nova" a death causes Adams to lose his nonreligious faith in the Virgin as a symbol of sexual force and to realize with renewed intensity that Christianity has failed. In both cases the disillusionment occurred specifically because of the contrast between the violence of the death and an example of tranquility, the uncaring tranquility of nature in the first case and of the "charming Church" (472) in the second. In "Chaos" Adams fled from his experience of chaos to the Alps where his senses gradually recovered their illusions about nature's order, stability, and beauty. But no sooner had this occurred than Europe was plunged into the social and political chaos of the Franco-Prussian War. From this new chaos Adams fled to Wenlock Abbey, where he finally found peace. There he received a letter asking him to teach history at Harvard College. The following chapter is primarily concerned with his experience teaching history at Harvard, the final result of the preparation for a career which is the principal meaning of "education" in the first half of the book. This experience and thus his first education proved a "Failure" (as he entitled the chapter) because he did not want to teach history as the chaos it is and could not falsify (that is, unify) it in any useful or satisfying way because it had not become scientific and hence had no value for young men preparing to live in a scientific world (300–301). In "Vis Nova" what is destroyed—or at least diminished—is the peace and pleasure he had found since boyhood in an imagined retreat to the Middle Ages. By this time his pleasure in that retreat had developed from the purely aesthetic attraction of Sir Walter Scott and the aesthetic, antiquarian attraction of Wenlock Abbey to the more contemporaneously viable sexual force which primarily attracted him in the Virgin and vitalized the aesthetic and antiquarian pleasure he also found in her and her churches. That pleasure and that sophisticated illusion was destroyed—or diminished—by the experience at Troyes, which dramatically illustrated the superiority of chaos to the Virgin. Where now could Adams go for the illusion of peace and order? He turned to himself and the creation of a formula of his own for the universe, which in the following two chapters proved to be his own attempt to give to history that scientific basis which might have made his experience at Harvard a success. The two chapters on "The Dynamic Theory of History" and "A Law of Acceleration" are therefore not only the final result of Adams' search for the "great generalization" (224) which is the principal meaning of "education" in the second half of the book, they are also the practical tool for want of which Adams failed at a career in the first half. Thus, in a sense, they represent the final result of both meanings of education, as Adams himself suggests when he calls his theory the "term of a nineteenth-century education" (472). The parallels between the two parts of the book seem to be deliberate; the difference is primarily the emphasis in the first half of the book on the death of the sister (which as the climax of the entire work is properly its most vivid episode) rather than on the failure at Harvard and the subordination in the second half of the experience of chaos to Adams' relatively successful creation of order in his Dynamic Theory.

60. The much-discussed last sentence of the book seems to me neither a "lapse of tone," as Levenson says (b, 347), nor the change of meaning Folsom sees (162; see also 174), but a complex piece of irony. (Cf. Spiller, a, 1103: "In his final testament of futility and affirmation, his vein [247] was comic in spite of the tragic intensity of his feelings. Wit alone could bear the burden.") It enables Adams to suggest that for sensitive natures the world has always been a hideous place and yet to do this lightly. It also enables him to express directly the profound wish that led him on his search for unity while at the same time making it clear by the excessiveness of the expression as well as the total context of the work in which it appears that he is being ironic. The irony is not bitter, but sad, and pitying, though not with the self-pity Levenson suggests, except in the sense that the self here is that of Everyman. For what Adams is expressing indirectly through his irony is pity for mankind and the human condition.

61. The other principal attempt to reach toward a symbolism in *The Education* that goes beyond the Virgin and the dynamo is that of MacLean. He asserts that the principal symbols of *The Education* are the window and the cross. By the window he means the "imaginative moments" in *The Education*—in many of which, he says, "Adams has actually included the literal frame of a window" (333)—which are—figuratively—embedded in the stonework of the prose and connected by the usually implicit symbol of the Cross (342). MacLean also says that one of the recurrent colors in the work is the color of Jesus' agony on the Cross (344). Individual aspects of these and other insights in the article might fruitfully be examined in a more systematic way. The window, for example, suggests the question: what is the significance, if any, of the fact that the apocalyptic vision of New York in the final chapter, which Adams ostensibly has as his ship comes up the bay to New York, is associated by him, as he is looking out his club window on Fifth Avenue, with Rome under Diocletian? Clearly it is when he is at rest rather than in motion that the imaginative association takes place; but how is the window implicated, if at all? MacLean's cluster of images as a whole, however, seems to me to have implications which violently distort the meaning of *The Education*. Together they suggest that *The Education* is a Christian church, a twentieth-century cathedral. This is the antithesis of my belief that *The Education* is a dynamo that constantly threatens to explode and

become an ocean of chaos. The explicit uses of the Cross mentioned by MacLean seem to me of relatively small importance. What MacLean refers to as the "hidden image" of the Cross lies, he says, "in the centre of the Adams text." He describes it cryptically as "the psychological point where the two dreams cross, of pleasure and pain . . . . playing into every irony, every paradox, every wish and defeat." A few lines further, he refers to "a central psychological cross. 'For he knew no longer the good from the bad' 'For he knew not where to turn'" (342–343). He seems to be referring here to Adams' response to what *The Education* calls the "warring, irreconcilable problems, irreducible opposites" (9) of human life: "Life was a double thing," Adams writes, in a sentence quoted by MacLean (342). These passages suggest that the essence of human life is division and therefore suffering. But the Christian Cross signifies not only such division and suffering (occasioned by the conflict of man's soul and his corrupted nature) but also the promise of ultimate reconciliation: the connection between the two pieces of the Cross is transformed into a fusion and thereby releases man from conflict into harmony with God. If that Cross is present in *The Education*, it is so only by (and for) contrast. Life there is what connects the warring opposites of human experience, opposites which can never be fused (except momentarily in art—and that is not the emphasis in *The Education*) and can be escaped only by a death which destroys an individual's identity and disperses his material remains amidst the chaos of the multiverse. Thus *if* there is any particular symbolic significance in the explicit uses of the Cross, it would seem to be that human life, not only in the twentieth century but at all times, is the life of the Cross without hope or possibility of redemption.

62. Critics agree that the dynamo is the principal symbol of *The Education*, as the Virgin is of *Chartres*. My claim that the drama and the ocean are the ultimate symbols of the two works does not necessarily contradict this position. The Virgin is the highest expression of the dramatic view of life; the dynamo is the final—or nearly final—expression of the view that reality is like an ocean. But it is curious that in a work in which it is the principal symbol the dynamo appears so rarely (as Maud, 387, notes). In *Chartres* the Virgin is central to over half the book; but in *The Education* the dynamo appears prominently in only one chapter, "The Virgin and the Dynamo," though it also appears, disguised, in "A Dynamic Theory of History." For whatever else "dynamic" means, it suggests that Adams' theory of history is the *dynamo*'s theory of history (Levenson, b, 341), a rational unification of reality which parallels the technological unification effected by the dynamo. For the dynamo is not itself multiplicity. It is the last—or nearly the last—manifestation of

man's power of giving unity to nature's multiplicity when that power is on the verge of collapse. After the dynamo man will—barring some unforeseeable, though possible, leap in his abilities—be unable to give unity to the forces he discovers and will be destroyed. These being the circumstances, it is appropriate that the dynamo should be a less powerful symbol in *The Education* than the ocean of colliding atoms which threatens to overwhelm it. The "dread atom-king" of "A Prayer to the Virgin of Chartres" does not seem so dreadful when, in the final chapter of *The Education*, the city (New York) and the country (America) of the dynamo are on the verge of collapse—or rather explosion—into the chaos of reality. Set against this danger the Dynamic Theory represents a slight possibility of hope, offset by a more rigorous application to man of the kinetic theory of gases. At this point, too, the movement toward chaos in Adams' life and world which he seemed to have halted for a moment by his rebellion and its expression in the Theory is shown to have continued all the while and to be threatening now more than ever to swallow up himself, his Theory, and the world.

An attack on Adams' dynamo and Virgin as symbols appears in Maud (384–388). He devotes one section to assessing "what artistic achievement [there is] in Adams' symbol-making." He first considers the dynamo (384–387), analyzing sentence-by-sentence the third paragraph of "The Dynamo and the Virgin" and some other passages from later paragraphs and from the "Prayer to the Dynamo." He denies, for one thing, that there is adequate evidence for considering the dynamo a symbol of multiplicity. In reply, it must be admitted, first, that Adams nowhere in *The Education* states the dynamo's meaning. It has to be inferred from (1) his statement that the dynamo "gave to history a new phase" (342); (2) his apparent dating of the beginning of that phase as 1900 (382–383); (3) his use of the dynamo as a symbol of that new phase in opposition to the Virgin as a symbol of the Middle Ages in the chapter title of "The Dynamo and The Virgin" (379); and (4) his juxtaposition of these symbols within the chapter in the statements (a) that "he turned from the Virgin to the Dynamo as though he were a Branly coherer" (384), (b) that the Virgin's predecessors, Diana of the Ephesians and the Oriental goddesses, were worshipped because they were "animated dynamo[s]" (384), and (c) that the Virgin exercised "vastly more attraction over the human mind than all the steam engines and dynamos ever dreamed of" (385). Thus (5) when, later (435), Adams says that in *Chartres* and *The Education* he is opposing thirteenth-century unity and twentieth-century multiplicity, it seems clear that the dynamo is his symbol for that multiplicity. Maud's main concern, however, is his belief that "we find much stage 'business' but little compelling significance" in the dynamo as a symbol. Here he refers to the fact that Adams' presentation of the dynamo consists more of metaphors expressing feeling than of rational analysis. Yet such a mode of presentation accords with Adams' conception in *The Education* both of education and of himself. In a late letter Adams says he wrote *The Education* to show that education consists in following the "intuitions of instinct" (to Margaret Chanler, Sept. 9, 1909, in Ford [1892–1918], 524). Here he calls that kind of education "accidental education." Yet Adams also depicts himself as too much a Bostonian and therefore a man of reason (387, 370) to apprehend or at least to present experience purely in terms of feeling. Hence his account in "The Dynamo and the Virgin" of his instinctive awareness of the opposition that would later generate his dynamic theory of history is expressed not wholly in terms of feeling and imagination but in a mixture of feeling and thought which might distress a poet for being too abstract as much as it distresses Maud for being too metaphorical. Maud also scores Adams' feelings about the dynamo, essentially because Adams' sense of its mysteriousness seems to him pretense. Specifically, he says of Adams' contention that there is an irreparable break in continuity between the steam engine and the dynamo that "we understand the dynamo, though Adams tries to convince us we don't." This supposed obfuscation, Maud believes, vitiates the value of the symbol, for "in myth-making there can be no self-deception; one cannot *pretend* not to understand." (Here Maud echoes Winters' charge—the charge that Campbell answers —that Adams establishes "a state of confusion for the sake of . . . wit . . . . The bewilderment is imposed on the experience arbitrarily.") Part of the problem here seems to be a personality conflict between two kinds of men: the one who is more impressed by his (and man's) ignorance even of the things he knows and the one who is impressed that man knows as much as he does. Adams' position is that of his friend, Samuel Langley, whom Maud calls "superstitious" because Langley insists on how little he knows about the things he studies and because he finds that the newly discovered rays do not fit into the mechanistic scientific theory of the universe conceived by Newton and developed further in the nineteenth century. Jordy (168) says that Langley was director of the Smithsonian Institution at the time Adams writes about him. That Adams truthfully reported his position is verified by a passage from an article by Langley (quoted by Samuels, III, 619 n. 44) in which he says that "we know little of the order of nature, and nothing at all of the 'laws of nature.'" Whatever Maud may think of Langley as a scientist, the agreement of Langley with Adams' position suggests that it was a viable position in Adams' time and also that Adams' adherence to it was not necessarily any more a pretense than Langley's was.

Maud's criticism of Adams' use of the Virgin (387–388) is more complex. (1) He seems to say that the Virgin is a poor symbol because, as depicted by Adams, she is no longer a viable symbol for the twentieth century. Here he has failed to note that Adams tries to make her viable by making her a symbol of sexual force, still a reality in the twentieth century, and of unity, also alive in the century. (He forgets, too, Adams' avowal that his works are addressed to that small group of persons for whom sexual force and the sense of unity are very much alive.) (2) Maud also believes that the Virgin fails as an attempt to evoke a formerly viable symbol. After asserting that *Chartres* "is notable for the way Adams identifies himself with the medieval mind," he criticizes him for acknowledging that he does not expect his nieces to believe in the Virgin. Maud apparently does not understand that *Chartres* is an expression of nostalgia for belief, in which Adams heightens the nostalgia and the sense of tragedy by making the Virgin as real as he can and then ironically evoking modern unbelief. (3) Again, Maud argues that the three chapters on theology at the end of *Chartres* tear apart a book which argues that "the real force of the period was the Virgin, who cared little for reason or logic." Here he exaggerates the amount of space devoted to theology as compared with the rest of the book—three of sixteen chapters, with one of the three devoted less to mystical theology than to mystics and mystical feeling—fails to observe that the Virgin dominated only one of the three centuries Adams is concerned with, and fails to note that the emphasis on reason in the last three chapters exemplifies the pattern of decline from feeling to a relative emphasis upon reason which Adams says characterizes man's movement in the three centuries. Maud also says that Adams does not take the time to "make us feel the importance of the particular kind of power She had." But surely *Chartres* does that? If he means that Adams doesn't mention the Virgin in the abstract, rationally developed versions of the theory (in *The Education*, "The Rule of Phase Applied to History," and "A Letter to American Teachers of History"), he should have gone on to notice that neither she *nor* the dynamo are mentioned in these versions. This fact suggests the extent to which both symbols were created by and for feeling rather than reason (see Appendix I, pp. 236–237, of the present text); consequently, it is not surprising that the Virgin is not much help mathematically, as Maud notes. But he complains that "as a symbol, She has been frittered away in the talk about forces. Once the symbols have been reduced to mathematical signs, they have the inherent weakness of inviting scrutiny as to their accuracy." But Adams doesn't—so far as I can see—reduce the Virgin to a mathematical symbol. Nor can I see that in *Chartres* she is at all "frittered away in the talk about forces." In *The Education* there is no attempt to evoke her

vividly, but, even if Adams' insistence that *Chartres* is a necessary predecessor and companion of *The Éducation* be disregarded—as it should
not be—the vivid evocations of femininity earlier in *The Education* help
vitalize the Virgin when she appears.

The best analysis of the meaning and use of both symbols and, therefore, by implication the best defense of them (in general as well as against
Maud), is in R. P. Blackmur's brilliant essay, "The Virgin and The
Dynamo," which consists primarily of a close reading of the same chapter
in *The Education* that Maud is concerned with.

63. Commentators have varied widely in considering Adams' attitude
toward his theory of history, partly because, in this case as in others, his
own expressed opinions vary widely. Omitting the fact that there are
those who believe Adams had different purposes in the three major versions
of the theory (in *The Education*, "The Rule," and "A Letter"), there are
three views of Adams' attitude: (1) those like Commager (b, 193) and
Chalfant (350–352, 324, 361–362), who believe he seriously proposed to
stimulate thought but made the content of the theory a *reductio ad absurdum*; (2) those like Stevenson (357), who believe he was creating aesthetic
metaphors to express a personal vision; and (3) those who believe he was
intellectually serious both in his purpose and in the content of his theory.
In this last group are three subgroups: (a) those like Wasser (12, 26–27),
who believe Adams thought he could find a valid theory of reality; (b)
those like Levenson (b, 341, 345, 370), who emphasize that Adams thought
of the theory as tentative and speculative; and (c) those like Hume (237–
238), who believe Adams sought a theory of reality with no real belief that
a valid one could be found. There are also many combinations of these
views, such as that in Jordy (161–163). The charge of a lack of seriousness
in the content of the theory is seriously countered by the inherent im-
probability that anyone would spend so many years of study and effort
simply to construct a *reductio ad absurdum*, even if the purpose was serious.
The strongest arguments against the second are again the inherent improb-
ability of anyone's spending so much time on scientific materials for a
wholly aesthetic construct and, as Stevenson herself notes, the "positive-
ness of date and preciseness of figure" (360) in the theory itself.

Of the citations to the theory in the letters, none of the eight clear
references to it as it appears in *The Education* treat it as other than a
serious intellectual effort; only one of six references to "The Rule"
treats it as unserious, and there "amusing" could well be a self-depreca-
tory term for "interesting." "A Letter" is treated differently: four references treat it as wholly a joke or a plaything; the other four emphasize its
function as a prod. Thus of twenty-six citations to the three main versions
of the theory, sixteen treat it with complete seriousness, five as a prod, five

as a joke. These statistics do not seem to support either views 1, 2, or 3c. The interpretations they do support are 3a or 3b. Of all the passages in the letters, those in the two about the "Titanic" sinking (to E. Cameron, April 16 and 21, 1912, Ford [1892–1918], pp. 594–595—see present text, pp. 219–222) would seem to be the most crucial. They were written at one of the peak emotional moments which appear in Adams' letters, and they have the ring of complete sincerity. Both refer seriously to predictions based on the theory in *The Education*, but both also suggest surprise as well as horror (and some satisfaction) at apparently being correct. This suggests to me that 3b is the view supported most strongly by the letters. (References relevant to the analysis are in Ford [1892–1918], 485, 495, 504, 505 [*The Education*]; 489 [*The Rule*]; 515, 528, 531, 533, 534, 535, 536, 537, 541, 546 [*A Letter*]; and Cater, 623, 646, 649, 697 [*The Education*]; 609, 647, 649–650, 675–676 [*The Rule*]; 682 [*A Letter*].) The "Preface" to "The Rule" given in Cater (esp. 783–784) also supports 3b. So, probably, does "The Tendency of History." But the assertion, implicitly in "A Letter" and explicitly in *The Education*, that reality is chaos (and a hint of the same view at the end of the "Preface" to "The Rule") suggests 3c (and argues against 3a). So do the last pages of *Chartres* (and the letter about its anarchism to Charles Milnes Gaskell, Dec. 20, 1904, in Ford [1892–1918], 444) and the ocean image in *Lodge*. Along with the brief statement of 3c by Hume cited above, excellent longer expositions are in Campbell and Kariel (though the latter seems to me to exaggerate Adams' optimism about the usefulness of his theory, partly because he misinterprets what Adams means by "force" in his Jan. 17, 1905, letter to H. O. Taylor, in Cater, 558–560).

64. The only other critic to analyze the philosophical material in *Lodge* is Samuels (III, 507–510). He says that "Adams's analysis suggests the strong philosophical affinity that existed between the younger man and himself" and then quotes the passage in which Adams says that "Lodge's dramatic motive . . . was . . . the idea of the Will, making the universe, but existing only as subject." Adams, he says, saw the "underlying theme" of both *Cain* and *Herakles* as "symbolic re-enactments of the process of self-knowledge and self-mastery" (507). *Herakles*, specifically, he believes, illustrates Adams' common search with Esther for a refuge from the ego in "a kind of mystical pantheism" (510). The theme of *Herakles*, he says, is "the mystical one of renunciation of this world for an ideal nonworld of contemplation and passivity, the ultimate discovery of perfect being" (509). Thus he sees Adams as sympathizing with Herakles, refers slightingly to "the stoical, pragmatic common-sense of King Creon who disturbs himself with no metaphysical questionings" (508), and believes that Adams' conclusion that "Creon's human solution" is "more paradoxical,

and . . . less logical, than the superhuman solution of Herakles" indicates Adams' preference for Herakles (510). But one fundamental difference between Adams' thought and Herakles' prevents Samuels from identifying Adams with Lodge's self-projection in his hero. Lodge, Adams says, "assumed that the world-soul or God was one and not many, order and not chaos, unity and not multiplicity, an assumption that Adams himself hesitated to make." Hence Samuels concludes that "if Herakles believes that he has become the God and partakes of the Deity it becomes doubtful [in Adams' view] that he has really completed the process of self-liberation. If he had, the self and the will would be supreme and the world subsumed under it." Samuels concludes that the "uncompromising act of liberation is not really liberation at all but merely escape from the claims of humanity . . . , not to become a Nietzschean superman of the unfettered will but rather through the will to destroy the will, that is to say, the self which is at the core of being human" (509). (I do not understand the preceding three sentences. In regard to the first two sentences, if [as Adams says in the passage Samuels quotes earlier] the Will is God, nature, all that is, but knowable only as "ourself," then would not Herakles' becoming God in the first sentence also be his becoming wholly the self and will Samuels mentions in the second sentence? But then, in the third sentence, Samuels says that self-liberation is the destruction of the will and the self. If he means by this the destruction of the personal and human will and self in order to realize a suprapersonal and suprahuman will and self—as he suggests in the following paragraphs—would that not be the partaking of the Deity which he rejects in the first sentence?) Clearly there are points of agreement between this interpretation and my own, specifically in Samuels' belief that Herakles did not represent Adams' ideal, which was also opposed to the Nietzschean superman; that Lodge believes far more in the unity of ultimate reality than Adams did; that Adams was concerned with self-mastery. Essentially, however, our interpretations are antithetical. Samuels views Adams as a neovitalist and mystical pantheist whose ethical sympathy is completely with Herakles, despite their metaphysical disagreement. I view Adams as believing that reality is a materialistic chaos (amidst which man's vision and creation of unity serve as a protective bulwark) whose criticism of Herakles reflects a fundamental and pervasive metaphysical disagreement *and* ethical hostility. Samuels mentions neither of the two pieces of external evidence which I use to support my interpretation, the letter to George Cabot Lodge on Dec. 2, 1908 (in Cater, 629), and that to Elizabeth Cameron on March 3, 1912 (in Ford [1892–1918], 588).

65. There has been much disagreement about Adams' attitude toward Abélard, St. Bernard of Clairvaux, St. Francis of Assisi, and St. Thomas

Aquinas. The controversy has centered around the first, third, and fourth
of these, because Bernard acts primarily as a foil for Abélard (as the title
of the chapter in which both appear—"Abélard"—indicates). My view of
Adams' interpretation of Abélard has appeared in other critics. Blackmur
identifies Abélard as the "extreme of intellect self-willed and anarchic"
(b, 2), and Hochfield recognizes that Adams sympathizes with his philosophy (a, 105). More specifically, Brunner points out (163, 243, 244) that
in Adams' view Abélard's nominalism led directly to the pluralism of
Karl Pearson described in "The Grammar of Science." Stevenson (326–
327) notes Adams' ambivalent identification with Abélard and Adams'
recognition that his individualism and nominalism posed a threat to the
whole structure of medieval life and thought. Adams' view of St. Francis
has been subject to more controversy. The most pervasive view emphasizes Adams' sympathy for Francis and finds its most extreme expression
in Samuels, who, in accordance with his belief that Adams' view is one
with that of the child, says that Adams

> turned toward the mystics, especially to Saint Francis, with a deep sense of
> fellow feeling. Who better than Saint Francis exemplified those epiphanies
> of ineffable feeling that he and his fellow Pre-Raphaelites sought? . . . Francis
> was elementary nature . . . . Higher praise Adams could not bestow . . . , Saint
> Francis' "Chant of the Sun," as freely adapted by Adams, could serve as a
> creed for Conservative Christian Anarchists like himself. (III, 293–295)

But the uncle—the old man—alludes to the disaster of the Children's
Crusade to prick the beautiful bubble of St. Francis' ultimate expression
of the child's illusion. In regard to St. Thomas the general opinion has
been that Adams admired him, or did him justice, or at least did not
condemn him, although he felt more affection for Francis. Rule, however,
argues that, in the chapter on Thomas, Adams' assertion that he is not
going to write of Thomas' thought in a philosophical way is merely cam-
ouflage for a "devastating analysis" (b, 220). It seems to me Rule correctly assesses what Adams does and that at times Adams not only plays
the twentieth-century Abélard, who delights in his work of destruction,
but takes the side of Bernard and Francis against all reason, an animus
heightened by Adams' skepticism of science. The over-all tone of the chapter, however, seems to me not hostile, as Rule suggests, but harmonious
with the general attitude of *Chartres* toward the Middle Ages—an awareness of the discrepancy between the dream and the reality which, though
ironic and pathetic, is ultimately tragic. The tone of the chapter is also
controlled by Adams' sense that though Thomas' work was built to
buttress a church rather than to save souls, Thomas believed that the
church he buttressed not only tried to save souls but was necessary for

the salvation of most souls (342). Perhaps the best evidence that Adams'
analysis is not primarily hostile is the book's final paragraph. Its tone is
that of tragedy, the tone which the nostalgia of the book constantly moves
toward and achieves at its climactic moments. Here Adams achieves it by
making Thomas' Gothic church sum up the church image as a whole as
"the cry of human suffering" (377). But if Rule is correct such a use of
Thomas would be an abrupt and unconvincing reversal of Adams' attitude
throughout the chapter. Moreover, the chapter itself would also be an
abrupt reversal of the tone of the rest of the book, a reversal which this
last paragraph would be a last-minute attempt to rectify.

66. Samuels is the only other critic to date to analyze the Fay article
(III, 580–582). In the main, Samuels accepts Fay's assertion that the
article was almost wholly Adams' work. His analysis concludes with the
comment that "the article would suggest that the passage of nearly a score
of years [since 'A Prayer to the Virgin of Chartres' and *Chartres*] had
brought him round, as his letters indicate and the allusions in the essay on
[*The Rule of*] *Phase*, to a more sympathetic appreciation of the theology of
Augustine and Thomas Aquinas and to a partial recantation of his exalta-
tion of instinct and intuition." But Samuels neither elaborates this statement nor spells out, here or earlier in the volume, what he views as the
steps by which Adams moved—from at least the time of "The Rule" in
1908—toward the position expressed in the Fay article. My own view is
that Adams' "partial recantation" can be seen even in *Chartres* and that
it is only in *Esther* (and "Buddha and Brahma") that intuition has the
kind of supremacy Samuels assigns to it.

67. Brunner views (275, 372, 381) the ocean in the latter part of *The
Education* as a "sea of phenomenalistic chaos" but believes that Adams
describes it as losing energy in accordance with the second law of thermodynamics: he speaks (372–373) of "the determined flow of nature, which
as vital force in *Chartres* or phenomenalistic chaos in *The Education*, flowed
always in the direction of" what he calls elsewhere the "dead ocean of
entropy" (275). In *The Education*, he says, Adams used "the symbolism
of water to suggest" both "the aqueous formlessness of the world that
science revealed to his reason" and

> the flow of time that was carrying this phenomenal world to its death . . . .
> Time was entropy . . . . There was thus beneath Henry Adams' protests in
> the *Education* that the world that science was revealing to human reason was
> a world of chaos, . . . a basic sense of [an] underlying . . . . unifying principle
> in entropy—the ultimate ocean of neutral oneness into which all things drifted
> at last. (373)

"By the time he had written ['A Prayer to the Virgin of Chartres'] in
1901," Brunner says, "Adams was working out . . . a theory of human

devolution" (27) based on the second law of thermodynamics, which was the basis for *Chartres, The Education,* and "The Rule," as well as "A Letter." But neither in Brunner's text nor in *The Education* (nor *Chartres*) do I find any evidence either for this interpretation of the water symbolism or of the dynamic theory of history. Brunner gives six examples of water images which seem to him to express the second law of thermodynamics. None of them seem to me to do so conclusively. For example, Brunner cites Adams' description of Russia as a "wall of archaic glacier," which was "as fixed, as ancient, as eternal, as the wall of archaic ice that blocked the ocean a few hundred miles to the northward, and more likely to advance" (411). But, if the glacier is the end result of entropy, would it advance? And would Adams say of Russia eventually that "inertia of race and bulk would require an immense force to overcome it, but in time it might perhaps be partially overcome" (448)? Again, Brunner cites Adams' ironic assertion that he would be "almost glad to act the part of horseshoe crab in Quincy Bay, and admit that . . . nothing ever changed . . . and that the woman would swim about the ocean of future time, as she had swum in the past . . . , unable to change" (448). Here, although in context it is clear that the woman will change, I see no implication that the ocean will do so. In *The Education* the closest approximation to evidence that I find for Brunner's belief that the dynamic theory is based upon the second law of thermodynamics is the second of the three possibilities for man's ultimate fate Adams suggests on p. 487, but this seems to receive no support from the rest of the book (see pp. 217–218 of chapter 8). Brunner's argument seems to hinge on the acceptance at face value (46) of statements made by Adams in his correspondence after 1909 about the relationship between his works from *Chartres* on, particularly the comment (quoted by Brunner [38]) in a letter to Raphael Pumpelly written on May 19, 1910, that "*Mont-Saint-Michel and Chartres* . . . . began the demonstration of the law which this *Letter* announces, and the *Education* illustrates" (in Ford [1892–1918], 542; see also HA to Elizabeth Cameron, Feb. 21, 1910, in *ibid.,* 536). It seems to me that recent Adams scholarship is correct in doubting, explicitly or implicitly, these statements and hence the validity of any attempt to make the second law of thermodynamics the key to all the versions of the dynamic theory (Hochfield, a, 133–134, 135–136; Levenson, b, 364, 366, 369 [though on p. 364 Levenson admits the possibility that "the dissipation of force through entropy was an underlying idea in *Mont-Saint-Michel and Chartres* and the *Education*"]; and especially Samuels, III, 418, 495, 651 n. 62). See also critical note 69.

68. As suggested by the concluding pages of chapters 7 and 8 of the present text, I believe that Adams' thought terminates in praise for the

King and Judge, who assumes responsibility for continuing civilization, and in horror at what Adams believes is the approaching dissolution of civilization. This view is the antithesis of that expressed in Hochfield: "Adams' last works evidence the craving of a religious mystic for universal dissolution, for an end to the torment of finite intelligence through union with the 'ultimate ocean of atoms'" (a, 139). In part the difference arises from Hochfield's making "A Letter" the terminus of Adams' thought— *Lodge* being only a personal postscript—whereas I view *Lodge*, the "Titanic" letters of 1912, the 1914 letter to Gaskell, the 1915 letter to Taylor, and the Fay essay as the crucial expression of his final views.

Another critic who views "A Letter" as the ultimate expression of Adams' thought is Brunner. But my thought is closer to his. He argues that Adams' work asserted that man as a reasoning being is a deterioration of man as an instinctive or intuitive being but that reason brings man closer to truth. More specifically, he says that Adams portrayed instinct as subject to the rational deterministic account of history which Adams called his dynamic theory (191–192, 232). In the end, Brunner believes, Adams also trained his skepticism on his own theory (421, 422) and turned to silence (422) as his final position. But Brunner also believes that, while Adams rejected the dynamic theory, he retained what Brunner asserts was always its controlling concept, the second law of thermodynamics—the philosophical equivalent of silence (422)—as the absolute of his thought (420, 421). See also Wagner, a, 77, 86, 93–94.

There seems to me some inconsistency between the assertion that Adams found reality unknowable (428–429) and the assertion that he accepted entropy as an absolute. Yet I agree with Brunner's account of the relationship between instinct and reason (31), between Adams' metaphysical vitalism (153, 188) and his scientific dynamic theory (although I do not agree with Brunner's belief that entropy is the basis for all versions of the theory [see critical note 67], and with his assertion that Adams eventually rejected both [31, 44]). I also agree that on the verge of his thought Adams emphasized man's inability to know and the wisdom of silence. But I do not believe that entropy was as pervasive or as important to Adams' later thought as Brunner does. Partly for this reason, Adams' concern with silence (e.g., the "Editor's Preface" to *The Education*, p. viii) seems to me primarily a concern with cessation of the will, not of the mind (*The Education*, 359).

Moreover, Adams' final emphasis seems to me not upon entropy, ignorance, and silence but upon chaos, not the chaos of death that entropy brings all things to but that absolute chaos—without even unity of direction—which Brunner calls "phenomenalistic chaos" and which Adams refers to when he suggests in "A Letter" that reality is "a chaos of anarchical energies" (241). This chaos Adams symbolizes not by the "dead ocean" of entropy of "A Letter" (Brunner's "ocean of nothingness beneath the phenomenal show of nature" [431]), but by the "shoreless ocean" of *Democracy* and the "Titanic" letters, the violent and savage ocean of *Esther*, the "ocean of colliding atoms" of *The Education*, and the restless, stormy (and also "shoreless") ocean of *Lodge*.

That reality is such a chaos means that reality is meaningless and therefore unknowable by man. In "The Rule," as Brunner points out, Adams says ("The Rule," 304–305) that man can know only the projection of his own mind, never reality. But in his other late works Adams seems to believe that man can know with some degree of certainty that reality is a meaningless chaos of forces (*Chartres*, 375; *The Education*, 288–289; "A Letter," 240–242). When Adams asserts the contrary, the assertion is generally a tactical device. In *The Education*, for example, he observes that since the child always sees unity, the old man, multiplicity, whether one viewed geology since 1867 as drifting toward unity or multiplicity would depend "on the age of the man who drifted." Yet in the next sentence he shows himself seeking for "some impersonal point for measure" of the actual drift of thought. He soon finds such a point and eventually discovers evidence which supports the validity of the old man's perspective (*The Education*, 398–401).

69. Jordy and Hochfield have also listed similarities between the versions of the theory. Jordy shares what seems to me the error of most critics up to his time—and some since (see Samuels, III, 418, 495, 651 n. 62), especially Brunner (see critical note 67)—of reading all the versions as if the second law of thermodynamics were central to each and therefore exaggerating the likenesses and the lack of differences between the versions (Levenson, b, 364, calls Brooks Adams the source for this interpretation). Jordy says that "from the start . . . Adams made [four] tacit assumptions . . . first, that of all the factors accounting for historical development the discovery and utilization of energy have been the most significant; second, that a choice was possible from among the three hypotheses relating to energy; third, that knowledge of the future of history was more important than of its past, because the former permitted the historian to distinguish the insignificant events of the past from the important (133) . . . . fourth [which Jordy calls the 'most important assumption'] . . . . Reason was the degradation of instinct" (138–139). Of these four points three at least are made explicitly in one or more of the three principal versions of the theory while the other (the third) is a valid inference from another explicitly made point. The first point here is implied in the first part of my seventh. But it fails to take into account the second part of my seventh, which in the modern period(s) has tended increasingly to become equally

important. His fourth point is explicitly made in two versions of the theory (and in *Chartres*). Surprisingly, considering Adams' avowal that *The Education* was written "to recall how Education may be shown to consist in following the intuitions of instinct" (to Margaret Chanler, Sept. 9, 1909, in Ford [1892–1918], 524), it is not explicitly made in chapters 33 and 34 of *The Education* (though see p. 370). Moreover, the term "degraded" has a specific connotation which belongs only to "A Letter." Jordy's second point, explicitly made in "A Letter," assumes the implicit presence of the second law of thermodynamics in all versions of the theory. His third point appears in the concern with prediction in my first and twelfth points. It does not appear in them in the form in which Jordy makes it because, though in itself a valid inference from what Adams says, it seems to me a distortion of Adams' view of his theory. Adams is interested in the future primarily because he wishes his work to be relevant and of service to the needs and interests of the future. Throughout his life he despised history as antiquarianism and sought to make of it a means of relating the past to both the present and the future (*The Education*, 302–303, 488. HA to Henry Osborn Taylor, Jan. 17, 1905; HA to [?], Oct. 6, 1899, in Cater, 559–560, 480).

Hochfield's list (a, 132–137) (avowedly concerned with likenesses which are relevant to his own study) includes five points: (1) "The Dynamic Theory, the *Rule*, and the *Letter* are all based on laws drawn from the physical sciences." (2) "The scientific description of reality implies an actual monism." (3) "Monistic unity permits the framing of single, all-inclusive laws" (see also a, 95–96). (4) "The . . . theory in all its forms is deterministic. The assumption of a monism changing according to a single law is equated in Adams' mind with an irreversible process—history cannot undo itself or retrace its steps." (5) "Each of the last writings contains prophecies . . . that are occasioned by Adams' determinism . . . . An air of catastrophe hangs over all three." My list includes most of these points. Hochfield's first three I have included in my third; his fourth is equivalent to my fifth; most of his fifth is in my twelfth (I added the comment about prophecies after reading his list). The basic difference between his list and my own is that his neglects the relativistic elements in the theory suggested in my first two points. Our principal specific disagreement is about a corollary of his third point. He says that "Adams leaped to the conclusion . . . that the unity of substance meant that only one law was necessary to describe its basic principle of motion" (a, 134). It seems to me that this is what Adams wanted and looked for (e.g., *The Education*, 489), and what he found in "A Letter." But I do not agree that it is a "respect in which [the three principal versions of the theory] are fundamentally similar" (a, 132) in what they actually say. Hochfield argues that Adams believed

that, although science had not settled on an ultimate generalization cover-
ing all experience, eventually it would do so and that

> in the meantime, he must plunge ahead and make his choice among the candi-
> dates for a universal law of history, hoping that physics would eventually
> vindicate him. The result is that each of his three late writings on history is
> founded on a different law of behavior of matter. Always watching the "hori-
> zon of science," Adams jumped from one law to another as each promised
> increased certainty. (a, 135)

This does not seem to me a valid analysis. In *The Education* Adams characterizes the ultimate goal of education defined as the effort to "run . . .
order through chaos" (12) as "some great generalization which would
finish one's clamor to be educated" (224). The quest there for this generalization leads him to the kinetic theory of gases, which he calls "the
final synthesis of science and its ultimate triumph" (431). Yet this generalization, though it embraces all reality, is, ironically, "an assertion of
ultimate chaos" (451). In order to create his Dynamic Theory of History
Adams has to distort it by "assuming relation" (435) where the kinetic
theory makes it clear that no relation exists. Hence the terms in which
Adams expresses the theory are not those of his ultimate generalization
but of a "gravitational theory," as Hochfield says (a, 135). So little is this
the law which Adams then felt "promised . . . certainty," however, that
in the preface to the first version of "The Rule," he characterizes the
Dynamic Theory in *The Education* as a "scientific formula, which affects
the terms of astronomy because every child is supposed to know the *so-
called* [italics added] law, as well as the fact of astronomy." When he adds
that "the statement in one set of terms implies that it can be made equally
well in all" (Cater, 782), he suggests that "The Rule" is fundamentally
not a better statement of the theory but a restatement of it in different
terms. Hochfield also argues that in "The Rule" the rule of phase is the
ultimate generalization Adams is looking for. But Adams calls the "law
of solutions . . . the latest and largest of possible generalizations" (269).
Later in the essay he says that "Nature is not so simple as to obey only one
law" (303). Only in "A Letter" does Adams find a single scientific law
which, because it both embraces all reality and describes the direction in
which reality (including history) moves, can be made the basis for his
theory.

LIST OF WORKS CITED

I. WORKS BY HENRY ADAMS

"American Finance, 1865–1869," *The Edinburgh Review*, CXXIX (April, 1869), 504–533.

"Buddha and Brahma," *Yale Review*, V (N.S.) (October, 1915), 82–89.

A Cycle of Adams Letters, 1861–1865. Edited by Worthington Chauncey Ford. 2 vols. Boston: Houghton Mifflin Co., 1920. (With Charles Francis Adams and Charles Francis Adams, Jr.).

Democracy: An American Novel. New York: Henry Holt and Co., 1908.

The Education of Henry Adams. Introduction by James Truslow Adams. The Modern Library. New York: Random House, Inc., 1931.

Esther: A Novel. By Francis Snow Compton [pseud.]. With an introduction by Robert E. Spiller. New York: Scholars' Fascimiles and Reprints, 1938.

"The Genesis of the Super-German," *Dublin Review*, CLXII (April, 1918), 224–233. [With Sigourney W. Fay. Signed by Fay.]

"The Great Secession Winter, 1860–1861," in *Proceedings*, Massachusetts Historical Society, XLIII (1909–1910), 656–687.

The Great Secession Winter of 1860–61 and Other Essays. Edited and with an introduction by George Hochfield. A Perpetua Book. New York: A. S. Barnes and Co., Inc., 1963.

Henry Adams and His Friends: A Collection of His Unpublished Letters. Compiled with a biographical introduction by Harold Dean Cater. Boston: Houghton Mifflin Co., 1947.

The History of the United States of America During the Administrations of Thomas Jefferson and James Madison. 9 vols. New York: Charles Scribner's Sons, 1889–1891.

"The Independents in the Canvass," *North American Review*, CXXIII (October, 1876), 426–477.

John Randolph. Boston: Houghton Mifflin Co., 1899.

"A Letter to American Teachers of History," in *The Degradation of the Democratic Dogma*. With an introduction by Brooks Adams. New York: The Macmillan Co., 1919.

Letters of Henry Adams, 1858–1891. Edited by Worthington Chauncey Ford. Boston: Houghton Mifflin Co., 1930.

Letters of Henry Adams, 1892–1918. Edited by Worthington Chauncey Ford. Boston: Houghton Mifflin Co., 1938.

Letters to a Niece and Prayer to the Virgin of Chartres. With a niece's memories by Mabel La Farge. Boston: Houghton Mifflin Co., 1920.

The Life of Albert Gallatin. Philadelphia: J. P. Lippincott and Co., 1879.

The Life of George Cabot Lodge. Boston: Houghton Mifflin Co., 1911.

"Men and Things in Washington," *Nation*, IX (November 25, 1869), 454–456.

Mont-Saint-Michel and Chartres. With an introduction by Ralph Adams Cram. Boston: Houghton Mifflin Co., 1933.

"The New York Gold Conspiracy," *Westminster Review*, XCIV (N.S.) (October 1, 1870), 411–436.

"Retrospect," *The Harvard Magazine*, III (March, 1857), 61–68.

Review of Alfred Lord Tennyson's *Queen Mary*, *North American Review*, CXXI (October, 1875), 422–429.

Review of Henry Cabot Lodge's *Life and Letters of George Cabot*, *Nation*, XXV (July 5, 1877), 12–13.

Review of John Gorham Palfrey's *History of New England*, *North American Review*, CXXI (October, 1875), 473–480.

Review of Hermann Eduard Von Holst's *The Constitutional and Political History of the United States*, *North American Review*, CXXIII (October, 1876), 328–361. (With Henry Cabot Lodge.)

"The Rule of Phase Applied to History," in *The Degradation of the Democratic Dogma*. With an introduction by Brooks Adams. New York: The Macmillan Co., 1919.

"The Session," *North American Review*, CVIII (April, 1869), 610–640.

"The Session," *North American Review*, CXI (July, 1870), 29–62.

"The Tendency of History," in *The Degradation of the Democratic Dogma*. With an introduction by Brooks Adams. New York: The Macmillan Co., 1919.

II. OTHER WORKS

Abrams, M. H. *A Glossary of Literary Terms*. New York: Holt, Rinehart and Winston, Inc., 1963.

Adams, Brooks. "The Heritage of Henry Adams," in *The Degradation of the Democratic Dogma*. New York: The Macmillan Co., 1919.

[Adams, Charles Francis, Jr.] Review of Henry Adams' *The Life of Albert Gallatin*, *Nation*, XXIX (August 21 and 28, 1879), 128–129, 144–145.

Adams, James Truslow. "Henry Adams and the New Physics," in *The Tempo of Modern Life*. New York: Albert and Charles Boni, Inc., 1931.

Adams, Marian (Mrs. Henry Adams). *Letters of Mrs. Henry Adams.* Edited by Ward Thoron. Boston: Little, Brown and Co., 1936.

Aiken, Henry. Foreword, in Henry Adams, *Democracy: An American Novel*. New York: The New American Library of World Literature, Inc., 1961.

Allers, Rudolf. "God," in *The Dictionary of Philosophy*. Edited by Dagobert Runes. New York: The Philosophical Library, 1942.

Anderson, Charles R. Introduction [to Henry Adams], in Anderson, *American Literary Masters*. New York: Holt, Rinehart and Winston, Inc., 1965.

Bassett, John Spencer. "Later Historians," in *The Cambridge History of American Literature*. Edited by William Peterfield Trent, *et al*. New York: G. P. Putnam's Sons, 1918–1921. Vol. II, pp. 171–200.

Baym, Max I. *The French Education of Henry Adams*. New York: Columbia University Press, 1951.

Bell, Millicent. "Adams' *Esther*: The Morality of Taste," *New England Quarterly*, IX (December, 1936), 564–582.

Blackmur, R. P. (a) "Adams Goes to School," *Kenyon Review*, XVII (Autumn, 1955), 597–623.

———. (b) "The Harmony of True Liberalism," *Sewanee Review*, LX (Winter, 1952), 1–27.

———. (c) "Henry Adams: Three Late Moments," *Kenyon Review*, II (Winter, 1940), 7–29.

———. (d) "The Novels of Henry Adams," *Sewanee Review*, LI (April–June, 1943), 281–304.

———. (e) "The Virgin and the Dynamo," *Magazine of Art*, XLV (April, 1952), 147–153.

Blunt, Hugh F. "The Mal-Education of Henry Adams," *The Catholic World*, CXLV (April, 1937), 46–52.

Brunner, John. "Henry Adams: His Decline and Fall." Ph.D. dissertation, UCLA, 1956.

Bunker, Robert M. "The Idea of Failure in Henry Adams, Charles Sanders Pierce, and Mark Twain." Ph. D. dissertation, University of New Mexico, 1955.

Campbell, Harry M. "Academic Criticism on Henry Adams: Confusion about Chaos," *Midcontinent American Studies Journal*, VII (Spring, 1966), 3–14.

Cargill, Oscar. "The Medievalism of Henry Adams," in *Essays and Studies in Honor of Carleton Brown*. New York: New York University Press, 1940.

Chalfant, Edward Allan. "Henry Adams and History." Ph.D. dissertation, University of Pennsylvania, 1954.

Colacurcio, Michael. (a) "*Democracy* and *Esther:* Henry Adams' Flirtation with Pragmatism," *American Quarterly*, XIX (Spring, 1967), 53–70.

———. (b) "The Dynamo and the Angelic Doctor: The Bias of Henry Adams' Medievalism," *American Quarterly*, XVII (Winter, 1965), 696–712.

Commager, Henry. (a) "Henry Adams," *South Atlantic Quarterly*, XXVI (July, 1927), 252–265.

———. (b) "Henry Adams," in *The Marcus W. Jernegan Essays in American Historiography* by his former students at the University of Chicago. Edited by William T. Hutchinson. Chicago: The University of Chicago Press, 1937.

Creek, Herbert. "The Medievalism of Henry Adams," *South Atlantic Quarterly*, XXIV (January, 1925), 86–97.

Folsom, James K. "Mutation as Metaphor in *The Education of Henry Adams*," *Journal of English Literary History*, XXX (June, 1963), 162–174.

Fuller, Louise Fant. "Henry Adams: Pilgrim to World's Fairs," *Tennessee Studies in Literature*, IX (1964), 1–10.

Gabriel, Ralph Henry. *The Course of American Democratic Thought: An Intellectual History since 1815*. New York: The Ronald Press, 1940.

Greifer, Elisha. "The Conservative Pose in America: The Adamses' Search for a Pre-Liberal Past," *The Western Political Quarterly*, XV (March, 1962), 5–16.

Gripkey, Sister Mary Vincentine. *The Blessed Virgin Mary as Mediatrix in the Latin and Old French Legend, Prior to the Fourteenth Century*. Washington, D.C.: Catholic University of America Press, 1938.

Harbert, Earl N. "Henry Adams' New England View: A Regional Angle of Vision?" *Tulane Studies in English*, XVI (1968), 107–134.

Hawthorne, Nathaniel. *The Complete Novels and Selected Tales of Nathaniel Hawthorne*. Edited with an introduction by Norman Holmes Pearson. The Modern Library. New York: Random House, Inc., 1937.

Healy, Sister M. Aquinas. "A Study of Non-Rational Elements in the Works of Henry Adams as Centralized in his Attitude toward Women." Ph.D. dissertation, University of Wisconsin, 1956.

Heeney, Sister St. Agnes. "The Cathedral in Four Major New England Authors: A Study in Symbolical Inspiration." Ph.D. dissertation, University of Pennsylvania, 1957.

Hochfield, George. (a) *Henry Adams: An Introduction and Interpretation.* New York: Holt, Rinehart and Winston, Inc., 1962.

——. (b) Introduction, in *The Great Secession Winter of 1860–61 and Other Essays.* Edited by George Hochfield. A Perpetua Book. New York: A. S. Barnes and Co., Inc., 1963.

Howe, Irving. *Politics and the Novel.* New York: Horizon Press Inc., 1957.

Hume, Robert A. *Runaway Star: An Appreciation of Henry Adams.* Ithaca, New York: Cornell University Press, 1951.

Jenkins, Iredell. "Naturalism," in *Dictionary of Philosophy.* Edited by Dagobert Runes. New York: The Philosophical Library, 1942, p. 205.

Jones, Joan. Unpublished seminar paper, University of Nebraska, 1966.

Jordy, William H. *Henry Adams: Scientific Historian.* New Haven: Yale University Press, 1952.

Kariel, Henry S. "The Limits of Social Science: Henry Adams' Quest for Order," *The American Political Science Review,* L (December, 1956), 1074–1092.

Koretz, Gene H. "Augustine's *Confessions* and *The Education of Henry Adams,*" *Comparative Literature,* XII (Summer, 1960), 193–206.

Levenson, J. C. (a) "Henry Adams and the Culture of Science," in *Studies in American Culture: Dominant Ideas and Images.* Edited by Joseph J. Kwiat and Mary C. Turpie. Minneapolis, Minn.: University of Minnesota Press, 1960.

——. (b) *The Mind and Art of Henry Adams.* Boston: Houghton Mifflin Co., 1957.

Lucas, F. L. *Tragedy in Relation to Aristotle's Poetics.* New York: Harcourt, Brace and Co., 1928.

Lydenberg, John. "Henry Adams and Lincoln Steffens," *South Atlantic Quarterly,* XLVIII (Jan. 1949) 42–64.

McIntyre, John P. "Henry Adams and the Unity of Chartres," *Twentieth Century Literature,* VII (January, 1962), 159–171.

MacLean, Kenneth. "Window and Cross in Henry Adams' *Education,*" *University of Toronto Quarterly,* XXVIII (July, 1959), 332–344.

Maud, Ralph. "Henry Adams: Irony and Impasse," *Essays in Criticism,* VIII (October, 1958), 381–392.

Maudsley, Henry. *Body and Will: Being an Essay Concerning Will in its Metaphysical, Physiological, and Pathological Aspects.* New York: D. Appleton and Co., 1884, 1894.

[Michaud, Joseph François.] *Michaud's History of the Crusades.* Translated by W. Robson. 3 vols. London: George Routledge and Co., 1852.

Milne, Gordon. *The American Political Novel.* Norman, Oklahoma: University of Oklahoma Press, 1966.

Murray, Henry. "Introduction to the issue 'Myth and Myth making,'" *Daedalus: Journal of the American Academy of Arts and Sciences*, LXXXVIII (Spring, 1959), 211–212.

Murray, James Augustus Henry (ed.). *A new English dictionary...* Oxford: The Clarendon Press, 1888–1928.

Nuhn, Ferner. "Henry Adams and the Hand of the Fathers," in *The Wind Blew From the East: A Study in the Orientation of American Culture*. New York: Harper and Brothers, Publishers, 1942.

Page, Evelyn. "'The Man Around the Corner'; An Episode in the Career of Henry Adams," *New England Quarterly*, XXIII (September, 1950), 401–403.

Quinlivan, Frances. "Irregularities of the Mental Mirror," *The Catholic World*, CCV (April, 1946), 58–65.

Roelofs, Gerrit H. "Henry Adams: Pessimism and the Intelligent Use of Doom," *Journal of English Literary History*, XVII (September, 1950), 214–239.

Rozwenc, Edwin C. "Henry Adams and the Federalist," in *Teachers of History: Essays in Honor of Laurence Bradford Packard*. Edited by H. Stuart Hughes. Ithaca, N.Y.: Cornell University Press, 1954.

Rule, Henry B. (a) "Henry Adams' Attack on Two Heroes of the Old South," *American Quarterly*, XIV (Summer, 1962, Part I), 174–184.

———. (b) "Irony in the Works of Henry Adams." Ph.D. dissertation, University of Colorado, 1960.

Samuels, Ernest. (a) "Henry Adams' Twentieth Century Virgin," *Christian Century*, LXXVII (October 5, 1960), 1143–1146.

———. (I) *The Young Henry Adams*. Cambridge: Harvard University Press, 1948.

———. (II) *Henry Adams: The Middle Years*. Cambridge: Harvard University Press, 1958.

———. (III) *Henry Adams: The Major Phase*. Cambridge: Harvard University Press, 1964.

Sandelin, Clarence Kenneth. "The Educational Philosophy of Henry Adams: A Brahmin Contribution to Critical Realism." Ph.D. dissertation, University of Wisconsin, 1956.

Saveth, Edward N. (a) "The Heroines of Henry Adams," *American Quarterly*, VIII (Fall, 1956), 216–230.

———. (b) Introduction, in Henry Adams, *The Education of Henry Adams and Other Selected Writings*. Edited by Edward N. Saveth. The Great Histories. New York: Washington Square Press, 1963.

Sayre, Robert F. *The Examined Self*. Princeton: Princeton University Press, 1964.

Sheen, Fulton J. *The World's First Love*. New York: McGraw-Hill Book Co., Inc., 1952.

Simonds, Katharine. "The Tragedy of Mrs. Henry Adams," *New England Quarterly*, IX (December, 1936), 564–582.

Smith, Henry Nash. *Virgin Land: The American West as Symbol and Myth*. Cambridge: Harvard University Press, 1950.

Speare, Morris Edmund. *The Political Novel: Its Development In England and in America*. New York: Oxford University Press, 1924.

Spiller, Robert. (a) "Henry Adams," in *Literary History of the United States*. Edited by Robert E. Spiller, Willard Thorp, Thomas H. Johnson, Henry Seidel Canby, *et al.* 3 vols. New York: The Macmillan Co., 1948. Vol. II, pp. 1080–1103.

———. (b) Introduction, in *Esther: A Novel*. By Francis Snow Compton [Henry Adams]. New York: Scholars' Facsimiles and Reprints, 1938.

Stephen, Sir Leslie. *History of English Thought in the Eighteenth Century*. 3rd ed. 2 vols. London: John Murray, 1902.

Stevenson, Elizabeth. *Henry Adams: A Biography*. New York: The Macmillan Co., 1955.

Tanner, Tony, "The Lost America—The Despair of Henry Adams and Mark Twain," *Modern Age*, V (Summer, 1961), 299–310.

Taylor, Henry Osborn. (a) *Deliverance*. New York: The Macmillan Co., 1915.

———. (b) Preface, in *Prophets, Poets, and Philosophers of the Ancient World* [new title for Taylor (a) above]. New York: The Macmillan Co., 1933.

———. (c) Review of *Mont-Saint-Michel and Chartres*, *American Historical Review*, XIX (April, 1914), 592–594.

Vandersee, Charles Andrew. "The Political Attitudes of Henry Adams." Ph.D. dissertation, UCLA, 1964.

Vann Woodward, C. *The Burden of Southern History*. Baton Rouge: Louisiana State University Press, 1960.

Wagner, Vernon. (a) "The Lotus of Henry Adams," *New England Quarterly*, XXVII (March, 1954), 75–94.

———. (b) *The Suspension of Henry Adams*. Detroit: Wayne State University Press, 1969.

Wasser, Henry. *The Scientific Thought of Henry Adams*. Thessalonike, [Greece]: [n.p.], 1956.

Welland, Dennis S. R. "Henry Adams . . . a Novelist," *Renaissance and Modern Studies*, III (1959), 25–50.

Wellek, René, and Warren, Austin. *Theory of Literature*. A Harvest Book. New York: Harcourt, Brace and Co., 1956.

Wilson, Edmund, "A Novel of Henry Adams," *The New Republic*, XLIV (October 14, 1925), 203.

Winters, Ivor. "Henry Adams: or The Creation of Confusion," in *The Anatomy of Nonsense*. Norfolk, Conn.: New Directions, 1943.

ACKNOWLEDGMENTS

Many individuals and institutions have helped to make this book possible. I am most grateful to my wife, who in the years I have been considering and reconsidering Henry Adams has been a constant source of encouragement and practical assistance. Our children too—Cathy, David, Thomas, and Susan—have frequently sacrificed a mother as well as a father to the necessities of scholarship. Professor Harry Clark of the University of Wisconsin, under whose direction the first draft of the manuscript was written, has been both an inspiring teacher and a warm and loyal friend. The generosity of my parents and brothers has made it possible for me to have far more time to work on the manuscript than I would otherwise have had. Others to whom I owe particular thanks are Professor John Brunner, whose professional generosity at a critical moment facilitated my decision to study Adams; Professor Merle Curti, of the University of Wisconsin, whose praise encouraged me to attempt the transformation of a dissertation into a book; Sister Mary Aquinas Healy, of Mount St. Mercy College, for many conversations about Adams and for her reading and criticism of two chapters of the original manuscript; Professors James Coberly, John Conder, and Earl Harbert of The George Washington University, the University of Wisconsin, and Tulane University, who each read and criticized a draft of the entire manuscript; and my colleagues at the University of Nebraska, especially Professors Robert Knoll and Dudley Bailey, whose support helped to bring this study to a conclusion. Finally, I would like to thank the typists who have worked on the manuscript, especially Miss Audria Shumard, and the institutions which have assisted me with grants of time or money or both: The George Washington University and especially the University of Nebraska.

GENERAL INDEX

Abélard, 97–99, 102, 103, 170, 301, N 65
American dream, 38, 61–64, 65, 67, 68–69, 71, 147–148, 155, 225–226. *See also* Liberal system of ideas, eighteenth-century
Aquinas, St. Thomas, 83, 87, 92, 93, 96, 101–106, 102–103 n 48, 108, 153–154, 157, 170, 171–172, 174, 187–188, 235, 279–283 N 48, 300–302 N 65; as symbol, 101–102, 172, 174, 187, 235
Art, 5–6, 40, 41, 44, 47, 56–57, 79, 81 n 30, 99, 102, 107, 108–112. *See also* Religion, and art
Augustine, St., 116, 175, 222–223, 284–285 N 49

Buddha, 161, 165, 170, 171, 184
"Buddha and Brahma," 38, 51 n 16, 150–151, 169–170, 171, 302 N 66

Christ, 54, 87, 161, 165, 171, 175, 178–179, 180, 181, 183
Circumstances. *See* Will and circumstances, relationship of

Dante, 109, 116, 128, 185
Darwinism. *See* Evolution, theory of
Democracy, 25, 26–28, 29, 32, 33–34, 35–36, 60, 61, 62–63, 64, 66, 68, 71, 73–74, 77, 121, 150, 250–251 N 6, 256–257 N 10; theme of in Adams' work, 3–4, 225–226, 227; belief in as ideal, 25, 26, 30–31, 32, 35, 61–62, 63, 68–69; George Washington as touchstone for ideal of, 26, 31, 32, 34, 34 n 17; relationship of to centralization in America, 26, 58–59, 61–62, 63–65, 66–67, 72–74, 75–77; drama of, 144, 145, 147–148; symbols of, 72–77, 199–203, 208, 214; failure of, 27, 29–30, 33, 34, 263–265 N 16
Democracy, 2, 37, 39, 47, 49, 55, 69, 121, 253–256 N 9, 256–257 N 10; explication of, 25–36; structure of, 25, 26, 27, 29, 33; characters of, 25–36 passim, 248–249 N 3, 249–250 N 4, 250 N 5,

250–251 N 6, 251–252 N 7; general symbolism in, 2, 26, 29–30, 35, 143, 153, 256–257 N 10; symbolism of characters, 26, 27–29, 31–32, 31 n 11, 33, 34, 169; symbolism of drama, 144–145, 146, 153, 168–169, 187; Mount Vernon as symbol, 26 n 2, 28, 29, 30–31, 31 n 11, 35, 36, 49; ocean as symbol, 35, 202–203, 212, 256–257 N 10, 305 N 68; star as symbol, 34, 34 n 17, 153, 169; George Washington as symbol, 26, 28, 29, 31, 31 n 11, 32, 34, 169
Determinism. *See* Will and circumstances, relationship of
Dichotomies, pervasiveness of in Adams' work, 23, 40, 56–57, 74, 160
Dynamic theory of history, 11–12, 38 n 2, 215, 227, 279 N 48, 287 N 54, 292–293 N 59; sources of, 130, 138 n 34, 291 N 58; purpose of, 78, 128–130, 151, 173–174, 182, 232 n 9, 244 n 11; development of, 78, 151–158; versions of, 78 n 3, 79–80, 130–133, 137–138, 215–216, 231–239, 307 N 69; symbolism and, 6, 10, 47, 135, 139, 151, 155–157, 213; relationship of to works, 9, 45, 77, 78–79, 113, 127, 159–160; relationship of to *Chartres*, 12, 84–85, 90, 96, 99, 100, 102, 105, 108–112 passim, 231, 233–235, 236–237; relationship of to second law of thermodynamics, 157–159, 302–303 N 67, 304 N 68; Adams' attitude toward, 11, 80, 128–130, 158–159, 206, 223–224, 227, 298–299 N 63

Education, 1, 113–139 passim (esp. 120–121, 127–128, 129, 132), 174; accidental, 120, 242, 245
Education of Henry Adams, The, 3, 46, 47, 73–74, 77, 78–81, 82, 89, 90, 154, 156 n 39, 157, 159–160, 162, 163–164, 167 n 69, 168 n 71, 169, 172–174, 177 n 92, 181 n 100, 182, 187–188, 190, 193, 197, 202, 203, 205–206, 214–221 passim, 221 n 50, 223–224, 230, 231–239, 242–246, 250 N 5, 283–285 N 49,

319

Education of Henry Adams, The—(cont.)
289–290 N 56, 290–291 N 58, 293 N 60,
302–303 N 67, 304–305 N 68,
305–307 N 69; explication of, 113–139;
structure of, 115, 127, 129, 269 N 20,
273 N 40, 285–286 N 51, 287 N 53,
288–289 N 55, 291–293 N 59; dynamic
theory in, 11–12, 78–80, 154–156,
156 n 39, 181–182, 215, 231–239, 298–
299 N 63, 305–307 N 69; general symbolism in, 4, 8–12; Ara Coeli as symbol,
113–115, 117, 120, 123–124, 128,
285 N 50, 286–287 N 52; Boston as
symbol, 117–120, 122, 124, 133–134,
287–288 N 54, 288–289 N 55; symbolism of death of sister, 5, 9, 127–128,
132, 134, 154–155, 211 n 29, 221,
221 n 50, 243, 287 N 54, 290 N 57,
291–293 N 59; dynamo as symbol, 11,
117, 123, 132, 138, 153, 205, 258–
259 N 12, 287–288 N 54, 290 N 56, 294–
296 N 62, 280 N 48; Garden of Eden
as symbol, 116, 117–118, 128, 130, 132,
137–138, 139; glacier as symbol, 122,
133–135, 139, 212–213, 303 N 67; ice
as symbol, 133–135, 134 n 27, 192, 209,
212–213, 216–217; ocean as symbol,
133, 135–139, 136 n 29, 136 n 31,
137 n 32, 193, 197, 202, 203, 205–206,
210 n 27, 210–213, 211 n 28, 211 n 29,
214, 217–218, 288 N 54, 290 N 56,
302–303 N 67, 305 N 68; Quincy as
symbol, 117–119, 127, 133–134, 287–
288 N 54, 288–289 N 55; raft as symbol, 136, 136 n 31, 137, 138, 202, 212,
221; Russia as symbol, 122–123, 126,
134–135, 138, 212; school as symbol,
118, 119, 120–121, 122, 133–135; ship
as symbol, 136–137, 136 n 29, 136 n 31,
221; snow as symbol, 133–135, 192,
209; steam as symbol, 133, 134 n 27,
138–139; Virgin as symbol, 5, 11, 117,
126, 129, 130–131, 132, 137–138, 187–
188, 190, 205, 236–237, 258–259, 287–
288 N 54, 289–290 N 56, 290 N 57,
294–298 N 62; wanderer as symbol,
116, 117, 120, 131, 137, 211, 229;
water as symbol, 133–139, 140, 210,
211

Esther, 2–3, 59, 69, 144–148, 169–170,
187–188, 198–199, 205–206, 208–209,
213, 242, 257 N 11, 258–259 N 12,
259–261 N 14; explication of, 37–57;
structure of, 40; general symbolism in,
2–3, 8; symbolism of characters, 40–56
passim, 257 N 11, 259 N 13; Church as
symbol, 40–41, 45, 47, 48, 53–56, 205;
Niagara Falls as symbol, 8, 40, 45–56,
205–206, 208, 213, 222, 242, 258–
259 N 12, 261–263 N 15; ocean as
symbol, 46–47, 46–47 n 9, 48, 55, 205,
206, 209, 257 N 11, 262 N 15,
305 N 68; symbolism of Petrarch's

sonnets, 40, 42–44, 45, 53; miscel-
laneous symbolism, 41, 45–46, 143,
144–146, 147, 169–170, 187, 198–199,
257 N 11
Evolution, theory of, 28, 52, 60, 115, 120,
121–122, 130–131, 136, 159, 260–261

Fay, Father, 176 n 89, 178, 179
Feeling, 145–146, 165–168, 247–248 N 1,
304 N 68; Adams' work and, 1–12;
truth and, 2–3, 14, 23–24, 50–51, 52,
100–101, 128, 131–132, 241–246, 304 N
68; modern man and, 90, 93, 237;
pre-modern man and, 79, 80–81, 96,
187–188; religion, art, and, 79, 98, 99,
178–181; symbolism and, 4, 6–10, 236–
237; dynamic theory and, 79, 107, 130–
132, 236–237; *Chartres* and, 90–93,
269–270 N 20, 278 N 46; reason and,
2–3, 8, 79, 80–81, 86, 92, 93, 95–102
passim, 106, 107, 130–132, 156 n 39,
172–181 passim, 186–190, 236–237,
241–246, 247–248 N 1, 269–270 N 20,
272 N 34, 278 N 46, 304 N 68
Francis of Assisi, St., 17, 99–102, 102–
103 n 48, 104, 112, 160–161, 170–174,
228, 235, 245, 300–301 N 65; as a
symbol, 99, 102, 160, 170–174, 228,
235, 301 N 65

Gallatin, Albert, Adams' *Life of. See Life
of Albert Gallatin, The*
"Genesis of the Super-German, The,"
178–181, 183, 189, 302 N 66
Goodness, natural, 3, 13–14, 19, 22, 25,
28, 34, 61–63, 69, 77, 226
"Great Secession Winter of 1860–61,
The," 6–7, 199, 219

History, 1–2, 3–4, 7, 59–61, 64, 66, 69,
72–73, 78, 109–115, 127, 128, 130, 137–
139, 142–160, 178–184, 203–209, 211,
212–216, 217–219, 222–227, 229, 244–
246, 274–275 N 43, 303–305 N 68. *See
also* Dynamic theory of history *and*
Will and circumstances, relationship of
*History of the United States During the
Administrations of Thomas Jefferson and
James Madison, The*, 2, 7, 37, 38, 150–
151, 198–199, 200, 212, 213–214;
explication of, 58–77; structure of,
263–265 N 16; determinism in, 37,
266–267 N 18; general symbolism in,
7–8, 69–70, 77; symbolism of drama,
63, 143, 146–150, 151, 155; flag as
symbol, 4–5, 69–72, 74, 75, 77 n 19;
ocean as symbol, 61, 69–70, 72–74,
73 n 16, 75, 76, 207–209, 212–216,
267–268 N 19; ship as symbol, 69–70,
74–77, 198–199, 200

Idealism, 140–141, 146, 155, 184; naturalness of to human beings, 79, 80, 107, 109, 112, 152, 153, 160, 205, 225; versions of, 13–14, 61–62, 63, 79, 129–132, 146, 147–148, 155, 158, 184–190, 212, 225–227; expressions of, 78–79, 86–87, 88–89, 94, 95, 96–106, 160–184, 185–186, 228–229; human embodiments of, 10–11, 13–22 passim, 25–36 passim, 62–66, 99–101, 160–164, 168, 169, 170–171, 172–173; fragility of, 60–61, 64–65, 88, 92, 95–96, 100–101, 105–108, 111, 145, 147, 152, 202–204, 209–210, 212; balance of with practicality, 29, 32, 36, 168–183, 190, 226; practicality of, 19, 59–60, 62, 68–69, 87, 108, 109–111, 112, 135, 152, 152 n 28, 173–174, 211, 227, 232; Adams' sympathy with, 27, 29, 65, 94, 184–186, 227–228; Adams' criticism of, 14, 17, 29, 32, 36, 59–61, 145–146, 165–168, 168–183, 185–186; Adams' attitude toward versions of, 10–11, 13–23 passim, 65, 68–69, 78, 81, 82, 84, 89–92, 189–190, 223–224, 225–226. See also Dynamic theory of history; Symbolism, drama and Virgin; Will and circumstances, relationship of
Illusion and reality, theme of, 3, 12, 23–24, 25, 57, 58–59, 61, 77, 78, 79–86, 109–112, 113, 117, 127–128, 133–134, 139, 140, 146, 147–148, 151–153, 154–156, 158–159, 225, 227–228
Instinct. See Feeling
Irony, 82, 95, 100, 112, 274 N 42, 293 N 60

Jefferson, Thomas, 14, 16, 19, 23, 62–66, 148, 168, 169
John Randolph, 7, 7 n 10, 168–169, 185–186; symbolism in, 7, 168–169, 185, 199–200

Kelvin, Lord, 158, 159, 175, 177, 217, 223
Kinetic theory of gases, 131, 135–136, 137, 138, 163, 211–212, 295 N 62

"Letter to American Teachers of History, A," 10, 158–159, 160, 182, 218, 236–237, 303–305 N 68; second law of thermodynamics in, 157–158, 223–224, 227, 302–303 N 67, 304–305 N 68, 305–306 N 69; symbolism in, 6, 157–158, 159, 160, 174, 188–189, 206, 214–217, 218–219, 302 N 67, 305 N 68; dynamic theory of history and, 223–224, 231–233, 235–238, 298–299 N 63, 302–303 N 67, 305–307 N 69

Liberal system of ideas, eighteenth-century, 10–11, 13–14, 63; influence on Albert Gallatin, 10–11, 13–24 passim, 63, 248 N 2. See also American dream
Life of Albert Gallatin, The, 2, 10–11, 37, 38, 61, 63, 69, 152, 153, 168, 170, 184, 187, 190, 248 N 2; explication of, 13–24; symbolism in, 10–11, 13, 23, 153, 168, 170, 184, 187, 190, 201–202, 203, 208, 219. See also Liberal system of ideas, eighteenth-century
Life of George Cabot Lodge, The, 170–171, 180, 186, 245; explication of, 159–168, 299–300 N 64; general symbolism in, 160; symbolism of complex nature, 163–166, 170; King and Judge as symbol, 160, 166–168, 167 n 69, 168 n 71, 170, 176, 180, 189, 299–300 N 64; ocean as symbol, 162–163, 209, 210, 305 N 68; Savior as symbol, 160, 164, 166–171 passim, 173, 177, 180, 186, 245, 246, 299–300 N 64; symbolism of simple nature, 160–165, 170
Lodge, George Cabot, Adams' Life of. See Life of George Cabot Lodge, The
Love, courteous, 94–95, 102, 108, 109, 110, 185, 187

Machine, 37, 59, 60, 61, 65, 126, 162, 185, 191–192, 221, 279 N 47, 290 N 56. See also Symbolism, machine
Man and nature, relationship of. See Nature and man, relationship of
Marcus Aurelius, 129, 175, 176, 230
"Men and Things in Washington," 144, 250 N 5; symbolism in, 143–144, 145, 146
Michael, St., 86, 86 n 38, 87
Military force, 60–61, 71, 85, 87, 121, 149, 177 n 92, 190
Mont-Saint-Michel and Chartres, 3, 8–9, 12, 113, 133, 157, 160–162, 163, 165, 170–172, 180, 183, 187, 188, 190, 205, 209–210, 242, 244–245, 246, 268–270 N 20, 273–274 N 41, 274 N 42, 274–275 N 43, 275–276 N 44, 279–283 N 48, 294 N 62, 300–302 N 65, 302–303 N 67; explication of, 78–112; structure of, 83, 91 n 42, 92, 107, 108–109, 269 N 20, 278 N 46, 278–279 N 47; general symbolism in, 4, 8–9; the child as symbol, 80–85, 87, 89–92, 91 n 42, 96, 99, 100–101, 102, 107, 108–109, 112, 117–120, 132, 155, 160–162, 164, 170, 176 n 89, 273 N 40, 275 N 44; symbolism of drama, 108–112, 133, 142, 149, 152–153, 183–186, 187, 190; dynamo as symbol, 96, 153, 157; journey as symbol, 81–83, 93, 100, 108, 229 (see also Education of

Mont-Saint-Michel and Chartres—(*cont.*)
Henry Adams, The, wanderer as
symbol); symbolism of literature of
courteous love, 94–96, 108, 109, 185;
symbolism of medieval architecture,
83, 86–88, 90–92, 94, 98, 99, 101, 102,
106–108, 107 n 50, 229; old man as
symbol, 80–85, 87, 90, 92, 96, 101–
102, 108–109, 120, 132, 153, 155, 160,
163, 170, 176 n 89, 273 N 40; ocean as
symbol, 84, 86, 205, 209–210; pilgrimage as symbol, 82, 83, 87, 91–92, 229;
Virgin as symbol, 5, 87, 88–96, 99,
106–112 passim, 170–171, 185–186,
187, 190, 205, 236–237, 258–259
N 12, 275 N 44, 276–278 N 45, 289–
290 N 56, 294–298 N 62
Moralism, 1–3, 121, 142, 143, 145, 148,
173–176, 180–181, 185, 186, 226; in
Gallatin, 13–14, 15, 22; in *Democracy*,
25–30, 31–36, 145, 249 N 3, 249–
250 N 4, 250 N 5, 251–252 N 7, 252–
253 N 8, 253–256 N 9; in *Esther*, 54;
in *The History*, 61–63, 65–69; in
Chartres, 85, 88–89, 94, 104–105, 170–
171; in *The Education*, 119, 121, 190;
in *Lodge*, 160–161, 163, 165–166
Multiplicity, Abélard and, 98–99, 102;
Adams' acceptance of, 128–129, 172–
173; Adams' rejection of, 78, 79, 129–
130, 135, 151; Adams' ultimate belief
in, 158–159, 190, 275–276 N 44, 304–
305 N 68; America and, 73–74, 76–77,
77 n 19, 181 n 100, 288 N 54; Ara
Coeli and, 120, 285 N 50, 286 N 52;
complex nature and, 163; death of
Adams' sister and, 5, 127–128,
290 N 57, 287 N 54; democracy and,
73 n 16, 74, 77, 226; dynamo and, 11,
132, 138, 287–288 N 54, 294–296 N 62;
education and, 120–121; *The Education*
and, 80–81, 86, 113–139, 211–213,
211 n 28, 243; "energy without direction" and, 175, 177–178, 177 n 92, 184;
the Fall and, 115; feeling and, 243–246
passim; Francis of Assisi, St., and, 100,
172, 173; the Germans and, 175,
177–181, 181 n 100; history and, 11,
78, 108, 243 n 9; human destructiveness and, 111, 227, 229–230; human
male and, 94, 180 n 99, 186; human
opposition to, 78, 79, 85–88, 94, 96–97,
100–102, 107, 108–111, 209–210;
human perception and, 117, 120; joining
unity and, 85, 96–97, 98, 102–106;
kinetic theory of gases and, 131–132,
135–136, 138; *Lodge* and, 162–163,
209–210; man's fate and, 217–219, 221,
223, 302 N 67, 303–304 N 68; Middle
Ages and, 102, 274–275 N 43; nominalism and, 99, 103; ocean and, 46–47, 84,
86, 133, 135–137, 138, 202–203, 209–
210, 261–262 N 15, 288 N 54,

302 N 67; old man and, 80, 85, 86,
102–103, 117, 120; post-Renaissance
world and, 79, 80, 85, 96, 102, 106, 234;
Quincy and, 117, 118, 119, 127, 133–
134, 287–288 N 54; reality and, 5, 37,
38 n 2, 78, 79, 84, 85, 86, 100, 101,
106, 127–128, 151, 154–160 passim,
163, 165, 181, 210–211, 217–219, 221,
223, 227, 232 n 9, 243, 243 n 9,
269 N 20, 274–275 N 43, 275–276 N 44,
287–288 N 54, 290 N 57, 291–293 N 59,
294–295 N 62, 302 N 67, 304–305 N 68;
reason and, 79, 130, 243–246 passim;
Rome and, 119; Satan and, 85, 86, 87–
88, 116, 119, 287 N 54; Savior and,
165–166, 180–181, 186; science and, 86,
102, 105–106, 107, 108, 130, 131–132;
steam and, 133, 136 n 29, 136 n 31,
138–139; twentieth century and, 80,
103, 106, 132, 139, 211, 219–224, 226,
234, 243 n 9; twentieth-century
America and, 73, 121, 122–127, 138–
139, 288 N 54; wanderer and, 116–117,
131, 137; war and, 177–178, 177 n 92,
181; Washington, D.C., and, 118–119,
288–290 N 55; Wenlock Abbey and,
286–287 N 52. *See also* Unity, and
multiplicity
Mysticism, 97, 98, 99–101, 102, 104, 128,
161

Napoleon Bonaparte, 70–71, 168, 169, 185
Naturalism, 37–38, 38 n 2, 39, 128, 227;
pessimistic, 38, 38 n 2, 78, 128, 227
Nature, as mechanical, 37, 140–160
passim; as chaos, 5, 37, 38 n 2, 78,
84–85, 100, 105–106, 127–128, 158–
159, 217, 227, 243, 275–276 N 44,
304–305 N 68; as personification, 127,
290 N 57
Nature and man, relationship of, 10–11,
13–14, 16–18, 20–22, 37–38, 97–100,
104–105, 116, 140–246 passim,
257 N 11, 258–259 N 12; in Adams'
thought, 5, 13–24 passim, 29–30,
55–56, 59, 100–101, 107, 118, 127,
127–129, 134, 266–267 N 18, 287–
288 N 54, 302–303 N 67, 303–
305 N 68; in characters of *Esther*, 44–50
passim, 52–56, 53 n 18, 259 N 13; in
the dynamic theory, 79, 109, 129,
130–132, 135, 136–138, 232–236
"New York Gold Conspiracy, The," 2, 7,
142, 143, 145, 146, 151; symbolism in,
7, 142, 143, 145, 146, 147
Nietzsche, 177–178, 179, 180, 181
Nominalism, 97–99, 102, 102 n 48, 103,
105, 170

Pantheism, 97, 99, 104, 105, 161, 162, 163
Phenomenalism, 136 n 29, 136 n 31,
302 N 67

Practicality, 229–230; human embodiments of, 14, 18–19, 25–36 passim, 168, 170, 172, 173–174, 176; balance of, with idealism, 29, 32, 36, 166–183, 186–190, 226; use of, to test validity, 1–2, 3, 34–36, 59–60; Adams' sympathy with, 18–19, 60–61 n 6, 65, 120, 186–190, 226; Adams' criticism of, 17, 27, 29, 32, 34, 65–66, 120–121, 166, 180–181, 183–184, 227, 253–256 N 9, 259–261 N 14. *See also* Will and circumstances, relationship of, *and* Idealism
"Prayer to the Virgin of Chartres, A," 11, 275 N 44, 295 N 62

Quixote, Don, 7, 101, 185–186, 228

Randolph, John, Adams' life of. *See John Randolph*
Realism, 97–98, 102 n 48, 103
Reason, 247–248 N 1, 304 N 68; Adams' work and, 1–12; truth and, 2–3, 23–24, 50–51, 52, 128, 131–132, 172, 173–174, 180, 241–246, 304 N 68; modern man and, 79, 80–81, 90, 93, 187; Middle Ages and, 96, 101, 102, 187–188; religion and, 99, 176, 178–181, symbolism and, 4, 6–10, 236–237; man's survival and, 172, 173–174, 180; dynamic theory and, 79, 107; particular works and, 80–81, 93, 96, 112, 236–238, 241–246, 269–270 N 20, 278 N 46, 305–306 N 69. *See also* Feeling, reason and
Religion, 14, 22, 25, 26, 30–31, 34–36, 38–42, 79, 85–92, 95–98, 99–104, 105, 112, 115, 117, 125–129, 130–132, 145–147, 150–151, 156 n 39, 160–172, 175–181, 176 n 89, 182–188, 209–210, 227, 245, 246, 271 N 31, 275–276 N 44, 276 N 45, 279–283 N 48, 287–288 N 54, 289–290 N 56, 290 N 57, 293–294 N 61, 294–298 N 62, 299–300 N 64, 300–302 N 65, 302 N 66; and art, 42, 79, 83, 87, 88, 108–112, 145–146, 227–229; and science, 4, 39, 41, 42, 44–45, 51–52, 56–57, 79, 93, 101–102, 104–106, 107, 130–132, 156, 226, 227, 233, 235
Rome, as city, 119–120, 125, 182–183, 288–289 N 55; as nation, 113–115, 123–125, 126, 144, 182–183, 223; as symbol, 119–120, 182, 288–289 N 55
Roosevelt, Theodore, 121, 125, 166, 168, 182, 221
Rousseau, Jean Jacques, 14, 16, 17, 23, 248 N 2
"Rule of Phase Applied to History, The," 3, 6, 156–157, 158, 162, 174, 188–189, 214–216, 218–219, 231–233, 235, 236–238, 298–299 N 63, 303 N 67, 305–

307 N 69; symbolism in, 6, 156–157, 174, 188–189, 214–215, 216, 218–219

Scholasticism, 97–99, 101–106
Schopenhauer, Arthur, 161, 177–178
Science, 1, 2, 10, 22–23, 42, 44–45, 50–52, 56–57, 60, 62–63, 75, 79, 85, 86, 90, 101–102, 105–107, 130–132, 136 n 29, 136 n 31, 138 n 34, 149–150, 154, 160, 169, 232, 237, 306–307 N 69. *See also* Religion, and science
Second law of thermodynamics, 157–159, 160, 216–217, 227, 236, 238, 302–303 N 67, 303–305 N 68, 305–307 N 69
Silence, 112, 304 N 68
Stoicism, 129, 133, 175–177, 176 n 90, 179–180, 182
Symbolism, 2–12 passim, 29, 69–70, 128–129, 140, 160, 174–178, 182–184, 189, 191–192, 193–194, 203–204, 219–223, 305 N 68. *See also under individual works*
—Virgin, 5, 11, 87, 88–96, 99, 106–112 passim, 117, 126, 129, 130–131, 132, 137–138, 170–171, 172, 185, 187–188, 189–190, 205, 236–237, 258–259 N 12, 275 N 44, 276–278 N 45, 287–288 N 54, 289–290 N 56, 290 N 57, 294–298 N 62
—Drama, 41, 108–112, 133, 140–141; political drama, 142–144, 145, 146, 182–183, 186; social drama involving King and Judge, 186–190; love drama, 146, 184–190; economic drama, 142–143, 146, 183–184; religious drama, 146, 147, 150–151, 182–183, 184, 186 (*See also* Symbolism, Savior); "energy without direction" as drama, 175, 177–181, 184
—Machine, 102–103 n 48, 103, 105, 139, 140–160 passim, 280 N 48; ship, 35, 46, 69–70, 74–77, 136–137, 136 n 29, 136 n 31, 191–203, 219–222, 221 n 50, 222 n 51; raft, 136, 136 n 31, 137, 138, 191, 194, 212, 221; dynamo, 11, 96, 117, 123, 132, 138, 153, 156–157, 205, 258–259 N 12, 280 N 48, 287–288 N 54, 290 N 56, 294–296 N 62
—Water, 133, 140, 191–192, 194–198; ocean, 35, 46–47, 46–47 n 9, 48, 55, 61, 69–70, 72–74, 73 n 16, 75, 76, 84, 86, 133, 135–139, 136 n 29, 136 n 31, 137 n 32, 162–163, 192–193, 194, 196–197, 201–203, 204, 205, 206, 207–223, 211 n 28, 211 n 29, 256 N 10, 257 N 11, 262 N 15, 267–268 N 19, 288 N 54, 290 N 56, 302–303 N 67, 305 N 68; ocean tides, 192, 196, 200, 203; river, 72–73, 192, 194, 203–209, 212–217; stream, 59, 192, 196, 207; Niagara Falls, 8, 40, 46–56, 192, 205–206, 222, 242, 258–259 N 12, 261–263 N 15; ice, 133–135, 134 n 27, 192, 209, 212–213,

Symbolism—(*cont.*)
216–217; glacier, 72–73, 122, 133–135, 139, 208–209, 212–213, 303 N 67; steam, 133, 134 n 27, 138–139
—Symbolic types: child, 80–85, 87, 89–92, 91 n 42, 96, 99, 100–101, 102, 107, 108–109, 112, 117–120, 132, 153, 155, 160–162, 164, 170, 176 n 89, 273 N 40, 275 N 44, 305 N 68; old man, 80–85, 87, 90, 92, 96–97, 101–102, 108–109, 120, 132, 153, 155, 170, 176 n 89, 273 N 40, 305 N 68; simple nature, 160–165, 170; complex nature, 163–166, 170; Savior, 160, 164–166, 167–168, 169, 170–174, 177, 180–181, 182, 183, 186, 187, 245, 246, 299–300 N 64; King and Judge, 160, 166–168, 167 n 69, 168 n 71, 169, 170, 174, 176–177, 180, 181–183, 184–185, 186–190, 228, 230, 299–300 N 64; impractical idealist, 168–184; practical idealist, 168–184

"Tendency of History, The," 151
Time, 81, 87, 95, 106, 117, 130, 131
Tristan and Isolde, 83, 109, 185
Truth, how attained, 1–3, 6–9, 11, 18–19, 22–23, 23–24, 25, 48, 50–51, 52, 59, 77, 80–81, 103, 105–106, 107, 111–112, 115, 116–117, 120–121, 127–128, 146–147, 149–150, 155–156, 157–159, 170, 172–173, 210, 225, 226, 241–246, 247–248 N 1, 291–293 N 59, 302 N 66, 303–305 N 68

Unity (major aspects); America and, 58–61, 63–69, 73–74, 76–77, 121–125, 154, 263–265 N 16, 288 N 54; art and, 42, 44, 56–57, 79, 102, 105–112 passim, 228, 229; Aquinas, St. Thomas and, 101–106, 108, 154, 172; Boston and, 117–120, 133–134, 287–288 N 54; child and, 80, 85, 86, 99, 117, 118, 127, 153, 155, 160–162, 164; church and, 86–87, 102, 105–107, 108, 111, 229; drama and, 108–112, 152, 154–156, 160, 164–165, 166, 183–184, 185–186; dynamic theory of history and, 78, 108, 129–130, 135, 137–138, 154, 159, 173–174, 181–182, 227, 232, 232 n 9, 235–236, 244 n 11, 287 N 54, 291–293 N 59; dynamo and, 156–157, 294–295 N 62; evolution and, 131, 159; feeling and, 79, 241–246 passim; St. Francis Assisi and, 99–100, 101–102, 104, 173, 174, 228; Garden of Eden and, 116,

128, 130, 132, 137; invalidity of in *The History*, 74, 76–77; invalidity of in *Chartres*, 78, 79, 80–81, 85, 86–88, 92, 95, 96, 99, 100–101, 103, 106–108, 109, 244, 274–275 N 43; invalidity of in *The Education*, 114, 117, 120, 125, 127–128, 131–139, 173, 190, 210–212, 221, 242–243, 244–246, 291–293 N 59; invalidity of in others, 151, 154–155, 158–159, 163–166, 210, 221, 227–228, 241–243, 299–300 N 64; King and Judge and, 166, 174, 181–182, 183, 185, 189, 228; love and, 88–89, 93–94, 185–188, 228; man's belief in, 78, 79, 109–112, 137, 226; mechanical analogy and, 151–159, 160, 191; middle ages and, 79, 81, 83, 85, 101–102, 105–106, 274–275 N 43, 287–288 N 54; multiplicity and (major passages), 11, 42, 44, 57, 72–81 passim, 85–87, 91–92, 96–109 passim, 114–115, 127–132, 147, 151–159 passim, 164–166, 172–174, 179–181, 186–187, 209–212, 219–221, 223–229 passim, 232–233, 235, 241–246, 269–270 N 20, 274–275 N 43, 291–293 N 59, 295 N 62, 303–305 N 68; reason and, 157, 172, 173–174, 188, 241–246 passim; religion and, 79, 86, 99, 107, 108, 130–132, 154, 156, 186, 229; Russia and, 122–123, 134–135; Savior and, 164–166, 173, 174, 183; school and, 118, 119, 134, 135; science and, 86, 105–106, 131; second law of thermodynamics and, 157–159, 227; Virgin and, 5, 79, 89, 99, 108, 110, 132, 137–138, 185, 229, 287–288 N 54; woman and, 79, 89, 90, 93–94, 125–128, 132, 137–138, 184–190, 228–229, 236

Washington, George, as a symbol, 26, 27, 29, 31, 31 n 11, 32, 34, 34 n 17, 121, 169, 288 N 54
Will and circumstances, relationship of, 3–4, 19, 37–38, 59–61, 64–66, 79, 81, 95, 104–105, 109, 127–130, 132, 136–139, 140–229 passim, 231–238 passim, 243, 246, 263 N 16, 265 N 16, 266–267 N 18, 290 N 57, 291–293 N 59, 298–299 N 63, 303–305 N 68, 306–307 N 69
William of Champeaux, 97–98, 170
Woman, and love, 39, 83, 88, 93–96, 184–190, 228; and sexual force, 5, 79, 89, 93, 125–127, 137, 138, 185, 190, 228, 236, 271 N 32, 289–290 N 56. *See also* Unity, woman and

INDEX OF WORKS DISCUSSED IN CRITICAL NOTES

Adams, Brooks, "The Heritage of Henry Adams," 305 N 69

Adams, Charles F., Jr., review of *The Life of Albert Gallatin*, 248 N 2

Adams, James T., "Henry Adams and the New Physics," 268–269 N 20

Aiken, Henry, Foreword to *Democracy*, 249 N 3, 250 N 5, 251 N 7, 252–253 N 8

Anderson, Charles R., Introduction to Henry Adams, 269–270 N 20, 273 N 40, 278 N 46, 286 N 51, 290 N 57, 290–291 N 58

Bassett, John Spencer, "Later Historians," 273 N 41

Baym, Max T., *The French Education of Henry Adams*, 290–291 N 58

Bell, Millicent, "Adams' *Esther* ...," 258 N 12

Blackmur, R. P., "Adams Goes to School," 287 N 53, 288 N 55; "The Harmony of True Liberalism," 301 N 65; "The Novels of Henry Adams," 259 N 13; "The Virgin and the Dynamo," 298 N 62

Blunt, Hugh F., "The Mal-Education of Henry Adams," 269 N 20, 276 N 45, 279 N 48

Brunner, John, "Henry Adams: His Decline and Fall," 248 N 1, 258 N 12, 265 N 16, 268 N 19, 273 N 40, 276 N 44, 277 N 45, 279 N 48, 284 N 49, 285 N 50, 301 N 65, 302–303 N 67, 304–305 N 68, 305 N 69

Campbell, Harry M., "Academic Criticism on Henry Adams ...," 276 N 44, 282 N 48, 296 N 62, 299 N 63

Cargill, Oscar, "The Medievalism of Henry Adams," 273 N 41, 275 N 44

Chalfant, Edward Allan, "Henry Adams and History," 267 N 18, 285 N 51, 287 N 53, 298 N 63

Colacurcio, Michael, "*Democracy* and *Esther* ...," 253–256 N 9, 258 N 12, 259–261 N 14; "The Dynamo and the Angelic Doctor ...," 269 N 20, 279–283 N 48

Commager, Henry, "Henry Adams" (1927), 275 N 44; "Henry Adams" (1937), 298 N 63

Creek, Herbert, "The Medievalism of Henry Adams," 268–269 N 20

Folsom, James K., "Mutation as Metaphor in *The Education of Henry Adams*," 286–287 N 52, 293 N 60

Gripkey, Sister Mary Vincentine, *The Blessed Virgin Mary as Mediatrix ...*, 276 N 45

Healy, Sister M. Aquinas, "A Study of Non-Rational Elements in the Works of Henry Adams ...," 247 N 1, 249 N 3, 250–251 N 6, 251 N 7, 256 N 10, 258 N 12, 276 N 44, 276 N 45, 289 N 56

Heeney, Sister St. Agnes, "The Cathedral in Four Major New England Authors ...," 276–277 N 45

Hochfield, George, *Henry Adams: An Interpretation*, 261 N 15, 263–265 N 16, 266 N 17, 267 N 18, 269 N 20, 301 N 65, 303 N 67, 304 N 68, 305–307 N 69; Introduction to *The Great Secession Winter of 1860–61 ...*, 258 N 12

Howe, Irving, *Politics and the Novel*, 249–250 N 4

Hume, Robert A., *Runaway Star*, 248 N 3, 250–251 N 6, 298–299 N 63

Jordy, William H., *Henry Adams: Scientific Historian*, 263 N 16, 266 N 18, 296 N 62, 298 N 63, 305–306 N 69

Kariel, Henry S., "The Limits of Social Science . . .," 299 N 63

Koretz, Gene H., "Augustine's *Confessions* and *The Education of Henry Adams*," 287 N 54, 290 N 57

Levenson, J. C., *The Mind and Art of Henry Adams*, 248 N 1, 250 N 5, 263 N 16, 268–269 N 20, 273 N 41, 278 N 46, 285 N 50, 285–286 N 51, 290 N 57, 291 N 59, 293 N 60, 298 N 63, 303 N 67

McIntyre, John P., "Henry Adams and the Unity of *Chartres*," 269 N 20, 273 N 40, 275 N 44

MacLean, Kenneth, "Window and Cross in Henry Adams' *Education*," 285 N 50, 286–287 N 52, 293–294 N 61

Maud, Ralph, "Henry Adams: Irony and Impasse," 294–298 N 62

Milne, Gordon, *The American Political Novel*, 250 N 6

Nuhn, Ferner, "Henry Adams and the Hand of the Fathers," 290 N 57

Page, Evelyn, "'The Man Around the Corner' . . .," 248 N 2

Roelofs, Gerrit H., "Henry Adams . . .," 290–291 N 58

Rule, Henry B., "Irony in the Works of Henry Adams," 249–250 N 4, 251–252 N 7, 258 N 12, 274 N 42, 279 N 48, 301–302 N 65

Samuels, Ernest, "Henry Adams' Twentieth Century Virgin," 276–278 N 45; *Henry Adams: The Major Phase*, 247 N 1, 268–269 N 20, 273 N 40, 274 N 43, 275 N 44, 276–277 N 45, 279 N 48, 285 N 51, 285–286, 291 N 58, 296 N 62; *Henry Adams: The Middle Years*, 248 N 2, 258 N 12, 263 N 16, 266 N 18, 267–268 N 19; *The Young Henry Adams*, 284 N 49

Sandelin, Clarence Kenneth, "The Educational Philosophy of Henry Adams . . .," 279 N 48

Saveth, Edward N., "The Heroines of Henry Adams," 249 N 3; Introduction to *The Education of Henry Adams* . . ., 266 N 18

Sayre, Robert F., *The Examined Self*, 284 N 49, 285 N 50, 286 N 51, 290 N 57

Sheen, Fulton J., *The World's First Love*, 276–278 N 45

Simonds, Katharine, "The Tragedy of Mrs. Henry Adams," 259 N 12

Speare, Morris Edmund, *The Political Novel* . . ., 250 N 6, 251 N 7

Spiller, Robert, "Henry Adams," 247 N 1, 269 N 20, 284 N 49, 293 N 60

Stevenson, Elizabeth, *Henry Adams* . . ., 248–249 N 3, 298 N 63, 301 N 65

Taylor, Henry Osborn, review of *Mont-Saint-Michel and Chartres*, 273 N 41

Vandersee, Charles Andrew, "The Political Attitudes of Henry Adams," 251 N 7, 266 N 18

Wagner, Vern, "The Lotus of Henry Adams," 304 N 68

Wasser, Henry, *The Scientific Thought of Henry Adams*, 247 N 1, 279 N 48, 298 N 63

Welland, Dennis S. R., "Henry Adams as a Novelist," 257 N 11, 258 N 12

Wilson, Edmund, "A Novel of Henry Adams," 248 N 3

Winters, Yvor, "Henry Adams . . .," 282 N 48, 296 N 62